D1038887

VINDICATING LINCOLN

VINDICATING LINCOLN

Defending the Politics of
Our Greatest President

THOMAS L. KRANNAWITTER

ROWMAN & LITTLEFIELD PUBLISHERS, INC.
Lanham • Boulder • New York • Toronto • Plymouth, UK

ROWMAN & LITTLEFIELD PUBLISHERS, INC.

Published in the United States of America
by Rowman & Littlefield Publishers, Inc.
A wholly owned subsidary of The Rowman & Littlefield Publishing Group, Inc.
4501 Forbes Boulevard, Suite 200, Lanham, Maryland 20706
www.rowmanlittlefield.com

Estover Road
Plymouth PL6 7PY
United Kingdom

Distributed by National Book Network

Copyright © 2008 by Thomas L. Krannawitter
First paperback edition 2010

All rights reserved. No part of this publication may be reproduced,
stored in a retrieval system, or transmitted in any form or by any
means, electronic, mechanical, photocopying, recording, or otherwise,
without the prior permission of the publisher.

British Library Cataloguing in Publication Information Available

Library of Congress Cataloging-in-Publication Data

The hardback edition of this book was previously cataloged by the Library of
Congress as follows:

Krannawitter, Thomas L., 1969–
 Vindicating Lincoln : defending the politics of our greatest president / Thomas
L. Krannawitter.
 p. cm.
 Includes bibliographical references and index.
 1. Lincoln, Abraham, 1809–1865—Political and social views. 2. United States—
Politics and government—1861–1865. 3. United States—Politics and
government—Philosophy. I. Title.
 E457.2.K69 2008
 973.7092—dc22   2007049628

ISBN: 978-0-7425-5972-1 (cloth : alk. paper)
ISBN: 978-0-7425-5973-8 (pbk. : alk. paper)
ISBN: 978-1-4422-0064-7 (electronic)

Printed in the United States of America

♾™ The paper used in this publication meets the minimum requirements of
American National Standard for Information Sciences—Permanence of Paper for
Printed Library Materials, ANSI/NISO Z39.48-1992.

To Lori,
who helped me to discover
the better angel of my nature

We have no higher duty, and no more pressing duty, than to remind ourselves and our students of political greatness, human greatness, of the peaks of human excellence. For we are supposed to train ourselves and others in seeing things as they are, and this means above all in seeing their greatness and their misery, their excellence and their vileness, their nobility and their triumphs, and therefore never to mistake mediocrity, however brilliant, for true greatness.

—Leo Strauss

We see in great men a brighter gleam of the Infinite. . . . In the greatness of Lincoln, the people of this nation are lifted up to their own greatness.

The place which Lincoln holds in the history of the nation is that of the man who finished what others had begun. . . . [The Founders] built a base that was sound and solid. They left plans by which it was to be finished. The base they made was the Union. The plans which they drew, and stated time and time again, were for a free people. But Lincoln rises above them all in one thing. He never halted; he never turned aside . . . he followed the truth through to the end. In this peculiar power it is not too much to say that he excels all other statesmen.

—Calvin Coolidge

CONTENTS

Acknowledgments   ix

Introduction   1

1   Was Lincoln a Racist?   *13*

2   Was the Kansas-Nebraska Act Pro-Choice or Pro-Slavery?   *47*

3   Who Was Right about the Founding, Lincoln or Taney?   *77*

4   Was Lincoln a "Child of His Age?"   *115*

5   Do States Possess a Constitutional Right of Secession?   *145*

6   Was the Civil War Caused by Slavery or Economics?   *205*

7   Was Lincoln's Goal to Preserve the Union or End Slavery?   *263*

8   Was Lincoln the Father of Big Government?   *289*

9   Was Lincoln a Tyrant?   *317*

Conclusion   337

Index   341

About the Author   355

ACKNOWLEDGMENTS

While working on this book, I have relied on the help, advice, and generosity of many people. First among them is Dr. Larry Arnn, president of Hillsdale College. Arnn is a great student of the greatest statesmen, and he is among the foremost teachers of statesmanship. He understands, as few do, the qualities of mind and character that the statesman must possess, and he is able, therefore, to teach by example, in addition to teaching from books. The Founding Fathers—Thomas Jefferson, James Madison, Alexander Hamilton, and George Washington above all—were models of statesmanship for Abraham Lincoln. He once described them as "iron men." In his tireless work to build upon all that is good and right in America, I believe Arnn ranks among the men of iron today.

I am also grateful for the support and encouragement offered by the Claremont Institute and its president, Brian Kennedy. Among political think tanks today, the Claremont Institute is distinguished by the fact that all of its work—from timely public policy studies, to scholarly books and essays, to educational programs, to the *Claremont Review of Books*—is informed by its singular mission: recovering the natural right principles of American constitutional government and free society and the statesmanship necessary to establish and protect them.

Chris Flannery, a friend, teacher, and colleague of mine, was the first to read sections of the manuscript before it was completed. Chris possesses that rare combination of a philosophic mind and the pen of a poet—his friends all wish they could write as well as he does. He was more than generous with his time, and he helped me to make this book better. His thoughtful comments and suggestions were right in every instance, and I thank him. Burton Folsom, who teaches with me at Hillsdale College and is among the premiere American economic historians, also read the manuscript in rough form, as did Harold Holzer, cochair of the United States Abraham Lincoln Bicentennial Commission, and Herman Belz, award-winning historian at the University of Maryland. I thank all of them and deeply appreciate their willingness to take the time to provide helpful suggestions. I also want to thank my editors at Rowman & Littlefield, Michael McGandy and Elaine McGarraugh, who have been patient and diligent in working with me. Alex Harner, a recent graduate of Hillsdale College, designed the maps I employ in chapter 2, and I appreciate his good work. I also want to thank my colleagues and friends at Hillsdale College for their willingness to discuss important matters in a congenial manner. I have learned much from them in the short time I have been there.

Nowhere is the debt of a student to his teachers more evident than in a book the student writes. My book is no exception. Whatever the reader might find to be intelligent and important in the pages that follow owes to the fact that I have been surrounded by excellent teachers. I alone am responsible for any and all mistakes.

Of the teachers who have most influenced my own intellectual development, the first to mention is my undergraduate instructor and advisor, Paul Basinski, with whom I studied at Fort Hays State University in my home state of Kansas. Professor Basinski introduced me to a world I did not know existed before I met him: the world of ideas. Like most American university students, when I first enrolled, I thought school was simply a place to acquire some kind of technical training and job skill. But as Professor Basinski introduced me to the great books of the Western philosophic tradition, I began to understand something of the higher purposes of higher education, purposes we are in danger of forgetting as vo-tech education replaces traditional liberal education.

Technical education is instrumental; it helps us to get a job and then to get the job done. In a word, technical education is *useful*. But its usefulness is precisely why it is not the highest kind of education. Useful technical knowledge or skills are desirable only so long as they produce the things we want: we want the skills of a pilot only until our airplane or ship reaches its destination; we want the skills of a physician only until our health is restored; we want the skills of an accountant only until our tax bill is settled. Technical education is a means of obtaining, and is therefore subordinate to, the objects it is used to produce or the ends it is used to serve. Technical education is a *servile* kind of education, in other words, because it is in the service of the necessities we need to live. Technical education is not and cannot be truly *liberal* education, because liberal education is education for a mind that is free, at least to some degree, from the slavish necessities of life, a mind that enjoys the leisure to contemplate the highest and permanent questions: What is good, true, and beautiful? What is the right way to live, and what is the purpose, end, or *telos* of human life? Is there a timeless reality that transcends time, and what might its nature be?

Liberal education presents a special challenge, therefore, because these questions have no simple or prepackaged answers. Merely understanding these questions and all they entail typically requires much time, effort, and reflection, with no guarantee of finding satisfactory answers. This leads some who are not liberally educated to dismiss liberal education because it is not especially *useful*. Indeed, liberal education is not especially useful in sailing a ship, curing an illness, or staving off the tax man in the way that the art or science of a pilot, medical doctor, or accountant is. But that is because the aim of liberal education is not merely to help us *do* something but to help us *understand* something, namely, ourselves and the world in which we live. Liberal education is education for its own sake—learning not for the sake of *doing*, but learning for the sake of understanding.

Liberal education, of course, has a stake in the political liberty without which there can be no liberal education. Thus, liberal education and political science reinforce one another; they are two sides of the same coin. Free minds study and teach the conditions of freedom so that free minds might continue to study and teach freely.

Political science arises from the fact that every human task is informed by some art or some science that instructs us how to do the task better. Each art produces a product or condition that is used for higher purposes. For example, the art of saddle-making produces saddles which are used by horsemen; the art of horsemanship produces riders who are used as cavalry by generals; the art of generalship is used by statesmen to secure victory. But if each practical art serves a higher purpose than itself, is there one highest art that does not point beyond itself? Is there a comprehensive art that instructs and gives order to all other arts? According to no less an authority than Aristotle (whom Thomas Aquinas admiringly called, "The Philosopher"), there is one such art: political science.

Consider the victory secured by the statesman. What should we do with victory? Should we continue to make war (we can always find new enemies, if needed) merely for the sake of war? Political science is the science of answering these highest practical questions by intensive study of human nature. In particular, political science teaches us that war is not the highest good; rather, war is in the service of the peace it might produce—but even peace is not the highest good. Once peace is won, we still must ask: What should we do with our peace? Political science answers that peace provides the opportunity to live well, to strive for moral and intellectual excellence. By studying political science, we discover that all human action points to the good life, the happy life, the life of virtue.

Contrary to a common misunderstanding today, happiness is not the satisfaction of any and all appetites. Rather, happiness arises from the cultivation of our moral and intellectual capacities, the cultivation of virtue. This is precisely why George Washington, in his First Inaugural Address, explained that there exists in human nature "an indissoluble union between virtue and happiness." Happiness requires good character because a people who lack good character will not be a happy people.

Washington understood, as all good political scientists do, that political society cannot ignore the character of its citizens. As free society requires limited, constitutional government, so limited, constitutional government requires citizens who are morally self-restrained and responsible. And as self-government requires good character, so the intellectual rigor of liberal education also requires self-restraint because minds enslaved to passions and appetites are not minds that can think freely or think well.

I continued my liberal education at the Claremont Graduate University in California. There, I encountered what I believe was the greatest graduate faculty in political science assembled in the United States at that time, many of whom were either students or students of students of the late Professor Leo Strauss. I enjoyed my time in Claremont so much that I probably would have stayed a graduate student forever, if only the pay were better. Mark Blitz, Charles Kesler, James Nichols, and Ralph Rossum were among the graduate faculty in Claremont most influential in my own intellectual development.

To my graduate professors Harry Jaffa and Harry Neumann, I owe more than I can ever hope to repay. Professor Neumann is unique among academics today. While many academics find themselves in the contradictory position of advancing a pet political cause, on the one hand, and grounding their political cause in the groundlessness of relativism and nihilism, on the other hand, Professor Neumann knows better. He presents himself as a defender of both relativism and nihilism. When American intellectuals and elites insist that there is no God, and there is no truth, and there is no right, Professor Neumann agrees. But he understands, as few others do, and he helps his students understand that philosophic nihilism offers no support for political advocacy of any kind. If nihilism is true, then all politics and all morality—indeed, all human life and all human choice— are nothing but meaningless sound and fury. But this cannot be. Every human being understands that his actions aim at some good, and that good is the basis of his politics. Every human being cannot help but strive to attain what he understands to be good. Thus, Professor Neumann teaches, if reality is political and moral, then nihilism cannot be true. This simple, but vital, lesson informs all of Professor Neumann's teaching—the human impossibility and unintelligibility of philosophic nihilism—a lesson that qualifies Professor Neumann as among the foremost moralists of our day.

Harry Jaffa, now professor emeritus at Claremont McKenna College and Claremont Graduate University, has spent a lifetime teaching and writing on subjects as diverse as classical and modern political philosophy, Thomas Aquinas, Shakespeare, the Bible, Mark Twain, Winston Churchill, and, most importantly, the American political tradition. His 1959 book on the Lincoln-Douglas debates, *Crisis of the House Divided*, is widely acknowledged as a watershed book in Lincoln scholarship, surpassed only by his 2000 sequel, *A New Birth of Freedom*. I believe in honesty in advertising, and I therefore disclose to the reader that I am a student of Jaffa's. To be fair, I should have concluded almost every paragraph with a footnote acknowledging Jaffa's teaching, but I knew the reader would tire of it, so let me state here that Jaffa's influence is present throughout the book. Any missteps I have made in the pages that follow—and I am confident that my teacher will point them out to me (I would be disappointed if he did not)—simply mean that I have to work harder to be a better student.

Jaffa is more than an academic, however; his influence extends to some of the most prominent political men of our day. At a 1999 dinner in Washington, D.C., Supreme Court Justice Clarence Thomas concluded his speech by asking the audience, which included a number of sitting members of Congress, to "raise a glass to our Founding Fathers, to Abraham Lincoln, and to Harry Jaffa, who reminds us of their great achievements in the fight for freedom and enables us to pass on their great legacy to a new generation of Americans."

For Jaffa, learning, writing, teaching, and challenging the politics of the day are not unrelated things. The late prominent constitutional scholar Martin Diamond used to joke in class about some of the "great books" colleges: "Socrates questioned the opinions of the ancient Athenians," Diamond would begin, "and if students go through a great books program, they too can question the opinions of the ancient Athenians; but if students go to Claremont and study with Harry Jaffa, they will question the opinions of Americans." Professor Jaffa is perhaps the closest thing to a living Socrates. But the challenge for a living Socrates today is different than it was for the ancient Athenian Socrates. Modern culture, politics, and academia are dominated by modern philosophic doctrines of relativism, positivism, historicism, and nihilism. From the modern point of view, man as a moral being who possesses a free will and a rational mind has become barely recognizable. He has been reduced to little more than the effects of various material and historical causes. And thus, the self-knowledge Socrates sought, the goal of genuine liberal education, has become increasingly difficult to attain because, looking through the corrosive lenses of false theories, man can no longer see himself. It has been Harry Jaffa's life work to unmask these doctrines, often disguised as mere academic scribbling, and to demonstrate to his fellow citizens that they are both theoretically false and politically dangerous. He has done this by providing a political and philosophical defense of the principles of the American founding, those moral and political ideas bound up in the eternal "laws of nature and of nature's God" that provide the only rational ground for a regime of civil and religious liberty.

Of no less significance is Professor Jaffa's work on statesmanship. Almost single-handedly, he has revived the classical idea of statesmanship and shown that it is not merely an object of historical curiosity but is relevant to our most vital interests today. By articulating the heights of political greatness—evidenced by such statesmen as George Washington, Abraham Lincoln, and Winston Churchill—Professor Jaffa helps to illuminate, and thereby make visible, human potential that we might otherwise have never seen on our own. By learning about human potential, we cannot help but learn something important about human nature and about ourselves. Thus, Harry Jaffa is above all a teacher. He is a teacher of the highest things. He is my teacher, and I thank him for opening my eyes so that I might see for myself the good, the true, and the beautiful.

My education would have been impossible if not for my loving and supportive parents, Don and Janice Krannawitter. They have never failed me, and whenever I was in need of someone to believe in me, they did. Their support for me reflects their devotion to one another. Through trials and tribulations, they have remained steadfast in their dedication to each other's welfare and the good of our family. It used to be commonplace in America that a husband and a wife would love and take care of each other and their children, and the children, in turn, would learn by the parents' example what it means to be a parent as well as a self-reliant, self-governing, responsible citizen. Sadly, this has become far less common. But in my own parents, I find a model of the familial responsibility that helped to make America great, and I extend to them my gratitude and respect. They deserve both.

Finally, I want to thank my wife, Lori. She listens when I want to talk. She gives me good advice. She keeps my life in order. She makes me happy.

The research and writing for this book have been no easy affair for her. During the many late nights and long weekends I spent working on this material, her patience was tried, but never failed. Most importantly, she has provided me with two beautiful children, Claire and Benjamin, who have brought more happiness into my life than I deserve. My wife has been good for me. She has made me better than I am, and I thank her from the bottom of my heart.

INTRODUCTION

In 1841, at the corner of Broadway and Ann Street in New York City, P. T. Barnum opened his American Museum filled with eccentricities on display for public viewing such as bearded ladies and Siamese twins. Following the publication of Robert Chamber's *Vestiges of the Natural History of Creation* (1844), Barnum unveiled the first live orangutan exhibit in America, labeling it "Connecting Link between Human and Brute Creation." But after Charles Darwin published his *Origin of Species* in 1859, Barnum replaced the orangutan with an eighteen-year-old black man from Georgia. In a caption above his head appeared the question "What Is It?"

Of course, an observer would know "it" was a man if he knew his nature, his human nature, which would also help the observer know why it was wrong to call a man an "it," as if he were merely a piece of property. Some used to consider this a self-evident truth. But the idea of truth, self-evident or otherwise, has long been out of vogue among many who consider themselves sophisticated. Modern minds are much more comfortable talking about *perspectives* or *truths* in the plural, rather than *truth*, the singularity of which suggests it might deserve a capital *T*. Perhaps, then, we do not need a category as problematic as *truth*; perhaps we can trust that it will be obvious to everyone with eyes to see that a man is a man? Then again, perhaps not.

Throughout history, few people have found it obvious that all human beings are equally human. It has been far more common across the ages for human beings to deny, rather than to acknowledge, the humanity they share with other human beings and the many moral and political implications that flow from such acknowledgment. Indeed, according to one of the most celebrated commentators on American democracy, Alexis de Tocqueville, the idea of human equality was virtually unknown in the ancient

1

world. According to Tocqueville, it required nothing less than the coming of Jesus Christ for human beings to see one another as equals—and even then, Tocqueville argues, equality has been more of a problem to be solved than a principle to be championed.[1]

On the eve of America's great civil war, the most entrenched apologists for slavery considered themselves good Christians and were taken aback by anyone who questioned their piety. Of course they were Christians, they insisted with righteous indignation, praising and promoting all biblical teachings, including the Golden Rule. Many of them simply saw no contradiction between the Golden Rule and slavery because they believed slaves were not fully human and, therefore, were not included in the injunction to do unto others as one would have others do unto oneself. The Golden Rule did not apply to horses and cattle in the fields; nor did it apply to "chattel" slaves. As American history has sadly witnessed, the failure to acknowledge the equal humanity of a fellow human being can transform any moral principle into a principle of tyranny and injustice. This is precisely why Abraham Lincoln argued that human equality "is the father of all moral principle."

Answering the simple, disturbing question posted above that poor soul's head in Barnum's museum turns out to be more difficult than one might at first think. It requires an objective standard of moral and political right. Lincoln followed the American Founders in identifying nature, human nature in particular, as that standard. But do we modern Americans still believe that human nature contains within itself some principle of how we ought to live? Or do we think of nature as something to be conquered, controlled, and used for any purposes we desire? If the latter is true, then how do we know which purposes we should pursue and which desires we should satisfy and which not? Once we conquer and control human nature, what do we do with it? What do we do with ourselves? If we grant a variety of "truths" and "perspectives," especially if they contradict one another, how do we determine which among them is really true? If we do not look to human nature as the foundation of morality, then how would we answer the question in Barnum's exhibit? Some observer might suggest that the eighteen-year-old is a man; others might say he is not a man but a beast. Who is right and how do we know? Reflecting on these problems reveals the challenge of self-government: combining government by consent with the equal protection of equal rights. Do others have a right to consent to laws that govern you if those laws ignore and violate your humanity, if those laws treat you as an "it" and violate your equal natural rights? Those who object and answer no understand that consensual government is not necessarily the same thing as just government. Historically, most human beings have been ruled without their consent; therefore, the question of self-government has not always been at the forefront of politics. But even when people have secured the right to consent to the government and laws under which they live, they have often consented to unjust governments and laws. Government by consent of the governed, or popular government, can be as tyrannical as the most undemocratic despotism; majority tyranny may be as brutal as tyranny by a minority. As Thomas Jefferson announced in his *Notes on the State of Virginia*, "An elective despotism was not the government we fought for."[2] But will an elective government secure justice? History has not answered this question, at least not unambiguously.

Indeed, the question of self-government, or democracy, seems to be more relevant today than it has been in a long time. After the terrorist attacks of September 11, 2001, American foreign policy under President George W. Bush has centered on the proposal that "regime change" in the Middle East, which in practice has meant democratizing certain tyrannical regimes, serves the interests of both U.S. national security and those who live in the Middle East. Throughout his many foreign policy speeches, President Bush seems to equate liberty with democracy, holding democracy to be the opposite of, and the cure for, tyranny. But what about the possibility of *democratic* tyranny? For example, Hamas, an Islamic terrorist group dedicated to the destruction of Israel, was victorious in the democratic 2006 Palestinian elections. Should supporters of the Bush administration consider the election of Hamas a foreign policy success or failure? Setting aside the troubling question of whether conditions allowed for a genuinely free and informed election, does democratic electoral victory legitimize the rule of Hamas? If the Hamas government is *democratic*, does it follow that it is *good* government? As the Hamas victory demonstrates, democracy is not necessarily the means for justice or the cure for tyranny. In some cases, democratic means might be employed for tyrannical ends.

History has not answered the question of whether an elective government will secure justice; nor can it. The question is sown permanently in the nature of man. Thus, in the famous opening paragraph of the first paper of *The Federalist*, Alexander Hamilton raises a question that every generation of Americans needs to ask: are human beings "really capable or not of establishing good government from reflection and choice," or are they "forever destined to depend for their political constitutions on accident and force?" The question arises because, by nature, men are neither beasts, which cannot form governments, nor gods, who do not need governments. Human beings are the in-between beings who possess reason, and through reason, human beings can know it is morally wrong to govern some men as if they were beasts (slaves) or permit others to govern as if they were gods (kings). Every legitimate moral teaching, from the laws of Moses to Plato's *Laws*, from the Golden Rule to the American Declaration of Independence, rests on the distinction between human and nonhuman beings, a distinction rooted in, and inseparable from, nature.

Throughout his political career, Abraham Lincoln worked tirelessly to shape public opinion, reminding his fellow Americans of the basic natural humanity of blacks, especially those held in the miserable bondage of chattel slavery. When the citizens of eleven states rejected his constitutional election as president and attempted to secede, fearing threats to their "peculiar institution" of slavery, Lincoln faced the awful choice of allowing the Union to crumble or drawing blood to preserve it. It is the essence of the American tragedy that in order for free government to survive, it had to endure such a terrible civil war.

Lincoln understood, as few of his contemporaries did and few scholars do today, that government by consent of the governed rests upon the idea of human equality. It is precisely because "all men are created equal" that it is wrong for one man to rule another without the other's consent. This moral principle finds its most eloquent and authoritative expression in the American Declaration of Independence, which states,

> We hold these Truths to be self-evident, that all Men are created equal, that they are endowed by their Creator with certain unalienable Rights, that among these are Life, Liberty and the pursuit of Happiness—That to secure these Rights, Governments are instituted among Men, deriving their just Powers from the Consent of the Governed.

Over the course of the four score and seven years that separated the Declaration of Independence and the Gettysburg Address, Lincoln believed that as Americans adopted opinions of moral neutrality toward slavery or came to believe it was a positively good institution, they were forgetting or abandoning what Lincoln called their "ancient faith" in human equality and, thereby, forfeiting the only ground upon which free society can be defended. No one worked harder than Lincoln to remind Americans of the noble principles of their nation's founding and to explain why those principles are both just and useful.

Today, as in Lincoln's day, the meaning of the American Founding has faded in the American mind. The most important political task before us today is to recover its principles, the principles of freedom, and submit our politics and our government to their guidance. From its inception, American self-government has been, and it must remain, an experiment. Success is not guaranteed; nor will it ever be final. America places its destiny in the hands of its citizens, and we are free to make of America what we will. This does not mean that Americans must make these fateful choices blindly or arbitrarily. In the principles of the American Founding, we can discover wisdom, truth, and the conditions of freedom that should guide us today.

For the sake of perpetuating the American experiment, this book aims to recover from accumulating neglect and misunderstanding the preeminent example of American statesmanship offered by Abraham Lincoln. From his life, we can learn the virtues necessary to sustain self-government. Thus, Lincoln's teachings remain as relevant in our day as they were in his. His story provides a window for citizens to see what the principles of their country mean, the obligations those principles impose on them, and the great challenges entailed in preserving them. The highest purpose of any book on Lincoln is not merely to prattle about the past. It is, rather, to explain, based on Lincoln's example, the principles and practices necessary for us to perpetuate our own freedom. It is to show that failing to recognize the humanity of fellow human beings is morally wrong for the very same principled reason that individual liberty and constitutional government by consent are morally right, issues that we can never ignore or forget if we care about preserving free society. By studying Lincoln with care and attention, Americans today can understand that his fight is their fight as well.

But Lincoln's reputation has been tarnished in some quarters of the American mind, while few educated Americans believe in the natural right principles that informed his political thought. Lincoln Day celebrations, for example, which were prominent and many only a couple of generations ago, have become almost extinct. No longer celebrated by many Americans, Lincoln's birthday (as well as Washington's) has been absorbed into the bland and meaningless President's Day, as if there were no important differences between the greatest and lowest who have occupied the office. I am not suggesting that Americans have completely forgotten Lincoln. Most American school children are still taught the basic historical dates and facts of his life, and millions of visitors continue to tour the Lincoln Memorial in Washington, D.C. But do Americans understand what Lincoln means or why he is important? Growing numbers of prominent scholars dismiss Lincoln's principles as irrelevant to our lives today. Others openly attack his politics, arguing that he was a traitor to the cause of free society and constitutional government. These teachers of teachers influence how Americans view the man once considered the greatest American president and, in turn, how Americans come to understand themselves and their country.[3]

While some school-aged American children might be able to recite Lincoln's Gettysburg Address, it is unclear whether they speak his words with reverence, or embarrassment, or, most likely, indifference.[4]

So, what is the status of Lincoln and his principles in America today? If his principles are alive and influential anywhere, one might expect them to be so in the Republican Party that Lincoln helped to establish by becoming the first successful Republican presidential candidate in 1860. Speaking as a representative from Mississippi, however, Trent Lott, who would later go on to become the Republican majority leader in the U.S. Senate, declared in 1984 that "the spirit of Jefferson Davis lives in the . . . Republican platform." Surely Lincoln would be turning in his grave if he knew that his Republican Party embodied the "spirit of Jefferson Davis." While Lincoln argued tirelessly that "all men are created equal," Davis believed that blacks were ordained by God to live in slavery. The state of Mississippi, which both Lott and Davis represented in the U.S. House and the U.S. Senate, declared in its 1861 Declaration of Secession from the federal union that "our position is thoroughly identified with the institution of slavery—the greatest material interest of the world," which "none but the black race can bear [because of their] exposure to the tropical sun."[5] Nothing could be farther removed from Lincoln's principles.

Perhaps the confirmation hearings of Supreme Court Justice Clarence Thomas best reveal the degree to which Americans have either rejected or forgotten those principles. Most Americans remember little about Thomas's controversial confirmation hearings in late 1991 except for Anita Hill's last-minute allegations of sexual harassment. But in the opening days of the hearings, before Hill stole the spotlight, the most troubling issue for members of the Senate Judiciary Committee was the fact that Thomas had given public speeches in which he defended the natural law principles of the American Founders and Abraham Lincoln. It was almost as if Thomas had declared the earth to be flat, so alien and unusual was his defense of the natural law in the committee members' eyes. They simply could not believe that an educated and intelligent mind in 1991 could believe in the natural law, something they considered antiquated and irrelevant to modern politics and law. In his opening remarks, for example, Senator Joseph Biden, a Democrat from Delaware who at that time chaired, and today continues to sit on, the Senate Judiciary Committee, exhorted Thomas to explain:

> Judge Thomas, you come before this committee . . . with a philosophy different from that which we have seen in any Supreme Court nominee in the nineteen years since I have been in the Senate. For, as has been

widely discussed and debated in the press, you are an adherent to the view that natural law philosophy should inform the Constitution. Finding out what you mean when you say that you would apply the natural law philosophy to the Constitution is, in my view, the single most important task of this committee and, in my view, your most significant obligation to this committee.[6]

It is telling that in his previous nineteen years in the Senate, Senator Biden had never encountered a nominee for the Supreme Court who believed in the natural law principles of the Founders and Lincoln! In light of Senator Biden's comment, it is no exaggeration to suggest that those principles have been almost universally abandoned, at least by educated and political elites. Intellectuals today, of both the left and the right, routinely dismiss the natural law and the idea of natural rights. In his 2004 *Rights From Wrongs*, for example, the prominent liberal law professor at Harvard University, Alan Dershowitz, asserts "[t]he truth is that a set of specific rights based on natural law simply does not exist" because the "[n]atural law is a human invention, much like religions that believe in an intervening God." Despite their political differences, Dershowitz echoes the quip from Alasdair MacIntyre, a conservative Catholic defender of traditionalism, in his widely influential book, *After Virtue*: "there are no [natural] rights, and belief in them is one with belief in witches and unicorns."[7] With statements like these coming from esteemed academics, it is little wonder that our elected officials are incredulous that someone today might actually believe in the natural rights principles of Lincoln and the Founders. As the senators continued to press Thomas about his seemingly strange attraction to the theory of natural law, Thomas explained that it was through Lincoln that he had learned about it: "Repeatedly, Lincoln referred to the notion that all men are created equal. And that was my attraction to, or beginning of my attraction to this [natural law] approach." At one point in the hearings, Thomas asked the senators if

> we can both agree that the founders of our country, or at least some of the drafters of our Constitution and our Declaration, believed in natural rights. And my point was simply that in understanding overall our constitutional government that it was important that we understood how they believed—or what they believed in natural law or natural rights.[8]

But the majority of the Senate Judiciary Committee was hardly in the mood to be instructed by Thomas about the natural law theory of the Founders and Lincoln. After long and intense hearings, the Senate barely confirmed Thomas's nomination to the Supreme Court on October 15, 1991, by a vote of 52–48, the closest confirmation vote within the past century. Today, Clarence Thomas is the only sitting member of the Supreme Court who explains and defends in his written opinions the natural right principles that informed the drafting and ratification of the U.S. Constitution, as well as Abraham Lincoln's principled defense of it. And for his dedication to those principles, he is subject to continuous criticisms, attacks, and insults.[9]

Among prominent academics, some attack Lincoln's character, calling him a racist and sometimes comparing him to Adolf Hitler, Joseph Stalin, and other murderous tyrants of the past century. The pages that follow examine these charges closely. But consider also the political effects of such attacks. When critics attempt to knock Lincoln out of the pantheon of American heroes, they add to the growing cynicism of American politics. After all, if Americans come to believe that the president reputed to be the greatest was in truth a scoundrel unworthy of respect, then surely they will view all lesser politicians as such, adding to the mistaken idea that there is nothing noble or beautiful about politics, that politics entails nothing more than base and greedy grabs for power. Such political cynicism, at best, breeds political apathy. The lower our view of politics becomes, the more we tune out of politics and tune in to our private pursuits and private interests. But if we do not pay attention to politics, then who will hold our government accountable to constitutional and moral standards? And if our government is not accountable to constitutional and moral standards, then how secure is our own liberty?

I am not suggesting that we look at Lincoln through rose-colored glasses in order to provide Americans with a much-needed heroic figure. We should not prop up Lincoln's reputation if he does not deserve it. If Lincoln deserves licks, then licks he should get. But, as I will demonstrate, the most serious attacks on Lincoln are sorely mistaken. The most urgent demands to knock Lincoln down in the estimate of the American mind are based on misunderstandings of Lincoln's words and actions. We should weigh the evidence and think long and hard, therefore, before we allow some to take an American hero away from the American people, a people already at risk of self-destructive cynicism. Perhaps the most urgent political task in America today is for Americans to recover an older view of politics, one that suggests politics as a means for accomplishing great and high-minded goals. There is no better way to recover that old view than by studying the examples of the great heroes and statesmen who have helped to make America the free country it is, Abraham Lincoln foremost among them.

No single book can provide an exhaustive account of the literature that has been produced about Lincoln and the Civil War. An estimated sixteen thousand volumes exist, and more are published each year. As Aristotle once remarked, however, it is pointless to review all opinions; we should limit our discussion to the most prominent and serious.[10] I have chosen, therefore, to respond to those books and articles that best represent and articulate the most powerful criticisms leveled against Lincoln. In the chapters that follow, I focus on the questions most frequently raised by those who challenge Lincoln's iconic status. Some of these questions relate directly to today's pressing political concerns. The question of racism, for example, persists in political disputes ranging from affirmative action and racial preferences to airport security measures and racial profiling. Lincoln is frequently invoked in these disputes, sometimes as a man of good intentions who simply failed to understand or defend the full implications of his principles and at other times as a man who had no principles. Later in the book, I address the question of Lincoln's fidelity to the Constitution in his presidential exercise of executive war powers, a subject headlined in newspapers today no less frequently than it was during the Civil War. Other subjects, such as the Kansas–Nebraska Act, *Dred Scott v. Sandford*, and the question of states' rights and state secession, are more historical, although each helps us to understand the nature of our union and the purposes and meaning of our Constitution. They also help us to judge whether Lincoln deserves to be celebrated, scorned, or ignored. By reviewing some of the most controversial literature, I consider various interpretations of Lincoln, including historicist assumptions that Lincoln was merely a child of his age and that his ideas were therefore bound to the nineteenth century, as well as more pointed accusations that Lincoln was a racist and related arguments that his speeches and deeds were motivated more by economics than by any moral concerns for blacks or slavery. Lincoln's many critics come from a variety of scholarly backgrounds and include academic historians and economists, as well as prominent political liberals and conservatives. A rejection of the natural right principles that informed Lincoln's statesmanship unites their otherwise disparate writings. They aim to vilify Lincoln and to persuade the American people to abandon his principles and example. In this book, I aim to vindicate Lincoln's statesmanship against misunderstandings, some willful some not, and to demonstrate in the process the superiority of Lincoln's understanding (and, necessarily, the Founders' understanding) of human nature over today's elite opinion, which increasingly influences public opinion.

The charges against Lincoln must be taken seriously, and answered if possible, because we stand to lose much if we lose the example of Lincoln. More than anyone else, Lincoln demonstrates a uniquely American kind of statesmanship—he represents the very possibility of democratic greatness. At least since Tocqueville's *Democracy in America*, many thoughtful commentators have lamented that American self-government renders true human greatness impossible, that the principle of equality causes an irresistible and irreversible leveling of the human condition, a condition in which mediocrity is considered a virtue and excellence a vice. America, then, presents the basic question of human potential in our democratic age. Can a political regime dedicated to the proposition that all men are created equal comprehend and accept the ways in which some men might be unequal? Does equality prevent Americans from appreciating the truly great and outstanding human being? Even if superior wisdom or goodness is possible, does the requirement of consent preclude the supremely wise from teaching the supremely vulgar? America finds the definitive answer to these questions—how to connect the high and the low, wisdom and consent—above all in the statesmanship of Abraham Lincoln.

Statesmanship is an old-fashioned word, one seldom used today, but we should reclaim it. People typically identify politics with power, politics being the means, power the end. But statesmanship is something higher. Statesmanship, too, is concerned with power, but it employs persuasion as well—it appeals both to our sense of justice and to our interests—in order to accomplish some common good. Statesmanship is required when no clear path connects the present to some preferred future state of affairs or when there is disagreement about which future state of affairs should be preferred. In politics, it is sometimes unclear how to achieve the greatest good or avoid the greatest evil. In political disputes, each of the competing arguments often contains some truth, while none is entirely true. Sometimes political reality presents multiple options that are all bad, and it is not clear which, if any, is less bad than the others. While never losing sight of the fixed principles of right, the statesman must simultaneously keep his eyes on the many changing particulars that surround him. Prudence, or practical judgment, therefore, is the virtue upon which statesmanship chiefly rests, although prudence will not be forthcoming if not fortified by moderation, justice, and courage. Lacking any special foreknowledge of the future, the statesman's job is to figure out the prudent course of action and then persuade others to join him and support the effort. The statesman can achieve little by himself; he needs the help of others. Thus, the statesman must possess a clear mind—he must be able to reason well—but he also needs the art of rhetoric. His prudence and reasoning will be of no avail unless he can speak and write in a way that moves and shapes the opinions of others. As an ancient maxim declares, the highest purpose of the statesman is to teach. Unlike the mere partisan, the statesman does not simply preach to his choir, although he may occasionally try to inspire or motivate it. Mainly, the statesman's speech always aims to teach and persuade others, especially those who hold contrary opinions. Elihu Root, a U.S. senator who also served as secretary of war under President William McKinley and secretary of state under President Theodore Roosevelt and was awarded the Nobel Peace Prize in 1912, captures the importance of rhetoric in Lincoln's statesmanship in an essay titled "Lincoln as Leader of Men":

> [Lincoln] was intensely practical. While he never for a moment lost sight of the great ends toward which he struggled, or wavered in his devotion to the eternal principles which justified those ends, he never assumed that his conclusions would be accepted merely because he knew they were right, however clearly he might state them. He did not expect other people to have their minds work as his mind worked, or to reach his conclusions because he thought they ought to reach them, or to feel as he felt because he thought they ought to feel so. He never relied upon authority or dictation or compulsion upon the minds of others.[11]

In the constant struggle to unite universal right with particular demands and desires that are not always right, the statesman may well lose sight of himself. Lincoln's statesmanship, however, is best revealed in his complete subordination of himself to his cause. Lincoln understood that what mattered most was not the life and career of Abraham Lincoln, but the principles of justice that his mind could comprehend and his labor could advance, however fleeting and limited his individual efforts might be:

> [Lincoln] liked to get on in the world, of course, as any normal man does; but the way he got on was by thinking about his job, not by thinking about himself. During all these years he was not thinking about making Abraham Lincoln famous; he was thinking about putting an end to slavery and preserving the Union. It is interesting to observe that the two who have attained the highest pinnacles are not to be found among the millions of Americans who have dreamed of power and fame for themselves. Washington and Lincoln reached their preeminence by thinking about their work and forgetting themselves.[12]

The truly great American statesman finds the source of his greatness in the timeless principle of equality. Few in history have begun life in such a low station and risen to such heights of preeminence as Abraham Lincoln. But in rising from the low to the high, Lincoln understood that the cause of his rise was something higher than himself, a principle that at once stands above all human beings while informing us that all human beings are equal in a decisive respect. In Lincoln, we see not only that American greatness and American statesmanship are possible, but that, in their most excellent forms, they elevate the souls of all men by teaching them the source of goodness and right, the natural right principle that all men are created equal.

NOTES

1. Harvey C. Mansfield and Delba Winthrop, eds., *Alexis de Tocqueville: Democracy in America* (Chicago: University of Chicago Press, 2000), 413.

2. Thomas Jefferson, "Notes on the State of Virginia," Query XIII, in *Jefferson: Writings*, ed. Merrill D. Peterson (New York: Library of America, 1984), 245.

3. William A. DeGregorio, *The Complete Book of U.S. Presidents*, 6th ed. (Fort Lee, NJ: Barricade Books, 2005), 796.

4. Barry Schwartz, "Postmodernity and Historical Reputation: Abraham Lincoln in the Late Twentieth-Century American Memory," *Social Forces* 77, no. 1 (September 1998): 63–103.

5. "A Declaration of the Immediate Causes Which Induce and Justify the Secession of the State of Mississippi from the Federal Union," January 9, 1861, Civil War Homepage, www.civil-war.net/pages/mississippi_declaration.asp (accessed June 1, 2007).

6. Sen. Joseph Biden, "Opening Statement before the U.S. Senate Judiciary Committee's Hearing on the Confirmation of Clarence Thomas to Be an Associate Justice to the U.S. Supreme Court," September 10, 1991, GPO Access, www.gpoaccess.gov/congress/senate/judiciary/sh102-1084pt1/6-21.pdf (accessed June 5, 2007). See also Lawrence Tribe, "Clarence Thomas and Natural Law," *New York Times*, July 15, 1991, A15.

7. See Alan Dershowitz, *Rights From Wrongs: A Secular Theory of the Origins of Rights* (New York: Basic Books, 2004), 62, and Alasdair MacIntyre, *After Virtue: A Study in Moral Theory* (Notre Dame, IN: University of Notre Dame Press, 1984), 69.

8. Clarence Thomas, "Response to Senator Biden during the U.S. Senate Judiciary Committee's Hearing on the Confirmation of Clarence Thomas to Be an Associate Justice to the U.S. Supreme Court," September 10, 1991, GPO Access, www.gpoaccess.gov/congress/senate/judiciary/sh102-1084pt1/107-175.pdf (accessed June 5, 2007). See also Clarence Thomas, *My Grandfather's Son: A Memoir* (New York: HarperCollins, 2007), 187–88, 221–22, 231.

9. The most recent example is Kevin Merida and Michael Fletcher, *Supreme Discomfort: The Divided Soul of Clarence Thomas* (New York: Doubleday, 2007).

10. Joe Sachs, trans., *Aristotle: Nicomachean Ethics* (Newburyport, MA: Focus Publishing, 2002), 3.

11. Elihu Root, "Lincoln as Leader of Men," in *Men and Policies: Addresses by Elihu Root*, ed. Robert Bacon and James Brown Scott (Cambridge, MA: Harvard University Press, 1924), 72.

12. Root, "Lincoln as Leader of Men," 72.

1

WAS LINCOLN A RACIST?

Lincoln said repeatedly in private and public, in Springfield and in the White House, that he was a White supremacist and that he wanted to deny Blacks equal rights because of their race.

> —Lerone Bennett Jr., *Forced into Glory:*
> *Abraham Lincoln's White Dream*

Let us discard all this quibbling about this man and the other man—this race and that race and the other race being inferior, and therefore they must be placed in an inferior position. . . . Let us discard all these things, and unite as one people throughout this land, until we shall once more stand up declaring that all men are created equal.

> —Abraham Lincoln, speech in Chicago, July 10, 1858

The first and most decisive question to ask about Abraham Lincoln is whether he really believed in human equality or was a racist and white supremacist, as Lerone Bennett insists in the epigraph above. Did Lincoln believe what he said at Gettysburg, that America was "conceived in liberty, and dedicated to the proposition that all men are created equal?" Was Lincoln himself so dedicated? Did he himself believe that all men are created equal?

We are compelled to ask these questions because, despite Lincoln's fame as the Great Emancipator, countless Lincoln critics since the Civil War have insisted that he spoke disingenuously of equality between whites and blacks, that he really believed blacks were inferior to whites, and that he advanced policies to keep blacks down whenever he could. If these accusations are true, then indeed Lincoln deserves contempt, not the elevated, perhaps un-rivaled, position he has occupied among America's most distinguished citizens. The matter is far from settled among those who write about and invoke Lincoln, but most seem to lean in the direction that Lincoln is guilty as charged.

In his recent book *Why Lincoln Matters*, former Democratic governor of New York Mario Cuomo, for example, quotes from scholars who defend Lincoln as a champion of color-blind principles and others who scorn him as a racist, but Cuomo himself never says which view he believes is correct.[1] Instead, he laments that "there are not many respected scholars or authors who would deny Lincoln held . . . unsavory racial views before he assumed the presidency."[2] U.S. Senator Barack Obama, in a 2005 feature essay in *Time* magazine, wrote, "[I] cannot swallow whole the view of Lincoln as the Great Emancipator. As a law professor and civil rights lawyer and as an African American, I am fully aware of his limited views on race."[3] According to journalist and author Michael Lind, Lincoln was simply a "white supremacist" whose "racial policies, intended to produce a homogenous, all-white America, seem repugnant in a postracist United States where not only racial integration but also racial intermarriage increase with each generation." Thankfully, Lind concludes, Lincoln-the-racist "is a figure of the past" whose beliefs have become "obsolete."[4] According to historian Clyde Wilson, "Lincoln . . . like ninety-eight percent of his voters and most Americans of several succeeding generations, was also a white supremacist."[5] Or as libertarian Charles Adams sums it up, "Lincoln believed in white supremacy."[6]

Broader implications flow from these charges, implications that reach beyond Lincoln and his reputation. In the United States, unlike most nations, questions of slavery, race, and equality reach to the very core of what America is. In America, we cast moral judgments (however much we talk about being nonjudgmental) on our fellow citizens based on whether they affirm the founding principle of equality; we might tolerate, but we tend to look down upon, citizens who disavow the equal rights of others. And, in the past at least, this dedication to equality inspired in many Americans a belief in the moral superiority of America, a view that America should serve as a kind of political and moral role model for the rest of the world. If, however, Americans and their most famed politician, Lincoln, have used the principle of equality merely as a cover for injustice, if Americans talk the talk of equality but walk the walk of racists, then America can be no role model. Just the opposite: one might well conclude that America is immoral and a fraud, a conclusion that many Americans (and many around the world) seemed to have reached.

In his recent, provocative book *White Guilt*, Shelby Steele raises the thorny question of why growing ranks of American intellectuals and political elites are reluctant to celebrate America—some even seem unwilling to defend America against its foreign enemies—while at the same time they are quick to embrace non-American cultures and customs. In short, why has multiculturalism replaced patriotism in America? The answer, at least in part, argues Steele, is to be found in the civil rights era of the 1960s, the moment when America "moved out of its long age of white racism and into a new age of white guilt."[7] The 1960s was the pivotal time, according to Steele, when racism, previously an asset for whites, quickly became a liability for them. Steele reminds us that as late as the 1950s, even the most prominent white political elites could tell n-word jokes in polite company without worry; but after the 1960s, any comment that smacked of racism would mortally injure any white politician's political career. Americans no longer found racism funny.

What Steele calls "white guilt," the admission by whites that they, or at least some among them, are either guilty of racism or complicit in it by association, led to an "enormous vacuum of moral authority." "The vacuum of moral authority that comes from simply knowing that one's race is associated with racism," Steele explains, requires white Americans to "acknowledge historical racism to show themselves redeemed of it." But once they acknowledge their past racism,

> they lose moral authority over everything having to do with race, equality, social justice, poverty, and so on. . . . The authority they lose transfers to the "victims" of historical racism and becomes their great power in society. This is why white guilt is quite literally the same thing as black power.[8]

It is good when racists come to acknowledge the injustice of their racism, of course, and work to end racist policies and practices. The problem, Steele argues, is that in their attempt to separate themselves from all things racist, many Americans wrongly identify America itself with racism. "When white supremacy was de-legitimized," writes Steele, "whites did not simply lose the authority to practice racism . . . [but] whites also lost a degree of their authority to stand proudly for the [principles] and ideas that had made the West a great civilization." In short, "after America admitted what was worst about itself, there was not enough authority left to support what was best."[9] After the 1960s, the new movement to cleanse America of racism insisted that any defense of Western, and especially American, principles, institutions, and history was synonymous with a defense of racism.

Steele argues persuasively that among today's white educated and political elites, perhaps more so in blue states than in red, most pay lip service to remedying present problems caused by past racism, but their main concern is a desire to clear their own consciences and feel good about themselves. They are much less interested in justice than in disassociating themselves from the stigmas of racism and bigotry, which in their view requires not only condemning racism but condemning America itself. White Americans ease their guilty feelings and redeem themselves from their past sins of racism, in other words, by rejecting everything America used to stand for.

Further, they demand that conscientious white Americans take responsibility for the problems caused by their racism, most visibly by supporting affirmative action and other government programs that offer preferences and subsidies to, and therefore help shoulder the responsibility for, victimized racial groups. By supporting racial preferences and programs, white Americans inoculate themselves against accusations of racism: after all, how could anyone who supports affirmative action be a racist? Accordingly, anyone who opposes racial preferences and programs is not taking responsibility for, and might well be suspected of, racism.[10] Anyone opposed to affirmative action, in other words, is part of the problem, not the solution. This is the widely known, but seldom admitted, reason why so many politicians (including many in red states) refuse to defend color-blind policies and campaign actively to end race-based preferences and discrimination: they are scared of being called racists and unsure they can defend themselves against such accusations.

But opposition to racial affirmative action policies does not equal racism. In fact, it is more consistent to oppose racial preferences, categories, and quotas while demanding equal treatment under the law, itself a logical and necessary inference from the American Founding's color-blind principle of human equality—*the* principle that provides the only true remedy for racist opinions and policies. Steele's description of the national guilt that gripped the American mind after the civil rights movements of the 1960s is probably right, but he never explains fully why much of that guilt was misplaced and fails to emphasize that however unjust parts of American history might seem, we should never forget that American politics rests on a foundation of justice, a lesson offered by the Founders and Lincoln that complements Steele's otherwise intelligent analysis.

It might sound strange at first, but the problem of slavery in the American Founding and the years following may best reveal America's goodness. That is, slavery was clearly a problem to be solved in America, but slavery is a problem only in a good regime; slavery is no problem in a bad one. We should not forget that throughout most of human history, slavery was commonplace and few if any considered it to be a problematic ill. "Slavery has existed from the dawn of human history right down to the 20th century, in the most primitive of human societies and in the most civilized," writes Orlando Patterson in *Slavery and Social Death*. "There is no region on earth that has not at some time harbored the institution. Probably there is no group of people whose ancestors were not at one time slaves or slaveowners."[11] Around the world and across the ages, societies accepted, practiced, and defended slavery as an institution rooted in tradition and law. In *The End of Racism*, for example, Dinesh D'Souza recounts the story of an English antislavery activist who led a campaign to suppress slavery in Sudan and found Africans unwilling to entertain the idea that slavery is a moral wrong: "It was in vain that I attempted to reason with them against the principles of slavery—they thought it wrong when they were themselves the sufferers, but were always ready to indulge in it when the preponderance of power lay upon their side." When both Britain and France were debating whether to end slavery in their respective colonies and territories in the 1830s and 1840s, tribal leaders from Gambia, Dahomey, the Congo, and other African nations sent delegations to London and Paris to protest, encouraging European powers to continue the slave trade from which these African nations had prospered. D'Souza concludes that "perhaps the fairest generalization is that no Africans opposed slavery in principle, they merely opposed their own enslavement."[12]

The views the Africans expressed were not uncommon. Prior to the American Founding, the only principled opposition to slavery was found in obscure and dense old philosophy books. But in America, slavery became a problem, and not merely an intellectual or abstract problem for philosophers to sort out in their spare time but a public and political problem that would not go away and eventually cost America a bloody civil war. This fact alone tells us much about the goodness of America. Having justified their own revolution and independence with the principle of equality, thereby placing equality front and center in their politics, Americans could not avoid a reckoning with the institution of slavery. America was destined for some kind of moral and political confrontation over the issue because, and only because, the nation was founded on the principle of human equality, a principle that stands diametrically opposed to slavery. Can that be said of any regime prior to America's establishment? Though founded on the principle of equality, American government and law offered protection for the institution of slavery. A house so divided could not stand indefinitely. And at the center of the confrontation over slavery stood Abraham Lincoln, whose election in November 1860 did as much as anything to bring about the Civil War.

LINCOLN IN SPEECH

It is impossible to peer into the soul of another human being and know with certainty his inner thoughts and motives.[13] The best I can do is infer Lincoln's intentions from his words and actions. I cannot prove beyond all doubt that Lincoln believed in the perfect equality of whites and blacks. I cannot claim to know Lincoln's mind as fully as Lincoln did. Many have argued that Lincoln spoke disingenuously of equality and simply said whatever getting elected required. But after close analysis of Lincoln's words and deeds, I find that argument unlikely, because there is much to suggest that Lincoln did in fact believe in the equal rights of whites and blacks, even if he often presented those beliefs in an esoteric manner. Lincoln's rhetorical strategies reveal much about his statesmanship as he constantly adjusted his language in order to gain an audience and win their support, while subtly reminding them of equality, without offending them.

Let us turn, then, to Lincoln's words. Below I offer two quotations from Lincoln that critics most frequently present as conclusive proof of his supposed views of white racial supremacy:

> [T]his is the true complexion of all I have ever said in regard to the institution of slavery and the black race. This is the whole of it, and anything that argues me into [Stephen Douglas's] idea of perfect social and political equality with the negro, is but a specious and fantastic arrangement of words, by which a man can prove a horse-chestnut to be a chestnut horse. I will say here, while upon this subject, that I have no purpose, directly or indirectly, to interfere with the institution of slavery in the States where it exists. I believe I have no lawful right to do so, and I have no inclination to do so. I have no purpose to introduce political and social equality between the white and the black races. There is a physical difference between the two, which, in my judgment, will probably forever forbid their living together upon the footing of perfect equality, and inasmuch as it becomes a necessity that there must be a difference, I, as well as Judge Douglas, am in favor of the race to which I belong having the superior position.[14]

Here is Lincoln again:

> I will say then that I am not, nor ever have been, in favor of bringing about in any way the social and political equality of the white and black races—that I am not nor ever have been in favor of making voters or jurors of negroes, nor of qualifying them to hold office, nor to intermarry with white people; and I will say in addition to this that there is a phys-

ical difference between the white and black races which I believe will forever forbid the two races living together on terms of social and political equality. And inasmuch as they cannot so live, while they do remain together there must be the position of superior and inferior, and I as much as any other man am in favor of having the superior position assigned to the white race.[15]

The first quotation comes from Lincoln's first debate with Stephen Douglas, held in Ottawa, Illinois, on August 21, 1858; the second quotation is from the fourth debate with Douglas in Charleston, Illinois, on September 18, 1858.

Thomas DiLorenzo, one of Lincoln's most vocal and unforgiving critics in recent years, who has written two well-received books aimed at discrediting him, believes Lincoln's words clearly indicate that he opposed racial equality of any kind. "Incredibly," DiLorenzo exclaims, "various Lincoln scholars take a statement like [the quotations above] and somehow conclude that Lincoln 'really' meant, 'I do have purpose to introduce political and racial equality.'" DiLorenzo's main complaint is that he believes most Lincoln scholars purposefully keep Lincoln's racism from the public view: "Mostly, [racist] statements like this are simply ignored and kept from the innocent eyes of American schoolchildren."[16] According to DiLorenzo, this is symptomatic of academics who comprise a "Lincoln cult" and who "do whatever is necessary to keep unflattering information about Lincoln from the public." "If they do dare to mention such facts, they spin their statements to mislead, misinform, and confuse the reader. One has to wonder: What purpose does all this deception and misinformation serve? If Lincoln was such a saint, why can't his record speak for itself?"[17]

In his best-selling book, *The Politically Incorrect Guide to American History*, Thomas Woods quotes the lines above from Lincoln's fourth debate with Douglas in Charleston, suggesting that the obvious racism in Lincoln's words offer a "reality check" about "Lincoln's views on race."[18] David Gordon, editor of the libertarian journal *The Mises Review*, is in disbelief that Lincoln might have considered blacks the equals of whites: "How can someone who says [what Lincoln says above] be regarded as a believer in equality between blacks and whites?"[19]

Even some writers who are friendlier toward Lincoln think his views on race were less than honorable. For example, in his biography of Lincoln, which won the 1996 Lincoln Prize, David Donald quotes Lincoln's opening remarks from the Charleston debate, commenting simply,

> This was a politically expedient thing to say in a state where the majority of the inhabitants were of Southern origin; perhaps it was a necessary thing

to say in a state where only ten years earlier seventy percent of the voters
had favored a constitutional amendment to exclude all blacks from Illinois.

More importantly, "it also represented Lincoln's deeply held personal
views," although Donald believes that Lincoln "had given little thought to
the status of free African-Americans" and "did not know whether [blacks]
could ever fit into a free society."[20] In *April 1865: The Month That Saved
America*, Jay Winik quotes Lincoln from the Ottawa debate and his 1858
speech in Chicago, which appears as the epigraph at the beginning of this
chapter ("Let us . . . unite as one people throughout this land, until we shall
once more stand up declaring that all men are created equal"), concluding
that Lincoln "was often caught in embarrassing contradictions."[21]

In a book review titled "What Did He Really Think about Race?"
published in the *New York Review of Books*, historian James McPherson
suggests that Lincoln was "a master of misdirection" and deliberately
used his rhetoric on race matters to hide his own belief in equality yet
"[appear] to appease [those who did not believe in equality] while ma-
nipulating them toward acceptance of radical policies." In a letter responding to McPherson's essay, however, Michael Lind dismisses
McPherson's argument with the mocking label "the Secret Lincoln hy-
pothesis." According to Lind, the view that Lincoln secretly believed in
the equal rights of whites and blacks but was reluctant to say so in public is merely an unsupported and desperate defense of Lincoln put up by
"twenty-first-century Americans embarrassed by some of the attitudes of
a great nineteenth-century American."[22]

These otherwise very different scholars share the assumption that Lincoln's rhetoric reveals racial hostility toward blacks, but they offer almost no
analysis of Lincoln's words and fail to identify precisely where they believe
Lincoln advocates white supremacy. In fact, the more closely one inspects
Lincoln's words—unlike politicians today, Lincoln did not rely on speech
writers and chose his words carefully—the more the evidence condemning
Lincoln as a racist seems to evaporate.

When Lincoln said, "I have no purpose to introduce political and social equality between the white and black races," he stated nothing but political fact. From the time he reentered national politics in 1854 (reacting to
the Kansas-Nebraska Act, which is discussed in chapter 2) until his 1860
campaign for president, Lincoln had in fact never proposed "to introduce
political and social equality between the white and black races." The core
of his political platform was the proposal to prohibit slavery from spreading
into the federal territories; in terms of policies related to slavery and race,

Lincoln only advocated repealing the Kansas-Nebraska Act and restoring the Missouri Compromise. On face value then, Lincoln's words are not a statement of racial supremacy; they only describe his campaign platform. Further, while he said it was not his purpose in 1858 to "introduce political and social equality between the white and black races," Lincoln never denied that he believed in their political and social equality, and he never said that he would not support policies of racial equality in the future should public opinion become more receptive to them.

"There is a physical difference between the two," Lincoln said next, "which in my judgment will probably forever forbid their living together upon the footing of perfect equality." Is there a physical difference between black and white human beings? Of course: blacks are black, and whites are white. And while this simple difference of skin color, in itself, does not imply or require political and social inequality, the distinction of color in America had become deeply entwined with slavery and questions of racial hierarchy. Lincoln was offering a sound sociological observation when he predicted that differing skin colors would "probably forever forbid their living together upon the footing of perfect equality." If the long and sad story of race relations in America teaches anything, it is that people of different skin colors have a difficult time seeing one another as equals, as fellow citizens, and as potential friends rather than as members of separate racial groups.

Seventy years earlier, in his *Notes on the State of Virginia*, Thomas Jefferson made the same argument Lincoln did later: unfortunately, it would be difficult for whites and blacks ever to view one another as equals. While Jefferson based his opinion partly on distinctions of skin color, he also entertained the possibility that blacks were physically and intellectually inferior to whites, that perhaps natural differences between the races did run deeper than skin color and would prevent blacks from ever establishing themselves as equals to whites within the horizon of civil society. Understanding Jefferson's political thought, especially his thoughts on race and slavery, is important to understanding Lincoln's because it was to the principles of Jefferson, whom Lincoln described as "the most distinguished politician of our history," that Lincoln returned time and again as he argued for the injustice of slavery.[23]

Captivated by modern science and the Enlightenment, Jefferson sought to base his opinions on evidence produced by scientific inquiry. When confronted with the question of whether blacks were equal to whites, Jefferson eschewed abstract speculation in favor of scientific observation and measurement, so he went about measuring, comparing, and contrasting various characteristics of whites and blacks to see if in fact there were differences. As he admitted, his observations of blacks were limited primarily to black slaves at Monticello and in surrounding areas, and therefore, "the opinion, that [blacks] are inferior in the faculties of reason and imagination, must be hazarded with great diffidence" because his sample was insufficiently large and not representative. Jefferson knew that asserting any scientific generalization "requires many observations, even where the subject may be submitted to the anatomical knife, to optical glasses, to analysis by fire, or by solvents." "How much more then," he cautioned, "where it is a faculty, not a substance, we are examining; where it eludes the research of all the senses; where the conditions of its existence are various and variously combined; where the effects of those which are present or absent bid defiance to calculation."[24]

His reservations, however, did not stop him from publishing his views on black inequality. In Query XIV of his *Notes on the State of Virginia*, Jefferson wrote about the differences he had observed between blacks and whites and the possible origins of black inferiority, describing at length black men and women's failure to measure up to whites in terms of physical beauty, expressiveness, memory, literary abilities, the advancement of reason and science, and other categories of comparison. Jefferson asserted his belief that blacks possessed "the moral sense" no less than whites, emphasizing that "we find among them numerous instances of the most rigid [moral] integrity, and as many as among their better instructed masters, of benevolence, gratitude, and unshaken fidelity." Nonetheless, "I advance it therefore as a suspicion only," Jefferson concluded, "that the blacks, whether originally a distinct race or made distinct by time and circumstances, are inferior to the whites in the endowments both of body and mind."[25]

While modern readers will surely find Jefferson's remarks repugnant, and while he may rightly be criticized for ignoring his own warning against generalizing about an entire racial group based on limited observations, it is important to note that Jefferson himself left open the possibility that the miserable conditions of slavery, not their nature, caused the inferior talents of the blacks he witnessed. As he wrote in a 1791 letter to Benjamin Banneker, the famed black scientist and architect of the Capitol in Washington, D.C.,

> Nobody wishes more than I do to see such proofs as you exhibit, that nature has given to our black brethren, talents equal to those of the other colors of men, and that the appearance of a want of them is owing merely to the degraded condition of their existence.[26]

In a letter to Henri Gregoire in 1809, Jefferson explained,

Be assured that no person living wishes more sincerely than I do, to see a complete refutation of the doubts I have myself entertained and expressed on the grade of understanding allotted to [blacks] by nature, and to find that in this respect they are on a par with ourselves. My doubts were the result of personal observation on the limited sphere of my own State, where the opportunities for the development of their genius were not favorable, and those of exercising it still less so. I expressed them therefore with great hesitation.

But Jefferson's argument did not end there: "Whatever be their degree of talent," he insisted, "*it is no measure of their rights.*" For Jefferson, whether people of different skin colors possessed different capacities might be an interesting scientific question, but he was also firm in his conviction that regardless of any differences scientific observation revealed, blacks had the same natural rights as whites. "Because Sir Isaac Newton was superior to others in understanding," Jefferson argued, "he was not therefore lord of the person or property of others."[27] Never in writing or in recorded speech did Lincoln entertain the kind of racial categories of human development that Jefferson did, but Lincoln did fully embrace the Jeffersonian dictum that any perceived inferiority of blacks to whites in certain respects was no measure of their rights. Lincoln defended this principle as true, and it is likely why Lincoln praised Jefferson so lavishly on various occasions.

Unlike in the ancient world, where neighboring tribes and cities enslaved one another through warfare and thus masters and slaves often looked quite similar to one another, slavery in America corresponded in large measure with color: virtually all slaves were black; none were white. When a human being looks at another human being, color is among the first sensory perceptions that strike the beholder, and when skin color is so closely tied to political and social status as it was with American slavery, moving society beyond color-consciousness to color-blindness becomes a daunting challenge. Jefferson was concerned that when American whites saw blacks, they would immediately associate them with slavery and therefore assign to them an inferior social rank; when American blacks saw whites, they would immediately associate them with the masters who oppressed them. Thus, Jefferson feared that widespread manumission might lead to a terrible race war in America:

Deep rooted prejudices entertained by the whites; ten thousand recollections, by the blacks, of the injuries they have sustained; new provocations; the real distinctions which nature has made; and many other circumstances, will divide us into parties, and produce convulsions which will probably never end but in the extermination of the one or the other race.[28]

Fearing that blacks and whites would never be able to live together freely and peacefully, Jefferson, and later Henry Clay and Lincoln among others, looked to some kind of plan for colonization (sending freed slaves to Africa or some other place far away from the United States to live independently) to solve the American race problem that slavery had created. If slavery could be eliminated in America, then colonization would be necessary for two reasons: First, it would protect whites against possible retaliation from former slaves seeking revenge. Second, colonization would offer security for blacks, who as free men might not be protected in America to the extent they were when they were considered to be valuable property as slaves.

Thankfully, Jefferson was wrong in his prediction—America has not suffered a genocidal war in which one race has exterminated the other— but it is also true that Americans, both white and black, have found it tremendously difficult to get beyond race and to see one another as fellow citizens without regard to color. Today, more than two centuries after Jefferson penned his prescient words, Americans continue to wrestle with the question of whether our laws should judge a man by the color of his skin or the content of his character.[29]

In his statements in Ottawa, Lincoln asserted a logical position with which most people would agree: "Inasmuch as it becomes a necessity that there must be a difference, I . . . am in favor of the race to which I belong, having the superior position." Lincoln did not endorse a political hierarchy based on race but indicated that such hierarchy may be "a necessity," an inescapable result of widespread racial opinions and assumptions. In such a case, anyone of any color, when presented with the choice of having his race assigned a superior or an inferior position in a given society, with no option of equal citizenship, would choose to have his race in the superior position. Lincoln's assertion is the flip side of the obvious statement that no man would wish to be enslaved. That in no way proves that Lincoln did not believe in the equality of rights of all men of all colors or that he did not hope American opinion would someday move in the direction of equal citizenship for all men of all colors. It simply demonstrates that so long as necessity required that there be an unjust hierarchy based on color, so long as the *American people* rejected color-blindness, Lincoln, like anyone else, would rather be on top than on bottom if forced to choose.

I draw a similar conclusion from the second quotation as well, which comes from the fourth joint debate with Douglas in Charleston, Illinois. Here, I only point out that in the Charleston speech, Lincoln clarified what he had never proposed in the past and what he was not proposing in 1858, namely, "the social and political equality of the white and black races," which included "making voters or jurors of negroes . . . qualifying them to hold office . . . [and allowing them to] intermarry with white people." In Charleston in 1858, he said, "I am not nor ever have been in favor" of these policies, which was true: he had never endorsed policies to make jurors or voters or officeholders of blacks or to make them eligible for marriage with whites, and he was proposing no such policies in 1858. In the context of his many other statements insisting on the equality of whites and blacks, it seems likely that his refusal to advocate such policies was more a matter of strategy than principle on his part: Lincoln knew that there was no possibility at all of getting such policies enacted into law, so why destroy his political career by proposing those policies to an audience that wanted nothing to do with them? Nowhere did Lincoln suggest that such policies would be wrong. Nor did he deny that he might support such policies in the future, perhaps when the American mind had cleansed itself of some of its racial prejudice and was better prepared to entertain the full implications of human equality.

More importantly, in both the first and the fourth debates and elsewhere, Lincoln insisted that blacks *were* equal to whites in the basic right to keep what they earned with their own labor. As Lincoln went on to say in Ottawa immediately following the section quoted above,

> But I hold that, notwithstanding all this, there is no reason in the world why the negro is not entitled to all the natural rights enumerated in the Declaration of Independence, the right to life, liberty, and the pursuit of happiness. I hold that he is as much entitled to these as the white man. I agree with Judge Douglas he is not my equal in many respects—certainly not in color, perhaps not in moral or intellectual endowment. But in the right to eat the bread, without the leave of anybody else, which his own hand earns, *he is my equal and the equal of Judge Douglas, and the equal of every living man.*[30]

Consider the implications of Lincoln's qualification of his position. If Lincoln could move public opinion to grant this basic precept of political right, that blacks have the right to own and acquire property, the other precepts of civil society and civil liberties could then be argued. John Locke, followed by James Madison and the other Founders, taught that the right to property originates in the fact that, by nature, each man owns himself and, by extension, the fruits of his labor.[31] Acknowledging a black man's right to property acknowledges his humanity. And as Locke argued further, "No man in civil society can be exempted from the laws of it."[32] If Lincoln could persuade Americans of all blacks' equal humanity and natural rights, and if

Americans were to act consistently with the terms of their own social contract, justice would demand either equal citizenship for blacks or the right to freely emigrate from the United States. In either case, holding blacks as chattel slaves violated the first principle of the Americans' social contract, human equality.

Locke argued that "absolute arbitrary power, or governing without settled standing laws," violates the end of civil society, which is "the enjoyment of [its members'] properties in peace and safety."[33] This end in turn points to the means by which civil society achieves it, that is, "the laws established in that society." As the laws are the means to "enjoying property in peace and safety," it follows that "the supreme power [within civil society] cannot take from any man any part of his property without his own consent."[34]

More generally, argued Locke, the laws lack authority without "the consent of society, over whom no body can have a power to make laws, but by their own consent and by authority received from them."[35] In a republican form of government, the requirement of consent usually takes the form of suffrage but at the same time points to, and underlies, the right of revolution, which citizens can exercise when suffrage is prevented or the end of civil society is negated. Under the social contract, legislative power to which the people consent "is limited to the public good of the society. It is a power that hath no other end but preservation, and therefore can never have a right to destroy, *enslave*, or designedly to impoverish the subjects."[36] Therefore, if blacks possess equal natural rights, and if the purpose of the republican form of government under which they live is to protect their natural rights through laws made with their consent, then withholding the power to consent by withholding the right of suffrage violates the social contract; the logic of the social contract demands nothing less than making voters of Negroes once their equal humanity and natural rights have been recognized. It also follows that if blacks have a natural right to consent to the laws under which they live, they deserve the civil right to be tried by juries of their peers when accused of breaking those laws and to sit on those juries themselves in judgment of their fellow citizens. Further, as civil rights or liberties are the legal means to the end of civil society, then black citizens should have equal civil rights and equal protection under the law. This means nothing less than that they should share equally in the private sphere of freedom intrinsic to a government of limited powers and, therefore, should be free to form associations and friendships with those of their choosing, including members of the opposite sex whom they want to marry, regardless of race.[37]

Before any of these necessary implications could be argued publicly, however, Americans first had to recognize the equal basic natural rights of blacks, which meant affirming their equal humanity—that a black man owned his person and property. This was no small task. Influenced by John C. Calhoun and others, including many prominent Christian preachers and theologians who argued for the "positive good of slavery," many Americans at the time questioned the basic humanity of black slaves and embraced a new view that slavery was their natural and appropriate condition in society.

Three forces—technology, modern political theory, and economics—merged and caused a massive transformation in how the American public viewed slavery and blacks. After Eli Whitney patented his cotton gin in 1794 in America (allowing raw cotton to be processed much more efficiently by machine rather than by hand), and as England perfected the power loom (using steam power to weave cotton threads into cloth) in the early nineteenth century, cotton became far more profitable than ever before, eventually giving rise to the phenomenon of "King Cotton" throughout the South. Thus, more and more white Americans had greater economic interest in the production of cotton—and the slave labor needed to harvest it. Those with economic interests in slavery were offered a clear conscience by new moral and political theories emanating from Europe, especially German political philosophy and Hegelianism in particular, which denied a common human nature uniting all human beings under one moral code and argued instead that different human "races" had evolved differently in history. Many intelligent Americans, both in the North and the South, interpreted these historicist or evolutionary philosophies as justification for the enslavement of people of African descent by people of European descent.

John H. Hopkins, for example, an Episcopal bishop of the diocese of Vermont, argued that blacks' natural inferiority "would prevent Negroes from achieving any type of equality in a racially mixed community." Even some of the most ardent antislavery advocates frequently described blacks in derogatory terms. As Robert Walker, the fourth territorial governor of Kansas, remarked in his 1855 inaugural address,

> Those who oppose slavery in Kansas do not base their opposition upon any philanthropic principles or any sympathy for the African race. For in their so-called constitution, framed at Topeka, they deem that entire race so inferior and degraded as to exclude them all forever from Kansas, whether they be bond or free.

Often Northerners' opinions were even more stinging. "Those niggers at the south," wrote Ephriam Hart of Connecticut, "are much happier than our free niggers [because Southern masters] treat their slaves as kindly as any one would his favorite race horse." In 1860, the *Democratic Standard* newspaper of Concord, New Hampshire, editorialized, "To us, the proposition that the negro is equal by nature, physically and mentally, to the white man, seems to be so absurd and preposterous, that we cannot conceive how it can be entertained by any intelligent and rational white man."[38] The growing popularity of such evolutionary, racist views signaled the growing rejection of the natural right principle that "all men are created equal."

Reacting against both the taunts and the accusations of abolitionists and the fear sparked by the prospect of slave rebellions—Nat Turner's slave rebellion, in which more than fifty white men, women, and children were murdered in cold blood, occurred the same year, 1831, that William Lloyd Garrison founded his provocative abolitionist newspaper, the *Liberator*—Southerners especially welcomed new arguments and theories that justified black slavery while they became increasingly irritated by abolitionist suggestions that slavery was wrong. Throughout much of the South, in fact, numerous policies sprang up to suppress antislavery speeches and publications. As Lincoln commented during his 1860 address at New York City's Cooper Union, it seemed that many Southerners (and some Northerners, such as Stephen Douglas) insisted on "suppressing all declarations that slavery is wrong, whether made in politics, in presses, in pulpits, or in private."[39] In parts of the country, public opinion, which forms the center of political and cultural gravity in America, had moved so far away from the self-evident truth of human equality that, in 1861, Alexander Stephens, speaking as the recently elected vice president of the Confederacy, stated with perfect confidence that anyone who continued to believe in the equality of the races suffered from a form of mental illness:

> Those at the North, who still [believe in the equality of blacks], with a zeal above knowledge, we justly denominate *fanatics*. All fanaticism springs from an aberration of the mind—from a defect in reasoning. *It is a species of insanity.* One of the most striking characteristics of insanity, in many instances, is forming correct conclusions from fancied or erroneous premises; so with the anti-slavery fanatics. Their conclusions are right if their premises were. They assume that the negro is equal, and hence conclude that he is entitled to equal privileges and rights with the white man. If their premises were correct, their conclusions would be logical and just—but their premise being wrong, their whole argument fails.[40]

Such was the climate of opinion in which Lincoln found himself: divided, unsettled, and often hostile to any suggestion that blacks possessed rights equal to those of whites. Getting American audiences to listen and then persuading them of the equality of blacks would require great, and perhaps unprecedented, rhetorical skills. No one, however, was more calculating in crafting his speech than Lincoln as he attempted to refute the new pro-slavery arguments while moving public opinion, without insulting the public, back in the direction of the founding principle of human equality.

In the fourth debate in Charleston, for example, after restating his belief that public opinion among whites would probably prevent blacks and whites from living on a plane of equality, and that if equality could not be achieved, he would prefer that whites occupy the superior rather than inferior position in society, Lincoln offered these comments:

> I say upon this occasion I do not perceive that because the white man is to have the superior position, the negro should be denied everything. I do not understand that because I do not want a negro woman for a slave I must necessarily want her for a wife. My understanding is that I can just let her alone. I am now in my fiftieth year, and I certainly never have had a black woman for either a slave or a wife. So it seems to me quite possible for us to get along without making either slaves or wives of negroes. I will add to this that I have never seen to my knowledge a man, woman or child who was in favor of producing a perfect equality, social and political, between negroes and white men. I recollect of but one distinguished instance that I ever heard of so frequently as to be entirely satisfied of its correctness—and that is the case of Judge Douglas' old friend Col. Richard M. Johnson.[41]

In denying that he necessarily wanted a Negro woman for a wife, Lincoln tried to separate himself from radical abolitionism. At the same time, he did not want to appear as an apologist for slavery. His solution was that whites needed not to take Negroes for wives or slaves, that whites could simply leave blacks alone. Curiously, however, he went on to say that he knew of only one instance in which someone was in favor of producing a "perfect equality" between whites and blacks, and that was the case of Douglas's old friend and political ally, Colonel Richard M. Johnson. Why would Lincoln insert the example of Johnson? Colonel Johnson, a prominent Democrat who had served in both the U.S. House and the Senate and as vice president under Martin Van Buren, was also widely known to live and have two children with a mulatto slave woman. Clearly, Lincoln invoked Johnson to embarrass Douglas; after all, Douglas was trying to portray Lincoln as a black-loving abolitionist who wanted to marry and sleep with Negroes. Lincoln could paint Douglas and the Democrats as hypocrites by pointing out that a Democrat, not a Republican, was best known for the kind of racial amalgamation that Democrats claimed to abhor.

But could Lincoln have included the example of Colonel Johnson for another reason? Lincoln gave us no details about Johnson's life, but Johnson's biography reveals that he had two daughters with Julia Chinn, a mulatto slave whom Johnson had inherited as part of his father's estate. We also know that Johnson provided for the education of his daughters and that both daughters married white men and were deeded part of Johnson's estate. When one of his daughters, Adaline, died in 1836, Johnson wrote the following to a friend:

> I thank you and all who administered to that lovely and innocent child in her final painful hour. She was a source of inexhaustible happiness and comfort to me. She was mild and prudent. She was wise in her counsel beyond her years and obedient to every thought and every advice of mine. . . . She was a firm and great prop to my happiness here, but she is gone where sorrow and sighing can never disturb her peaceful and quiet blossom. She is happy, but has left me unhappy in mourning her loss.[42]

Colonel Johnson and Julia Chinn never married because Johnson's home state of Kentucky prohibited the legal marriage between whites and blacks. But his beautiful and moving letter hints at how he understood his relationship to Chinn and their children. The laws of Kentucky notwithstanding, Johnson loved Chinn as his wife, and he adored his daughters as affectionately as any parent ever has. When he looked at Chinn and his children, he did not see color; he saw human beings, the dearly beloved members of his family. The vast majority of white Americans in 1858, in the North and South, were not prepared to look at blacks the way Colonel Johnson looked at Julia Chinn and his daughters. But perhaps Lincoln was thinking of more than his immediate audience when he included Johnson in his remarks. Perhaps Lincoln intended Johnson to serve as a model for Americans in 1858 as well as for future Americans seeking to learn what "perfect equality" means.

Americans today find it difficult to understand the grip racial views had on the American mind that Lincoln was trying to influence in the 1850s. Anyone seeking to advance the principle of equality through electoral politics had to speak carefully to the American people. As historian Philip Paludan writes, "Most white people disliked blacks as a group, as a race that was inferior and corrosive of ideals they cherished. They did not want blacks to live, shop, play, learn, celebrate, worship, or even be buried anywhere near them."[43] In *A People's Contest*, Paludan relates stories of Northern whites fighting for the Union army who refused to serve with black soldiers:

Many white troops refused to serve with Negroes in the Union-saving struggle. Seeing themselves involved in a noble enterprise, sharing the camaraderie that binds soldiers together in intimacies as well as suffering and death, whites feared that the presence of black soldiers would debase the cause and bring them down to the level of "niggers." A corporal in a New York regiment announced, "We don't want to fight side by side with the nigger. We think we are a too superior race for that."[44]

Given this state of opinion, no white man could hope to be elected dog-catcher, much less to a higher office, if he asserted publicly the equality of the black and white races.

In one of his books attacking Lincoln, DiLorenzo spends an entire chapter describing the racism and white supremacy deeply rooted in antebellum "Yankee" thought, yet he nowhere acknowledges the constraints that the widely held racism he describes placed on political speech. A far more thoughtful account of the limitations popular opinion placed on speech in America can be found in Alexis de Tocqueville's masterly work *Democracy in America*:

> In America, the majority draws a formidable circle around thought. Inside those limits, the writer [or speaker] is free; but unhappiness awaits him if he dares to leave them. It is not that he has to fear an auto-da-fé, but he is the butt of mortifications of all kinds and of persecutions every day. A political career is closed to him; he has offended the only power that has the capacity to open it up. . . . [Thus,] he yields, and finally he bends under the effort of each day and returns to silence as if he felt remorse for having spoken the truth.[45]

DiLorenzo possesses none of Tocqueville's appreciation for rhetoric and its limitations, and he never considers how Lincoln might appeal to the prejudices of his audience, especially if Lincoln did not share those prejudices. Instead, DiLorenzo simply chalks Lincoln up as another nineteenth-century racist. "As a man of his time," DiLorenzo asserts, "Lincoln held views that can only be described as the views of a white racist."[46] But this ignores the possibility that Lincoln tried to improve the moral opinions of his audience while crafting his speech to attract and not offend them.

When Lincoln was running for the U.S. Senate in 1858, one of the most powerful criticisms his opponent, Stephen Douglas, made against him was that he was a "Black Republican" who wanted to live and have intimate relations with blacks, charges met with enthusiastic applause from Douglas supporters in the audience, mixed with hissing and booing aimed at Lincoln.

Any argument Lincoln might have made for the full equality of blacks, any argument that openly called for the immediate writing into law of the full moral and political implications of the principles of the Declaration of Independence, would have generated fierce opposition and hostility. No one who hoped to advance these principles in elected political office could possibly make such arguments in public, however much he may have believed them to be true. This is why abolitionists were almost irrelevant politically: they were seen as zealots and lunatics far outside the political mainstream.

Though modern Americans may find them uncomfortable, these are nonetheless simple, sad, and undeniable facts of American life in the middle of the nineteenth century. We must view Lincoln's rhetoric in light of this reality if we are to understand the political confines within which he had to work.

In his debates with Douglas and elsewhere, Lincoln did not openly endorse policies demanding full political and social equality for blacks, but he also never denied that such policies were right or questioned the truthfulness of the proposition that all men are created equal. What are we to make of this? Lincoln certainly catered to the prejudices of his audience as much as necessity required of him, but, I would quickly add, he also consistently reserved for himself ground upon which to defend the principle of human equality and all its implications more comprehensively at some later date. In his 1854 speech in Peoria, Illinois, Lincoln lamented,

> When southern people tell us they are no more responsible for the origin of slavery, than we; I acknowledge the fact. When it is said that the institution exists and that it is very difficult to get rid of it, in any satisfactory way, I can understand and appreciate the saying. I surely will not blame them for not doing what I should not know how to do myself. If all earthly power were given to me, I should not know what to do, as to the existing institution.[47]

For reasons mentioned above, the idea of freeing slaves and then colonizing them somewhere outside the United States appealed to Lincoln because it may have appeared to be the only possible solution. Lincoln asked rhetorically whether Americans could "free [blacks], and make them politically and socially our equals?" He first responded that his "own feelings would not admit of this," but then quickly shifted attention away from his own opinion, not wanting to clarify or defend it, to emphasize what was more important, the opinions of his fellow Americans: even "if mine would," Lincoln said, "we well know that those of the great mass of white people will not." If Lincoln believed that blacks should be the free social and political equals of whites, he knew that openly stating such views would be political and possibly even lit-eral suicide, which might explain the ambiguity in his statements and his un-willingness to expand on his personal opinions regarding race-related policies. In addition, Lincoln knew that his opinions were far less important and less influential than the opinions of the voting American people. And whether or not public opinion was just or right was not the only question: "Whether this feeling accords with justice and sound judgment," Lincoln continued in his Peoria speech, "is not the sole question, if indeed, it is part of it. A universal feeling, whether well or ill-founded, can not be safely disregarded" because "universal feeling," or public opinion, places important limitations on what can be achieved through public policy.[48] However much one might lament or loathe public opinion, those who hope to bring about political change in America cannot ignore it. Lincoln concluded that "we cannot, then, make [blacks] equals" precisely because he understood all too well the racial opin-ions of the vast majority of whites in America.[49]

In a self-governing republic, the emancipation of slaves requires the consent of the governed. Where the people do not want emancipation, emancipation will not happen. Lincoln understood that his first job was to reshape public opinion so that, at a minimum, Americans would discuss the possibility of emancipation. Rather than evincing racism, as Lincoln critics then and now contend, Lincoln's position demonstrates a prudential con-cern for the formation of public opinion, public policy, and the rule of law. But when opportunities presented themselves, Lincoln clearly stated his dis-approval of slavery: "As I would not be a slave, so I would not be a master. This expresses my idea of democracy. Whatever differs from this, to the ex-tent of the difference, is no democracy."[50]

LINCOLN IN ACTION

With slavery standing in direct opposition to self-government, only two op-tions in trying to free the slaves presented themselves to Lincoln: make them equal citizens in America or help them establish self-government of their own someplace else. Neither option was easy. Public opinion presented mas-sive obstacles to the former, while the latter was probably physically impos-sible. As early as his 1854 speech in Peoria, Lincoln explored the many dif-ficulties that would plague any colonization effort:

> My first impulse would be to free all the slaves, and send them to Liberia—
> to their own native land. But a moment's reflection would convince me,

that whatever of high hope, as I think there is, there may be in this, in the long run, its sudden execution is impossible. If they were all landed there in a day, they would all perish in the next ten days; and there are not surplus shipping and surplus money enough in the world to carry them there in many times ten days.[51]

Fully aware of the daunting challenges presented by slavery, Lincoln moved ahead on both fronts, refining and channeling his rhetoric in an attempt to persuade Americans of the injustice of slavery while acknowledging that the problem of slavery in America might, in theory, require colonization as a solution, however difficult it may be to execute in practice. A generation earlier, abolitionist Benjamin Lundy, who was William Lloyd Garrison's mentor, lamented that purchasing the freedom of all American slaves and transporting them to a foreign land would require "all the wealth of Croesus" and would therefore be as futile as trying to "bail dry the old ocean with a thimble."[52] Late in his life, Lincoln learned first-hand the practical difficulties of colonization. The only colonization plan he actually sponsored was an 1863 expedition to the Caribbean in which blacks participated voluntarily and which Congress funded fully. When after only a few months it turned into a debacle, Lincoln sent a ship to bring the colonists back to the United States. Never again did he speak seriously about colonization for blacks, pressing instead for whites and blacks to learn to live together as free Americans.[53]

For historian Lerone Bennett, who has produced perhaps the single largest tome attacking Lincoln, the obstacles Lincoln faced and his response to them in no way vindicate him as a statesman. What matters most for Bennett are the facts that Lincoln failed to endorse black suffrage and to endorse policies allowing blacks to testify in court and serve on juries. Bennett also reminds us that Lincoln supported the fugitive slave law, which allowed slave owners to recover slaves who ran away to free states, and supported the repressive Illinois black code, which, among other things, prohibited free blacks from taking up residence in the state. For Bennett, these failings prove beyond dispute that Lincoln was a racist. Here is what Bennett writes, for example, on the subject of Lincoln's support for the fugitive slave law:

> The case against the "great emancipator" myth is clear, and compelling. As an Illinois citizen, as a lawyer, legislator, congressman and politician, he personally supported the infamous Fugitive Slave Law and asked his neighbors to go out into the streets and hunt down fugitive slaves and return them to slavery. As president, he ordered the return of fugitive slaves to slavemasters, supported proslavery generals who returned slaves to slavemasters, and struggled to keep from destroying the institution of

slavery. . . . He continued to oppose immediate emancipation, going to his death arguing for the proposition that men and women should be judged not by the content of their character but by the color of their skin. These are facts, unimpeachable facts.[54]

Bennett adds that he thinks Lincoln was "enthusiastic" about the idea of colonization for former black slaves, which proves to his satisfaction that Lincoln did not believe in the proposition that all men are created equal. Mark Graber, in a recent book on *Dred Scott v. Sandford* (discussed in chapter 3), seems to agree with Bennett, placing the subject of colonization entirely within the context of racism: "Racism was well grounded in American political thought from the very beginning." Colonization was defended by "Americans who opposed slavery . . . [and] believed white supremacy the higher constitutional value. Slaves could be freed only when doing so furthered or at least did not weaken white racial hegemony."[55] The truth is that Lincoln was never "enthusiastic" about colonization. He never formulated a clear and concrete policy of colonization for the simple reason that no supporter of colonization, beginning with Jefferson, ever had a clear plan of how it could actually work. Far more importantly, however, Lincoln supported colonization because he thought most white Americans were not prepared to accept blacks as equals and fellow citizens, and he saw no other way to solve the problem of slavery. As I have already discussed, few white Americans of the antebellum period, in the North as well as the South, would have accepted black citizenship. Further, in the *Dred Scott* case in 1857, the Supreme Court decided that no blacks, free or slave, could be American citizens, even if whites wanted them to be. The burden for Lincoln critics is to show how policies of emancipation and equal citizenship for all blacks could have become public law in the middle of the nineteenth century in any way other than that achieved by Abraham Lincoln.

Both during his one term in Congress and as president, Lincoln advocated plans for the gradual elimination of slavery coupled with compensation for slave owners, that is, payment to owners for forgoing their slave property. In a chapter titled "Lincolnia: The Fantasy Plan for Banishing Blacks," Bennett heaps scorn on Lincoln's endorsement of a plan for the gradual, compensated emancipation of slaves and their colonization:

> The new president's racial policy was based on the wildest idea ever presented to the American people by an American president. What Lincoln proposed officially and publicly was that the United States government buy the slaves then deport them to Africa or South America. . . . Like most nineteenth-century racists, Lincoln pretended to believe that Blacks had to live in tropical climes, although he knew it required marshals and

the massed White population to keep slaves from running away to the arctic zone of Chicago, which was founded by a free Black man, Jean Baptiste Pointe DuSable, more than fifty years before the Lincolns arrived in Illinois.[56]

Bennett is especially disturbed because Lincoln recommended obedience to the fugitive slave law, but Bennett never asks why he did so. Lincoln found the fugitive slave law, which rendered it almost impossible for any free black man accused of being a runaway slave to prove his innocence and retain his freedom, appallingly immoral. But he counseled Americans to obey it because he thought they should obey *all* laws. The fugitive slave law was a statutory enforcement of the Fugitive Slave Clause of the Constitution (Article IV, Section 2), and therefore disobeying or undermining the fugitive slave law would be tantamount to disobeying or undermining the Constitution itself. Lincoln understood well that, absent the rule of law, there is only anarchy, and anarchy quickly turns into tyranny of one form or another. And what is tyranny but the rule of violence, where might makes right and the strongest rule, which is but itself a condition of slavery? In Lincoln's mind, slavery and the rule of force represent the antithesis of equality and the rule of law, a theme that Lincoln first articulated in an early speech in 1838 before the Young Men's Lyceum in Springfield, Illinois:

> Let reverence for the laws, be breathed by every American mother, to the lisping babe, that prattles on her lap—let it be taught in schools, in seminaries, and in colleges; let it be written in Primmers, spelling books, and in Almanacs; let it be preached from the pulpit, proclaimed in legislative halls, and enforced in courts of justice. And, in short, let it become the *political religion* of the nation; and let the old and the young, the rich and the poor, the grave and the gay, of all sexes and tongues, and colors and conditions, sacrifice unceasingly upon its altars.[57]

Lincoln did not mean to suggest that American law was flawless or beyond improvement, but he thought it best to work within the system of law to change the law via the consent of the governed. Here, Lincoln parted ways with abolitionists who picked and chose which laws they would and would not obey. Lincoln saw in the abolitionists' disregard for the law an evil equal to slavery because the lawlessness that abolitionism encouraged would simply replace one form of slavery with another. If one man may ignore a law he believes unjust, why may not some other man ignore some other law he believes unjust for some other reason? And when many men believe that only laws to their liking are to be followed, is the rule of law possible absent violent enforcement? Thus Jefferson, in his inaugural address as president, sounded a call for an American "political faith" quite similar to Lincoln's Lyceum message, teaching Americans that the founding principles of civil and religious liberty, and the laws that enshrine them,

> should be the creed of our political faith, the text of civic institution, the touchstone by which to try the services of those we trust; and should we wander from them in moments of error and alarm, let us hasten to retrace our steps and to retain the road which alone leads to peace, liberty, and safety.[58]

Bennett and those who share his critique of Lincoln are modern-day versions of abolitionists. Bennett's frustration with Lincoln springs from his insistence that Lincoln should have demanded immediate emancipation for all slaves and full social and political equality for all blacks, with no reservation, hesitation, compromise, or concern for obtaining the consent of the governed. Thankfully, Lincoln understood better than the Bennetts of our day, and the William Lloyd Garrisons and John Browns of his own day, that preserving the rule of law, placing slavery on the course to ultimate extinction, and protecting the equal rights of all men of all colors were all inseparable aspects of one supreme goal: a free and just society.

By the 1850s, America had achieved an unprecedented degree of government by consent of the governed. Large numbers of free Americans were consenting, primarily by exercising their right to vote, to the laws and government under which they lived. But the American experiment in self-government was incomplete; it remained flawed. In addition, large numbers of people in America were being ruled without their consent, foremost among them, those being held as chattel slaves. Abolitionists such as Garrison and Brown—the former burned copies of the Constitution to show his utter disdain for it, and the latter engaged in cold-blooded murder to strike a blow against slavery—had no qualms about undermining the rule of law and abandoning the Constitution in what they perceived to be a righteous war against slavery. Had they been successful, the society they formed would likely have been a lawless place in which righteous conviction would be held as authoritative over man-made laws. Such a state of lawlessness might well have unleashed a form of tyranny more widespread, more miserable, and more difficult to eradicate than that of black slavery. Lincoln, on the other hand, wanted to preserve the realm of consent that had been achieved, while extending the right of consent to include everyone living under American law. This meant operating within the system of law and ensuring that all the laws, even odious ones like the fugitive slave law, be enforced until they could be changed or repealed through the consent of the governed.

Lincoln's desire to preserve the rule of law and to work within a lawful framework toward the elimination of slavery is precisely why he emphasized the importance of public opinion, something ignored by both the abolitionists of Lincoln's day and modern-day abolitionists such as Bennett. In order to implement policies leading to the elimination of slavery in a self-governing republic, one in which the people are the source of the law, Lincoln understood that first public opinion needed to be shaped to support such policies. "In this and like communities," he said during the first joint debate with Douglas in 1858, "public sentiment is everything. With public sentiment, nothing can fail; without it nothing can succeed. Consequently he who moulds public sentiment, goes deeper than he who enacts statutes or pronounces decisions. He makes statutes and decisions possible or impossible to be executed."[59] This is why Lincoln emphasized the corrupting influence of Douglas's "popular sovereignty" doctrine, according to which Douglas often said that he "didn't care" whether slavery was voted up or down: "Judge Douglas is a man of vast influence, so great that it is enough for many men to profess to believe anything, when they once find out that Judge Douglas professes to believe it." Against the sway of men like Douglas, the fiery and fanatical rhetoric of the abolitionists, and even the fanatical and murderous actions of abolitionists like John Brown, had little influence. In fact, Lincoln argued just the opposite: abolitionism lessened the credibility of the antislavery movement while adding fuel to the Southern resolve to defend slavery and the Southern way of life.

Bennett fairly points out that Lincoln sometimes supported, or in most cases simply did not oppose, various laws that were oppressive to blacks. But this is far from the whole story. The evidence should be presented in light of the question, what choice did Lincoln have? As a thought experiment, suppose that in the 1840s and 1850s Lincoln had publicly demanded that blacks be legally permitted to vote, sit on juries, and marry white people. As a politician seeking to influence public policy by getting elected to public office, how successful might he have been? Policies such as the Illinois black codes and the federal fugitive slave law, as oppressive as they were for blacks, had widespread support from the voting white people of Illinois. Suppose someone other than Lincoln, some imaginary person who genuinely believed in universal, natural human equality, came to Illinois in the 1840s or 1850s and tried to improve racial justice in the state. Suppose he wanted to move both public opinion and public policy in the direction of color-blind law and equal civil rights. How might he be advised to speak to the people of Illinois? Though a difficult question to answer, it is one the statesman cannot avoid. Should he stand and threaten violence like John Brown, who committed murder in Kansas and was later hanged for treason in 1859 after a failed attempt to capture a federal weapons depot at Harpers Ferry, Virginia, and incite a slave rebellion? Or should he, like William Lloyd Garrison, thunder that the Constitution was a pact with hell because it offered concessions to slavery? Consider Garrison's abolitionist rhetoric in 1831:

> I will be as harsh as truth, and as uncompromising as justice. On this subject [of slavery] I do not wish to think, or to speak, or to write, with moderation. No! No! Tell a man whose house is on fire to give a moderate alarm; tell the mother to gradually extricate her babe from the fire into which it has fallen.—But urge me not to use moderation in a cause like the present. I am in earnest—I will not equivocate—I will not excuse—I will not retreat a single inch—AND I WILL BE HEARD.[60]

Though an evil as great as slavery may inspire such passionate outbursts, they are in vain unless someone can gather the discordant winds of public opinion and channel public support toward the goal of ending the institution. If Lincoln had presented himself the way abolitionists like Brown or Garrison did, he would not likely have been elected to any office; more likely, he would have been run out of town, and possibly lynched or shot (abolitionist Elijah Lovejoy's printing press was thrown into the river four times before he was eventually murdered by a white mob tired of his persistent attacks on slavery). Certainly an abolitionist Lincoln would never have had the opportunity to serve the American antislavery cause as well as only President Lincoln could. As Frederick Douglass explained in an 1876 speech at the dedication of the Freedmen's Memorial Monument to Abraham Lincoln in Washington, D.C.'s Lincoln Park, "Viewed from the genuine abolition ground, Mr. Lincoln seemed tardy, cold, dull, and indifferent." Douglass understood, however, that Lincoln was more political, therefore more effective in bringing about an end to slavery, than the abolitionists: "But measuring him by the sentiment of his country, a sentiment he was bound as a statesman to consult, he was swift, zealous, radical, and determined."[61]

When looking back at history, it is easy to forget or ignore the very real obstacles that a statesman of the time could not. By recalling the great political challenges of the past—and few in human history have faced the kinds of challenges Lincoln did—it becomes possible to distinguish statesmen from ordinary politicians on the one hand and from zealots more concerned with righteousness than political success on the other. All statesmen are politicians, to be sure, but not all politicians are statesmen. The statesman possesses the practical wisdom needed to maneuver around or overcome the many obstacles that stand in the way of justice, wisdom that results from deep study of both permanent and timely things. This is not to suggest that a statesman's decisions are easy or simple. Often the right path of action is neither illuminated nor agreed upon. Confusion, self-doubt, and uncertainty often cannot be avoided, especially in times of dire political exigency, when success or failure, freedom or slavery, life or death might be on the line. But in the most difficult and trying circumstances, where ordinary human beings are likely to give up, give in, or simply flee, the statesman remains doggedly persistent in his purposes. Indeed, no description of statesmanship would be complete if it did not include persistence. That persistency is seen in Lincoln's long story of lifting himself out of dirt poverty, working tirelessly to educate himself in the crudest manner befitting a poor man's son, coming back from failures time and again both in his business ventures and in politics, and finally achieving the pinnacle of public office. Lincoln's persistency becomes even more visible in his years as president when virtually everyone, including former friends and political allies, abandoned him as the American people and their elected politicians grew tired of, and angry about, the war Lincoln would not let end without victory and when he suffered the most degrading insults about his mind, his character, and even his looks (Lincoln was routinely mocked as a "duffer," a "hick," a "baboon," and a "giraffe," and one of his own generals, Joseph Hooker, once called him a "played-out imbecile"). But amidst the carnage and confusion of war, and in spite of deep depression, illnesses, and occasional paralyzing migraines, Lincoln was a rock. At times, Lincoln argued that he was doing what he believed reason dictated; at others, he intimated that an inscrutable Providence was more responsible for events than he himself. In any case, he did not budge, he did not waiver, and he did not fail to do his duty as he understood it.

To repeat what I wrote earlier, no one can prove the goodness of Lincoln's soul beyond question; there will always be doubt, as well as those who will use it to try to strike a blow against Lincoln's reputation and propel their own careers in the process. But we can judge Lincoln by his words and actions, and it is not overly generous to suppose that a man with the best intentions and the best understanding of justice, if he found himself in the same political situation Lincoln did, would conduct himself in much the same way as Abraham Lincoln. Lincoln's challenge was to move opinion back toward the principles of the Declaration of Independence while avoiding the fanaticism of abolitionism and to uphold the rule of law and protection of property rights while avoiding the fanaticism of the pro-slavery camp. In this, Lincoln's skill was unmatched. In the words of Elihu Root:

> Lincoln never made the mistake of using words—either oral or written—merely for his own satisfaction. Many fine sentiments are uttered

about public affairs, which are not really designed to have an effect upon anybody except the speaker or writer whose feelings are gratified by expression. They are like the use of expletives—profane and otherwise—which simply relieve the feelings of the speaker. Lincoln never made this mistake. When he spoke or wrote, his objective was always the mind of somebody else.

Root offers a telling example of how Lincoln could appeal to the interests and judgments of others in a way that allowed him to advance right while securing the support he needed from his audience:

> His method with individuals is well illustrated by the incident when a committee of gentlemen called upon him to object to the use of negro troops. They said they were all patriotic citizens, that their sons were serving in the Union Army, and were cultivated gentlemen, and they objected to having negroes put upon the same level. Mr. Lincoln said: "Well, gentlemen, if you would rather have your sons die for a black man than have a black man die for your sons, I suppose there is nothing more to be said." This was a wholly new view of the subject. The objectors were prepared to stand for all time against arguments designed to force them to abandon their prejudice. Lincoln, however, had instantly found the line of least resistance, which left the prejudice undisturbed and at the same time left them nothing to say; so the objection ended.[62]

The art of rhetoric Root attributes to Lincoln is the art of the statesman. In *Federalist* 10, James Madison remarked, "Enlightened statesmen will not always be at the helm." But in some instances, when the public forgets the principles of the freedom they enjoy and that their government is supposed to secure, statesmanship may be indispensable. The antebellum and Civil War periods were such instances, and Lincoln was the indispensable statesman, fully aware of the extent to which racism had corrupted the American mind and tireless in his efforts to recover the only principle by which racism can be condemned, the principle of human equality enshrined in the Declaration of Independence.

NOTES

1. In his highly entertaining book, *Land of Lincoln*, Andrew Ferguson quotes Bob Rogers, who designed the new Abraham Lincoln Presidential Library and Museum in Springfield, Illinois: "We're not in the business of shoving anything down anybody's throat. After six years of living with Abraham Lincoln, I can give him to you anyway you want, cold or hot, jazz or classical. I can give you scandalous Lincoln,

conservative Lincoln, liberal Lincoln, racist Lincoln, Lincoln over easy or Lincoln scrambled." Andrew Ferguson, *Land of Lincoln* (New York: Atlantic Monthly Press, 2007), 109.

2. Mario M. Cuomo, *Why Lincoln Matters: Today More Than Ever* (New York: Harcourt Press, 2004), 157.

3. Barack Obama, "What I See in Lincoln's Eyes," *Time*, July 4, 2005, 74.

4. Michael Lind, *What Lincoln Believed: The Values and Convictions of America's Greatest President* (New York: Doubleday, 2004), 264.

5. Clyde Wilson, "DiLorenzo and His Critics," June 18, 2002, LewRockwell .com, www.lewrockwell.com/orig/wilson7.html (accessed May 15, 2007).

6. Charles Adams, *When in the Course of Human Events: Arguing the Case for Southern Secession* (Lanham, MD: Rowman & Littlefield, 2000), 159.

7. Shelby Steele, *White Guilt: How Blacks and Whites Together Destroyed the Promise of the Civil Rights Era* (New York: HarperCollins Publishers, 2006), 21.

8. Steele, *White Guilt*, 24.

9. Steele, *White Guilt*, 109–10.

10. The suspicion of racism on the part of anyone who opposes affirmative action is not limited to Americans with white skin. Ward Connerly, who is black, led efforts to eliminate race-based preferences and discrimination in California (1996), Washington State (1998), and Michigan (2006), and he has been denounced repeatedly in print and in public speech as an "Uncle Tom," an "Oreo," a "sellout," and a "house slave."

11. Orlando Patterson, *Slavery and Social Death: A Comparative Study* (Cambridge, MA: Harvard University Press, 1982), vii.

12. Dinesh D'Souza, *The End of Racism* (New York: The Free Press, 1995), 105–106.

13. To my knowledge, the best attempt to explore and explain Lincoln's character is Douglas O. Wilson, *Honor's Voice: The Transformation of Abraham Lincoln* (New York: Alfred A. Knopf, Inc., 1998).

14. Roy P. Basler, ed., *The Collected Works of Abraham Lincoln* (New Brunswick, NJ: Rutgers University Press, 1953), III:16. Cited hereafter as Lincoln, *Collected Works*. Lincoln repeated this statement almost verbatim in the sixth debate with Douglas, October 13, 1858, and again in a speech in Columbus, Ohio, September 16, 1859. Cf. Lincoln, *Collected Works*, III:249, 402.

15. Lincoln, *Collected Works*, III:145–46.

16. Thomas DiLorenzo, *Lincoln Unmasked: What You're Not Supposed to Know about Dishonest Abe* (New York: Crown Forum, 2006), 27.

17. DiLorenzo, *Lincoln Unmasked*, 12.

18. Thomas E. Woods Jr., *The Politically Incorrect Guide to American History* (Washington, DC: Regnery Publishing, 2004), 66–67.

19. David Gordon, "The Indefensible Abe," *Mises Review* (summer 2001), www.mises.org/misesreview_detail.asp?control=179&sortorder=issue (accessed July 20, 2007).

20. David Herbert Donald, *Lincoln* (New York: Simon & Schuster, 1995), 221.

21. Jay Winik, *April 1865: The Month That Saved America* (New York: Harper-Collins, 2001), 238.

22. James McPherson, "What Did He Really Think about Race?" review of *The Radical and the Republican: Frederick Douglass, Abraham Lincoln, and the Triumph of Antislavery Politics*, by James Oakes, *The New York Review of Books*, March 29, 2007, www.nybooks.com/articles/19994 (accessed April 1, 2007).

23. Lincoln, *Collected Works*, III:372, II:249.

24. Thomas Jefferson, "Notes on the State of Virginia," Query XIII, in *Jefferson: Writings*, ed. Merrill D. Peterson (New York: Library of America, 1984), 256–75. Cited hereafter as Jefferson, *Jefferson: Writings*.

25. Jefferson, *Jefferson: Writings*, 270.

26. Jefferson, *Jefferson: Writings*, 982.

27. Jefferson, *Jefferson: Writings*, 1202 (emphasis added).

28. Jefferson, *Jefferson: Writings*, 264.

29. See, e.g., Ward Connerly, *Creating Equal: My Fight Against Race Preferences* (San Francisco: Encounter Books, 2000).

30. Lincoln, *Collected Works*, III:16 (emphasis in original).

31. C. B. Macpherson, ed., *John Locke: Second Treatise of Government* (Indianapolis: Hackett Publishing Co., 1980). See also James Madison's essay, "On Property." Some scholars have made much of the fact that Locke speculated in the slave trade, investing for example in the Royal African Company, a slave-trading company, and he also advised Lord Proprietor of Carolina Anthony Ashley Cooper, who later became the first Earl of Shaftesbury, in which capacity he may have contributed to the writing of the slave provisions of the Fundamental Constitutions of Carolina. See, e.g., James Farr, "'So Vile and Miserable an Estate': The Problem of Slavery in Locke's Political Thought," *Political Theory* 14, no. 2 (May 1986): 263–89, and Wayne Glausser, "Three Approaches to Locke and the Slave Trade," *Journal of the History of Ideas* 51, no. 2 (April–June 1990): 199–216. The main charge against Locke is hypocrisy—that he personally benefited from slavery while making theoretical arguments against it. I find these arguments against Locke to be neither all that important nor interesting. Even if the charges are true, to say that Locke failed to live up to his own principles is merely to say something that is true of every human being who is less than an angel. Further, his personal actions have no bearing on the merits of his arguments. Regardless of his personal actions, Locke's arguments are among the foremost defending human equality and liberty and condemning slavery. Would Locke's detractors have us abandon the principled defense of liberty simply because the man who best articulated those principles did not live in perfect accord with them?

32. Macpherson, *John Locke: Second Treatise of Government*, ch. VII, 51.

33. Macpherson, *John Locke: Second Treatise of Government*, ch. XI, 69, 72.

34. Macpherson, *John Locke: Second Treatise of Government*, ch. XI, 73.

35. Macpherson, *John Locke: Second Treatise of Government*, ch. XI, 70.

36. Macpherson, *John Locke: Second Treatise of Government*, ch. XI, 71 (emphasis added).

37. In the 1967 case *Loving v. Virginia* (388 U.S. 1), the U.S. Supreme Court struck down a Virginia statute prohibiting interracial marriage on the grounds that "distinctions between citizens solely because of their ancestry [or race] are odious to a free people whose institutions are founded upon the doctrine of equality." The Court concluded that "marriage is one of the 'basic civil rights of man,' fundamental to our very existence and survival. To deny this fundamental freedom on so unsupportable a basis as the racial classifications embodied in these statutes, classifications so directly subversive of the principle of equality at the heart of the Fourteenth Amendment, is surely to deprive all the State's citizens of liberty without due process of law. The Fourteenth Amendment requires that the freedom of choice to marry not be restricted by invidious racial discriminations. Under our Constitution, the freedom to marry, or not marry, a person of another race resides with the individual and cannot be infringed by the State."

38. Eugene H. Berwanger, "Negrophobia in Northern Proslavery and Antislavery Thought," *Phylon* 33, no. 3 (1972): 266, 268, 269.

39. Lincoln, *Collected Works*, III:548. See also David Brion Davis, *Inhuman Bondage: The Rise and Fall of Bondage in the New World* (New York: Oxford University Press, 2006).

40. Alexander Stephens, "Cornerstone Speech," in *Alexander H. Stephens in Public and Private with Letters and Speeches* (Philadelphia: National Publishing, 1866), 721.

41. Lincoln, *Collected Works*, III:146.

42. Leland Winfield Meyer, *The Life and Times of Colonel Richard M. Johnson of Kentucky* (New York: AMS Press, 1967), 322. See also Harry V. Jaffa, *A New Birth of Freedom: Abraham Lincoln and the Coming of the Civil War* (Lanham, MD: Rowman & Littlefield, 2000), 331–32.

43. Philip Shaw Paludan, *The Presidency of Abraham Lincoln* (Lawrence: University of Kansas Press, 1994), 221.

44. Philip Shaw Paludan, *"A People's Contest": The Union and Civil War, 1861–1865* (Lawrence: University of Kansas Press, 1996), 209.

45. Harvey C. Mansfield and Delba Winthrop, trans., *Alexis de Tocqueville's Democracy in America* (Chicago: University of Chicago Press, 2000), 244.

46. DiLorenzo, *Lincoln Unmasked*, 28.

47. Lincoln, *Collected Works*, II:255.

48. Lincoln, *Collected Works*, II:256.

49. Lincoln, *Collected Works*, II:256.

50. Lincoln, *Collected Works*, II:532.

51. Lincoln, *Collected Works*, II:255.

52. Quoted in William E. Cain, ed., *William Lloyd Garrison and the Fight against Slavery: Selections from* The Liberator (Boston: Bedford Books, 1995), 10.

53. Benjamin P. Thomas, *Abraham Lincoln: A Biography* (New York: Barnes & Noble, 1994 [1952]), 361–63. As president, Lincoln seriously entertained a proposal

for colonizing freed blacks in Chiriqui, Panama, but eventually opted for l'Ile à Vache, Haiti, as the preferred site. For details of Lincoln's failed experiment in colonization, see James D. Lockett, "Abraham Lincoln and Colonization: An Episode That Ends in Tragedy at l'Ile à Vache, Haiti, 1863–1864," *Journal of Black Studies* 21, no. 4 (June 1991): 428–44, and Paul J. Scheips, "Lincoln and the Chiriqui Colonization Project," *Journal of Negro History* 37, no. 4 (October 1952): 418–53.

54. Lerone Bennett Jr., *Forced into Glory: Abraham Lincoln's White Dream* (Chicago: Johnson Publishing Co., 2000), 37.

55. Mark Graber, *Dred Scott and the Problem of Constitutional Evil* (New York: Cambridge University Press, 2006), 78–79.

56. Bennett, *Forced into Glory*, 381, 385.

57. Lincoln, *Collected Works*, I:112.

58. Jefferson, First Inaugural Address, March 4, 1801, in Jefferson, *Jefferson: Writings*, 495.

59. Lincoln, *Collected Works*, III:27.

60. Cain, *William Lloyd Garrison and the Fight against Slavery*, 72.

61. John W. Blassingame and John R. McKivigan, eds., *The Frederick Douglass Papers* (New Haven, CT: Yale University Press, 1991), IV:436. See also James Oakes, *The Radical and the Republican: Frederick Douglass, Abraham Lincoln, and the Triumph of Antislavery Politics* (New York: W.W. Norton & Co., 2007).

62. Elihu Root, "Lincoln as Leader of Men," in *Men and Policies: Addresses by Elihu Root*, ed. Robert Bacon and James Brown Scott (Cambridge, MA: Harvard University Press, 1924), 72–73.

2

WAS THE KANSAS-NEBRASKA ACT
PRO-CHOICE OR PRO-SLAVERY?

> Lincoln certainly would not have felt obliged to push for leg-
> islation or court rulings that would have prohibited all abor-
> tions . . . [so long] as no one would ever be compelled to have
> an abortion or to use contraceptives in violation of their reli-
> gious beliefs.
>
> —Mario Cuomo, *Why Lincoln Matters*

> [The Kansas-Nebraska Act] is wrong; wrong in its direct ef-
> fect, letting slavery into Kansas and Nebraska—and wrong in
> its prospective principle, allowing it to spread to every other
> part of the wide world, where men can be found inclined to
> take it. This declared indifference [is really a] covert real zeal
> for the spread of slavery, [which] I can not but hate.
>
> —Abraham Lincoln, speech at Peoria, Illinois,
> October 16, 1854

In *Why Lincoln Matters*, former New York governor Mario Cuomo suggests that the principles Abraham Lincoln championed are the same principles that the pro-choice side in the abortion debate champions today. But
Lincoln confronted the question of freedom of choice in the controversy
over the Kansas-Nebraska Act, and he came down on precisely the opposite ground that Cuomo attributes to him. If Cuomo thinks Lincoln's opposition to the Kansas-Nebraska Act and the extension of slavery somehow
indicates that he would have taken a pro-choice stand on abortion, then
Cuomo either misunderstands the controversy over slavery extension, or he

misunderstands Lincoln, or perhaps both. Nevertheless, Cuomo rightly suggests similarities between the controversy over abortion today and the controversy over slavery extension in the 1850s.

In the 1973 case of *Roe v. Wade*, the U.S. Supreme Court argued that the Constitution protects a woman's "right to choose" to terminate a pregnancy through abortion, a right encompassed by a larger "right to privacy" that has "roots" in the Ninth Amendment's reservation of rights to the people, as well as in the Fourteenth Amendment's protection of liberty.[1] More than three decades later, public opinion in America remains deeply divided between those who affirm an allegedly morally neutral "pro-choice" position—neither advocating nor condemning abortion—and "pro-lifers," who argue that one cannot be neutral on a question of moral right and wrong, that there is no "right to choose" to end the life of another human being, and that therefore abortion is a destruction of freedom and self-government.

The fight over abortion, however, is not the first to divide Americans over the question of a "right to choose" and differing definitions of freedom and self-government. In 1854, U.S. Senator Stephen Douglas of Illinois defended his Kansas-Nebraska Act with the principle of "popular sovereignty"; he took a position of moral neutrality regarding slavery, which he described as his not caring whether slavery was voted "up or down" but only for the "sacred right" of the people "to choose" whether they wanted slavery in the territories or not. Douglas's doctrine of "popular sovereignty" eventually caused an irreparable split in the Democratic Party (thanks in no small measure to the political efforts of Lincoln), which allowed for Lincoln's election and thus initiated the chain of events culminating in the Civil War.

All the same, is it fair to invoke Lincoln in the modern debates over abortion? Cuomo certainly thinks so. The only opposition to abortion, Cuomo insists, is strictly grounded in irrational religious dogma. But Lincoln never offered a confession of sectarian religious faith. From this, Cuomo concludes that Lincoln would be "pro-choice" because, in Cuomo's words, "no one would ever be compelled to have an abortion in violation of their religious beliefs."[2] No more succinct statement could be made of Stephen Douglas's "popular sovereignty" doctrine regarding slavery: those who want slavery should be free to choose it, and those who do not want it should be free to choose not to have it. In Cuomo's account, Lincoln stands perfectly aligned with Douglas's "pro-choice" principle of the Kansas-Nebraska Act, a measure Lincoln vigorously opposed from the moment of its adoption.

If, in his writing, Cuomo too quickly identifies Lincoln with the pro-choice principle of the Kansas-Nebraska Act, others say too little about it. Consider Thomas DiLorenzo, who is among the most clamorous of Lincoln critics. Perhaps more important than what DiLorenzo writes is what he does not write: throughout the pages of *The Real Lincoln* and *Lincoln Unmasked*, DiLorenzo almost never mentions the Kansas-Nebraska Act.[3]

In one brief passage in *The Real Lincoln*, DiLorenzo alludes to the act, but he suggests nothing about the escalation in the fights over slavery that it caused. Instead, DiLorenzo only remarks that Republicans like Lincoln opposed the Kansas-Nebraska Act because they were Negrophobes who did not want blacks migrating into federal territories.[4] In his *Lincoln Unmasked*, DiLorenzo writes, "Even when the Republicans did oppose the extension of slavery into the new territories, it was motivated much more by politics and economics than by humanitarianism." "In fact," DiLorenzo continues, "Lincoln and other party leaders explicitly stated that they wanted to preserve the territories for the white race." But DiLorenzo never quotes anything Lincoln "explicitly stated." Instead, he quotes historian Eugene Berwanger, who wrote,

> Republicans made no pretense of being concerned with the fate of the Negro and insisted that theirs was a party of white labor. By introducing a note of white supremacy, they hoped to win the votes of the Negrophobes and the anti-abolitionists who were opposed to the extension of slavery.[5]

DiLorenzo never explains why it might be wrong for "Negrophobes" and "antiabolitionists" to vote against the extension of slavery or why it might be wrong for Republicans to vie for those votes. More importantly, however, both DiLorenzo and Berwanger miss the fact that Lincoln's central criticism of the Kansas-Nebraska Act was emphatically moral. As I demonstrate in chapter 1, Lincoln certainly appealed to the racist views of his audience time and again (without ever conceding that those views were right or that he shared them), but he did so in order to advance a noble and moral cause, that is, halting the spread of slavery, which DiLorenzo fails to acknowledge. Those who genuinely seek to know "the real Lincoln" cannot ignore the Kansas-Nebraska Act and the politics surrounding it.

TERRITORIAL EXPANSION: SEEDS OF CONFLICT

In 1803, President Thomas Jefferson acquired from France a massive tract of land stretching from the Gulf Coast to Canada, from the Mississippi River to the Rocky Mountains, more than doubling the geographical size of the United States. This was the Louisiana Purchase, and it included what would later become some of the most fertile farmland in the world (see map 1). But as Americans prepared to settle their new western frontier, a thorny problem arose regarding slavery: should slavery be allowed to spread into the new territory or not?

During the next two decades, the controversy heated up between those who wanted slavery prohibited from the territory and those who demanded that it be allowed to spread. In 1820, the conflict came to a head over the question of whether Missouri, located entirely within the Louisiana Purchase territory, could enter the Union as a slave state. Amidst public alarm and threats of secession and disunion, which Jefferson likened to "a fire bell in the night," the Missouri Compromise was reached and public tranquility restored, at least for the moment. The 1820 Missouri Compromise allowed Missouri into the Union as a slave state but prohibited slavery in all the remaining territory purchased from France that lay north of 36°30′ latitude, an extension of Missouri's southern border (see map 2).

For three decades, the Missouri Compromise remained unchallenged as America's national policy regarding slavery in the federal territories. By 1850, however, slavery had again become a source of national political turmoil. Soon after war erupted between the United States and Mexico in 1846, Congressman David Wilmot, a Democrat from Pennsylvania, introduced his Wilmot Proviso, which stipulated that slavery would be prohibited in any land the United States acquired from the Mexican War. The response by Southern defenders of slavery was uncompromising: they would accept no limitation on slavery in newly acquired territories. Wilmot's proviso passed through the House of Representatives multiple times, only to be rejected each time by the U.S. Senate.

In the midst of the imbroglio over the Wilmot Proviso, gold was discovered in California. As the prospect of instant riches brought thousands of Americans to the West Coast in 1849, California skipped over the usual territorial organization and sought to be admitted to the Union as a state. But the state constitution proposed by Californians prohibited slavery, adding more fuel to the intense fights in Congress between those opposed to, and those supporting, the spread of slavery. California's antislavery constitution outraged Southerners, who interpreted it as an undeserved slight against the Southern way of life.

The controversies over the Wilmot Proviso, California, and slavery boiled over in Congress, as no compromise seemed possible and Southerners both in Congress and at home talked more and more openly of disunion.

Louisiana Purchase Territory

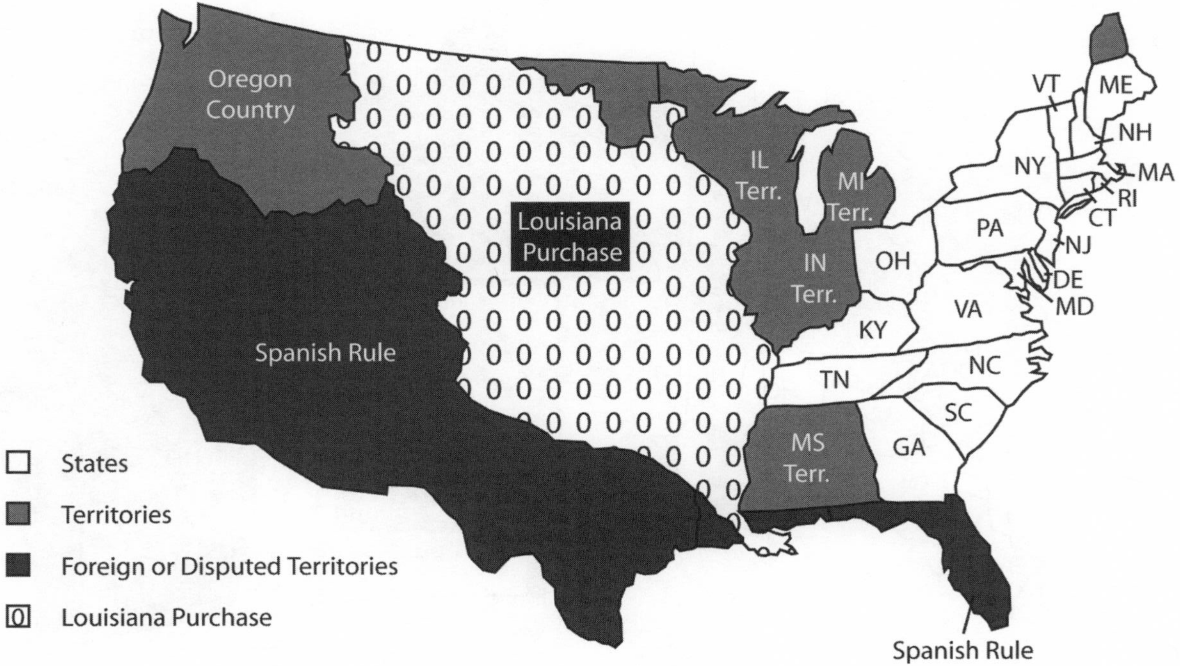

States

Territories

Foreign or Disputed Territories

Louisiana Purchase

Oregon Country

Spanish Rule

Louisiana Purchase

Spanish Rule

IL Terr.

MI Terr.

IN Terr.

OH

KY

TN

MS Terr.

GA

SC

NC

VA

PA

NY

VT

ME

NH

MA

RI

CT

NJ

DE

MD

Map 1

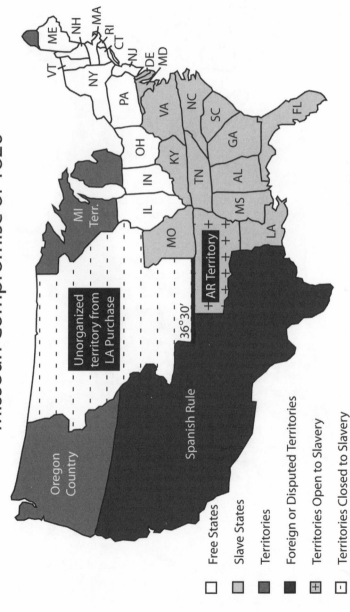

Missouri Compromise of 1820

Free States

Slave States

Territories

Foreign or Disputed Territories

Territories Open to Slavery

Territories Closed to Slavery

Map 2

Oregon Country

Unorganized territory from LA Purchase

36°30′

Spanish Rule

AR Territory

MO

MI Terr.

IL

IN

OH

PA

NY

VT

ME

NH

MA

RI

CT

NJ

DE

MD

VA

KY

TN

NC

SC

GA

AL

MS

LA

FL

From the Southern point of view, any compromise over slavery would result in the addition of free states—California and any states formed from the southwest territory would be free under the terms of the Wilmot Proviso—which in turn would make the slave-holding states of the South a diminishing minority in Congress. This development they equated with abolitionism and would not tolerate. Historian David Potter explains the incompatible views driving the crisis of 1850:

> Southerners believed, with fearful conviction, that abolition would literally destroy southern society. It would subject "the two races to the greatest calamity, and the [Southern] section to poverty, desolation, and wretchedness." Regardless of whether their fears were realistic or fantastic, the dominating fact is that they believed that abolition would produce a "holocaust of blood," and they resisted anything which might lead to abolition as if they were resisting the holocaust itself.[6]

From the Southern point of view, the question of slavery in the territories and new states pointed to concerns beyond the sectional balance of power in Congress. Many Southerners perceived attacks on slavery as attacks on Southern honor.[7] In late 1849, Robert Toombs of Georgia took to the floor of the House of Representatives and openly declared,

> I do not hesitate to avow before this House and Country, and in the presence of the living God, that if, by your legislation, you seek to drive us from the territories of California and New Mexico, purchased by the common blood and treasure of the whole people, and to abolish slavery in this District, thereby attempting to fix a national degradation upon half the states of this confederacy, I am for disunion.[8]

When "Old Rough and Ready" Zachary Taylor, a Southerner, a career military man, and a hero from the Mexican War, assumed the presidency in 1849, he refused to make concessions with anyone who threatened disunion. In a stormy meeting in February 1850, Taylor told a group of disunion-favoring Southerners that if executing the laws and maintaining the Union required force, he would personally lead the army and hang persons "taken in rebellion against the Union . . . with less reluctance than he had hanged deserters and spies in Mexico." President Taylor was sure in early 1850 that Southern disunionists would back down if confronted by strong policy.

We will never know whether he was right. Taylor died in office only a few months later after attending a Fourth of July celebration. He was replaced by his vice president, Millard Fillmore, who was far more disposed toward compromise with Southern "fire eaters." Shortly afterward, Congress passed the various components of the Compromise of 1850, which President Fillmore signed into law in September.

It is interesting to speculate about the likely result had Taylor lived to stand by his policy and defend the Union. He might have been correct that the Southern bark in 1850 was worse than its bite and that, despite all their fiery rhetoric to the contrary, Southerners would have acquiesced when faced with a president, a Southern president no less, determined to use force to protect the Union's integrity. But not everyone agreed. Daniel Webster, among others, speculated that "if General Taylor had lived, we should have had a civil war."[9] A civil war in 1850 would likely have been less bloody and shorter than the Civil War that began eleven years later because national sentiment still predominated over sectionalism in many parts of the country, and particularly in the South, there was still widespread desire for union as evidenced by the fact that Southern unionists, such as Taylor and Andrew Jackson a generation before him, were capable of winning the presidency. In 1850, the South had not yet fully come to view itself as a unified political people, while many in the North were sympathetic toward Southerners who were insulted and outraged by abolitionist jabs against their way of life. These facts alone would have made the edge of an 1850 war less sharp than it became in 1861. Consider also the military capacity to wage war, as the economic, technological, and manufacturing abilities of both the North and the South, but especially the North, were greater in 1861 than they had been in 1850. While we can never know with certainty, it may well be correct that "the refusal of Congress to follow [Taylor's] policy cost the republic ten years of avoidable strife, ending in a titanic civil war."[10]

The Compromise of 1850 featured five key provisions that Henry Clay had been unable to pass as one omnibus bill but which finally received majority support in Congress under the stewardship of Stephen Douglas, whose national celebrity was greatly boosted after he broke the bill into pieces and shepherded each into law individually:

1. California was admitted as a free state.
2. The Texas boundary was settled, and Texas was compensated for debts incurred during the Mexican War.
3. New Mexico was granted territorial status with slavery neither explicitly allowed nor prohibited.
4. A fugitive slave law was passed that required federal officers to assist slaveholders seeking the return of fugitive slaves.
5. The slave trade was abolished in the District of Columbia.

These measures preserved peace, and the Missouri Compromise remained the law of the land in the Louisiana Purchase territory north of the 36°30′ line. But not for long. The Kansas-Nebraska Act, signed into law on May 30, 1854, by President Franklin Pierce, overturned the Missouri Compromise and the public peace that rested upon it. As David Potter comments, no event has "swung American history away from its charted course so suddenly or so sharply as the Kansas-Nebraska Act," which brought anti- and pro-slavery forces into an unprecedented and violent political clash, preparing the way for Abraham Lincoln's presidency as the ominous clouds of civil war gathered.[11]

FROM RAILROADS TO SLAVERY

The Kansas-Nebraska Act began as a railroad measure. Bound up in the nineteenth-century spirit of Manifest Destiny was a widespread desire to connect the American West and East with one or more railroad lines. And everyone wanted in on the railroad action. From New Orleans to Vicksburg to St. Louis, cities and states lobbied fiercely to be the connecting point between a rail line running west to the Pacific and another running east, vying for the promise of population and economic growth, not to mention the government subsidies, that would follow the tracks. Throughout the 1830s and 1840s, even men with reputations as strict constitutionalists opposed to government funding of internal improvements, such as South Carolina's John C. Calhoun, were willing to put aside their constitutional scruples with the prospect of landing a federally subsidized railroad in their region.[12]

One of the most prominent and persistent railroad advocates was Democratic senator Stephen Douglas of Illinois, who was intent on seeing a rail line run from Chicago to the West Coast. One problem Douglas faced in securing a line from Chicago was that most of the territory west of Illinois, land the United States had acquired in the Louisiana Purchase, lacked any kind of territorial organization. As one railroad advocate lamented, "Why, everybody is talking about a railroad to the Pacific. In the name of God, how is the railroad to be made if you will never let people live on the lands through which the road passes?"[13] Thus was born Douglas's bill to organize the territories of Kansas and Nebraska.

Key members of Congress agreed to support the bill, but some legislators from slave states (such as Dave Atchison of Missouri) insisted that slave owners be allowed to settle in the newly organized territory, bringing their slaves with them. Douglas's original bill said nothing about slavery, but both the Kansas and Nebraska territories lay north of the 36°30' line, an area in which the 1820 Missouri Compromise prohibited slavery.

Here was the rub: Douglas needed to attract support from Southern slave states if his Kansas-Nebraska Bill was to pass, but that support would come at the expense of lifting the 1820 congressional ban on slavery in the territories above 36°30'. The solution was clear, and clearly it would be difficult to reach. Douglas would amend his bill expressly to repeal the Missouri Compromise's prohibition against slavery in the territories based on the doctrine of "popular sovereignty," according to which slavery could be allowed or prohibited in a territory depending on the desires of the people residing there. "It will raise a hell of a storm," predicted Douglas. But even this seasoned politician had no idea of the power of the forces he was about to unleash.

Before Douglas's bill received a vote in either house of Congress, six "Independent Democrats" published an attack on Douglas in the January 24, 1854, issue of the Washington, D.C., weekly newspaper *National Era*. The Kansas-Nebraska Bill, they wrote, represented a "gross violation of a sacred pledge" to keep the territories north of 36°30' free of slavery. It was part of an "atrocious plot" to turn free land into "a dreary region of despotism, inhabited by masters and slaves."[14] After the *National Era* article, Douglas's Kansas-Nebraska proposal was no longer a railroad bill; it had become a slavery bill (see map 3).

The following months witnessed some of the most heated debates in the history of the U.S. Congress, reigniting the tempers of free-soil and slave advocates, each viewing the other as mortal enemies (two years later, in 1856, Congressman Preston Brooks of South Carolina would beat Massachusetts senator Charles Sumner within an inch of his life right inside the Senate chambers). With much politicking and lobbying for support, Douglas's bill finally passed in late May, 1854. The Missouri Compromise, with its congressional prohibition against the spread of slavery, was repealed and replaced by the Douglas doctrine of "popular sovereignty" as the new governing principle throughout all the Louisiana Purchase territories. After the Kansas-Nebraska Act became law, slavery could spread throughout the territory if the people residing there chose to allow it.

But identifying the popular will of the people was not easy. Pro-slavery and free-soil men from bordering states poured into Kansas in an attempt to give greater numbers and greater votes to their respective sides, stirring up conflicts that quickly turned violent in the streets of Kansas. For two years after the passage of the Kansas-Nebraska Act, from 1855

Kansas Nebraska Act of 1854

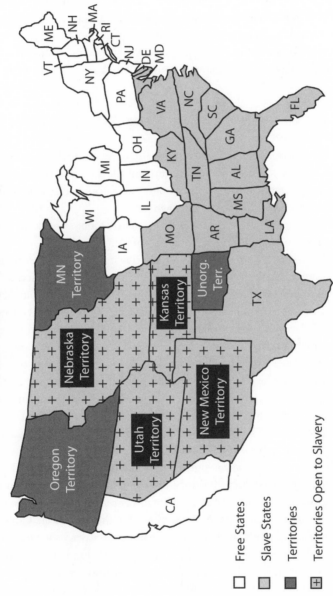

Free States

Slave States

Territories

Territories Open to Slavery

Map 3

through 1856, "Bleeding Kansas" would demonstrate that the act had done nothing to settle the fight over slavery; rather, the fighting became more intense. Further, no railroad would be laid until the sons of the North and South had finished butchering one another in places like Antietam, Shiloh, and Gettysburg. Of the many unintended consequences of the Kansas-Nebraska Act, perhaps the most important was its effect on the spirit of a dejected Illinois lawyer-cum-politician.

LINCOLN OPPOSES THE KANSAS-NEBRASKA ACT

In 1854, Abraham Lincoln was a political failure. Though he had served in the Illinois state legislature and one term in the U.S. House of Representatives, unsuccessful bids for appointments and nominations, as well as lost elections, checkered his political career.

The passage of Kansas-Nebraska propelled Lincoln back into national politics. He saw the adoption of the act and the doctrine of popular sovereignty as symptoms of a larger and terribly troubling transformation of public opinion. America had been founded in the firm conviction that all men are created equal and that slavery is therefore wrong, despite acknowledgment of the many challenges of eliminating the practice. Reflecting on the fate of slavery in America in light of the Americans' pronouncement of equality, John Jay, for example, urged in a 1786 letter, "It is much to be wished that slavery may be abolished. . . . To contend for our own liberty, and to deny that blessing to others, is an inconsistency not to be excused."[15] From the point of view of the Founding and the Declaration of Independence, slavery was immoral; therefore, the problem of eliminating slavery had to be solved. The most pressing question for the Founders was not *whether* but *how* to get rid of slavery.

Not everyone, however, agrees with Lincoln's view that the Founding was principally antislavery. "History does not support Lincoln's antislavery constitutionalism," argues Mark Graber in his recent book on *Dred Scott v. Sandford*, because "the persons responsible for the American Constitution were far more concerned that controversies over slavery *be settled peaceably* than that they be resolved *in favor of liberty.*"[16] Citing certain South Carolinians who believed slavery would be "a relatively enduring institution," Graber concludes that there existed no consensus on the immorality of slavery at the time of the Founding and that Lincoln wrongly argued that the Founders had placed slavery "in the course of ultimate extinction." But Graber sometimes seems to forget the Founders' faith in education and the triumph of truth, which he admits elsewhere.[17]

"Prior to the great [American] revolution," John Jay commented in 1788, "the great majority or rather the great body of our people had been so long accustomed to the practice and convenience of having slaves, that very few among them even doubted the propriety and rectitude of it." But he then compared the natural right principles of the Declaration of Independence to "a little lump of leaven which was put into three measures of meal," optimistically concluding that Americans "have good reason to hope and to believe that if the natural operations of truth are constantly watched and assisted, but not forced and precipitated, that end we all aim at [the end of slavery] will finally be attained in this country."[18]

The widespread opposition to slavery during the Founding followed from the recognition that all men are created equal in terms of their natural rights, combined with the recognition that black slaves were men, not property, by nature. The compromises over slavery in the Constitution, including the Three-Fifths, Slave Importation, and Fugitive Slave clauses, resulted precisely from the universal recognition that black slaves were persons. There were no disputes at the Constitutional Convention, for example, over whether to count mules or horses or oxen as part of a state's population, but there was intense fighting over whether to count slaves because every member of the convention understood that slaves, unlike mules, horses, and oxen, were human beings. The records of the convention are clear on this subject. When debating whether to prohibit the importation of slaves from Africa, for example, delegate Oliver Ellsworth of Connecticut argued that such a prohibition was not necessary because "as population increases, poor laborers will be so plenty as to render slaves useless. Slavery in time will not be a speck in our Country." He also pointed out that provisions had already been "made in Connecticut for abolishing [slavery]," that "the abolition ha[d] already taken place in Massachusetts," and that he had every expectation that slavery would continue to dwindle in the United States.[19] Luther Martin of Maryland, however, insisted that the importation of slaves be prohibited because slavery "was inconsistent with the principles of the revolution"; therefore, it would be "dishonorable to the American character to have such a feature [protecting the slave trade] in the Constitution."[20] George Mason of Virginia seconded Martin's opinion, adding that "every master of slaves is born a petty tyrant. They bring the judgment of heaven on a Country."[21] After much wrangling, fighting, and negotiating, the convention agreed to allow Congress to stop the Atlantic slave trade after a period of twenty years (found in Article I, Section 9 of the Constitution).

In general, the American Founders believed in the principles of the Declaration of Independence and expected that increasing numbers of Americans would eventually accept those principles as true and therefore come to oppose, and in due time put an end to, slavery. George Washington was almost boastful when he announced that the "foundation of our Empire was not laid in the gloomy age of ignorance and superstition, but at an epoch when the rights of mankind were better understood and more clearly defined, than at any former period."[22] "All eyes are opened, or opening, to the rights of man," Thomas Jefferson confidently asserted, because the "general spread of the light of science has already laid open to every view the palpable truth" that all men are created equal.[23] Lincoln did not need to argue that *every* American in 1776 or 1787 fully understood and affirmed the natural right principle of human equality and all of its implications. He needed merely to argue that the American regime was rooted in, and the leading minds of the Founding affirmed, the moral principle of equality, which rendered slavery immoral and thereby jeopardized slavery's future in America.

Almost contradicting himself, Graber argues that "breaking up the constitutional convention or refusing to ratify over slavery would not have alleviated the present condition of black slaves," and therefore antislavery delegates were right to think "that tolerating a decaying institution was a reasonable price to pay for union."[24] In other words, while they compromised on ending slavery immediately, delegates to the convention did believe that slavery was a "decaying institution," which is another way of saying it was "in the course of ultimate extinction." Here Graber suggests that history *does* seem to support Lincoln's antislavery constitutionalism, although earlier I quoted him stating just the opposite.

The Kansas-Nebraska Act presented slavery in a new light, asking Americans to refrain from judging slavery as either right or wrong, and offered instead a position of moral neutrality, or what we today might call "nonjudgmentalism," toward slavery. Lincoln saw perhaps more clearly than anyone that people who were morally neutral on slavery would have little reason to oppose those who taught that slavery was a moral good and little incentive to oppose policies that allowed slavery to spread. If one is neutral on a subject such as slavery, after all, why would one care if it proliferates? And, in Lincoln's opinion, once the American people had allowed slavery to spread and embraced slavery as a moral good, they would have forfeited any moral defense of their own freedom. The fundamental moral problem of freedom versus slavery came to dominate all of Lincoln's political thought after the passage of Kansas-Nebraska Act, focusing his attention on the principle of human equality from 1854 until his assassination in 1865. Understanding that statesmanship often requires cooperation and compromise, Lincoln, too, was willing to make many concessions and alliances, but he would not budge on one part of his political platform: his demand for the repeal of the Kansas-Nebraska Act and the reinstatement of the Missouri Compromise complete with its prohibition against the spread of slavery.

Douglas's "popular sovereignty" meant that Congress would no longer prohibit slavery in the territories. Rather, white settlers in the territories could invite slavery in or keep it out as they pleased. Douglas never tired of saying that he did not "care if slavery [was] voted up or down." For Lincoln, this moral ambiguity regarding slavery represented the dissolution of all moral principle. There can be no middle ground between the views that slavery, as a moral wrong, should be contained and placed in the course of ultimate extinction or, as a moral right, should be championed and allowed to spread. "If slavery is right," Lincoln argued in his 1860 address at New York's Cooper Institute, "all words, acts, laws, and constitutions against it are themselves wrong, and should be silenced, and swept away," and "if it is right, we cannot justly object to its nationality—its universality; [but] if it is wrong, [slave proponents] cannot justly insist upon its extension—its enlargement."[25] Either all human beings share a common nature and equal natural rights, or they do not. Slavery must be right, or it must be wrong. And "if slavery is not wrong," said Lincoln, "nothing is wrong." As Lincoln explained in his 1854 Peoria speech,

> [The Kansas-Nebraska Act] is wrong; wrong in its direct effect, letting slavery into Kansas and Nebraska—and wrong in its prospective principle, allowing it to spread to every other part of the wide world, where men can be found inclined to take it. This declared indifference, but as I must think, covert real zeal for the spread of slavery, I can not but hate. I hate it because of the monstrous injustice of slavery itself . . . [and] because it forces so many really good men amongst ourselves into an open war with the very fundamental principles of civil liberty—criticizing the Declaration of Independence, and insisting that there is no right principle of action but self-interest.[26]

Lincoln understood that "popular sovereignty," or the right of self-government, is right so long as it is understood to refer to what James Madison called the "social compact," that is, free people voluntarily governing themselves in recognition of, and for the protection of, their equal natural rights. But "popular sovereignty" had no proper application to slavery. Divorced from the principle of human equality and the purpose of protecting equal natural rights, "popular sovereignty" became a justification for majority tyranny: "When the white man governs himself, that is self-government; but when he governs himself and also governs another man . . . that is despotism." Drawing upon the principles of the Declaration of Independence, Lincoln argued, "my ancient faith teaches me that 'all men are created equal,' and that there can be no moral right in connection with one man's making a slave of another."[27]

Douglas and others presented "popular sovereignty" as synonymous with liberty, the freedom to choose how one wants to live. Lincoln understood, however, that liberty defined as the freedom to enslave others is no liberty at all. In short, the entire controversy over Kansas-Nebraska and the extension of slavery into the territories turned on the meaning of liberty. "The world has never had a good definition of the word liberty," Lincoln remarked during an 1864 speech in Baltimore, "and the American people, just now, are much in want of one."

> We all declare for liberty; but in using the same *word* we do not all mean the same *thing*. With some the word liberty may mean for each man to do as he pleases with himself, and the product of his labor; while with others the same word may mean for some men to do as they please with other men, and the product of other men's labor. Here are two, not only different, but incompatible things, called by the same name—*liberty*. And it follows that each of the things is, by the respective parties, called by two different and incompatible names—liberty and tyranny.
>
> The shepherd drives the wolf from the sheep's throat, for which the sheep thanks the shepherd as a *liberator*, while the wolf denounces him for the same act as the destroyer of liberty, especially as the sheep was a black one. Plainly the sheep and the wolf are not agreed upon a definition of the word liberty; and precisely the same difference prevails today among us human creatures.[28]

Lincoln saw, as few did, that in the course of the nineteenth century, America was abandoning or forgetting the basic principles upon which a free society rests and increasingly accepting slavery, first as a morally neutral institution and then as a morally good institution. For Lincoln, the Kansas-Nebraska Act was the most visible sign of this rejection of the principle of equality, which is why Lincoln fought so hard to oppose it. Forgetting that the principle of equal natural rights precedes and legitimizes self-government, that government neither creates nor legitimizes rights, America was becoming a house divided against itself over the question of slavery and stood on the brink of abandoning the principle of freedom for the principle of slavery.

Lincoln sounded this theme in his widely circulated "house divided" speech delivered in June 1858 as he accepted the Republican nomination to challenge Democrat Stephen Douglas for his seat representing Illinois in the U.S. Senate (Lincoln lost, and Douglas was reelected). Perhaps no other speech went so far not only in describing the growing split in America over whether slavery was right or wrong but in driving the opposed sides even further apart:

> I believe this government cannot endure permanently half slave and half free. I do not expect the Union to be dissolved—I do not expect the house to fall—but I do expect it will cease to be divided. It will become all one thing, or all the other. Either the opponents of slavery will arrest the further spread of it, and place it where the public mind shall rest in the belief that it is in the course of ultimate extinction; or its advocates will push it forward, till it shall become alike lawful in all the States, old as well as new—North as well as South.[29]

No one made it clearer than Lincoln that the principles of freedom and slavery were mutually exclusive. If one was right, the other must be wrong. Eventually, Lincoln predicted, America would have to make up its mind and become all free or all slave. And after a large portion of Americans proclaimed moral "indifference" toward slavery, there would be little or no resistance against a movement toward national slavery. This is why Lincoln argued in Peoria that the supposed "declared indifference" toward slavery was in fact merely a disguised "covert real zeal for the spread of slavery." Lincoln understood that the most effective way to win popular support for the spread of slavery was not by preaching pro-slavery doctrines, which might ruffle moral and religious feathers, but instead by encouraging a "pro-choice" position of moral neutrality over slavery, which would allow citizens to avoid the controversies and divisiveness that necessarily accompany moral judgments.

FREEDOM, CHOICE, AND SELF-GOVERNMENT

Using "popular sovereignty" to market his Kansas-Nebraska policy, Douglas presented himself as a "pro-choice" candidate, insisting (at least in public) that slavery was neither right nor wrong and that only a given people should decide whether they should have slavery or not; or in Lincoln's words, "if one man [chooses to] enslave another, no third man should object." Douglas's position was correct if slavery represented a morally neutral alternative; that is, if there was no objectively correct answer to the moral question of whether slavery was right or wrong. But if slavery was wrong, then, as Lincoln remarked, there is "no right to do wrong." In his "house divided" speech and elsewhere, Lincoln made clear the political implications that followed moral ambiguity or confusion over slavery. In particular, if slavery could not be condemned as wrong, then freedom could not be defended as right. That is why Lincoln predicted that ultimately either freedom or slavery would become the universally accepted principle and policy of America.

In the fall of 1858, Lincoln and Douglas met for a series of seven public debates as Lincoln challenged Douglas for his seat in the U.S. Senate. In the first debate, Douglas opened by reading the portion of Lincoln's "house divided" speech quoted above, which caused a number of Lincoln supporters in the audience to cheer, "Good, good." Douglas responded, "I am delighted to hear you Black Republicans say 'good.' I have no doubt that doctrine expresses your sentiments, and I will prove to you now, if you will listen to me, that it is revolutionary and destructive of the existence of this Government." Douglas then explained,

> Mr. Lincoln, in the extract from which I have read, says that this government cannot endure permanently in the same condition in which it was made by its framers—divided into free and slave States. . . . Why can it not exist divided into free and slave states? Washington, Jefferson, Franklin, Madison, Hamilton, Jay, and the great men of that day, made this Government divided into free states and slave states, and left each state perfectly free to do as it pleased on the subject of slavery. Why can it not exist on the same principles on which our fathers made it?[30]

According to Douglas, the vitality of American government and society resulted from the different states' great diversity of policies, lifestyles, and opinions. Lincoln was dangerous and radical, Douglas argued, because he wanted to replace the diversity that had flourished in American since the Founding with a new policy of uniformity, forcing one national policy and one set of principles on Americans who were happier with different policies and different principles for people with different interests across the country:

> [The Founders] knew when they framed the Constitution that in a country as wide and broad as this, with such a variety of climate, production and interest, the people necessarily required different laws and institutions in different localities. They knew that the laws and regulations which would suit the granite hills of New Hampshire would be unsuited to the rice plantations of South Carolina, and they, therefore, provided that each State should retain its own Legislature and its own sovereignty, with the full and complete power to do as it pleased within its own limits, in all that was local and not national.[31]

As Douglas summed up during the third debate, "Our government was formed on the principle of diversity in the local institutions and laws and not on that of uniformity."[32] He identified freedom and self-government with diversity, with the right of different people to choose diverse policies based on diverse ideas and principles. Douglas interpreted any attempt to limit diversity in America as a limit on freedom. Most importantly, warned Douglas, Lincoln was advancing uniformity on something far more important than granite quarries or rice plantations. He was promoting the dangerous idea that up and down America, blacks should uniformly be viewed as equal human beings with equal rights:

> Mr. Lincoln, following the example and lead of all the little Abolition orators who go around and lecture in the basements of schools and churches, reads from the Declaration of Independence, that all men were created equal, and then asks, how can you deprive a negro of that equality which God and the Declaration of Independence awards to him?[33]

"I do not question Mr. Lincoln's conscientious belief that the negro was made his equal and hence is his brother," Douglas said mockingly, "[but] for my own part, I do not regard the negro as my equal, and positively deny that he is my brother." According to Douglas, it was precisely their differing interpretations of human equality and their divergent views on the personhood of slaves that separated him and Lincoln:

> If you desire negro citizenship, if you desire to allow them to come into the state and settle with the white man, if you desire them to vote on an equality with yourselves, and to make them eligible to hold office, to serve on juries, and to adjudge your rights, then support Mr. Lincoln and the Black Republican party, who are in favor of the citizenship of the negro. For one, I am opposed to negro citizenship in any and every form. I believe this Government was made on the white basis. I believe it was made by white men for the benefit of white men and their posterity for ever, and I am in favor of confining citizenship to white men, men of European birth and descent, instead of conferring it upon negroes, Indians, and other inferior races.[34]

Douglas not only identified himself with a view of racial hierarchy—he clearly affirmed a belief that the white race was superior to others—but he also identified the Founders with such racial views, a rhetorical strategy some commentators have missed.

Modern scholars sometimes mistake the political landscape of the twentieth or twenty-first centuries, that is, one characterized by the split between conservatives and liberals, for that of the nineteenth century. The influential conservative writer Russell Kirk, for example, has tried to argue that conservatives should embrace Lincoln because Lincoln, too, was a conservative. In an essay titled "The Measure of Abraham Lincoln," Kirk quotes from Lincoln's 1860 Cooper Union Address in which Lincoln asks rhetorically, "What is conservatism? Is it not adherence to the old and tried, against the new and untried?"[35] Kirk believes this proves Lincoln to have been no political liberal in the modern, progressive sense of the term.

But Kirk seems to miss the fact that the pressing political disputes of the 1850s were not between "conservatives" and "liberals" as we understand those terms today; rather, they were disputes over what it means to be a conservative. Both Lincoln and Douglas were "conservative" candidates in the 1858 election in the sense that both claimed to be conserving the principles and policies of the American Founders. Each claimed the authority of the Founders for himself, while each characterized the other as offering radically new principles and polices in opposition to those of the Founders.[36] Neither Lincoln nor Douglas embraced anything like the idea of an "evolving Constitution"; nor did either suggest that new "progressive" principles of justice should be substituted for the original principles of the Founders. Kirk could have found many similar statements by Douglas praising the "old and tried against the new and untried," for Douglas, too, claimed to be a conservative. Thus, Kirk misses the most important political lesson of Lincoln's politics: we study the Lincoln-Douglas debates not to establish who was a progressive liberal and who was a conservative but to determine whether Lincoln or Douglas was the true conservative.

Kirk's failure to see this is evidenced when he writes that Lincoln "took the middle path between [fire-eaters and abolitionists] not out of any misapplication of the doctrine of the golden mean, but because he held by the principle that the unity and security of the United States transcended any fanatic scheme of uniformity."[37] Yet, as I have just shown, it was precisely Douglas's charge that Lincoln was in fact trying to impose "uniformity" on the United States; if Douglas was wrong about Lincoln, Kirk does not explain why or how. Further, Lincoln himself argued that all Americans must be uniform in their dedication to the principle of human equality and equal natural rights, and he predicted that America would become uniformly free or slave depending on whether they remained so dedicated. Both the words of Douglas and of Lincoln himself seem to refute Kirk's analysis of Lincoln. Further, if conservatism is measured by adherence to the old and tried, to tradition for the sake of tradition, then it would seem that, on Kirk's ground, both Lincoln and Douglas are equally conservative; that is, there is no principled difference between the most distinct political rivals of the antebellum era and therefore no principled standard by which we might judge who was right and who was wrong, who had the better argument and who did not. Yet in the very same speech from which Kirk quotes Lincoln's comment regarding conservatism, Lincoln also stated clearly that we are not "bound to follow implicitly in whatever our fathers did"—we are not bound to follow tradition—but we should either follow our fathers or "supplant the opinions and policy of our fathers" according to "evidence so conclusive" and "arguments so clear." We should do whatever prudential reason dictates, in other words, because in the final analysis reason understands that what is good is more important and more authoritative than what is old.

It seems Kirk failed to appreciate fully the extent to which Douglas rooted his arguments and policies in multiple appeals to tradition, including both the American political and the Christian traditions, as he appealed repeatedly to the authority of the American Founders and biblical revelation for his views on race:

> [Lincoln] holds that the negro was born his equal and yours, and that he was endowed with equality by the Almighty. . . . Now, I do not believe that the Almighty ever intended the negro to be the equal of the white man. If he did, he has been a long time demonstrating the fact.

According to Douglas, he, not Lincoln, held the moral high ground on two counts. First, Douglas believed that his was the morally correct view of how blacks should be treated: as beings with higher dignity than ordinary farm animals but not possessing the same rights as whites; beings whose place in society should be determined by whites. Second, he was defending the diversity of interests, the rights of different groups of people to choose freely their own local institutions and local practices, which was the hallmark of free society:

> I hold that humanity and Christianity both require that the negro shall have and enjoy every right, every privilege, and every immunity consistent with the safety of the society in which he lives. . . . The question then arises, what rights and privileges are consistent with the public good? This is a question which each state and each territory must decide for itself—Illinois has decided it for herself.[38]

As different people in different parts of America had different views on what was "consistent with the public good," Douglas concluded, the morally correct position was to allow different groups of people to choose for themselves whether blacks should be free men with equal rights, nonresidents with only limited rights, or slaves with no legal rights at all—all in the name of the "public good."

On its surface, there is a powerful appeal in Douglas's position—there is a certain logical connection between individuals living freely and people of diverse "values" choosing for themselves or their communities the lifestyles they desire—which is why Douglas's principle of "popular sovereignty" continues to find modern defenders in those who celebrate "diversity," "tolerance," "nonjudgmentalism," and other precepts of multiculturalism. Like Douglas, modern multiculturalists observe that among different people there exist differing conceptions of right and wrong and they typically proceed to argue that therefore there is no one objective moral standard that ought to apply uniformly to all people. To borrow a multicultural term, if different people have different "values," then there can be no one *true* set of "values."

Judge Robert Bork, for example, a prominent conservative jurist nominated by President Ronald Reagan for the U.S. Supreme Court only to be rejected by Senate Democrats after highly publicized confirmation hearings in 1987, has written that he doubts "moral philosophy can ever" discover an objectively true principle of right that everyone will affirm "simply [because] it never has." Bork argues that there is "no principled way to make the necessary distinctions" between right and wrong, and therefore we ought to "put such [moral] issues to a vote and . . . the majority morality prevails."[39] Right, in other words, is whatever the majority chooses to be right. Thus, Bork affirms the same "pro-choice" principle of moral neutrality that Douglas affirmed.

Justice Antonin Scalia has offered arguments similar to Bork's. During a 1996 address at the Gregorian Pontifical University in Rome, Scalia insisted that self-government means that "if the people want abortion, the state should permit abortion in a democracy." If one substitutes the word "slavery" for "abortion," Scalia's statement appears to agree in principle with Douglas's doctrine of "popular sovereignty." When an audience member pressed Scalia on whether the rights of minorities should be protected regardless of what the majority wants, Scalia responded, "The whole theory of democracy, my dear fellow, is that the majority rules; that is the whole theory of it. You protect minorities only because the majority determines that there are certain minority positions that deserve protection."[40] Both Bork and Scalia seem to equate moral right with "the majority morality"— right is whatever the majority says it is—which is tantamount to equating morality with power (the majority represents power in a democracy). This itself merely restates the old sophism at the heart of Douglas's "popular sovereignty" that might makes right, a sophism that Lincoln exposed repeatedly and subjected to a devastating moral and political critique.

Lincoln understood that as the alleged rightfulness of "popular sovereignty" rested on the rightfulness of unqualified majoritarianism, therefore, ultimately, on power, Douglas's argument could easily be turned against itself, undermining the freedom of choice and the diversity Douglas wanted to celebrate. For example, in Douglas's terms, a majority might conclude that the "public good" required the enslavement of some *white* minority no less than the enslavement of the black minority. Against this charge, Douglas had no answer. Lincoln was right: any argument for the enslavement of blacks could be turned to justify the enslavement of whites or any other arbitrary class of people. As Lincoln understood, by undermining the principle of human equality and therefore undermining the argument against slavery, Douglas's "popular sovereignty" was bad for blacks, bad for whites, and bad for freedom-loving people of all colors all over the world.

In a July 10, 1858, speech in Chicago, Lincoln asked what united Americans when many in fact came from strikingly different backgrounds that included various ethnicities, religions, and cultures:

> [In addition to Americans who are] descended by blood from our ancestors—[there are] among us perhaps half our people who are not descendants at all of these men. . . . If they look back through this history to trace their connection with those days by blood, they find they have none . . . but when they look through that old Declaration of Independence they find that those old men say that "We hold these truths to be self-evident, that all men are created equal," and then they feel that that moral sentiment taught in that day evidences their relation to those men, that it is the father of all moral principle in them, and that they have a right to claim it as though they were blood of the blood, and flesh of the flesh of the men who wrote that Declaration, and so they are. That is the electric cord in that Declaration that links the hearts of patriotic and liberty-loving men together that will link those patriotic hearts as long as the love of freedom exists in the minds of men throughout the world.[41]

In Lincoln's formulation, legitimate and rightful diversity results from universality. Diverse institutions, habits, and customs are good, in other words, but only when understood in light of the universal and equal rights of all human beings. It is the uniform agreement that "all men are created equal" that allows for and limits the free development of diverse interests and talents. Properly understood, equality means that all human beings possess the equal rights and equal liberty to live free and diverse lives, but that freedom does not include the freedom to live irresponsibly or to injure the rights of others; in other words, everyone does not have an equal right to do anything he or she chooses. As Lincoln never stopped emphasizing, Douglas celebrated the diversity of views regarding slavery while forgetting the universal principle upon which legitimate diversity rested:

> For the purpose of squaring things with [Douglas's] idea of "don't care if slavery is voted up or voted down" . . . we have Judge Douglas giving his exposition of what the Declaration of Independence means, and we have him saying that the people of America are equal to the people of England [and that Negroes and other inferior races are not included]. Now I ask you in all soberness, if all these things, if indulged in, if ratified, if confirmed and endorsed, if taught to our children, and repeated to them, do not tend to rub out the sentiment of liberty in the country, and to transform this Government into a government of some other form.

Lincoln's statesmanship comes to light in his ability to peer through the fog of popular opinion and popular movements and to see the political dangers and intellectual errors of arguments that were winning popular support. We should not forget that many Americans quickly adopted and celebrated Douglas's "popular sovereignty" doctrine. After Douglas broke ranks with the Buchanan administration in late 1857 and early 1858 over the Lecompton constitution—the pro-slavery constitution that purportedly represented the popular will of the people of Kansas but which in fact was the result of a rigged election staged by pro-slavery "border ruffians" from Missouri—many prominent and influential Republicans were trying to persuade Douglas to abandon the Democratic Party and become a Republican.[42] Yet Lincoln saw with unusual clarity that the arguments Douglas advanced as an apology for the "right to choose" slavery were in fact the same old arguments that kings had used for generations as a defense for their unjust rule without the consent of the ruled:

> Those arguments that are made, that the inferior race are to be treated with as much allowance as they are capable of enjoying; that as much is to be done for them as their condition will allow. What are these arguments? They are the arguments that kings have made for enslaving the people in all ages of the world. You will find that all the arguments in favor of king-craft were of this class; they always bestrode the necks of the people, not that they wanted to do it, but because the people were better off for being ridden. That is their argument, and this argument of [Stephen Douglas's] is the same old serpent that says you work and I eat, you toil and I will enjoy the fruits of it. Turn it whatever way you will— whether it comes from the mouth of a King, an excuse for enslaving the people of his country, or from the mouth of men of one race as a reason for enslaving the men of another race, it is all the same old serpent.[43]

In the growing fights over slavery, the meaning of the Declaration of Independence, particularly the meaning of its ringing phrase "all men are created equal," became the central focus of political controversy. Lincoln pointed out why that controversy was so important for all Americans:

> I hold if that course of argumentation that is made for the purpose of convincing the public mind that we should not care about this, should be granted, it does not stop with the negro. I should like to know if taking this old Declaration of Independence, which declares that all men are equal upon principle, and making exceptions to it, where will it stop? If one man says it does not mean a negro, why not another say it does not mean some other man?[44]

I mentioned Mario Cuomo at the beginning of the chapter as trying to equate Lincoln with a "pro-choice" position. Anyone who wants to defend "choice," whether in terms of abortion today or slavery yesterday, faces serious problems for their argument when confronted with the Declaration of Independence and its principle of equal natural rights. Cuomo maneuvers around this problem by insisting that the Declaration has no legally binding authority, that it "is not a law and therefore is not subjected to rigorous interpretation and enforcement."[45] It is puzzling how anyone can write a book titled *Why Lincoln Matters* and suggest that the Declaration *does not matter*, that it is not subject to "rigorous interpretation." Yet Kevin Gutzman repeats Cuomo's view in *The Politically Incorrect Guide to the Constitution*, in which he states that the "first three sections of the Declaration . . . had no legal effect" but merely contained "hortatory language."[46] Lincoln certainly believed that the Declaration mattered and offered a "rigorous interpretation" of the the many moral, political, and legal consequences that flowed from it. In fact, both Lincoln and Douglas spent more time during their debates arguing over the correct interpretation of the Declaration than on any other subject. Even those who rejected the principles of the Declaration, such as John C. Calhoun, spent much time trying to offer a "rigorous interpretation" of the document, if only in an attempt to refute it. And, as I discuss in the next chapter, the most infamous Supreme Court decision, *Dred Scott v. Sandford*, turned on nothing other than an "interpretation [however incorrect] and enforcement" of the Declaration of Independence.

Cuomo fails to understand that the question of the Declaration's meaning was important not necessarily because of its legal status as statutory or constitutional law—although in its 1878 revision of the U.S. Code, Congress listed the Declaration as the first among America's "organic laws" and every congressional enabling act since the Civil War for the admission of a new state into the Union included a statutory requirement that the constitution of the new state "shall not be repugnant to the Declaration of Independence."[47] Rather, the Declaration was important because virtually all Americans accepted it as the supreme statement of the American regime's principles. In many respects, the text of the Constitution embodies its principles. Consider, for example, the Constitution's preamble, which lists securing "the blessings of liberty to ourselves and our posterity" as the ultimate purpose for ordaining and establishing the Constitution. What is a "blessing" other than a gift from God? Is not the Constitution's recognition that human beings possess "blessings of liberty" identical in principle to the Declaration's statement that "all men" are "endowed by their Creator" with an "unalienable" right to "liberty?" Does not the idea of God-given natural rights explain why the Constitution's Ninth Amendment acknowledges that people possess rights in addition to the "certain rights" enumerated in the Constitution? Consider also that while the Constitution offers multiple protections for "persons," the Constitution nowhere answers the question of who is and who is not a person. The answer to that question, at least for the Founders and for Lincoln, is to be found in the "laws of nature" and the fact that human persons differ in their nature from property.

Contrary to Cuomo, Lincoln, Douglas, and virtually all the leading political lights of the 1850s agreed that the Declaration was the principle source for answering these kinds of important legal and political questions. Thus, it mattered greatly what those serving in public office and drafting public policy, as well as those who elected them, understood the Declaration to mean.

In the concluding debate with Douglas, Lincoln acknowledged that some men had of late come to reject fully the Declaration's principle that "all men are created equal":

> I know that more than three years ago there were men who, finding this assertion constantly in the way of their schemes to bring about the ascendancy and perpetuation of slavery, *denied the truth of it*. I know that [John C.] Calhoun and all the politicians of his school denied the truth of the Declaration. I know that it ran along in the mouth of some Southern men for a period of years, ending at last in that shameful though rather forcible declaration of [Senator John] Pettit of Indiana, upon the floor of the United States Senate, that the Declaration of Independence was in that respect "a self-evident lie," rather than a self-evident truth.[48]

But Douglas's position differed from that of Calhoun (whose arguments I discuss at length in chapter 5), who openly rejected the Declaration's principles. Claiming to champion the American Founding and to affirm the Declaration, he never once presented himself as an enemy or opponent of the Founders and their principles. But in fact, Lincoln argued, Douglas "had ventured to assail [the Declaration] in the sneaking way of pretending to believe it and then asserting it did not include the negro." By seducing the American mind into believing that the Declaration's recognition of human equality did not include blacks, Douglas had derailed the American Founding Fathers' principles and policies, policies resting on the conviction that slavery was wrong because equality was right, policies that allowed "the public mind [to] rest in the belief that [slavery] is in the course of ultimate extinction." In his effort to return slavery to a "course of ultimate extinction," Lincoln summarized his own position as "nothing more than a return to the policy of the fathers."

At the Gettysburg cemetery five years after his debates with Douglas and in the midst of the Civil War, Lincoln spoke to his fellow Americans:

> Four score and seven years ago our fathers brought forth on this continent, a new nation, conceived in Liberty, and dedicated to the proposition that all men are created equal. Now we are engaged in a great civil war, testing whether that nation, or any nation so conceived and so dedicated, can long endure.[49]

For his insistence on the wrongness of slavery and for his repeated calls to preserve the Union while reinstating the terms of the Missouri Compromise and restricting the spread of slavery, Lincoln was twice elected to the highest office in America. He would preside over the bloodiest conflict in American history, a conflict caused in large part by his own refusal to let Americans ignore all that was at stake in the fight over slavery. On Good Friday, April 14, 1865, four years to the day after the surrender of Fort Sumter, an assassin's bullet cut Lincoln's life short.

From the passage of the Kansas-Nebraska Act until his untimely death, opposition to slavery formed the core of Lincoln's statesmanship, as evidenced foremost by his continued opposition to the Kansas-Nebraska Act itself. The Kansas-Nebraska Act denied human equality and brought into stark relief the consequences of abandoning this central principle, turning the question of one man's right to enslave another into a matter of mere personal interest and power. But "popular sovereignty," viewed by many as nothing but an affirmation of freedom and choice, was terribly seductive, nonetheless, precisely because it offered an easy way out of a difficult moral problem without forcing citizens to take a stand.

In January 1861, as he awaited inauguration as president, Lincoln despaired that Congress's recent creation of the Colorado Territory, whose territorial charter did not prohibit slavery, was a sign that Douglas's "popular sovereignty" had won out in the American mind:

> Lincoln was upset at the Republicans in Congress, who during the secession winter voted to admit [the] Colorado [Territory] with no provision regarding slavery. While preparing to leave Springfield for Washington, Lincoln told [Joseph] Gillespie, "It seems to me that Douglas got the best of it at the election last fall. I am left to face an empty treasury and a great rebellion, while my own party endorses his popular sovereignty idea, and applies it in legislation."[50]

Mario Cuomo seems comfortable with "pro-choice" arguments, and he seems to adore Abraham Lincoln, so he finds it quite consistent to try to describe Lincoln as a "pro-choicer." But insofar as Lincoln identified the "right to choose" with Douglas's notion of "popular sovereignty" and refusal to admit the equal personhood and natural rights of blacks, nothing could be farther removed from Lincoln's moral and political thought. Lincoln was consistent and unwavering in his demand that freedom, choice, and self-government be understood within the moral and political framework of the "laws of nature and of Nature's God," first and foremost in the natural right principle of human equality. In 1857, three years after the passage of the Kansas-Nebraska Act, the debate over the meaning of the "right to choose" was ratcheted up a level as Douglas's principle that the people in a territory could choose to exclude slavery was replaced by the Supreme Court's decision in *Dred Scott*: a slave owner could take his slave property anywhere into the territories he chose, and no one, not Congress and not even the people living there, could stop him.

NOTES

1. *Roe v. Wade*, 410 U.S. 113 at 152.
2. Mario M. Cuomo, *Why Lincoln Matters: Today More Than Ever* (New York: Harcourt Press, 2004), 135.
3. Thomas J. DiLorenzo, *The Real Lincoln: A New Look at Abraham Lincoln, His Agenda, and an Unnecessary War* (Roseville, CA: Prima Publishing, 2002), and *Lincoln Unmasked: What You're Not Supposed to Know about Dishonest Abe* (New York: Crown Forum, 2006).
4. DiLorenzo, *The Real Lincoln*, 21–22.
5. DiLorenzo, *Lincoln Unmasked*, 100–101.

6. David M. Potter, *The Impending Crisis, 1848–1861* (New York: Harper & Row, 1976), 93–94.

7. Bertram Wyatt-Brown argues persuasively that the Civil War cannot be fully comprehended without an understanding of the meaning and importance of honor in Southern antebellum society. See Bertram Wyatt-Brown, *Southern Honor: Ethics and Behavior in the Old South* (New York: Oxford University Press, 1982).

8. Quoted in Potter, *The Impending Crisis*, 94.

9. Henry W. Hilliard, *Politics and Pen Pictures at Home and Abroad* (New York: G. P. Putnam, 1892), 231.

10. Potter, *The Impending Crisis*, 95.

11. Potter, *The Impending Crisis*, 167.

12. Potter, *The Impending Crisis*, 155. See also Irving H. Bartlett, *John C. Calhoun: A Biography* (New York: W. W. Norton & Co., 1993), 231.

13. Potter, *The Impending Crisis*, 155.

14. Potter, *The Impending Crisis*, 163.

15. John Jay, letter to R. Lushington, March 15, 1786, quoted in Matthew Spalding, ed., *The Founders' Almanac* (Washington, DC: Heritage Foundation, 2001), 207.

16. Mark Graber, *Dred Scott and the Problem of Constitutional Evil* (New York: Cambridge University Press, 2006), 229 (emphasis added).

17. Graber, *Dred Scott and the Problem of Constitutional Evil*, 232–43.

18. John Jay to the president of the Society for Promoting the Manumission of Slaves, June 1788, in Henry P. Johnston, *The Correspondence and Public Papers of John Jay* (New York: G. P. Putnam's Sons, 1890), III:340.

19. Max Farrand, *The Records of the Federal Convention of 1787* (New Haven, CT: Yale University Press, 1911), II:371.

20. Farrand, *The Records of the Federal Convention of 1787*, II:364.

21. Farrand, *The Records of the Federal Convention of 1787*, II:370.

22. George Washington, "Circular Letter to State Governments," in *Washington: Writings* (New York: Library of America, 1997), 517.

23. Thomas Jefferson, letter to Roger Weightman, in *Jefferson: Writings*, ed. Merrill D. Peterson (New York: Library of America, 1984), 1517.

24. Graber, *Dred Scott and the Problem of Constitutional Evil*, 107.

25. Roy P. Basler, ed., *The Collected Works of Abraham Lincoln* (New Brunswick, NJ: Rutgers University Press, 1953), III:549, IV:29. Cited hereafter as Lincoln, *Collected Works*.

26. Lincoln, *Collected Works*, II:255.

27. Lincoln, *Collected Works*, II:266.

28. Lincoln, *Collected Works*, VII:301–302.

29. Lincoln, *Collected Works*, II:461.

30. Lincoln, *Collected Works*, III:8.

31. Lincoln, *Collected Works*, III:8.

32. Lincoln, *Collected Works*, III:112.

33. Lincoln, *Collected Works*, III:9.

34. Lincoln, *Collected Works*, III:9.

35. Russell Kirk, "The Measure of Abraham Lincoln," *The Month* 2, no. 4 (1954): 197–206.

36. David Zarefsky, *Lincoln, Douglas, and Slavery: In the Crucible of Public Debate* (Chicago: University of Chicago Press, 1993).

37. Kirk, "The Measure of Abraham Lincoln," 200.

38. Lincoln, *Collected Works*, III:9–10.

39. Robert H. Bork, *The Tempting of America: The Political Seduction of the Law* (New York: The Free Press, 1990), 254, 258–59.

40. Quoted in Robbie George, "The Tyrant State," *First Things* 67 (November 1996): 41.

41. Lincoln, *Collected Works*, II:499–500.

42. Allen C. Guelzo, *Lincoln and Douglas: The Debates that Defined America* (New York: Simon & Schuster, 2008), 41–54.

43. Lincoln, *Collected Works*, II:500.

44. Lincoln, *Collected Works*, II:500.

45. Cuomo, *Why Lincoln Matters*, 137–38.

46. Kevin R. C. Gutzman, *The Politically Incorrect Guide to the Constitution* (Washington, DC: Regnery Publishing, 2007), 11.

47. Richard H. Cox, *Four Pillars of Constitutionalism: The Organic Laws of the United States* (New York: Prometheus Books, 1998).

48. Lincoln, *Collected Works*, III:301.

49. Lincoln, *Collected Works*, VII:23.

50. Michael Burlingame, *The Inner World of Abraham Lincoln* (Urbana: University of Illinois Press, 1994), 200.

3

WHO WAS RIGHT ABOUT THE FOUNDING, LINCOLN OR TANEY?

I do not believe that the meaning of the Constitution was for-ever "fixed" at the Philadelphia Convention. Nor do I find the wisdom, foresight, and sense of justice exhibited by the framers particularly profound. . . . Writing for the Supreme Court in 1857, Chief Justice Taney penned the following passage in the *Dred Scott* case:

> [Blacks] had for more than a century before been regarded as beings of an inferior order, and altogether unfit to associate with the white race . . . and so far inferior that they had no rights which the white man was bound to respect. . . .

And so, nearly seven decades after the Constitutional Con-vention, the Supreme Court reaffirmed the prevailing opinion of the framers regarding the rights of Negroes in America.

—Justice Thurgood Marshall, "Reflections on the Bicentennial of the United States Constitution," November 1987

We think the *Dred Scott* decision is erroneous. We know the court that made it, has often over-ruled its own decisions, and we shall do what we can to have it to over-rule this. . . . The *Dred Scott* decision was . . . based on assumed historical facts which were not really true.

—Abraham Lincoln, speech at Springfield, Illinois, June 26, 1857

I recently led a civic education workshop for middle and high school teachers during which I presented the different views of the Framers of the Constitution offered by Abraham Lincoln and Chief Justice Roger Taney. In a nutshell, I explained, Lincoln argued that the Founders truly believed in human equality, that black slaves were no less persons than whites, and that slavery was wrong and ought to be eliminated as soon as circumstances permitted, and he further argued that they had offered as much protection for liberty and as little protection for slavery in the Constitution and in public policy as political necessity would allow, confining slavery to where it already existed and cutting off both its supply and its extension.

Taney asserted exactly the opposite: that the Founders did not mean to include blacks when they said "all men are created equal," that they considered blacks to be nothing other than property, that they had few if any moral objections to slavery, and that they had intended for the Constitution to offer perpetual protection for slavery and to deny national citizenship to all blacks, whether slave or free.

After analyzing numerous original source documents from Lincoln, Taney, and the Founders, one of the teachers raised his hand in exasperation, explaining that for twenty-five years he had been teaching American government, and all along he had unknowingly been teaching Taney's view of the Founding, not Lincoln's. He went on to explain that he had not taught Lincoln's view because he had never encountered it, that all the American history and government textbooks simply parroted Taney's groundless description of the Founders, and that he felt cheated by his own (mis)education. I told him that his mistaken view of the Founders and his lack of understanding of Lincoln were understandable, perhaps even excusable to some extent, because no less a mind than Thurgood Marshall, the first black Supreme Court justice and reputedly a great civil rights jurist, ignored Lincoln and looked to Taney as his guide to the original intent of the Founders' Constitution.

As the epigraphs above make clear, Justice Marshall and Lincoln had strikingly different views of the Supreme Court's decision in *Dred Scott v. Sandford.* Marshall, on the one hand, appeals to Taney's majority opinion as authoritative and dispositive of what the Founders believed regarding the personhood and rights of blacks. Lincoln, on the other hand, comes very close to accusing Taney of outright lying about the Founders. So, who is right about *Dred Scott,* Thurgood Marshall or Abraham Lincoln? Who is right about the meaning of the Founding and the Founders' Constitution, Chief Justice Taney or Lincoln?

The question entails more than mere historical curiosity. It is a question of the status of our Constitution. Over the past century, a concentrated and highly successful movement has aimed at diminishing the authority of the Constitution in American politics and government. Many have dismissed the Constitution on two main charges: it is old, and it is racist. The first charge stems from a theoretical critique of the Constitution, arguing that the Constitution of 1787 as it was originally understood is outdated, that its principles are no longer relevant to, or sufficient for, modern American society, and that the only constitution suited for an evolving America is an evolving, or "living," one. I address this argument in chapter 8.

The second critique of the Constitution, which in practice supports the "living constitution" doctrine, rests on accusations that the original Constitution was an immoral and racist document. Modern Americans, therefore, have no moral obligation to follow or support an immoral Constitution from a racist past. This critique informs Justice Marshall's negative assessment of the Constitution. It also explains in part why generations of blacks in America have consistently voted against those who claim to champion its original intent. When political conservatives talk about limited government, federalism, and states' rights, many black citizens think these terms are mere disguises for black codes, Jim Crow, and slavery. Indeed, blacks and other minorities will embrace no political movement to restore the Constitution in American politics unless it can be demonstrated to their satisfaction that the Constitution is compatible with—or rather, inseparable from—the principles of individual rights, equal protection of the laws, and freedom instead of racism, slavery, and forced segregation.

Lincoln insisted at length that the Court wrongly decided *Dred Scott* because it wrongly viewed the Constitution as a pro-slavery, and emphatically not a pro-freedom, document. Indeed, no event in American history has so clearly focused on the question of whether the Constitution is a pro-freedom or pro-slavery document more than the *Dred Scott* case, and no one opposed the *Dred Scott* decision more vigorously than Lincoln. Any attempt to vindicate Lincoln, therefore, requires a vindication of his critique of *Dred Scott*.

THE SIGNIFICANCE OF *DRED SCOTT V. SANDFORD*

On March 6, 1857, the U.S. Supreme Court handed down its opinion in *Dred Scott v. Sandford,* one of the most infamous decisions in the Court's history and one of the central events leading to the Civil War.[1] The most comprehensive, authoritative, and critical analysis of the *Dred Scott* case is Don Fehrenbacher's *The Dred Scott Case: Its Significance in American Law and Politics,* published in 1978.[2] Taney's majority opinion in *Dred Scott* has found few defenders, including the authors of later Supreme Court opinions, which generally are highly critical and occasionally denunciatory of Taney's reasoning. In his recent *Dred Scott and the Problem of Constitutional Evil*, Mark Graber has distinguished himself by offering an intelligent and well-researched attempt to argue that Taney's opinion was at least as plausible as Lincoln's, if not more so; therefore, I will address Graber's claims at some length.[3]

I also want to make clear, however, that while Taney's *Dred Scott* decision has been widely condemned and criticized (Graber notwithstanding), key elements of Taney's constitutionalism remain very much alive and part of our jurisprudence today. As I will demonstrate, Taney's opinion turned in large measure on the Fifth Amendment's protection for a person's life, liberty, and property and on the question of whether a slave was a "person" to be protected or "property," in which case only the slave's owner was offered protection. As he tried to answer that question, Taney refused to consider the natural law distinction between persons and property, relying instead on the (supposed) authority of earlier lawmakers and what they determined to be persons versus property. Lincoln understood with unusual perspicuity that the definitional meaning of personhood was the real crux of the matter, that even the greatest pro-liberty constitution imaginable would be transformed into a constitution of tyranny if some human persons could be defined as nonpersons and therefore be placed outside the protection of the laws.

In the previous chapter, I mentioned the 1973 abortion case of *Roe v. Wade*, decided more than a century after *Dred Scott*, for which Justice Harry Blackmun wrote the majority opinion. In *Roe*, like *Dred Scott*, the argument turned on the meaning of "person," the difference being that in *Roe* the question was whether an unborn child is a "person" whose life, liberty, and property are protected by the Fourteenth Amendment (rather than the Fifth Amendment). Blackmun acknowledged the difficulty that "the Constitution does not define 'person' in so many words," and therefore a judge (or lawmaker) must look for some principle by which to distinguish what is and is not a person.[4] And, like Taney, Blackmun also refused to consider the natural law distinction between persons versus property, relying instead on the authority of earlier lawmakers to determine that "the word 'person,' as used in the Fourteenth Amendment, does not include the unborn."[5] Simply labeling unborn children or any other group, by this reasoning, as something other than "persons" (for example, as "embryos" or "fetuses") can therefore exempt them from the Fourteenth Amendment's protection. It seems fair, therefore, to ask what progress we've made in the century separating *Dred*

Scott from *Roe*. For just as *Roe* has divided Americans today, so *Dred Scott* divided Americans on the eve of the Civil War. And just as Lincoln, above all others, helped Americans think through the problems of *Dred Scott*, so his natural right principles might help us think through similar problems of legal definitions and constitutionalism today.

The first half of Taney's opinion raised the question of whether blacks could be citizens of the United States and allowed to file suit in federal courts; the second asked whether Congress possessed constitutional power to prohibit slavery from federal territories, as it had done through the Missouri Compromise of 1820. The Court's answer to both questions was no: blacks could not be American citizens and therefore could not sue in federal courts, and the Constitution did not grant Congress the power to prohibit slavery from the territories. The Court declared the Missouri Compromise unconstitutional.

Many critics at the time, including free-soil Republicans and abolitionists alike, opposed *Dred Scott*. Lincoln, however, not only opposed *Dred Scott* but hammered it like a wedge to divide the Democratic Party into two opposing factions. Southern Democrats championed the argument of *Dred Scott*, insisting that the Missouri Compromise had been unconstitutional and that every slave owner had a constitutional right to take his slaves into any territory owned and regulated by the U.S. government. "As interpreted by slaveholders," Graber comments, "*Dred Scott* required Congress to pass a federal slave code when territories failed to respect Southern property rights."[6] Northern Democrats, while initially supportive of the Court's opinion, ultimately rallied behind Stephen Douglas's doctrine of "popular sovereignty" and were unwilling to support the Southern demand for a federal slave code for all federally controlled territories. For Douglas Democrats, the "popular sovereignty" right of a people in a territory to choose whether to permit or prohibit slavery trumped the right of a slave owner seeking to move with his slaves into federal territory. No one did more than Abraham Lincoln to highlight the opposition between the two Democratic positions: slavery as a constitutional right versus slavery as an institution subject to the will of the people who lived in the territories. Lincoln emphasized that any Southerner who believed the *Dred Scott* position was right could not at the same time support the Democratic platform of Stephen Douglas, and any Northern Democrat who affirmed the "popular sovereignty" doctrine of Douglas could not join Southern Democrats in celebrating *Dred Scott*.

Lincoln's statesmanship is again on display in his use of *Dred Scott*, which he himself believed was seriously mistaken and ought to be overturned by a future Court, as a teaching moment to remind citizens why the Court's ruling was wrong; at the same time, Lincoln used *Dred Scott* to his own political advantage and to the disadvantage of those Democrats on the wrong side of the slavery question. It is not uncommon for modern scholars to argue, as Graber does, that "racist and other ascriptive ideologies are as rooted in the American political tradition as liberal, democratic, and republican ideals" and that "racism was well grounded in American political thought from the very beginning."[7] But Lincoln argued that the Supreme Court's interpretation of the Founding, which identified the leading principles of American constitutionalism with racism and white supremacy, was untrue and wholly at odds with the principles of civil liberty and free society, undermining the good reputation of the Declaration of Independence and the Constitution by asserting that both were pro-slavery documents. For Lincoln, therefore, the dispute over *Dred Scott* was one over the meaning of America and the principles that informed American politics and constitutionalism.

TANEY'S OPINION PART I: STANDING

Dred Scott was a black slave who lived with his owner, Dr. John Emerson, a surgeon in the U.S. Army stationed in the slave state of Missouri. Dred Scott sued for his freedom after Emerson took him to Rock Island, Illinois, and then to Fort Snelling, located in the northern area (north of 36°30' latitude) of the Louisiana Territory (what would later become the state of Minnesota), before being returned to Missouri. Slavery was prohibited in Rock Island under the state laws of Illinois; the Missouri Compromise of 1820 prohibited slavery in the Louisiana Territory north of 36°30'. Scott argued that by virtue of both Illinois law and federal law, he was a free man and was being held as a slave illegally upon his return to Missouri. Originating in a Missouri state court, Dred Scott's case dragged on for more than a decade, working its way up to the Missouri Supreme Court and then into the federal court system, finally resulting in a ruling from the U.S. Supreme Court in 1857.

Chief Justice Taney wrote the majority opinion for the Court, a long and often rambling essay, which was supported by concurring opinions offered by Justices James Wayne, Samuel Nelson, Robert Grier, John Campbell, and John Catron, as well as a separate opinion concurring in the result by Justice Peter Daniel (two justices, John McLean and Benjamin Robbins Curtis, each offered dissenting opinions). The first and main question Taney raised was whether Dred Scott had standing to sue in any federal court:

> The question is simply this: can a negro, whose ancestors were imported into this country, and sold as slaves, become a member of the political community formed and brought into existence by the Constitution of the United States, and as such become entitled to all the rights, and privileges, and immunities, guarantied by that instrument to the citizen? One of which rights is the privilege of suing in a court of the United States in the cases specified in the Constitution.[8]

By allowing Dred Scott to sue in state courts, Missouri had implicitly acknowledged that Scott possessed some minimal level of state citizenship: he was enough of a citizen to bring suit in state court. But regardless of what criteria Missouri (or any other state) used to discriminate between those who possessed state citizenship and those who did not, Taney indicated that the question of federal citizenship, and therefore of who could sue in federal courts, was a different one altogether. If Dred Scott was found to lack federal citizenship, then he would lack standing in federal courts and his case would be dismissed.[9]

In order to determine whether Dred Scott could be a citizen of the United States and therefore sue in federal courts, Taney turned to the question of who was and who was not a citizen of the United States "within the meaning of the Constitution." In particular, Taney asked whether blacks could be U.S. citizens, framing the question entirely in the context of race: "The question then arises, whether the provisions of the Constitution, in relation to the personal rights and privileges to which the citizen of a State should be entitled, embraced the negro African race."[10]

Taney argued clearly and persuasively that in his capacity as a Supreme Court justice, he was bound by the original intent of those who framed and ratified the Constitution, whatever those intentions might have been. He would not, he claimed, distort or invent new interpretations of the Constitution in order to reach a desired result:

> No one, we presume, supposes that any change in public opinion or feeling, in relation to this unfortunate race, in the civilized nations of Europe or in this country, should induce the court to give to the words of the Constitution a more liberal construction in their favor than they were intended to bear when the instrument was framed and adopted. Such an argument would be altogether inadmissible in any tribunal called on to interpret it. If any of its provisions are deemed unjust, there is a mode prescribed in the instrument itself by which it may be amended; but while it remains unaltered, it must be construed now as it was understood at the time of its adoption.[11]

The Constitution announces in its preamble that it is "We the people" who "ordain and establish this Constitution for the United States of America" in order, among other purposes, to "secure the Blessings of Liberty to ourselves and our Posterity." Who, Taney asked, are "the people" for whom the Constitution is meant to offer protection? Which people were included in "We the people?"

Taney identified "the people" of the Constitution as the same people who had declared independence from the British Crown and successfully fought a revolution to secure their sovereignty as an independent nation. In the last chapter, I cited Mario Cuomo, who tried to argue that the Declaration "is not a law and therefore is not subjected to rigorous interpretation and enforcement."[12] The primary and authoritative text for Chief Justice Taney, however, was precisely the Declaration of Independence of July 4, 1776, and Lincoln agreed with Taney on the binding authority of the Declaration, differing from Taney only in his understanding of what the Declaration meant.

According to Taney, the people for whom the Declaration was written were the constituent members of the "more perfect union" organized under the Constitution, among whom justice was to be established and domestic tranquility insured, their common defense provided for and their general welfare promoted. Citizenship originated with these constituent members, the original members of the American social compact; those who were not members of the constituency were not citizens "within the meaning of the Constitution" and, furthermore, could not become citizens unless the meaning of the original Constitution was altered by constitutional amendment. The central and simple question for Taney was whether blacks were intended to be included in the Declaration's opening statement of principle: "We hold these truths to be self evident, that all men are created equal." In a sweeping response, Taney asserted,

> In the opinion of the court, the legislation and histories of the times, and the language used in the Declaration of Independence, show, that neither the class of persons who had been imported as slaves, nor their descendants, *whether they had become free or not*, were then acknowledged as a part of the people, nor intended to be included in the general words used in that memorable instrument.[13]

According to Taney, not only were *black slaves* not included in the Declaration of Independence, but neither were *free blacks* living in America at the time of the Founding.

Taney acknowledged that the alleged racist views of earlier Americans might be difficult to accept for the more enlightened, more liberal Americans of his day:

> It is difficult at this day to realize the state of public opinion in relation to that unfortunate race, which prevailed in the civilized and enlightened portions of the world at the time of the Declaration of Independence, and when the Constitution of the United States was framed and adopted.[14]

But as unfortunate and unjust as the opinions of the Founders might have been, the Court could not ignore the overwhelming and compelling evidence that demonstrated beyond doubt the Founders' opinions of the inferiority of blacks:

> They had for more than a century before been regarded as beings of an inferior order, and altogether unfit to associate with the white race, either in social or political relations; and so far inferior, that they had no rights which the white man was bound to respect; and that the negro might justly and lawfully be reduced to slavery for his benefit. He was bought and sold, and treated as an ordinary article of merchandise and traffic, whenever a profit could be made by it. This opinion was at that time fixed and universal in the civilized portion of the white race. It was regarded as an axiom in morals as well as in politics, which no one thought of disputing, or supposed to be open to dispute; and men in every grade and position in society daily and habitually acted upon it in their private pursuits, as well as in matters of public concern, without doubting for a moment the correctness of this opinion.[15]

When Taney turned to confront directly the language of the Declaration of Independence, he found more pro-slavery opinions. The Declaration's second paragraph famously begins,

> We hold these truths to be self-evident: that all men are created equal; that they are endowed by their Creator with certain unalienable rights; that among them is life, liberty, and the pursuit of happiness; that to secure these rights, Governments are instituted, deriving their just powers from the consent of the governed.

According to Taney,

> The general words above quoted *would seem to embrace the whole human family*, and if they were used in a similar instrument at this day would be

so understood. But it is too clear for dispute, that the enslaved African race were not intended to be included, and formed no part of the people who framed and adopted this declaration.[16]

How did Taney know what the authors of the Declaration intended with regard to blacks? The men who framed the Declaration, Taney argued, "were great men—high in literary acquirements—high in their sense of honor, and incapable of asserting principles inconsistent with those on which they were acting." If the language, as understood in that day, "would embrace [blacks], the conduct of the distinguished men who framed the Declaration of Independence would have been utterly and flagrantly inconsistent with the principles they asserted; and instead of the sympathy of mankind, to which they so confidently appeared, they would have deserved and received universal rebuke and reprobation."[17]

As the Founders lived in an age of slavery, any statement of moral condemnation against slavery would have amounted to hypocrisy, of which, being "great men . . . high in their sense of honor," they were incapable. Therefore, they must have believed slavery to be good, and they must have intended to exclude blacks from the Declaration's principle of human equality. For Taney, these are the only two plausible views about the Founders: they were either hypocrites or racists. Identifying them as racists was the more respectable view, Taney believed, because at least then they could be defended as being consistent. Therefore, Taney determined, all blacks, whether slave or free, "were never thought of or spoken of except as property."

Because Dred Scott was a member of the "African race," he could not be a citizen of the community for whom the Declaration and Constitution were written. "Upon a full and careful consideration of the subject," Taney concluded,

> the court is of opinion, that, upon the facts stated in the plea in abatement Dred Scott was not a citizen . . . within the meaning of the Constitution of the United States, and not entitled as such to sue in its courts; and, consequently, that the Circuit Court had no jurisdiction of the case.[18]

Whatever the merits of his case might be, Dred Scott could not sue in American courts. His case could not be heard.

TANEY'S OPINION PART II: MISSOURI COMPROMISE

But Taney was hardly finished; he reached this conclusion only halfway through his written opinion. The second half attacked the Missouri Compromise, becoming only the second instance in its history when the Supreme Court exercised judicial review and struck down a law that Congress had passed and the president had signed (the first instance was *Marbury v. Madison* in 1803). The issue Taney raised next was whether Dred Scott's stay in Illinois and then in federal territory made him a free man. The question was entirely hypothetical, at least insofar as Dred Scott was concerned. Whatever answer the Court might reach, it had no bearing on Dred Scott's life because the first half of the Court's opinion denied him standing. But Taney thought it interesting nonetheless to speculate about what might have happened had the Court considered Dred Scott's argument.

Dred Scott traveled first to Illinois and then into federal territory, but Taney chose to address Scott's stay in the territory first. The territory where Dred Scott resided (Fort Snelling) was north of 36°30′, an area in which the Missouri Compromise of 1820 had prohibited slavery. Dred Scott claimed that once he entered free federal territory, where slavery was prohibited, he was no longer a slave but a free man, and his removal back to Missouri as slave property was therefore illegal. The main question for Taney, however, was not the technical legal question of whether the Missouri Compromise did in fact transform Scott into a free man; instead, he focused on whether Congress possessed the constitutional authority to pass the Missouri Comprise into law. "The difficulty which meets us at the threshold of this part of the inquiry," wrote Taney, "is whether Congress was authorized to pass this law under any of the powers granted to it by the Constitution." If not, Taney reminded his readers, "it is the duty of this court to declare it void and inoperative, and incapable of conferring freedom upon any one who is held as a slave under the laws of any one of the States."[19]

Taney knew that Article IV, Section 2 of the Constitution granted power to Congress "to dispose of and make all needful rules and regulations respecting the territory or other property belonging to the United States." He also knew that one of the first official acts of the First Congress assembled under the Constitution was the reauthorization of the Northwest Ordinance of 1787, which prohibited slavery in the Northwest Territory (federally owned land that would later become the states of Ohio, Indiana, Illinois, Michigan, and Wisconsin and part of Minnesota). The question of whether Congress possessed the constitutional authority to prohibit slavery in territorial land seemed to have been settled by no lesser authority than the First Congress, which included James Madison and other members of the 1787 Constitutional Convention that had met in Philadelphia. Claiming to follow the original intent of the Constitution's framers, Taney was, it seemed, in a pickle: if he denied Congress's right to prohibit slavery from federal territory, he could not help but deny the right of the First Congress of the Founding to prohibit slavery from the Northwest Territory.

Not so fast, cautioned Taney:

> In the judgment of the court, [Article IV, Section 2 of the Constitution] had no bearing on the present controversy, and the power there given, whatever it may be, is confined, and was intended to be confined, to the territory which at that time belonged to, or was claimed by, the United States, and was within their boundaries as settled by the treaty with Great Britain, and can have no influence upon a territory afterwards acquired from a foreign Government.[20]

Taney emphasized the singular form of the word "territory" in Article IV, Section 2. "It does not speak of any territory," he noted, "nor of Territories, but uses language which, according to its legitimate meaning, points to a particular thing." In other words, the Constitution empowers Congress "to dispose of and make all needful rules and regulations" only for one territory: the territory owned by the United States at the time of the adoption of the Constitution, the Northwest Territory. Article IV, Section 2 did not apply to, and Congress therefore lacked any power to legislate for, "a territory afterwards acquired from a foreign Government," such as the Louisiana Territory purchased by the United States in 1803.

According to Taney, the only section of the Constitution that grants Congress the power "to make all needful rules and regulations" for American territories had no application to the question of whether Congress had constitutional power to pass the Missouri Compromise and prohibit slavery in the Louisiana Territory north of 36°30'. If Article IV, Section 2 did not empower Congress to pass the Missouri Compromise, and if Congress possesses only those powers delegated to it by the Constitution, Taney reasoned, then Congress did not possess the constitutional power to pass the Missouri Compromise. It was unconstitutional.

But, Taney was quick to point out, there were more problems with the Missouri Compromise. If the section of the Constitution concerning the "territory" and "other property belonging to the United States" did not pertain to the Louisiana Territory, in what way did the powers of the Constitution extend over territories the nation acquired? For Taney, the Constitution extends over the territories as a kind of shield, protecting the rights of American citizens as they migrate from states into territorial land. Among the protections offered by the Constitution are those found in the Fifth Amendment, including the provision that "no person shall . . . be deprived of life, liberty, or property, without due process of law." The question regarding congressional prohibition of slavery in federal territories, then, turned on whether a slave was a person or a piece of property. If the slave was a person, then, theoretically at least, he could make a Fifth Amendment claim that holding him in bondage deprived him of his liberty without due process; but if the slave was merely a piece of property, and Congress prohibited slavery through legislation, then the slave owner could make a Fifth Amendment claim that he had been deprived of his property without due process of law.

In answering the question of whether slaves were persons or property in the context of the Fifth Amendment's protections of life, liberty, and property, Taney relied on his own conclusion from the first half of his decision: blacks were considered nothing more than property by the Founders. Slaves, therefore, were not "persons" within the meaning of the Fifth Amendment and were to be offered no protection of life, liberty, or property. Slave owners traveling to federal territories, however, had full Fifth Amendment protection of their slave property, as they would for any other kind of property. By prohibiting slavery in part of the Louisiana Territory, the Missouri Compromise violated slave owners' Fifth Amendment property rights. Thus, Taney struck down the Missouri Compromise on two grounds: it was unconstitutional because Congress lacked the constitutional authority to pass it and because it violated the Fifth Amendment's protection of the right to property. So, far from having any power to prohibit or restrict slavery, Taney concluded, "the only power conferred [to Congress] is the power coupled with the duty of guarding and protecting the [slave] owner in his rights."[21] According to the Supreme Court, it was Congress's duty to protect slavery in all federal territories outside the Northwest Territory. *Dred Scott* gave constitutional authority to policies demanded by Southern Democrats: full and expansive federal protection for slavery in the territories. As Lincoln never tired of pointing out, *Dred Scott* contradicted the "popular sovereignty" doctrine of Stephen Douglas and Northern Democrats. Anyone who stood with Taney could not stand with Douglas.

LINCOLN CHALLENGES TANEY

On June 26, 1857, Lincoln gave a speech dedicated almost entirely to Taney's opinion in *Dred Scott*. Lincoln's basic criticism was that Taney had fabricated the historical record regarding slavery and the treatment of blacks in the United States and had twisted the meaning of the principles of the American

Founding beyond recognition. In Lincoln's view, *Dred Scott* was unsound and not only should be ignored as a precedent for future cases but, in fact, should be overturned. "We believe . . . in obedience to, and respect for the judicial department of government," Lincoln wrote, "but we think the *Dred Scott* decision is erroneous. We know the court that made it, has often over-ruled its own decisions, and we shall do what we can to have it to over-rule this."[22]

"Chief Justice Taney, in delivering the opinion of the majority of the Court," Lincoln noted, "insists at great length that negroes were no part of the people who made, or for whom was made, the Declaration of Independence, or the Constitution of the United States." But, as Justice Curtis demonstrated in his dissenting opinion, "in five of the then-thirteen states, to wit, New Hampshire, Massachusetts, New York, New Jersey and North Carolina, free negroes were voters, and, in proportion to their numbers, had the same part in making the Constitution that the white people had."[23] It was simply historically untrue, Lincoln argued, to say that blacks formed no part of the people for whom the Declaration and Constitution were written.

Lincoln also challenged Taney's assumption that the public estimate of the black man was more favorable in 1857 than it had been at the time of the American Founding. After quoting the Declaration's statement of human equality, Taney alleged that "the general words above quoted would seem to embrace the whole human family, and if they were used in a similar instrument at this day would be so understood." Taney took a progressive view of public opinion, holding that public opinion was far more enlightened in 1857 than it had been in 1776, that Americans in 1857 had a fuller understanding of human equality than the Founders in 1776. Lincoln disagreed. "It is grossly incorrect to say or assume, that the public estimate of the negro is more favorable now than it was at the origin of the government," he argued. "The change between then and now is decidedly the other way; and [the] ultimate destiny [of blacks] has never appeared so hopeless as in the last three or four years." Lincoln then pointed to the many changes in public policy that revealed the change in opinions regarding American blacks:

> In two of the five States—New Jersey and North Carolina—that then gave the free negro the right of voting, the right has since been taken away; and in a third—New York—it has been greatly abridged; while it has not been extended, so far as I know, to a single additional State, though the number of the States has more than doubled. In those days, as I understand, masters could, at their own pleasure, emancipate their slaves; but since then, such legal restraints have been made upon emancipation, as to amount almost to prohibition. In those days, Legislatures

held the unquestioned power to abolish slavery, in their respective States; but now it is becoming quite fashionable for State Constitutions to withhold that power from the Legislatures. In those days, by common consent, the spread of the black man's bondage to new countries was prohibited; but now, Congress decides that it will not continue the prohibition, and the Supreme Court decides that it *could* not if it would.[24]

Lincoln believed America was moving away from seeing slavery as an evil to be tolerated out of necessity but gradually eliminated whenever possible, toward viewing slavery as a positive good, an institution that contributed to the welfare of slaves and slave owners alike. This deterioration in the moral climate of America, Lincoln maintained, resulted from Americans' forgetting, or rejecting, the principles of the Founding, foremost the Declaration's principle of human equality. "In those days," he remarked,

> our Declaration of Independence was held sacred by all, and thought to include all; but now, to aid in making the bondage of the negro universal and eternal, it is assailed, and sneered at, and construed, and hawked at, and torn, till, if its framers could rise from their graves, they could not at all recognize it. All the powers of earth seem rapidly combining against him. Mammon is after him; ambition follows, and philosophy follows, and the theology of the day is fast joining the cry.[25]

America was losing its moral light, which emanated from the principle of equality, the father of all moral principles, as Lincoln described it in his 1858 speech in Chicago. This is why Lincoln viewed with such alarm Taney's perversion of the meaning of the Declaration, a perversion he believed further clouded the moral and political guidance offered by the principles of the Founding. In his speech on *Dred Scott*, Lincoln focused on the fact that while "Chief Justice Taney . . . admit[ted] that the language of the Declaration is broad enough to include the whole human family," he asserted that "the authors of that instrument did not intend to include negroes, by the fact that they did not at once, actually place them on an equality with the whites." Lincoln immediately pointed out that neither did they "place all white people on an equality with one or another," then offered his own understanding of what the authors of the Declaration meant when they declared it to be a self-evident truth that all men are created equal:

> I think the authors of that notable instrument intended to include all men, but they did not intend to declare all men equal in all respects. They did not mean to say all were equal in color, size, intellect, moral

developments, or social capacity. They defined with tolerable distinct-
ness, in what respects they did consider all men created equal—equal in
"certain inalienable rights, among which are life, liberty, and the pursuit
of happiness." This they said, and this they meant.

"They did not mean to assert the obvious untruth," Lincoln explained in
plain language, "that all were then actually enjoying that equality, nor yet, that
they were about to confer it immediately upon them. In fact they had no
power to confer such a boon." Lincoln understood the principle of human
equality and equal natural rights to be, simultaneously, a descriptive statement
of what men are by nature—they are equal in their natural rights—as well as
a normative statement of how men should live in civil society—they should
aim to protect the equal natural rights of others as best they can.

> [The Founders] meant simply to declare the *right*, so that the *enforcement*
> of it might follow as fast as circumstances should permit. They meant to
> set up a standard maxim for free society, which should be familiar to all,
> and revered by all; constantly looked to, constantly labored for, and even
> though never perfectly attained, constantly approximated, and thereby
> constantly spreading and deepening its influence, and augmenting the
> happiness and value of life to all people of all colors everywhere.[26]

Lincoln next offered a remarkable observation, one that every generation of Americans ought to consider:

> The assertion that "all men are created equal" was of no practical use in
> effecting our separation from Great Britain; and it was placed in the De-
> claration, not for that, but for future use. Its authors meant it to be,
> thank God, it is now proving itself, a stumbling block to those who in
> after times might seek to turn a free people back into the hateful paths
> of despotism. They knew the proneness of prosperity to breed tyrants,
> and they meant when such should re-appear in this fair land and com-
> mence their vocation they should find left for them at least one hard nut
> to crack.[27]

Lincoln is undoubtedly correct on this point: the Founders did not need to
announce the principle of equality in order to separate themselves from
British rule and gain their independence. They only needed military victory. More precisely, the Americans needed only for the British to grow
tired of fighting and go home, thus leaving the Americans to rule themselves as they desired. Many scholars and critics of the Founding today are
quick to emphasize what the Founders failed to do in terms of achieving

full, perfect, and immediate justice. Lincoln certainly understood such criticisms, but as a statesman looking to preserve and expand free society for his own generation, as well as for later generations, he also saw the Founding in a different and better light, one that is not much discussed today. Instead of focusing the attention of Americans on what the Founders did *not* do, Lincoln asked Americans to reflect on what the Founders *did* do.

Before asking why the Founders did not immediately wipe out slavery (which it was beyond their power to do and which no other nation had done), for example, Lincoln in effect asks, why did the Founders justify their independence in terms of universal human equality? And whatever the answer might be, is it not a wonderful thing that they did? Do we not owe them much for doing so? Are we not a freer, happier, and ultimately more just society for having laid the foundation of our regime on the cornerstone of the "laws of nature and of nature's God" and the equality of natural rights those natural laws demand?

Notice also what Lincoln says above: the principle of equality does not belong merely to 1776. In fact, it was not, he argues, especially useful in 1776. Rather, the principle of equality is more useful for us today! Lincoln says that there is a "proneness of prosperity to breed tyrants," that as Americans become wealthy and prosperous, they become comfortable, and as they become comfortable, it becomes easy for them to forget the vigilance with which they must always guard against unjust encroachments on their liberties. But if and when tyranny begins to stir in America, it cannot succeed unless and until it drives the idea of equality from the American mind; for the tyrant-to-be will find in America "at least one hard nut to crack," the bedrock principle of equality by which civilized men understand that the only legitimate government is government by consent of the governed.

Lincoln wrote these words in 1857, and he believed that the principle of equality was in certain respects more important in 1857 than it had been in 1776. It seems reasonable that if he were here today, he might remind Americans that that principle continues to be more important today than it was in 1776. The question is whether anyone in America today believes that. Do we understand and teach our children and students that the principle of natural human equality is the foundation of justice and security for freedom today, or do we treat it like a historical artifact from the past, an interesting, if naïve and outdated, idea that some people used to discuss and debate in the late eighteenth century? Do we hold, as Lincoln did, that the principle of natural human equality cuts across time, that it is not merely a product of a particular culture or historical epoch but a timeless standard that applies to all cultures and all epochs, including our own?

While Taney was right that some African blacks were "bought and sold" during the period of the American Founding, he was wrong to generalize the treatment of all blacks by all whites from the way some whites treated some blacks in America. More importantly, mountains of historical evidence refute his groundless assertion that black slavery "was regarded as an axiom in morals as well as in politics, which no one thought of disputing, or supposed to be open to dispute." As discussed in chapter 1, it was amazing, if not miraculous, that in the American Founding a nation of slave owners at once declared their own independence upon the principle that "all men are created equal," while declaring slavery to be an evil and injustice that ought to be removed. Consider these statements by leading minds of the Founding era:

- George Washington: "There is not a man living who wishes more sincerely than I do, to see a plan adopted for the abolition of [slavery]."[28]
- John Adams: "Every measure of prudence ought to be assumed for the eventual total extirpation of slavery from the United States. . . . I have throughout my whole life, held the practice of slavery in abhorrence."[29]
- Benjamin Franklin: "Slavery is an atrocious debasement of human nature."[30]
- Alexander Hamilton: "The laws of certain states . . . give an ownership in the service of Negroes as personal property. . . . But being men, by the laws of God and nature, they were capable of acquiring liberty—and when the captor in war thought fit to give them liberty, the gift was not only valid, but irrevocable."[31]
- James Madison: "We have seen the mere distinction of color made in the most enlightened period of time a ground of the most oppressive dominion by man over man."[32]
- Thomas Jefferson: "The whole commerce between master and slave is a perpetual exercise of the most boisterous passions, the most unremitting despotism on the one part, and degrading submissions on the other.[33]

These opinions can be multiplied many times, while there is little, if any, documentary evidence suggesting that anyone of the Founding generation believed that blacks "had no rights which the white man was bound to respect." When slavery was defended, such as in the course of the Constitutional Convention, it was not as a moral good; nor were the humanity and equal rights of black slaves denied. Rather, slavery was defended simply as a matter of economic interest. The fact was that many white people had deep economic interests tied to black slave labor, and while they were therefore very cautious about any proposal that would suddenly end slavery and cause economic injury to those who depended on the institution, they never for a moment denied its massive injustice and moral wrong. Thus, it was no accident that as antislavery opinions spread, as increasing numbers of Americans came to understand that slavery directly contradicted the natural right principles of their own revolution, antislavery movements gained momentum. Prior to the American Revolution, slavery was lawful in all thirteen colonies under English law, but in the short period between the Declaration of Independence of 1776 and 1800, only twenty-four years, half of the original states either abolished slavery or adopted policies for its gradual elimination, and significant antislavery forces were at work in the remaining states. These facts Taney ignored.

He also ignored the unmistakable meaning of the very documents he claimed to have read, foremost the Declaration of Independence and the Constitution. Taney was surely aware that the Declaration of Independence had undergone revisions before it was adopted by the Continental Congress in 1776. The central section of the Declaration offers a litany of charges against the British king George III for crimes against the natural rights of humanity. In the original draft of the Declaration, penned by Thomas Jefferson, the longest indictment was reserved for the king's inhumane perpetuation of chattel slavery within the colonies:

> He has waged cruel war against human nature itself, violating its most sacred rights of life and liberty in the persons of a distant people who never offended him, captivating and carrying them into slavery in another hemisphere, or to incur miserable death in their transportation thither. This piratical warfare, the opprobrium of infidel powers, is the warfare of the Christian king of Great Britain. Determined to keep open a market where MEN should be bought and sold, he has prostituted his negative for suppressing every legislative attempt to prohibit or to restrain this execrable commerce.[34]

It strains every fiber of credulity to imagine that Jefferson or any of the Founders, who deemed it a "cruel war against human nature" to "keep open a market where MEN should be bought and sold"—Jefferson described this in the next sentence of the draft Declaration as an "assemblage of horrors"—believed at the same time that blacks should never be "thought of or spoken of except as property."

From the Founders' point of view, the distinction between a person and a piece of property arises in nature. By nature, a person is a being who owns himself, who possesses a free will and a rational mind and is therefore morally responsible for his actions. Property, on the other hand, whether living or not, has no free will or rational mind and is not morally culpable. A human being is a person because of his human nature, while a cow or horse or piece of land can become a person's property because it does not share human nature. Natural right, upon which the entire political philosophy of the American Founding rests, is derived from the natural distinction between human and nonhuman beings, as only human beings can discern by their own reason that it is wrong to treat other human beings as if they were property.

Natural right, as the standard of right for human behavior and human law, is perhaps presented best in James Madison's discussion of the Constitution's Three-Fifths Clause in *Federalist* 54. According to Madison, slavery was the most divisive problem the 1787 Constitutional Convention in Philadelphia faced and threatened the convention's success more than any of the controversies between big and little states or other sectional differences. After the delegates agreed on a bicameral legislature with equal representation for each state in the Senate and proportional representation for each in the House of Representatives, the problem of slavery reared its head and nearly caused the convention to dissolve.

The controversy centered on whether slaves should be counted as part of a state's population for the purposes of apportioning congressional representation. Southern states, which possessed the bulk of slaves in America, demanded that each slave be counted as a full person because, after all, they were equally persons and would be living under the laws of the Constitution no less than any other American. By counting their slaves toward their total population, slave states stood to benefit from increased representation in the House that, in turn, would also increase their number of state electors in the Electoral College (determined by adding the number of representatives plus two senators for each state) that elects the president. They backed their demand for counting slaves as whole persons with threats of walking out of the convention and refusing to join any new constitutional union. Northern delegates, which included some of the most determined opponents of slavery, faced two options: they could compromise with the South, or they could demand that each slave be counted as zero for the purposes of determining state population and the number of representatives a state would send to the House of Representatives. Had they done the latter, they might have applauded themselves for defending their cherished principles. The South, however, might very well have followed through on its threats, left the Constitutional Convention, and established an independent Southern confederacy. And if the Southern delegates had left the

Philadelphia Convention over the issue of slavery, the South might be expected to enshrine strict and harsh protections for the institution in any new constitution that it adopted. This would have sealed the fates of millions of black slaves in the South, placing Southern slave policies beyond the reach of Northern antislavery opinion and making slavery, in effect, perpetual. Fortunately, Northern delegates, while some stood to offer condemnations of slavery, nevertheless chose prudential compromise over imprudent inflexibility. A compromise was reached as both Northerners and Southerners agreed to add "to the whole number of free persons . . . three-fifths of all other persons."[35] With the three-fifths compromise in place, a constitutional union of both Northern and Southern states could be formed, offering at least some possibility of addressing the problem of slavery through peaceful means, such as persuasion and free elections.

Madison believed the omission of the words "slave" and "slavery" from the Constitution signaled the Founding generation's general opinion that slavery was wrong. During the Constitutional Convention, Madison "thought it wrong to admit in the Constitution the idea that there could be property in men" because "slaves are not like merchandise" or other forms of property; instead, they are human beings.[36] When Madison turned to defend the Constitution in the *Federalist,* he refused to defend the Three-Fifths Clause and its relation to slavery in his own name. In *Federalist* 54, which is the only number that discusses slavery, Madison placed almost all of his comments in quotation marks as observations that might be offered by "one of our southern brethren."

> "We subscribe to the doctrine," might one of our southern brethren observe, "that representation relates more immediately to persons, and taxation more immediately to property, and we join in the application of this distinction to the case of our slaves. But we must deny the fact that slaves are considered merely as property, and in no respect whatever as persons. The true state of the case is that they partake of both these qualities."[37]

Continuing to place his words in the mouth of a fictional Southerner, Madison proceeded to explain that the laws considered black slaves to be persons in some respects and property in others:

> "In being compelled to labor, not for himself, but for a master; in being vendible by one master to another master; and in being subject at all times to be restrained in his liberty and chastised in his body, by the capricious will of another—the slave *may appear to be* degraded from the

human rank, and classed with those irrational animals which fall under the legal denomination of property. In being protected, on the other hand, in his life and in his limbs, against the violence of all others, even the master of his labor and his liberty; and in being punishable himself for all violence committed against others—the slave is no less evidently regarded by the law as a member of the society, not as a part of the irrational creation; as a moral person, not as a mere article of property." (emphasis added)

In writing that "the true state of the case" was that slaves were both property and persons, Madison meant that the laws treated them as property in some instances and as persons in others. Thus, it was the "true state of the case" that the laws considered slaves to be both property and persons. For instance, each slave state had a criminal code for slaves, while there were no such criminal laws applicable to cattle, horses, or other irrational animals. Why? Because each slave state implicitly recognized the humanity of slaves, at least insofar as each slave state held slaves accountable for their actions. But by denying their equal rights to life, liberty, and the pursuit of happiness, laws creating and regulating slavery simultaneously denied the slaves' humanity. "The Federal Constitution therefore," Madison continued, "decides with great propriety on the case of our slaves, when it views them in the mixed character of persons and of property. This is in fact their true character." "It is the character bestowed on them by the laws under which they live," wrote Madison, "because it is only under the pretext that the laws have transformed the negroes into subjects of property, that a place is disputed them in the computation of numbers."

Had no one recognized the humanity of slaves, had the entire Founding generation viewed blacks as nothing other than property, as Taney insisted, then there would never have been a controversy over whether to count slaves as part of a state's population. The controversy that led to the adoption of the Three-Fifths Clause arose precisely because the delegates to the Philadelphia Convention recognized the equal humanity of those being held in slavery. According to Madison, some blacks had been considered slave property "only under the pretext" of the laws. But Madison emphasized that the law was not the final authority on the nature of black slaves, that nature itself revealed that slaves were human beings who possessed the same human nature as the free men and women among whom they lived. Indicating his disapproval of slave laws and suggesting what needed to be done to correct them, Madison concluded that "if the laws were to restore the rights which have been taken away, the negroes could no longer be refused an equal share of representation with the other inhabitants." Unjust slave laws violated the natural rights of black slaves, and under the proposed Constitution, it would be up to each state to decide for itself what to do about slavery. But Madison was clear that if the laws were to be good, justice would require that the laws "restore the rights which have been taken away" from black slaves. Yet, while Madison relied on the distinction between law and nature to determine the nature of blacks, Taney refused to do so.

In *Dred Scott and the Problem of Constitutional Evil*, Mark Graber offers a serious attempt to defend Taney's argument in *Dred Scott*. While Graber acknowledges that Taney "overreached when [he] claimed that 'the African race never have been acknowledged as belonging to the family of nations,'" he argues that "the denial of black citizenship in *Dred Scott* does not, however, depend on Taney's ahistorical reading of the Declaration of Independence." Graber draws upon historical evidence that some Americans during the Founding period believed that "people of different races could not occupy the same civic space."[38] Indeed, John Jay presents a similar argument in the *Federalist*:

> With equal pleasure I have as often taken notice that Providence has been pleased to give this one connected country to one united people— a people descended from the same ancestors, speaking the same language, professing the same religion, attached to the same principles of government, very similar in their manners and customs, and who, by their joint counsels, arms, and efforts, fighting side by side throughout a long and bloody war, have nobly established general liberty and independence.[39]

But it must also be kept in mind that Jay's argument in the *Federalist* appears within the context of encouraging Americans to stay united for their own safety and well-being, reminding them of the many cultural, religious, economic, and other bonds that support the American union.

The fact that some Americans raised questions about the cultural and/or racial homogeneity of the American people does not, however, address what Taney thought was most important for his argument. In denying the possibility that blacks might be citizens, Taney did not argue primarily from historical evidence. In fact, very little evidence was presented: for example, he almost never quoted from any of the leading Founders when discussing their views of blacks, slavery, and citizenship. Taney took recourse to what he presented as first principles and then based his argument upon (a peculiar version of) the social compact theory of the Founding. For Taney, it was emphatically important to identify who were and who were not the original members of the body politic; thus, it was critical to determine whether blacks were part of the sovereign people who declared independence in 1776.

THE POLITICS OF TANEY'S JURISPRUDENCE

How could a man as learned as the chief justice of the Supreme Court not know that the Founders acknowledged the humanity of blacks? How could he have been so profoundly wrong in his account of the principles and opinions of the American Founders? In his speech on the *Dred Scott* case, Lincoln intimated that Taney had not been fully honest in his account of the Founding. Historical evidence suggests that Lincoln might very well have been right.

In an 1818 case in Maryland, a Christian preacher, Jacob Gruber, had delivered a moving antislavery speech in the presence of more than four hundred blacks and was subsequently charged by a grand jury for attempting to incite a slave rebellion with his rhetoric. A then young Roger Taney was assigned as Gruber's defense lawyer. What follows is an excerpt from Taney's statement delivered in court defending Gruber's right to publicly criticize the institution of slavery:

> Any man has a right to publish his opinions on that subject [slavery] whenever he pleases. It is a subject of national concern, and may at all times be freely discussed. Mr. Gruber did quote the language of our great act of national independence, and insisted on the principles contained in that venerated instrument. He did rebuke those masters, who, in the exercise of power, are deaf to the calls of humanity; and he warned them of the evils they might bring upon themselves. He did speak with abhorrence of those reptiles, who live by trading in human flesh, and enrich themselves by tearing the husband from the wife—the infant from the bosom of the mother. . . . A hard necessity, indeed, compels us to endure the evil of slavery for a time. . . . Yet while it continues it is a blot on our national character, and every real lover of freedom confidently hopes that it will be effectually, though it must be gradually, wiped away; and earnestly looks for the means, by which this necessary object may best be attained. And until it shall be accomplished, until the time shall come when we can point without a blush, to the language of the Declaration of Independence, every friend of humanity will seek to lighten the galling chain of slavery, and better, to the utmost of his power, the wretched condition of the slave.[40]

Taney's language in 1818 might easily be confused for Lincoln's language in the 1850s, so powerfully did he denounce slavery and so persuasively did he defend the Declaration's principle of equality. Moreover, Taney did more than offer a defense of Gruber on account of the law, which would be expected of any defense attorney. After arguing that slavery was among the greatest of earthly evils, Taney willingly put himself at risk, threatening to make the same argument against slavery, using the same language as Gruber had, right there in the courtroom and to accept whatever punishment might be meted out to them both. "Shall I content myself with saying he had a right to [denounce slavery]?" Taney asked the judge and jury, "that there is no law to punish him?"

> So far is he from being the object of punishment in any form of proceeding, that [I am] prepared to maintain the same principles, and to use, if necessary, the same language here in the temple of justice, and in the presence of those who are the ministers of the law.

But that was the Taney of 1818. By 1857, as he sat down to pen his opinion in *Dred Scott*, the political landscape had been greatly transformed. As a lifelong Democrat, Taney must have been aware that the emergence of the new Republican Party threatened his party's status as the national, majority party. He could not have been unaware of the election results of 1856, the first election in which the Republicans fielded a candidate for president. Democrat James Buchanan won that election, but his Republican rival, John C. Fremont, showed strong electoral support. Among the three parties that offered candidates in the 1856 presidential election—the Democratic, Republican, and American (or Know-Nothing) parties—the breakdown of the popular vote was as follows:

Democrat:	1.833 million votes
Republican:	1.340 million votes
American:	872,000 votes[41]

Certainly, important differences separated the Republican Party and the American, or "Know-Nothing," Party, which included a large number of Southern Whigs. Nonetheless, if the Republican Party could absorb the American Party votes, the Republicans would emerge as the new majority party in the next election. Might Roger Taney have used his position as chief justice of the Supreme Court to intervene politically and try to offer his Democratic Party a political advantage by injuring the Republican cause?

Consider that the 1856 Republican platform (as well as the 1860 platform) connected the self-evident truth "that all men are endowed with the inalienable right to life, liberty, and the pursuit of happiness" with the language of the Fifth Amendment, through which the Founders "ordained that no person shall be deprived of life, liberty, or property, without due process of law." The Constitution's Fifth Amendment, Republicans concluded, prohibited "all attempts . . . of establishing slavery in the territories of the United States." Republicans denied that either Congress or a territorial legislature had any authority "to give legal existence to slavery in the any territory of the United States, while the present Constitution shall be maintained." This would explain why Taney went out of his way, in what many critics complained were merely obiter dicta, or incidental remarks that were not legally binding, to argue that rather than prohibiting slavery from the territories, the Fifth Amendment positively obligated Congress to offer federal protection for the institution throughout them. Or could it be coincidence that Taney's 1857 argument regarding the Fifth Amendment was a direct assault on the constitutional premise of the 1856 Republican platform? What better way to assist Democrats than by declaring the central purpose of the newly formed Republican Party, which was also the central policy demand of Abraham Lincoln, that is, the restoration of the Missouri Compromise, to be unconstitutional?

As I have mentioned, the principle controversy over the Fifth Amendment and slavery involved whether to consider the slave as a *person* who had been denied his liberty without due process of law or as *property* that a slave owner could not be denied. In addition to his strange reading of the Declaration of Independence, Taney also looked to the Constitution itself to determine whether the Founders considered blacks, slave or free, to be persons or property. In particular, Taney took notice of the Slave Importation Clause (Article I, Section 9), which prohibited Congress from abolishing the importation of African slaves prior to the year 1808, as well as the Fugitive Slave Clause (Article IV, Section 2), which allowed for runaway slaves to "be delivered up on claim of the party to whom such service or labor may be due." According to Taney, both of these constitutional provisions "point[ed] directly and specifically to the negro race as a separate class of persons, and show[ed] clearly that they were not regarded as a portion of the people or citizens of the Government then formed."[42] "These two provisions show, conclusively," Taney argued, "that neither the description of persons therein referred to, nor their descendants, were embraced in any of the other provisions of the Constitution." Taney overlooked the fact that both constitutional clauses pertained to "persons" and neither had any necessary bearing on free blacks.

More importantly, however, Taney was interested in only two of the three slavery clauses of the Constitution. Throughout his entire opinion, he never referenced or mentioned the Three-Fifths Clause of Article I, Section 2. Why might this be? Taney's entire argument rested upon the premise that the framers of the Constitution considered blacks as nothing other than property and that the Constitution "makes no distinction between [slave] property and other property owned by a citizen." In fact, the Constitution *does* make a distinction between slave property and other forms of property, most clearly in the Three-Fifths Clause. If the Constitution made "no distinction" between slave property and other forms of property, is it not peculiar that slaves were the only form of "property" that counted toward determining how much political representation a state would be afforded in the national government? Again, horses and cattle were not counted as part of a state's population, according to the Constitution, but slaves were because the Constitution recognized their humanity, even if it failed to grant them full representation. Had Taney addressed the Three-Fifths Clause, it would have been impossible to maintain that there was no constitutional distinction between slave property and other property. Thus, Taney's strategy: ignore the Three-Fifths Clause altogether.

While only God knows for sure what was in the mind of Chief Justice Taney, it is plausible that he offered his strained interpretation of the Founders' Declaration of Independence and Constitution, despite his protests to the contrary, precisely in order to reach the partisan result he desired, one that might undermine the Republican Party and provide a political boost for his own Democratic Party. Lincoln certainly believed that political intrigue lay behind the contorted logic of *Dred Scott*. In his 1858 "house divided" speech, as he accepted the Republican nomination to challenge Douglas for his Senate seat, Lincoln suggested nothing less than a conspiracy, which included Chief Justice Taney, as well as Senator Douglas, former President Franklin Pierce, and then President James Buchanan, to ensure the spread of slavery throughout the United States. The alternatives as presented by Lincoln could not have been clearer:

> If we could first know where we are, and whither we are tending, we could then better judge what to do, and how to do it. We are now far into the fifth year, since a policy was initiated, with the avowed object, and confident promise, of putting an end to slavery agitation. Under the operation of that policy, that agitation has not only, not ceased, but has constantly augmented. In my opinion, it will not cease, until a crisis shall have been reached, and passed. "A house divided against itself cannot stand." I believe this government cannot endure, permanently half slave and half free. I do not expect the Union to be dissolved—I do not expect the

house to fall—but I do expect it will cease to be divided. It will become all one thing, or all the other. Either the opponents of slavery, will arrest the further spread of it, and place it where the public mind shall rest in the belief that it is in course of ultimate extinction; or its advocates will push it forward, till it shall become alike lawful in all the States, old as well as new—North as well as South.[43]

Lincoln detected an overarching strategy to advance slavery, of which *Dred Scott* was only the most recent tactic. Douglas's Kansas-Nebraska Act of 1854 determined that Congress would not decide the fate of slavery in the territories, leaving it up to the people of the territories to decide for themselves. Taney's decision in *Dred Scott*, however, insisted that neither Congress nor the people *could* prevent slavery in the territories even if they *wanted* to. But if neither the people of a territory nor Congress could prohibit slavery, what about the people of a *state*? If the Southern slave owner had a constitutional right to take his slave property into federal territory, did he not also have a constitutional right to take his slave property into any state? As Lincoln warned, "We shall lie down pleasantly dreaming that the people of Missouri are on the verge of making their State free; and we shall awake to the reality, instead, that the Supreme Court has made Illinois a slave State."[44] All that was needed was another Supreme Court decision following the *Dred Scott* case "declaring that the Constitution of the United States does not permit a *state* to exclude slavery from its limits." "This," Lincoln suggested, would not be terribly controversial if Douglas's "doctrine of 'care not whether slavery be voted *down* or voted *up*' shall gain upon the public mind sufficiently to give promise that such a decision can be maintained when made." Lincoln lamented,

> Such a decision is all that slavery now lacks of being alike lawful in all the States.
>
> Welcome or unwelcome, such decision *is* probably coming, and will soon be upon us, unless the power of the present political dynasty shall be met and overthrown.[45]

Probably unbeknownst to Lincoln, at least one state-level court case a year after *Dred Scott* evidenced that Lincoln's dire warning that the courts could nationalize slavery might be realized sooner rather than later. In an otherwise obscure case, *In Re Archy*, the California Supreme Court relied upon the U.S. Supreme Court's ruling in *Dred Scott* to determine whether a slave owner from Mississippi could bring his slave property as he traveled to California, whose state constitution prohibited slavery.[46] The case concerned Charles A. Stovall, a citizen of Mississippi, who went to California and took with him his nineteen-year-old black slave, Archy. Archy escaped while in California and was later arrested by California police, at which time Stovall petitioned the California Supreme Court for a writ of habeas corpus for the recovery of his slave. The legal question before the Court was whether Stovall possessed a legal right to his slave property after bringing Archy into a free state whose constitution disallowed slavery. Attempting to persuade the Court, Stovall's legal counsel argued that "we have the sanction of positive law for slavery even in California."

> As has been before argued, slavery exists by virtue of the Constitution and laws of the United States in all the territories of the Union, and in all of the States where it has not been excluded by positive law enacted by their law-making power. So that, in California, slavery having been planted here by the operation of the Constitution of the United States, it must continue to exist here until the Legislature, by the enactment of sufficient prohibitions and penalties, has asserted the paramount sovereignty of the State.[47]

Stovall's attorney cited *Dred Scott* as the legal authority for the above assertion. His concluding argument, that slavery must continue to exist in California "until the Legislature, by the enactment of sufficient prohibitions and penalties, has asserted the paramount sovereignty of the State," was, of course, what Lincoln predicted the Supreme Court would strike down in a follow-up case to *Dred Scott*. For if a slave owner possessed a constitutional right to his slave property, then the California legislature, or any state legislature, could not prohibit slavery because to do so would violate the property rights of slave owners seeking to bring their slaves into the respective state.

The opinion of the California Supreme Court, authored by Justice Peter Burnett, also relied on the *Dred Scott* decision. "It must be concluded that, where slavery exists, the right of property of the master in the slave must follow as a necessary incident," Burnett argued, because "this right of property is recognized by the Constitution of the United States." Echoing Taney's argument, Burnett continued,

> The right of property having been recognized by the supreme law of the land, certain logical results must follow this recognition. If property, it must, from the nature of the case, be entitled, so far as the action of the federal government is concerned, to the same protection as other property. If permitted to exist by the general law, then it must be protected by the general law, so far as that general law would protect any

other property. No distinction can be made by this law between the different descriptions of private property.[48]

Burnett raised another question: when citizens of other states

> come to visit [California] for health or pleasure, shall they be permitted to bring their domestic servants with them, to attend upon them or their families as waiters? The citizens of the free States can bring their confidential servants with them—why should not the citizens of the slave States be allowed the same privilege?

Burnett attempted to argue at the conclusion of his opinion that California nonetheless retained the sovereign right to exclude slavery from its jurisdiction; therefore, only those slave owners who were temporarily visiting California could bring their slaves with them, while slave owners whose stay in California was prolonged forfeited their legal claim of ownership over their slaves. Burnett's conclusion, however, seemed to be undermined by his own argument in agreement with Taney that the Constitution recognizes a right to slave property equal to every other kind of property right, the precise argument Lincoln predicted the U.S. Supreme Court would eventually make, an argument it perhaps would have made had *In Re Archy* been challenged and argued before the Supreme Court. And in the case of young Archy, the California Supreme Court said that Archy's owner, Charles Stovall, was exempt from the rules the court had just laid down and ordered that police authorities release Archy and return him to his owner.[49]

Not unlike Taney, Lincoln too was aware of the election results of 1856 and believed they explained in large measure Taney's argument in the *Dred Scott* case. "It is my opinion," Lincoln remarked in his fifth debate with Douglas, "that the *Dred Scott* decision, as it is, never would have been made in its present form if the party that made it had not been sustained previously by the elections." And a "new *Dred Scott* decision, deciding against the right of the people of the States to exclude slavery," Lincoln urged, "will never be made, if that [Democratic] party is not sustained by the elections."[50] If Taney was using the influence of the Court to bolster the hegemony of the Democratic Party, Lincoln seemed to reason, then what better way for the American people to signal their disapproval to the Court than by voting against Democrats in upcoming elections? Lincoln, of course, hoped that as American voters turned away from the Democratic Party, they would embrace Republican principles and candidates. Lincoln not only needed to refute Democrats who were advancing pro-slavery arguments in defense of the *Dred Scott* ruling, he also needed to persuade his fellow Republicans that Douglas was not an ally of any Republican opposed to slavery, even though Douglas had worked to defeat the pro-slavery Lecompton constitution and many Republicans were openly courting Douglas to join Republican ranks. "How can [Douglas] oppose the advances of slavery," Lincoln asked in his "house divided" speech, when "[h]e don't care anything about it?" As Lincoln never failed to point out, Douglas's "avowed mission" was to impress upon the "public heart" to "care nothing about" slavery. If the day ever came when a second *Dred Scott* case would prevent all states from prohibiting slavery, the reaction on the part of the American people might well be a collective yawn of disinterest: such disinterest, Lincoln worried, was the practical effect of Douglas's popular sovereignty doctrine. The Republican cause, therefore, "must be entrusted to, and conducted by its own undoubted friends, those . . . who *do care*" whether slavery expands or dies.[51] Thus, as Lincoln tried to secure his own election to the Senate in 1858, he was also looking ahead to a Republican victory in 1860, and he wanted to make sure that any Republican victory would be won on the principle of freedom, not slavery:

> Two years ago the Republicans of the nation mustered over thirteen hundred thousand strong. We did this under the single impulse of resistance to a common danger, with every external circumstance against us. Of strange, discordant, and even, hostile elements, we gathered from the four winds, and formed and fought the battle through, under the constant hot fire of a disciplined, proud, and pampered enemy. Did we brave all *then*, to *falter* now?—*now*—when that same enemy is *wavering*, dissevered and belligerent? The result is not doubtful. We shall not fail— if we stand firm, we shall not fail.[52]

For Lincoln, the success of the United States, continued devotion to the central principles of human equality and free society, and the success of the new Republican Party were inseparable from one another. While Lincoln lost the 1858 senatorial election to Douglas, his ability, as demonstrated in the joint debates and elsewhere, to dismantle Douglas's "popular sovereignty" doctrine and to illuminate its incompatibility with Taney's *Dred Scott* decision paved the way for his nomination, and ultimately his election, to the presidency in 1860.

DRED SCOTT AND THE MODERN AMERICAN MIND

Taney's entire argument in *Dred Scott*, both his assertion that blacks could not be citizens and the opinion that the Missouri Compromise was unconstitutional, rested upon the premise that blacks were considered nothing but property because they were excluded from the Declaration's proposition that all men are created equal. That premise crumbled under the weight of Lincoln's principled and true defense of the original meaning of the Declaration's statement of human equality. But while Lincoln's argument was superior to Taney's in terms of reason, it would take a civil war and three constitutional amendments to reverse in practice the Supreme Court's shameful decision in *Dred Scott*.[53]

Americans today might find it puzzling that the American people of Lincoln's day did not widely and immediately accept Lincoln's views, so flimsy and self-serving was Taney's opinion. But even in our own time, many educated minds do not seem to understand Lincoln's principled opposition to *Dred Scott* or its importance. In *The Real Lincoln*, for example, Thomas DiLorenzo virtually ignores the *Dred Scott* case; he mentions it in only two sentences: one incorrectly summarizes the Court's decision; the other mentions Lincoln's speech on *Dred Scott* only to comment that Lincoln "couldn't resist once again criticizing Andrew Jackson's refusal thirty years earlier to recharter the Bank of the United States . . . [making] it a point to champion the nationalization of money and to demonize Jackson and the Democrats for their opposition to it."[54] In his speech, however, Lincoln invoked Jackson not to "champion the nationalization of money" but to highlight the incredible hypocrisy of Douglas Democrats. In the wake of the *Dred Scott* case, Democrats demanded unquestioning agreement with Supreme Court decisions, yet Douglas himself had often celebrated the great Democrat Andrew Jackson for his willingness to disagree with and challenge Supreme Court rulings. "The course of argument that Judge Douglas makes use of upon this subject [*Dred Scott*]," Lincoln reminded his audience in Galesburg, Illinois, "is preparing the public mind for that new *Dred Scott* decision."

> I have asked him again to point out to me the reasons for his firm adherence to the *Dred Scott* decision as it is. I have turned his attention to the fact that General Jackson differed with him in regard to the political obligation of a Supreme Court decision. . . . So far in this controversy I can get no answer at all from Judge Douglas upon these subjects. Not one can I get from him, except that he swells himself up and says, "All of us who stand by the decision of the Supreme Court are the friends of the Constitution; all you fellows that dare question it in any way, are the enemies of the Constitution."[55]

In his more recent book, *Lincoln Unmasked*, DiLorenzo again mentions *Dred Scott* only twice, and both references are tangential to other subjects.[56] Nowhere does DiLorenzo attempt to understand or explain the Court's opinion in *Dred Scott* or its influence on American history and politics.

Mark Graber, who does confront *Dred Scott* head-on and offers a lengthy and intelligent analysis of the Court's opinion, concludes with a defense of Taney—and any defense of Taney is intrinsically an attack on Lincoln. For Graber, the ultimate purpose of the Constitution was, or should have been, to balance the sectional interests so that no section would benefit at the expense of another, thereby facilitating "domestic tranquility" through amicable relations within the Union. The sectional controversies over slavery in the 1850s, which led to greater hostilities between the North and South, had the effect of "frustrating" the original constitutional compact. In particular, the South found itself with far less political power and influence over national policy in the 1850s than it had bargained for in 1787. Thus, Graber argues, a readjustment of the constitutional agreement was needed to help restore equity to Southerners who had been on the losing end of a demographic shift in political power. In Graber's opinion, *Dred Scott* was largely correct, or at least defensible, as a prescribed readjustment: "*Dred Scott* was a sound application of the version of neoclassical contract theory—adopted in many European countries, approved by many American legal commentators, and followed by occasional American judicial decisions—that authorizes courts to reformulate frustrated agreements."[57]

Graber reserves his most serious indictment not for Taney but for the U.S. Constitution:

> The Taney Court's decision in 1857 did not cause the Civil War by declaring that Congress could not ban slavery in the territories and that former slaves could not become citizens, no matter how morally wrong and constitutionally egregious that ruling was. . . . Secession and civil war occurred when [the Constitution] permitted a sectional coalition to take power, a coalition committed to making slavery policies that were unacceptable to a geographically concentrated minority whose support was necessary for maintaining the antebellum constitutional order.[58]

But, as Graber acknowledges, the Constitution of 1787, which ultimately allowed a sectional majority to control the powers of the national government and therefore dictate slave policy to a sectional minority, was understood at the time of the Founding "as sufficiently proslavery to be ratified in the South and sufficiently antislavery to be ratified in the North."[59] In addition, we ought not to forget that in several states, the Constitution was ratified by the thinnest margins of votes. Thus, a constitution that was considerably more antislavery, or one that was considerably more pro-slavery, would not likely have been ratified. If Graber thinks the Constitution of 1787 was defective or inadequate, especially because it was suffused with "constitutional evil" in the form of slavery, how would he have improved upon it? What alternative constitution should have been proposed at the Constitutional Convention?

Graber suggests that a better constitution would have anticipated sectional controversies and prevented one section of the country from dominating another through sectional policies or laws. "The Constitution caused the Civil War," Graber argues, "by failing to establish institutions that would facilitate the constitutional politics necessary for the national government to make policies acceptable to crucial elites in both sections of the country."[60] It is imaginable that a constitution might provide greater obstacles to sectional control of the government, for example, a constitution that required two-thirds, three-quarters, or some other supermajority in order to pass legislation. But let us suppose that such an alternative constitution might have delayed, or even prevented, the Civil War. This still does not solve the problem of slavery. To paraphrase Lincoln's second inaugural address, it might have prevented the drawing of blood by the sword, while blood would continue to be drawn by the lash. In the words of the Constitution, sometimes it might be impossible to "establish justice" and "insure domestic tranquility" at the same time—one might come at the cost of the other. Reflecting on these deeply rooted problems reveals the genuinely tragic character of the American dilemma over slavery. In 1776, justice required American independence and union. American independence and union, in turn, depended upon forming a constitutional order that offered some measure of protection for slavery. But the institution of slavery stood in direct opposition to the principles of American independence and union. Slavery was the height of injustice. As the American Founders were resolved to build their new regime on the foundation of natural justice, so it was America's tragic fate to resolve the contradiction of human slavery, which could not have been glossed over or dissolved by any constitutional design.

According to Graber, the real culprit was not Taney but Lincoln, who "failed the Constitution by forgetting that his obligation to adopt a plausible interpretation of the Constitution that best preserved the social peace was constitutionally higher than his obligation to adopt a plausible interpretation of the Constitution that best promoted justice."[61] But Graber fails to appreciate fully the moral and political dilemma of slavery in America because he is too quick to assume that "preserving the social peace" was more important than "promoting justice." It is not unreasonable to suggest that from the slave point of view, promoting justice was vastly more important than preserving the social peace. The "social peace" that Graber suggests Lincoln and others should have preserved was a living hell for those in bondage. Nonetheless, argues Graber, Lincoln was wrong to insist on the immorality of slavery and to advance policies aimed at stopping its spread with a view to its ultimate demise: "Lincoln's commitment to implementing antislavery policies without Southern consent took advantage of slave-state political weaknesses."[62] Lincoln's "claim that the persons responsible for the Constitution intended to place slavery 'in the course of ultimate extinction,'" Graber urges, "was faulty constitutional history." Who, according to Graber, possessed the true constitutional history? "Taney," Graber answers, "was more faithful [than Lincoln] to the original Constitution."[63]

It would be problematic if the many misinformed opinions about Lincoln and the Constitution were confined to academic scribblers. But the problem is larger than that. People of influence and power are more persuaded by Taney's account of the principles of the Founders and their Constitution than by Lincoln's, whose natural rights arguments seem to be almost unknown among many thinkers, writers, jurists, and politicians. Thus, we witness Supreme Court Justice Thurgood Marshall in 1987 looking not to Lincoln but to Taney for guidance in understanding the original intent of the Constitution. And, to be sure, if Taney's account of the Constitution is true, there is little reason why Americans should respect their Constitution or their country. Indeed, if America was as ignoble from the beginning as Taney insisted it was, then there is little reason for Americans to respect America itself.

Americans ought to recall, however, that the equal protection of equal rights is *the* American ideal, enshrined forever in the proposition that all men are created equal. And it is right. Racism is wrong precisely because equality is right. Any morally serious critique of the sin of racism rests on the American principle of equality. In other words, acknowledging past sins of racism in America in no way requires us to abandon the principles of America. Rather, just the opposite is true. The more we understand the injustice of racism, the more we should love and cherish the true principles upon which America was founded; and the more we study and learn what the principles of the Founding mean, the more we understand why racism is wrong. Rather than looking down at America as a shamefully racist country, Americans should be thankful that they live in the first country to be founded upon the principle of human equality, a beautiful principle that stands directly opposed to the ugliness of racism. And Americans should respect their Constitution, not because it was perfect in some utopian sense—no human constitution will ever be perfect—but because it marked the greatest effort in human history to form a government that operates by the consent of the governed and aims for the equal protection of equal rights. In his understanding of the goodness of the principles of the Founding and the connection between those principles and the U.S. Constitution, there is no greater student, and therefore there is no greater teacher, of the American political tradition than Abraham Lincoln.

NOTES

1. *Scott v. Sandford,* 60 U.S. 393.
2. Don Fehrenbacher, *The Dred Scott Case: Its Significance in American Law and Politics* (New York: Oxford University Press, 1978).
3. Mark Graber, *Dred Scott and the Problem of Constitutional Evil* (New York: Cambridge University Press, 2006).
4. *Roe v. Wade,* 410 U.S. 113 at 157.
5. *Roe v. Wade,* 410 U.S. 113 at 158.
6. Graber, *Dred Scott and the Problem of Constitutional Evil,* 138.
7. Graber, *Dred Scott and the Problem of Constitutional Evil,* 78.
8. *Scott v. Sandford,* 403.
9. Mark Graber argues that while Taney may have overstated his case ("blacks had never been regarded as a part of the people or citizens of the state"), Taney's general historical point is true: many of the blacks who may have voted at the time of the Founding were not necessarily considered citizens. See Graber, *Dred Scott and the Problem of Constitutional Evil,* 47–57.
10. *Scott v. Sandford,* 406.
11. *Scott v. Sandford,* 426.
12. Mario M. Cuomo, *Why Lincoln Matters: Today More Than Ever* (New York: Harcourt Press, 2004), 137.
13. *Scott v. Sandford,* 407 (emphasis added).
14. *Scott v. Sandford,* 407.
15. *Scott v. Sandford,* 407.
16. *Scott v. Sandford,* 410 (emphasis added).
17. *Scott v. Sandford,* 410.
18. *Scott v. Sandford,* 426–27.
19. *Scott v. Sandford,* 432.
20. *Scott v. Sandford,* 432
21. *Scott v. Sandford,* 452.
22. Roy P. Basler, ed., *The Collected Works of Abraham Lincoln* (New Brunswick, NJ: Rutgers University Press, 1953), II:401. Cited hereafter as Lincoln, *Collected Works.*
23. Lincoln, *Collected Works,* II:403 (emphasis added).
24. Lincoln, *Collected Works,* II:404.
25. Lincoln, *Collected Works,* II:404.
26. Lincoln, *Collected Works,* II:406.

27. Lincoln, *Collected Works*, II:406.

28. George Washington to Morris, April 12, 1786, in *George Washington: A Collection*, ed. W. B. Allen (Indianapolis: Liberty Classics, 1989), 319.

29. John Adams to Evans, June 8, 1819, in *Selected Writings of John and John Quincy Adams*, ed. Adrienne Koch and William Peden (New York: Knopf, 1946), 209.

30. Ben Franklin, "An Address to the Public from the Pennsylvania Society for Promoting the Abolition of Slavery," in *Benjamin Franklin: Writings*, ed. J. A. Leo Lemay (New York: Library of America, 1987), 1154.

31. Alexander Hamilton, "Philo Camillus No. 2," in *Papers of Alexander Hamilton,* ed. Harold C. Syrett (New York: Columbia University Press, 1961–1979), XIX:101–102.

32. James Madison, speech at the Constitutional Convention, June 6, 1787, in Max Farrand, *The Records of the Federal Convention of 1787* (New Haven, CT: Yale University Press, 1911), I:135.

33. Thomas Jefferson, "Notes on the State of Virginia: Query XVIII," in *Jefferson: Writings*, ed. Merrill D. Peterson (New York: Library of America, 1984), 288. See also Thomas G. West, *Vindicating the Founders: Race, Sex, Class, and Justice in the Origins of America* (Lanham, MD: Rowman & Littlefield, 1997), ch. 1.

34. Jefferson, *Jefferson: Writings,* 22.

35. United States Constitution, Art. I, sec. 2.

36. Farrand, *The Records of the Federal Convention of 1787*, II:417.

37. Charles R. Kesler and Clinton Rossiter, eds., *The Federalist Papers* (New York: Signet Classic, 2003), 334.

38. Graber, *Dred Scott and the Problem of Constitutional Evil*, 56–57.

39. Kesler and Rossiter, *The Federalist Papers*, 32.

40. Clement Eaton, *Freedom of Thought in the Old South* (Durham, NC: Duke University Press, 1940), 131. See also Harry V. Jaffa, *A New Birth of Freedom: Abraham Lincoln and the Coming of the Civil War* (Lanham, MD: Rowman & Littlefield, 2000), 219–20.

41. David M. Potter, *The Impending Crisis, 1848–1861* (New York: Harper and Row, 1976), 266.

42. Graber, *Dred Scott and the Problem of Constitutional Evil*, 411.

43. Lincoln, *Collected Works*, II:461–62.

44. Lincoln, *Collected Works*, II:467.

45. Lincoln, *Collected Works*, II:467.

46. *In Re Archy*, 9 Cal. 147 (1858). Edward J. Erler, a political scientist at California State University, San Bernardino, and a devoted student of Abraham Lincoln, discovered this case and brought it to my attention.

47. *Archy*, 9 Cal. 147.

48. *Archy*, 9 Cal. 147, 162.

49. *Archy*, 9 Cal. 147, 171.

50. Lincoln, *Collected Works*, III:232.

51. Lincoln, *Collected Works*, II:467–68.

52. Lincoln, *Collected Works*, II:468.

53. The Thirteenth Amendment prohibited slavery throughout the United States. The Fourteenth Amendment guaranteed citizenship to "all persons born or naturalized in the United States and subject to the jurisdiction thereof." The Fifteenth Amendment ensured that "the right of citizens of the United States to vote shall not be denied or abridged by the United States or by any state on account of race."

54. Thomas DiLorenzo, *The Real Lincoln: A New Look at Abraham Lincoln, His Agenda, and an Unnecessary War* (Roseville, CA: Prima Publishing, 2002), 68, 123.

55. Lincoln, *Collected Works*, III:232–33.

56. Thomas DiLorenzo, *Lincoln Unmasked: What You're Not Supposed to Know about Dishonest Abe* (New York: Crown Forum, 2006), 50, 94.

57. Graber, *Dred Scott and the Problem of Constitutional Evil*, 216.

58. Graber, *Dred Scott and the Problem of Constitutional Evil*, 250–51.

59. Graber, *Dred Scott and the Problem of Constitutional Evil*, 12.

60. Graber, *Dred Scott and the Problem of Constitutional Evil*, 167.

61. Graber, *Dred Scott and the Problem of Constitutional Evil*, 251.

62. Graber, *Dred Scott and the Problem of Constitutional Evil*, 216–17.

63. Graber, *Dred Scott and the Problem of Constitutional Evil*, 13.

4

WAS LINCOLN A
"CHILD OF HIS AGE?"

Lincoln was a creature of his age.

—Thomas Woods, *The Politically Incorrect*
Guide to American History

The concept of human rights is a product of historical development. It is closely associated with specific social, political,
and economic conditions and the specific history, culture, and
values of a particular country. . . . Thus, one should not and
cannot think of the human rights standard and model of certain countries [e.g., the American Declaration of Indepen-
dence] as the only proper ones and demand all countries to
comply with them.

—Liu Huaqiu, Chinese delegate to the UN Conference on
Human Rights, June 17, 1993

[The principle of equal natural rights in the Declaration of
Independence is] an abstract truth, applicable to all men and
all times.

—Abraham Lincoln, letter to Henry Pierce and others,
April 6, 1859

On September 14, 2002, city officials in Ottawa, Illinois, the site of the
first debate between Abraham Lincoln and Stephen Douglas in 1858,
unveiled two beautiful bronze sculptures of both men poised forever in the
midst of heated argumentation in the town square very near the exact spot

where they actually stood some 144 years earlier. I was there for the unveiling because I was speaking on a panel with a number of distinguished academics, mostly historians, all of whom had been invited to Ottawa to offer scholarly papers on Lincoln and his legacy as part of the weekend ceremonies.

After the panel presentations and the question-and-answer session that followed, an elderly gentleman from the audience confronted me. He told me that he was a lifelong resident of Ottawa and a longtime admirer of Lincoln. He went on to explain that as Ottawa was home of the first Lincoln-Douglas debate, the city hosted countless conferences, speeches, and various gatherings and presentations about Lincoln and Douglas and related matters. He said he had attended almost all of them, that most of them were serious and educational, and that he had learned plenty about the story of Lincoln and the details of his life. But, he said pointedly, my speech was different from anything he had heard before because it was the first time he could recall an academic standing up and defending Lincoln's principles as *true*—not merely repeating what Lincoln thought or said or did but offering a defense of Lincoln's ideas as right not only for Lincoln's time but for our time as well. He patted me on the back and thanked me for doing what he had heard no other academic do: vindicating Lincoln by vindicating his ideas. Indeed, that is what I want to do. I believe Lincoln's ideas deserve to be vindicated because I believe that they *are* true—not merely that they *were* true in the middle of the nineteenth century but that they *continue* to be true today.

I did not catch the gentleman's name, but I believe he is largely correct. In the academic literature, rarely does a Lincoln scholar ask whether Lincoln's principles are true. Lincoln's ideas, more often than not, are presented as largely, if not entirely, products of Lincoln's history and culture. Lincoln was a man of his age, or, at best, a man who was slightly ahead of it (typically meaning he was slightly less racist and less bigoted than most Americans of his time). This, of course, raises the question, are all men and their ideas merely products of their history and time, or is it possible that the human mind (including Lincoln's) can comprehend timeless truths? Most Lincoln scholars simply ignore this question even though it is, in a decisive respect, more important than and prior to all questions about what Lincoln said or did. I think the question must be raised, and answered if possible, if we are to know whether the study of Lincoln (or anyone else in history) is relevant to us or if it is mere trivia.

HISTORICISM IN THE HISTORICAL MIND

Many academics assume that we cannot know whether Lincoln's principles are true because they assume that historical research does not extend beyond stating what Lincoln (and others of his day) said and did. The reason is that the question of whether Lincoln's principles are true—not of *what* Lincoln believed but *whether* his beliefs are true—is not a historical but rather a philosophical one. Is there some unchanging realm within which historical change takes place? In particular, is human nature unchanging, and can the human mind discern unchanging truths about unchanging human nature? Typical historians do not bother to give these questions much thought. Instead, they tend to exclude these thorny philosophic issues from their historical research and confine their historical verdicts to the historical context they happen to be studying.

Many Lincoln scholars are good at describing what Lincoln and others around him did and said, and the best scholars explain what those things meant in their time. An unusually thoughtful and patient historian (or a scholar from another academic discipline) might explain that judging the ideas of someone from a different or past culture is at best an unscientific "value judgment," at worst an act of bigotry, because the "values" of the one judging differ from the "values" of the one being judged; therefore, such prejudiced judgment is not admissible in the arena of respectable academic scholarship. The bottom line: we can know what Lincoln said and did, and we might even know if he had the better argument *of his time*, but we cannot know if his ideas or principles are true, simply.

At least since the German theorist G. W. F. Hegel published his *Philosophy of History* in the early nineteenth century, it has been common for intellectuals to describe thinkers from the past as "children of their age" or "men of their time" and to attribute their (allegedly) antiquated ideas to the historical and cultural forces that preceded them.[1] The premise of this view, rightly called *historicism*, is a widely held conviction that human nature, and thus human thought, is evolutionary, that both change as history progresses, and therefore that ideas are more or less bound to the historical context in which they appear. But what if a thinker does not understand his own ideas to be bound by time or place? What if he believes in "an abstract truth applicable to all men and all times," as Lincoln indicates in one of the epigraphs above? In his 1854 Peoria speech, Lincoln offered a clear rejection of the historicist idea: "Repeal the Missouri compromise—repeal all compromises—repeal the Declaration of Independence—repeal all past history, *you still cannot repeal human nature.*"[2] And in his 1860 address at New York's Cooper Institute, Lincoln argued that "[h]uman action can be modified to some extent, but *human nature cannot be changed.*"[3] What is the historicist who believes that human nature *can* be repealed or changed to make of Lincoln's statements?

In a 2000 review of Thomas West's *Vindicating the Founders* (which served as a model for *Vindicating Lincoln*), historian Joseph Ellis criticizes West for suggesting that the principles of the Founders should serve as a guide for

American politics today. West's proposals stem from his belief (like Lincoln's) that human nature is fundamentally unchanging and therefore some ideas entertained by some human beings might be immutable and immune from historical change. In particular, West argues, the natural right principles of political justice, the core of which is formed by the self-evident truth that all men are created equal, remain valid for our generation, just as they were for the generation of the Founders. According to Ellis, however, West makes a grave mistake in believing "that ideas are like migratory birds that can take off in the eighteenth century and land intact in our time."[4]

Ellis's quip is not at all uncommon among academics. In certain respects, Ellis merely restates what historian Richard Hofstadter had cavalierly written more than a half-century earlier in his influential *The American Political Tradition and the Men Who Made It* (1948): "But no man who is as well abreast of modern science as the Fathers were of eighteenth-century science believes any longer in unchanging human nature."[5] Hofstadter assumed that no sophisticated person could doubt the basic Hegelian premise that human nature and human ideas are evolutionary; he assumed, without offering any proof, that there is no permanent human nature and therefore no permanent truths or principles that apply to human beings throughout time. But this historicist position hardly originated with Hofstadter. A generation earlier, in 1922, Carl Becker produced what perhaps is still the most comprehensive theoretical and literary analysis of the Declaration of Independence in *The Declaration of Independence: A Study in the History of Ideas*. Near the end, however, Becker argued that "to ask whether the natural rights philosophy of the Declaration of Independence is true or false is essentially a meaningless question" because the Declaration was "founded upon a superficial knowledge of history," as well as "a naïve faith in the instinctive virtues of human nature." "This faith," Becker almost seemed to lament, "could not survive the harsh realities of the modern world" as increasing "scientific criticism steadily dissolv[ed] its own 'universal and eternal laws' into a multiplicity of incomplete and temporary hypotheses."[6]

Thus, from 1922 through 2000, from Becker to Hofstadter to Ellis, we see three accomplished, influential, and widely honored scholars of American history and politics, all of whom seem to be in perfect agreement that historicism is not only true but incontrovertible.

Without question, there have been many changes in historical research paradigms over the past century of scholarship; in Lincoln and Civil War historiography in particular, historians now pay far more attention to slavery and race as major causes for the sectional conflicts preceding the war than earlier generations of historians did. Yet, the basic premise of historicism—that the ideas of Lincoln and his contemporaries were decisively nineteenth-century ideas that are of little relevance to us today and therefore cannot be judged as right or wrong by modern standards—has not much changed. Ellis's assertion that the ideas of one century cannot "land intact" in another and Hofstadter's insistence that no one "believes any longer in unchanging human nature" fairly describe the intellectual framework within which scholars understand and describe Lincoln. Few academics today who write about Lincoln, in other words, would agree with Lincoln that there is "an abstract truth applicable to all men and all times." Few academics, therefore, can understand Lincoln as Lincoln might have understood himself.

HISTORICISM AND THE "NEEDLESS WAR THESIS"

Following the rise of historical "revisionism" in the 1930s and 1940s, many leading Lincoln scholars either explicitly or implicitly adopted the revisionist thesis that the Civil War had been a "needless" or an "unnecessary" war. This thesis continues to appear in popular Lincoln literature today: Thomas DiLorenzo's 2002 book, for example, is subtitled *A New Look at Abraham Lincoln, His Agenda, and an Unnecessary War.*

The Civil War that Lincoln waged was unnecessary or needless, the revisionists argued, because there is never a *reason* for war. As James G. Randall, one of the fathers of revisionism, explained, "In contrast to the normal and basically valid demand for peace, the desire for war, or the whipping up of hostile feeling by those who begin a war, is artificial, unnatural, and abnormal."[7] In his widely acclaimed *Lincoln the President*, Randall argued that "one of the most colossal misconceptions is the theory that fundamental motives produce war. The glaring and obvious fact is the artificiality of warmaking agitation."[8] "The [Civil War] was the work of politicians and pious cranks!" revisionist Avery Craven exclaimed. "The peoples knew little of each other as realities. They were both fighting mythical devils."[9] The Civil War, as summed up by revisionist Philip Auchampaugh, was "a needless and heartless Brothers' War caused by uncontrolled and irrational emotions."[10]

Was the Civil War a "needless war?" Certainly, it was a costly war. More than six hundred thousand dead Americans, widespread and devastating destruction of property, unprecedented economic debt, and untold emotional torment and suffering were among the terrible sacrifices exacted from the American people. But what were the political, moral, and economic costs borne by millions of blacks who had been held in the most dreadful bondage as chattel slaves? Approximately four million souls were held in slavery in America on the eve of the Civil War. How does one place a price tag on their suffering? In Lincoln's mind, the price that ultimately had to be paid for the sin of slavery was great, maybe more than America could bear. "Every drop of blood drawn with the lash," he foreboded in his second inaugural address, might need to be repaid with "another drawn with the sword."

In presenting the Civil War as "needless," revisionist academics employed a distinction, largely of their own making, between reason, realism, and peace on the one hand and emotionalism, extremism, and war on the other.[11] According to revisionists, the extremism of those who brought about the Civil War was nowhere more apparent than in the strongly held moral "values" of anti- and pro-slavery men, "values" rooted in nothing but irrational emotions. Some in the North, especially Lincoln, insisted that slavery was wrong, while some in the South insisted with equal vigor that slavery was right. Had the anti- and pro-slavery men been "realists," had they been historicists themselves and understood that their own "values" were as contrived and arbitrary as their opponents', war would never have come.

One of the most striking features of "needless war" scholarship prior to the civil rights era of the 1960s was that Stephen Douglas (and James Buchanan to a lesser extent) became the object of vindication precisely because of his refusal to take a public moral stand on the question of slavery. Douglas's "nonjudgmentalism" and his unwavering defense of "diversity," long before those relativistic words became fashionable in American politics and education, led revisionists to argue that it was Douglas, not Lincoln, who understood the "realism" of peace and the "emotionalism" of "artificial" value judgments that lead to war. George Fort Milton's massive 1934 biography of Stephen Douglas was typical. In *The Eve of Conflict: Stephen A. Douglas and the Needless War*, Milton heralds Douglas as a lone voice of calming reason during a period of turbulent storms of irrational emotionalism. "Emotion," Milton writes, "was the basic quality of the renewed anti-slavery drive." While acknowledging the complex and interconnected forces informing the debate over slavery, including "social forces, economic determinants, differences in group cultures, religious factors and moral ideas," Milton nonetheless argues that "running through all these, translating the static into the dynamic and giving unity and coherence, was an overwhelming emotional drive."[12] Douglas "set out to fight the whole brood of emotion-born agitations" by advising all Americans to refrain from making any moral judgments about slavery or slave owners.[13] But, Milton laments, the "realism" of Douglas did not carry the day. Instead, the "emotionalism" of "extremists," including Northern abolitionists, Southern "fire-eaters," and Abraham Lincoln above all, prevailed as public emotions were whipped into such a fevered frenzy that it became impossible to prevent the spilling of blood.

If Lincoln could respond to the revisionist historians, I think he would find it very strange to suggest that morality is "artificial." I think he would also find the historicist premise of revisionism problematic because Lincoln did not think that human nature changes with time. In his seventh and last debate with Douglas, Lincoln argued with especial poignancy that right and wrong are eternal and never change because human nature never changes:

> That is the real issue. That is the issue that will continue in this country when these poor tongues of Judge Douglas and myself shall be silent. It is the eternal struggle between these two principles—right and wrong— throughout the world. They are the two principles that have stood face to face from the beginning of time; and will ever continue to struggle. The one is the common right of humanity and the other the divine right of kings. It is the same principle in whatever shape it develops itself. It is the same spirit that says, "You work and toil and earn bread, and I'll eat it." No matter in what shape it comes, whether from the mouth of a king who seeks to bestride the people of his own nation and live by the fruit of their labor, or from one race of men as an apology for enslaving another race, it is the same tyrannical principle.[14]

Read Lincoln's words again: right and wrong "have stood face to face from the beginning of time." Isn't Lincoln right? Right and wrong will never morph together or transform into something else. Right and wrong "will ever continue to struggle," as Lincoln said, because the nature of human beings, the human capacity for virtue as well as vice, never changes. In being a mixture of reason and passion, intellect and instinct, the nature of human beings today is exactly what it was in the days of Lincoln and the days before him.

Consider, for example, that no moral teaching comes with an expiration date. If one asked Americans to make a list of the most important moralists throughout human history, Jesus Christ would probably be at the top of many lists. For those with some education in philosophy or history, Aristotle and Immanuel Kant would probably rank high, along with other philosophers and theologians. Without denying the important differences between, say, the moral teachings of Jesus's Golden Rule, Aristotle's exposition of moral virtue, and Kant's morality of the categorical imperative, it is interesting that not one of them claims to expire after some date—not one has a "sunset clause" that stipulates some new moral code will be needed after the current one they propose becomes outdated. Jesus, Aristotle, and Kant, while disagreeing on a number of important matters, all assume that what is morally right will *always* be morally right. Why is this? Moral teaching presents itself as valid always and everywhere because all moral teaching assumes that human nature is unchanging and that what is morally right in one time will be morally right in another.

If you are not persuaded, ask yourself this question: what would it mean to say that right is historical, that what is right for human beings evolves over time? Is it conceivable that there might come a day in evolutionary history when the Golden Rule is no longer valid? Is it conceivable that vice might someday replace virtue as a moral good, that cowardliness or recklessness might someday become more virtuous than courage, for example, or that pettiness or vanity might become morally superior to magnanimity? In short, is it conceivable that what you know to be right might someday become wrong, and what you know to be wrong might someday become right? Historicist theorists such as Karl Marx and Friedrich Engels might answer yes. "We reject every attempt to impose on us any moral dogma whatsoever as an eternal, ultimate and forever immutable ethical law," Engels insisted, because he denied "that the moral world has . . . permanent principles that stand above history."[15] But very few ordinary people think that morality is evolutionary or progressive. Certainly Lincoln did not think so.

Precisely because he believed right and wrong do not change, Lincoln worried that as Americans came to embrace slavery, the nation was taking steps backward, not forward. Embracing slavery as a "good" did not signal moral progress, for Lincoln, but moral degeneracy. Further, he understood that the injustice black slaves suffered was far from "artificial" but rather all too real and all too painful. As he said in 1854, "I hate [slavery] because of the monstrous injustice."[16] Lincoln believed that if the moral principle of human equality was true—and he did believe it was true—then any nation that ignores or rejects it can find only suffering and failure. He agreed with George Washington, who had argued in his first inaugural address that "the propitious smiles of Heaven can never be expected on a nation that disregards the eternal rules of order and right which Heaven itself has ordained."[17] Lincoln understood the fight over slavery as much more than a mere dispute over the public policy issue of the day. "Slavery is founded in the selfishness of man's nature—opposition to it, in his love of justice," explained Lincoln. "These principles are in an eternal antagonism; and when brought into collision so fiercely, as slavery extension brings them, shocks, and throes, and convulsions must ceaselessly follow."[18]

With a conviction that right and wrong are both real and unchanging, Lincoln believed that compromising on the principle of slavery ignored or concealed the real evil of the institution and therefore would not lead to peace. Historical revisionists, however, prided themselves on their supposed "realism," according to which they refused to acknowledge moral right and wrong (which they believed were "artificial"). If Lincoln could respond, he would no doubt defend the reality of right and wrong, but he might also suggest that the revisionists' own concocted belief that there is no right and wrong is itself artificial.

Lincoln also understood, as few others of his time did, that as white Americans accepted arguments defending black slavery, to the degree these arguments shaped the American mind, whites were accepting the principle of their own enslavement. In a surviving fragment of a speech from 1854, Lincoln demonstrated the alternatives between universal freedom and universal slavery this way:

> If A can prove, however conclusively, that he may, of right, enslave B— why may not B snatch the same argument, and prove equally, that he may enslave A?
>
> You say A is white, and B is black. It is *color*, then; the lighter having the right to enslave the darker? Take care. By this rule, you are to be slave to the first man you meet, with a fairer skin than your own.
>
> You do not mean *color* exactly?—You mean the whites are *intellectually* the superior of blacks, and, therefore, have the right to enslave them? Take care again. By this rule, you are to be slave to the first man you meet, with an intellect superior to your own.
>
> But, say you, it is a question of *interest*; and, if you can make it your *interest*, you have the right to enslave another. Very well. And if he can make it his interest, he has the right to enslave you.[19]

Lincoln understood that any argument justifying the enslavement of black men equally justified the enslavement of white men and men of all different colors. Throughout his speeches and writings, Lincoln demonstrated repeatedly why chattel slavery was unjust and injurious to black slaves. But he also tried to teach his audience of free whites that the argument for slavery was harmful not only to blacks but to whites as well because it undermined the ground of freedom that whites claimed for themselves. In an 1858 speech in Edwardsville, Illinois, which Lincoln delivered between his debates with Douglas, Lincoln explained in stark terms how pro-slavery principles threatened the freedom of white people no less than that of black people:

> When by all these means you [whites] have succeeded in dehumanizing the negro; when you have put him down, and made it forever impossible

for him to be but as the beasts of the field; when you have extinguished his soul, and placed him where the ray of hope is blown out in darkness like that which broods over the spirits of the damned; are you quite sure the demon which you have roused *will not turn and rend you*? What constitutes the bulwark of our own liberty and independence? . . . Our reliance is in the *love of liberty* which God has planted in our bosoms. Our defense is in the preservation of the spirit which prizes liberty as the heritage of all men, in all lands, every where. Destroy this spirit, and you have planted the seeds of despotism around your own doors. Familiarize yourselves with the chains of bondage, and you are preparing your own limbs to wear them. Accustomed to trample on the rights of those around you, you have lost the genius of your own independence, and become the fit subjects of the first cunning tyrant who rises.[20]

The only principle upon which the argument for freedom could be defended and the argument for slavery defeated was the immutable principle of human equality. For defending the principle that freedom is morally superior to slavery, a generation of revisionist historians labeled Lincoln an "extremist" driven by "emotionalism."

Many scholars have challenged the "needless war" thesis. Ironically, many scholars during and after the 1960s rejected the historical revisionism that denounced Lincoln for too strongly emphasizing the moral problems of race and slavery in favor of "new history," or "social history," which seems almost fixated on the morality of race and slavery (as well as gender, class, and sexual orientation). But the "needless war" thesis is not dead. Michael Holt, whose earlier masterpiece *The Rise and Fall of the American Whig Party* earned him well-deserved academic acclaim, wrote in his 2005 *The Fate of Their Country: Politicians, Slavery Extension, and the Coming of the Civil War* that "shortsighted politicians . . . used the emotionally charged and largely chimerical (i.e., wildly fanciful and unrealistic) issue of slavery's extension westward to pursue the election of their candidates and settle political scores, all the while inexorably dragging the nation toward disunion." DiLorenzo then quotes that sentence approvingly in his most recent book attacking Lincoln, *Lincoln Unmasked*.[21] The "needless war" thesis lives on.

HISTORICISM AND LINCOLN HISTORIANS TODAY

The problems that plagued the revisionists continue to produce the kind of confusion expressed by historian David Donald (a student of the revisionist historian James G. Randall) in his 1995 biography, *Lincoln*, which was awarded the distinguished Lincoln Prize by the Lincoln and Soldiers Institute at Gettysburg College.[22] There is much solid historical information and analysis in Donald's *Lincoln*, and it is a good introduction to the story of Lincoln's life. But when Donald gets to the Lincoln-Douglas debates, he seems almost baffled over why Lincoln and Douglas spent so much time debating the morality of slavery in 1858:

> The controversy over whether the framers of the Declaration of Independence intended to include blacks in announcing that all men are created equal dealt with an interesting, if ultimately unresolvable, historiographical problem, but it was not easy to see just what it had to do with the choice of a senator for Illinois in 1858.[23]

It is odd that Donald suggests that the questions of slavery and the equal rights of blacks had little to do with the job of a U.S. senator in 1858, only four years after the passage of the Kansas-Nebraska Act and the founding of the Republican Party, which demanded the reinstatement of the Missouri Compromise's prohibition against the spread of slavery; less than two years since "Bleeding Kansas" and since Congressman Preston Brooks nearly beat Senator Charles Sumner to death right in the Senate chamber; only a year after *Dred Scott v. Sandford*; and in the midst of the most rancorous fights in Congress over slavery.

More importantly, when Donald characterizes the question of whether the Declaration's proposition of human equality included blacks as an "unresolvable historiographical problem," he denies the very ground of Lincoln's politics. Throughout Lincoln's many pronouncements on the meaning of equality in the Declaration and its relationship to chattel slavery, he made two basic arguments: First, the Declaration's principle of human equality is a self-evident truth precisely because of its universality, because it is rooted in the human nature that all human beings of all colors possess. According to Lincoln, it is a logical and necessary inference that blacks must be included in the Declaration's principle of human equality. To exclude any number of human beings is to fail to understand the self-evidence of the truth of human equality. Second, Lincoln argued that the Founders understood the universality of human equality and believed that blacks were included in the Declaration's principle of equality. Both reason and the historical account of what the Founders believed, according to Lincoln, make it clear that blacks were included in the Declaration's terms. Donald, however, implies that Lincoln's second argument was wrong because the question of what the Founders believed was "unresolvable." Further, Donald makes no attempt to explain or understand whether Lincoln's first argument was right. But if we cannot know whether black men are "men" as the word is used in the Declaration, and if we cannot know whether the Founders included all human beings of all colors when they wrote and ratified the Declaration, then indeed Lincoln appears as nothing but a wily agitator unnecessarily whipping up public emotion over the question of slavery. Donald suggests as much when he writes that during the debates "Lincoln and Douglas naturally exaggerated their differences," some of which were real and others "imaginary," according to Donald.[24] While Donald does not explicitly endorse the "needless war" thesis in his Lincoln biography, its presence is undeniable.

Perhaps most telling about the minds of Lincoln scholars is not what they write but what they do not write. The best mainstream scholars argue that Lincoln was indeed guided by principles of political and moral right, and some do a fine job of explaining how Lincoln understood those principles. But one almost never finds in Lincoln scholarship a defense of those principles *as being true*, or even an attempt to discover if they might be true or if they might apply to us today. After surveying many of the leading Lincoln books, I have concluded that Ellis's remark—that ideas are not migratory birds capable of time travel—sums up the intellectual framework of most Lincoln scholarship. The typical assumption in most Lincoln books, whether stated or unstated, is that Lincoln's ideas lived and died with Lincoln and that whatever meaning they might have had in the nineteenth century, they are irrelevant to our world today. It is simply impossible to know whether Lincoln's ideas are true or not.

Another example of the modern historical mind is the late Philip Paludan, a history professor and Lincoln scholar of much note. His 1994 *The Presidency of Abraham Lincoln*, like Donald's book, won the prestigious Lincoln Prize, and Paludan was named to the advisory committee of the U.S. Abraham Lincoln Bicentennial Commission before his untimely death in 2007.[25] His earlier *"A People's Contest": The Union and Civil War, 1861–1865* is an exhaustive social, cultural, and economic history of the Civil War period. I have learned much from his books and essays, in fact, and it is not from ingratitude that I raise questions about his scholarship. But nowhere in the pages of Paludan's writings does he attempt to discover whether the principles championed by Lincoln are true. I believe I can explain why, but I should warn the reader that trying to pin down Paludan is no easy matter and requires an extended analysis of his writings in order to reveal the subtle historicism that informs his scholarship.

Paludan comes closest to arguing for the truthfulness of Lincoln's principles in an essay titled "Emancipating the Republic: Lincoln and the Means

and Ends of Slavery," which he contributed to *"We Cannot Escape History":
Lincoln and the Last Best Hope of Earth,* a volume edited by the prize-winning historian James McPherson. Paludan argues that, for Lincoln, there
was an intrinsic connection between the principles of the Declaration of
Independence and the U.S. Constitution, but he does not consider whether
that connection is true, whether the Declaration and Constitution truly are
bound together by principle.

Paludan asserts and goes far in proving that Lincoln "was equally committed to the political constitutional system and to the ideal of equality.
Both mattered profoundly to him, and he believed that one could not be
achieved without the other. He fashioned a connection between them, not
during the war years, but before."[26] He writes that "Lincoln's reconciliation
of the Constitution and Declaration rested on both logic and history."
"When Lincoln turned historian," he continues, "the past that he found and
fashioned revealed freedom's Constitution, not slavery's." According to
Paludan, Lincoln saw the events of 1776 and 1787 as constituting one
Founding, not two separate foundings, but he also writes that "Lincoln used
history *to integrate* ideals and institutions."[27] Was the connection between the
principles of the Declaration and the structure of the Constitution present
in the Founding, or was it created by Lincoln's attempt "to integrate" them?
A couple of pages later Paludan reminds us that "Lincoln so interwove the
ideals of the Declaration with the Constitution and the processes of self-
government that attempts to unravel the threads dissolve in his thought."
Did Lincoln *discover* the objective meanings of the Declaration and Constitution and their connection, or was he a master intellectual weaver, threading together and *creating* ideas that were never intended by the authors of
those documents? Paludan does not tell us.

Paludan cites Harry Jaffa as an authority and quotes the following approvingly from Jaffa's essay titled "The Emancipation Proclamation"[28]:

> There has been a tendency to see the two phases of the war as corre
> sponding to the phases in which, first the Constitution, and then the
> Declaration of Independence, were looked to for the principles which
> needed to be vindicated. Needless to say, this implies a tension, if not a
> contradiction, between these two documents, as sources and statements
> of moral and political obligation. But there is no evidence that Lincoln
> himself was ever aware of any such tension or contradiction.[29]

Paludan then comments, "By that I think [Jaffa] means that during the war
Lincoln *integrated* the ideals and institutions of the nation's founding." While
Paludan agrees there was no contradiction *for Lincoln* between the principles

of the Declaration of Independence and the Constitution, he leaves unanswered the supreme question of whether Lincoln's view is correct or not.

Where Paludan once seemed to agree with Jaffa, later in his career he took a critical stance toward Jaffa's latest work on Lincoln, *A New Birth of Freedom*, mainly disagreeing with Jaffa's argument that Lincoln's principles were, and remain, true. "Jaffa is aware," notes Paludan in a 2002 review essay, "that by analyzing thought more than exploring history he will be accused of confusing poetry with history."[30] Paludan quotes Jaffa's reply to this charge, "as Lincoln in effect did reply," that history may require a poet for a people who can describe their "failings and sufferings as intrinsic to the uniqueness of their role as a chosen people." Paludan, however, is not persuaded:

> While it is true that historical circumstances call forth high poets, readers—*especially historian readers*—may have some doubts that we can take that poetry out of history, treating it as an abiding truth rather than as a text that sometimes reflects the blindness of the poet as well as the people he prophecies for. . . . By treating Lincoln's words as immortal truths, Jaffa stumbles, missing the historical environment and the limitations it imposes on its actors.[31]

Throughout *A New Birth of Freedom,* Jaffa goes to great lengths to demonstrate not only Lincoln's principled goals but the calculating prudence he exercised, knowing each step of the way how far public opinion would allow him to reach. This is nowhere better illustrated than in Jaffa's two chapters on Lincoln's first inaugural address, in which he makes visible for the reader the many uncertainties and the "historical environment" confronting Lincoln as he was sworn into office, as well as the "limitations" they imposed on Lincoln's words and actions.

"To contemplate Lincoln's inaugural address," Jaffa explains, "we must try to remove from memory everything that came after it. We must ourselves feel something of the uncertainties that Lincoln felt, to understand how his words reflected his awareness of these uncertainties." Seven states had already seceded when Lincoln took the oath of office on March 4, 1861. Would the South fight to defend its alleged right of secession, and if so, for how long and how hard? Lincoln did not know. Would the North fight to maintain the Union, and if so, for how long and how hard? Lincoln did not know this either. "In composing his inaugural, Lincoln had to articulate the cause of the Union and of the overriding importance of the elected government of the Union taking possession of the offices to which it had been elected," Jaffa reminds his readers, and "he had to do so in a manner calculated to make his fellow-citizens willing to fight for this government, without actually conceding that it would be necessary to fight."

> It was indispensable, because of the eight slave states still in the Union, that [Lincoln] present himself as no less an apostle of peace than of Union. He must not give any countenance to the charge of aggression. He must declare the indissolubility of the Union, and yet declare his pacific intentions, at one and the same time. Although he could not say so, Lincoln certainly knew that the Union would not be preserved without war. But for him to say so, at this juncture, would probably make it impossible to win such a war. The tension between these two imperatives, which set the parameters within which the speech had to be composed, is obvious.[32]

When Paludan refers to "the limitations" that a given "historical environment" places on any historical actor, he cannot mean that Jaffa has ignored the limitations that prudence placed on Lincoln's words and actions. Rather, the key to understanding Paludan's criticism is found in his remark that Jaffa is wrong to treat Lincoln's words as more than poetry that "reflects the blindness of the poet as well as the people he prophecies for," as if those words might enshrine "an abiding truth." The readers most attuned to this problem, according to the historian Paludan, are "historian readers," who may harbor "some doubts" that we can "take that poetry *out of history.*" Paludan, it seems, doubts that Ellis's birds can fly from Lincoln's century to our own.

Paludan understands that "Jaffa's modern goal goes beyond simply providing historical information and interpretation, or even proclaiming Lincoln's genius," rightly identifying Jaffa's purpose as nothing less than "offering an antidote to . . . the premises of historicism, positivism, relativism, and nihilism." Paludan, however, thinks Jaffa exaggerates the influence of these modern doctrines. But he can point to only one historian who he believes has defended the principles of the Declaration of Independence as true and right—that historian is Paludan himself. As evidence, he points the reader to his article "Emancipating the Republic: Lincoln and the Means and Ends of Slavery," which I mentioned above.

Paludan essentially accuses Jaffa of yanking Lincoln out of historical context by treating Lincoln's words as if they might be true, not merely for Lincoln's age but for all ages. Paludan believes that in doing so, Jaffa misses the power of the arguments put forth by Lincoln's antagonists, especially Stephen Douglas, Roger Taney, and John C. Calhoun. "Inspired by his admiration for Lincoln, Jaffa almost never credits the thoughts of Lincoln's opponents." According to Paludan, Jaffa does not see the logic and power of the arguments of Douglas, Taney, or Calhoun because Jaffa views their arguments in light of what he believes to be the unchanging truths captured in Lincoln's words. Were Jaffa to understand better the historical limitations of the "truths" spoken by Lincoln, then he would come to a better appreciation of the "truths" that informed Lincoln's political enemies as well. Lincoln and his enemies were all nineteenth-century men with nineteenth-century ideas; therefore, they were not nearly as far apart from one another as they themselves might have (mistakenly) thought.

Jaffa's defense of the principle of equality in the Declaration of Independence, writes Paludan, rests "on the fact of natural law that everyone who can speak and reason is equally a human being. Since anyone could see that blacks could speak and reason, Lincoln's enemies denied, contrary to reason, an obvious equality."[33] But the problem was not as simple as Paludan makes it out to be. It was not obvious to many that a black man was a man, or if it was obvious, that did not stop many white men from denying it. The evolutionary opinions of the day, originating in eighteenth-century European philosophy and later given scientific credibility by Charles Darwin and others, suggested to many a hierarchy of races within the human species, or that there simply was no distinct human species.[34] Paludan insists that the equality defended by Jaffa is "certainly obvious to us," meaning equality of natural rights is obvious to Americans today. But if that equality rests "on the fact of natural law," as Paludan states earlier, what about the fact that very few educated Americans believe that the natural law is real? As I mentioned in the introduction, when Clarence Thomas was nominated to the Supreme Court in 1991, U.S. senators were incredulous that Thomas, a highly educated and intelligent man, had ventured to offer a public defense of the natural law. I would argue just the opposite of what Paludan argues: neither the equality of the Declaration of Independence (meaning equality of natural rights) nor the natural law upon which it rests is "obvious to us" today. Just the opposite, the natural rights and natural law principles of the Declaration are virtually unknown to the modern American mind.

In what is perhaps a moment of unguarded honesty, Paludan explains what he believes the Declaration of Independence means and why Taney and Calhoun were at least partly right in denying the Declaration's principle of equality. "The Declaration only guarantees full equality for people who are created equal," Paludan asserts, "and it is not necessarily true that because people can speak and reason that they are equal or deserve equal treatment." According to Paludan,

Taney and Calhoun and company simply determined that, while blacks were at some level human, they could neither reason nor speak at the level of white human beings. They were not equal human beings. Hence slaves deserved compassion, better treatment than animals, but not the right to be free. Slaves were not capable of acting like responsible free people; they had not been created equal.[35]

Surely the most zealous slave apologist of the antebellum South could not have provided a better defense of slavery. It is unclear what Paludan means when he writes, "The Declaration only guarantees full equality for people who are created equal." The Declaration of Independence does not *guarantee* anything. The Declaration offers a principle of natural right that encompasses the moral and political obligations bound up in the natural distinction between men and God on the one hand and men and beasts on the other. As no man ought to rule over others without their consent as if he were God, so no man ought to be ruled without his consent as if he were a beast. But these principles of how men *ought* to act are no guarantee that they *will* act accordingly.

Compare what Paludan writes above to what Lincoln said in his speech on *Dred Scott*: in the Declaration's principle that all men are created equal,

[the Founders] meant to set up a standard maxim for free society, which should be familiar to all, and revered by all; constantly looked to, constantly labored for, and even though never perfectly attained, constantly approximated, and thereby constantly spreading and deepening its influence, and augmenting the happiness and value of life to all people of all colors everywhere.[36]

Lincoln understood, as Paludan apparently does not, that the principle of natural equality is a moral principle we strive for, not a guarantee of how people will act today or tomorrow.

When Paludan writes that Taney and Calhoun believed "slaves deserved compassion, better treatment than animals, but not the right to be free," he ignores the fact that both Taney and Calhoun abolished any meaningful distinction between free blacks and slaves; for both Taney and Calhoun, the political hierarchy of who deserves freedom and the protection of the laws and who does not is constructed solely along racial lines (Taney is discussed chapter 3, and Calhoun will be discussed at length in chapter 5).

But Paludan's larger point seems to be that Taney and Calhoun had *reasons* for their opinions, just as Lincoln had his reasons. Each was a reasonable man of his time, in other words. This is what Paludan thinks Jaffa misses because he treats Lincoln's principles as timeless and true: unlike Jaffa, the historian Paludan understands that all political men are really children of their ages, and therefore Lincoln's thought is best understood in light of his time, as is the thinking of Taney or Calhoun. To elevate Lincoln's principles to the status of truth distorts the historical picture, argues Paludan; therefore, Jaffa makes Taney and Calhoun out to be greater villains than in fact they were. If Jaffa took a more sympathetic view of Taney and quit insisting that the principle of equality is true simply, then he might see that Taney believed in "levels of equality," which informed his interpretation of the Constitution as a pro-slavery document. According to Paludan, "It is possible that Taney's failure was that he made the price of black inequality to be disproportionate to their actual inequality. Blacks might deserve the rights to decent treatment, and still not deserve full freedom."[37] How recognizing "levels of equality" is different from making an apology for slavery, Paludan does not say. But we know from the historical evidence of Taney's participation in the 1812 *Gruber* case (which Jaffa notes and which I discuss in chapter 3) that there was more to Taney's thinking on race and slavery than he let on in *Dred Scott*.

More importantly, Paludan fails to see the problem at the core of his assertion that blacks did not "deserve" full freedom. Why does one's color determine whether one is deserving of freedom? If the political philosophy of the Declaration of Independence means anything, it means an arbitrary characteristic such as skin color has no bearing in determining which men deserve freedom. This is precisely what is meant by the universal assertion that all men possess equally the natural rights to life, liberty, and the pursuit of happiness.

More telling is Paludan's comment that the age of Taney and Calhoun "did not find many modern ideas obvious." Lincoln, of course, lived in the nineteenth century, just like Taney and Calhoun; if they could not find modern ideas obvious, could Lincoln? It would certainly strike Lincoln (and the Founders) as strange to describe the principle of human equality, which Lincoln repeatedly calls "ancient," as a "modern idea" because the principle of human equality is at home no less in the Declaration than in the Bible, as well as in the books of Aristotle and Cicero—hardly "modern" texts.

Consider, for example, the biblical injunction to do unto others as one would have others do unto oneself. Who was Jesus's intended audience when he offered the Golden Rule? Was the Golden Rule intended for the several disciples standing immediately before Jesus, or was it intended for all human beings and all times? The Golden Rule applies to all mankind throughout all time precisely because "all men are created equal." Jesus, in other words, assumed the principle of human equality no less than Thomas Jefferson did.

Thomas Jefferson—and who knows more about the meaning of the Declaration of Independence than Jefferson?—explained that the purpose of the Declaration was "not to find out new principles, or new arguments"; rather, "all its authority rests then on the harmonizing sentiments of the day, whether expressed in conversation, in letters, printed essays, or in the elementary books of public right, as Aristotle, Cicero, Locke, Sidney, &c."[38] Jefferson indicated four authors among the "books of public right," two ancients (Aristotle and Cicero) and two moderns (John Locke and Algernon Sidney). For Jefferson, the ideas enshrined in the Declaration can be found in certain old books, as well as in certain new ones, because the foundation of "public right" is natural right, itself rooted in unchanging and eternal human nature that can be discerned by unassisted human reason anywhere and at anytime. In this decisive respect, an ancient mind, such as Aristotle or Cicero, might have discovered and understood more of the unchanging truth than a more modern mind, such as Taney or Calhoun (or perhaps even some academics today). But Paludan seems to reject precisely the idea that ancient minds might be more enlightened than modern ones.

Indicating his preference for the doctrine of a "living" or "evolving" Constitution, Paludan comments that "Taney's constitution might have denied a federal judge the right to make distinctions that a modern judge would make." Taney's Constitution differs from the Constitution interpreted by modern judges, apparently, because Taney lived long ago, and modern judges live today. The unstated premise of Paludan's comment is that the meaning of the Constitution changes with time; it was one thing in Taney's age, and it is another in our age.

In *The Presidency of Abraham Lincoln*, Paludan identifies the "proposition that all men are created equal" with the electoral process, but not in the sense that equality is the ground from which popular government arises, as Jefferson and Lincoln understood. For Paludan, it was through the "electoral process that popular government chose values, carried out ideals, demonstrated and discovered *the unfolding meaning* of the propositions it was founded to defend."[39] I can only conclude that, for Paludan, the proposition of equality enshrined in the Declaration of Independence has no objective and unchanging meaning; its meaning evolves as history moves through the processes of politics and elections. It seems that for Paludan, the historical processes of politics define the proposition; the proposition does not define or guide the historical processes of politics. Americans ought not—nay, cannot—look back to the Founding to understand what the proposition of equality means. Rather, they must look to themselves to discover its "unfolding meaning." The proposition of equality means whatever the Americans of a given age deem or want it to mean. And who in a given age will determine the meaning of equality and the justice that rests upon it? Those who possess power and define for others the meanings of terms, of course. What is this other than the old principle that might makes right?

Lincoln opened his Gettysburg Address by reminding Americans of the actions undertaken four score and seven years earlier, in 1776, when "our fathers brought forth on this continent, a new nation, conceived in Liberty, and dedicated to the proposition that all men are created equal." But for Paludan, the meaning of 1776 was inaccessible to the American people of 1863 (and by implication remains inaccessible to us today) because the Declaration of Independence was much more a statement of irrational, religious "values" than an assertion of objective and unchanging moral facts. In his 1988 *"A People's Contest": The Union and Civil War, 1861–1865*, Paludan asserts that "the definition of the nation itself, subscribed to by both major parties and by minor parties as well, had at its core a set of religious values and ideals."[40] Certainly no one can contest that religion influenced the events of the American Founding. We need only glance at George Washington's first inaugural address, in which he interpreted the American people as a people protected by Divine Providence.

But Paludan makes no distinction between religion, which he characterizes as a "sentiment," and the principles enshrined in the Declaration and other documents of the Founding era. He explicitly contrasts the "rationalistic environment of the American Revolution" with the Declaration of Independence, which, according to Paludan, spoke in religious terms "of self evident truths emerging from the laws of nature and nature's God to which this nation pledged its faith." In the concluding line of the Declaration, however, the "nation" did *not* pledge its "faith" to the "laws of nature and nature's God"; rather, the individual signers of the Declaration mutually pledged *"to each other* our Lives, our Fortunes and Sacred Honor," although they offered their pledge to one another with "a firm reliance on the protection of divine providence."

But Paludan's larger point is that the Declaration's statement of principles is really a form of irrational religion or religious faith. Religion, by definition, rests on a faith in the supernatural, a power or being above or outside the scope of reason. By comparing the Declaration to religion, Paludan implies that the principles of the Declaration are nothing more than objects of irrational faith or sentiment, not rational ideas to be discovered and articulated through reason. Further, as religions change through history and religious doctrines evolve, so does the religious meaning of the principle of human equality. Human equality cannot be the "sheet anchor of American republicanism," which Lincoln believed it was. For Paludan, there is no sheet anchor. The ship of the American republic is adrift, following the currents of history.

Falling into the trap of historicism, Paludan identifies the progress of knowledge with the progress of time. Ideas can be old or new, but they cannot be true throughout time—this forms Paludan's core critique of Jaffa. In the end, writes Paludan, Jaffa needs to judge Lincoln's villains "against their standards as well as ours." Jaffa would likely agree, but I suspect from the foregoing that, for Paludan, the emphasis should be on "their" standards, not "ours."

Paludan admits that when illuminated in the light of Jaffa's coherent rationalism, "Lincoln [becomes] a more coherent thinker." But this is more Jaffa's mind at work than Lincoln's, according to Paludan. By making Lincoln better than he was, Jaffa "weakens Lincoln's adversaries" and "diminishes the extent of Lincoln's intellectual achievements," which also causes Jaffa to fail to see that Taney and Calhoun, "for all their evil deeds and arguments, were not stupid." But given Paludan's historicist premise—they had their standards in the nineteenth century, while we have ours today—it is impossible to see how we can know that their deeds and arguments were "evil." If we cannot know that the ideas of Taney and Calhoun were evil, how can we know if the ideas of Lincoln were good? If the birds of goodness cannot fly from one century to another, neither can the birds of evil. If ideas cannot transcend time, if Lincoln's ideas are trapped in the nineteenth century, then there is nothing inherently important or true to learn from Lincoln. Lincoln becomes irrelevant to later generations. At best, he and his ideas become objects of antiquarianism, quaint and interesting for those with a peculiar interest in old things but of no particular importance for us today. Not only has Paludan, who spent the better part of a lifetime studying Lincoln and explaining the world in which he lived and died, made Lincoln inaccessible and irrelevant to us, but from Paludan's historicist horizon, it is impossible to know whether Lincoln deserves praise or contempt.

THE PROBLEMS OF HISTORICISM

In a 1941 address on German nihilism given at the New School for Social Research, Leo Strauss, one of the few modern academics who questioned the intellectual coherency of historicism, demonstrated the intrinsic connection between the historicist assumption that human ideas are products of historical forces and the depreciation of human reason. Strauss argued, rightly I believe, that there are two fundamental alternatives for understanding human beings in the past (and the present): either human nature, and therefore human reason, is changeable, or it is not. "If reason is changeable," Strauss argued, then "it is dependent on those forces which cause its changes; it is a servant or slave of the emotions and it will be hard to make a distinction which is not arbitrary between noble and base emotions once one has denied the rulership of reason."[41]

According to the historicist thesis, human reason does not freely observe, judge, and comprehend the orderly universe in which human reason finds itself. Rather, it is merely an effect of which history or historical culture is the efficient cause. You, the reader, in other words, do not have the freedom to think for yourself; your thoughts, your ideas, and the categories with which your mind makes sense of the world have been determined for you in varying degrees by the historical and cultural forces that surround you. This historicist account of human reason is sometimes presented today under the banner of *multiculturalism*, according to which it is argued that different people who live in different times or different cultures necessarily possess different "values," which the different times and cultures cause. None of these diverse cultural "values" are better or worse than the others because there is no objective standard of *better* or *worse*, right or wrong. Every decision about what constitutes better and what constitutes worse is itself a *value judgment* informed by cultural bias or prejudice. This multicultural view explains the statement by Liu Huaqiu, the Chinese delegate to the UN Conference on Human Rights quoted in one of the epigraphs at the beginning of the chapter, who insists that the principle that all human beings are created equal and possess equal natural rights is merely an expression of American culture that other people and other nations need not accept as true.

Whether one labels it "multiculturalism" or "historicism," the argument culminates in the conclusion that there is no unchanging, objectively true right and wrong that human reason can discover. Once one has granted the historicist premise that human nature and human reason change with time, it is difficult, if not impossible, to make any objective distinction between what is noble and base, right and wrong. Lincoln said in his 1838 Young Men's Lyceum speech that the preservation of the rule of law and free society depends on our ability to distinguish between "passion" and "reason, cold, calculating, unimpassioned reason."[42] Lincoln echoed *Federalist* 49 in which James Madison had argued that the supreme goal of a well-designed constitution is self-government in the classical sense of the term, the rule of reason over passion: "[T]he reason alone of the public . . . ought to control and regulate the government," Madison explained, while the "passions ought to be controlled and regulated by the government."[43] Madison's *Federalist*, in turn, echoed the argument of classical political philosophy, especially Plato's *Laws*, that law rests upon and is legitimized by reason, the rightful ruler of passion. But according to historicism (and multiculturalism), the human mind cannot make a distinction between reason and passion because there is no principled difference between them; what one might call reason is in truth a function of various historical and cultural passions.

But historicism is fatally flawed by a contradiction within its own argument. Every historicist academic who asserts that Lincoln (or any figure from the past) was a "man of his time" or a "child of his age" assumes that Lincoln's mind was confined to the prejudices of his day: as a nineteenth-century man, Lincoln was limited to understanding nineteenth-century ideas. But what about the academic who makes the assertion? Is his mind limited to the time and culture in which he finds himself?[44] More to the point: in one of the epigraphs at the beginning of the chapter, I quote the historian Thomas Woods asserting in 2004 that Lincoln was a "creature of his age." Is Woods a creature of *his* age? Does Woods think that his own judgment (that Lincoln was a "creature of his age") is merely a reflection of Woods's own historical culture and therefore subject to historical change? Or does Woods claim to be telling us something he believes is *true*? I suspect the latter. Thomas Woods believes that his mind and his reason are free to discover unchanging *truth*. But then, why should we not also assume that Lincoln's mind and reason possessed the same freedom? Why, in other words, is Lincoln a "creature of his age" if Woods is not?

The historicist contradiction can be resolved in one of two ways: The first is to argue that all minds and all truths are relative to history.[45] Woods could be consistent if he said that just as Lincoln was a "creature of his age," so too is Woods himself; therefore, any arguments Woods puts forth in his book are not *true* but merely reflect the cultural biases of his particular place and time. This is to say that there is no Truth with a capital *T*, only *truths* that might be true for certain people at certain times. The problem with this solution is that no one believes there is *no* Truth. Even the argument that *there is no truth* has to be presented as being *true* and thereby undermines itself.

The second way to resolve the contradiction of historicism is to reject historicism and the idea that human nature and human reason evolve in history. We do not need to affirm that all ideas are relative to history. Rather, one can affirm that some ideas transcend time, that there might be Truth, and that human reason is unchanging in the sense that human reason always was and always will be, in principle, capable of discerning the permanent Truths of the world, Truths that exist outside of time, not in time. It is certainly undeniable that among different people in different places and in different times, there exists great diversity in terms of customs, laws, and religions; but it is also undeniable that for all their diversity, human beings are everywhere and always united in that they are the only creatures capable of asking the fundamental moral question, how should we live our lives? Human reason and the fact that human beings alone can question whether they ought to obey their appetites make this capacity possible. In their ability to reason about and question how they live, human beings today are the same as human beings thousands of years ago. That is one truth not affected by time.

Strauss pointed his students and readers toward the second solution as he offered a devastating critique of historicism that allowed educated minds in good conscience to entertain the possibility that some truths or ideas or principles might be eternal and not time bound. But Strauss's influence within academic circles has been limited for at least two reasons, one practical and the other theoretical. The practical problem is that Strauss challenged what has become orthodoxy among academics: the very historicism asserted so confidently by Becker, Hofstadter, and Ellis and assumed by Donald, Paludan, and Woods. Scholars are not likely to abandon the intellectual ground upon which they have built academic careers and reputations.

The theoretical problem is more difficult. The critique of historicism is precisely that, a critique. It is not a positive argument or a proof; it is the dismantling of an erroneous argument. But if historicism is not true, then what is the alternative? Where is the proof that there *is* a universal, unchanging human nature and human reason that can comprehend universal ideas? Here is the rub that leaves many academics unsatisfied: universal human nature cannot be proved, at least not in any empirical or scientific sense that would persuade academic skeptics, because any "proof" of human nature necessarily assumes human nature before the proof even begins. Let me explain.

If I attempt to prove that you are a human being, what is it about *me* that authorizes *me* to conduct such a proof? Do not both you and I assume that I am a human being capable of offering proofs (i.e., reasoning) *before* I attempt to prove anything? You would never sit in front of a dog or a cow or a horse waiting for it to explain a scientific proof, but you might sit and wait for me to explain a proof. Why? What is it that you *know* about me that makes me different from the dog or the cow or the horse? Is it not that

I possess reason (however limited and faulty it might be) and that I am a human being in a way the dog and the cow and the horse cannot be?

Ask further when I try to explain my proof of human nature to you, what it is that qualifies *you* to be a proper *audience* as opposed to a dog, cow, or horse? I assume that most readers would agree with me that it would be ridiculous for me to spend time explaining my proof to a room full of dogs or cows or horses. But how can I know the difference between a reasoning human being on the one hand, and a dog, cow, or horse on the other, if that knowledge requires scientific or philosophic proof? *Who* or *what* will give the proof and *who* or *what* will be capable of understanding it? The answer, of course, is *human beings*.

As my thought experiment shows, we already know the difference between human beings and nonhuman beings *before* any philosophic or scientific proof is offered; in fact, our commonsense knowledge of human nature precedes all philosophic or scientific inquiry. Stated differently, universal human nature and human beings' ability to reason cannot be proved demonstrably, but they are the ground of all demonstrable proofs. Everyone, including the historicist academic, assumes he is a human being capable of reasoning *before* he begins to reason about whether he is a human being capable of reasoning. Everyone, including the historicist academic, assumes the members of his audience are human beings capable of reasoning *before* he asks them to reason with him and question whether they themselves are human beings capable of reasoning. Human knowledge of human nature is prescientific and prephilosophic. It is what some used to call "common sense," but that term carries little authority among the ranks of academics, which is why they are reluctant to give up the theory of historicism: they are so enamored with the world of theory (as opposed to the actual world in which they live) that they demand a philosophic or scientific proof of the (commonsense) alternative to historicism—nothing less than a philosophic or scientific proof of universal human nature will satisfy them—which, as I have explained, is impossible.

Thus continues the present historicist trend in Lincoln scholarship: more and more books on Lincoln are being published every year, and we know more and more details of his day-to-day life, yet Lincoln is increasingly alienated from our modern minds as we alienate our minds from Lincoln's.

In his essay "Postmodernity and Historical Reputation: Abraham Lincoln in Late Twentieth-Century American Memory," sociologist Barry Schwartz rightly equates *postmodernism* with the rejection of *metanarratives*, which means the rejection of "abstract theories and concepts" that provide the self-identity of a nation or group of people.[46] Schwartz argues that for a long time, the story of Lincoln was the supreme metanarrative of the American people; that is, it was by reference to Lincoln and the principles he defended that Americans understood what it meant to be an American. But Schwartz also argues that Americans have forgotten Lincoln's importance and relevance as they have become increasingly disillusioned with all metanarratives and increasingly convinced that all "abstract theories and concepts" are nothing but stories contrived to keep people happy or in line. Americans have abandoned Lincoln as they have become more postmodern, and the surest sign that they have become postmodern is their abandonment of Lincoln.

Schwartz seems to lament the current state of affairs, what he calls a sad phenomenon of "the fading hero," although he never considers that he might be contributing to the problem he bemoans. It is difficult to persuade Americans to embrace the principles of Lincoln if academics like Schwartz keep referring to those principles as "metanarratives" rather than defending them as *true*. (Lincoln would never have said, "Fourscore and seven years ago our fathers brought forth on this continent a new nation . . . dedicated to the *metanarrative* that all men are created equal.") Nevertheless, Schwartz rightly suggests that many Americans today view Lincoln's principles as frozen in the nineteenth century, as relics from the past, while Lincoln believed the principles he discovered are true everywhere and always. Until we confront our own intellectual prejudice in favor of historicism and postmodernism, until we become open-minded enough to consider the possibility that some principles might be true always and everywhere and are not merely "metanarratives," modern Americans who believe Lincoln was a "creature of his age" will find it difficult to understand, much less respect, a man who believed in an "abstract truth applicable to all men and all time."

NOTES

1. In *The Philosophy of History*, which was based on a series of lectures he delivered in 1822 and later, Hegel argued that "the history of mankind does not begin with a conscious aim of any kind," but instead "the whole process of History is directed to rendering this unconscious impulse [into] a conscious one." That is, prior to Hegel's "discovery" that History forms the minds of men, rather than men's minds forming history, no human being, according to Hegel, was conscious of the fact that he was a historical figure, that his thoughts were limited to his historical epoch, that he could not access timeless truth. Every thinking human being in his-

tory, in other words, confused his own time-bound thoughts for timeless truth. In Hegel's thought, there is no timeless truth, except the "truth" that all human thought is historical thought. This conviction informed Hegel's famous line, "every man is a child of his age," found in his book *The Philosophy of Right*. See Georg W. F. Hegel, *The Philosophy of History* (New York: Prometheus Books, 1991 [1837]), 25. See also Georg W. F. Hegel, *The Philosophy of Right* (New York: Prometheus Books, 1996 [1821]), xxviii.

2. Roy P. Basler, ed., *The Collected Works of Abraham Lincoln* (New Brunswick, NJ: Rutgers University Press, 1953), II:271. Cited hereafter as Lincoln, *Collected Works*.

3. Lincoln, *Collected Works*, III:541 (emphasis added).

4. Joseph J. Ellis, "Who Owns the Eighteenth Century?" in *William and Mary Quarterly* 57, no. 2 (April 2000): 417–21.

5. Richard Hofstadter, *The American Political Tradition and the Men Who Made It* (New York: Vintage Books, 1974 [1948]), 20–21.

6. Carl Becker, *The Declaration of Independence: A Study in the History of Ideas* (New York: Vintage Books, 1958 [1922]), 277–79.

7. James G. Randall, *Lincoln the Liberal Statesman* (New York: Dodd, Mead, & Co., 1947), 88.

8. James G. Randall, *Lincoln the President: Springfield to Gettysburg* (London: Eyre and Spottiswoode, 1947), I:76.

9. Avery Craven, "Coming of the War between the States: An Interpretation," *Journal of Southern History* 2, no. 3 (August 1936): 305.

10. Philip G. Auchampaugh, *James Buchanan and His Cabinet on the Eve of Secession* (Pennsylvania: Privately printed, 1926), 201.

11. Thomas J. Pressly, *Americans Interpret Their Civil War* (New York: The Free Press, 1962 [1954]), 293.

12. George Fort Milton, *The Eve of Conflict: Stephen A. Douglas and the Needless War* (New York: Octagon Books, 1980 [1934]), 160.

13. Milton, *The Eve of Conflict*, 169.

14. Lincoln, *Collected Works*, III:315.

15. Robert C. Tucker, *The Marx-Engels Reader*, 2nd ed. (New York: W. W. Norton & Co., 1978), 726.

16. Lincoln, *Collected Works*, II:255.

17. George Washington, First Inaugural Address, in *Washington: Writings* (New York: Library of America, 1997), 733.

18. Lincoln, *Collected Works*, II:271.

19. Lincoln, *Collected Works*, II:222–23.

20. Lincoln, *Collected Works*, III:95 (emphases in original).

21. Thomas DiLorenzo, *Lincoln Unmasked: What You're Not Supposed to Know about Dishonest Abe* (New York: Crown Forum, 2006), 177.

22. David Herbert Donald, *Lincoln* (New York: Simon & Schuster, 1995).

23. Donald, *Lincoln*, 226.

24. Donald, *Lincoln*, 225.

25. Sadly, Professor Paludan passed away on August 1, 2007, while I was making the final edits to the book manuscript.

26. Philip Shaw Paludan, "Emancipating the Republic: Lincoln and the Means and Ends of Slavery," in *"We Cannot Escape History": Lincoln and the Last Best Hope of Earth*, ed. James McPherson (Urbana: University of Illinois Press, 1995), 48.

27. Paludan, "Emancipating the Republic," 53 (emphasis added).

28. Harry V. Jaffa, "The Emancipation Proclamation," in *One Hundred Years of Emancipation*, ed. Robert Goldwin (Chicago: Rand McNally, 1964).

29. Paludan, "Emancipating the Republic," 59, quoting from Jaffa, "The Emancipation Proclamation," 23.

30. Philip Shaw Paludan, "Review Essay of *A New Birth of Freedom: Abraham Lincoln and the Coming of the Civil War*," *Journal of the Abraham Lincoln Association* 23 (2002): 61–70.

31. Paludan, "Review Essay of *A New Birth of Freedom*," 63 (emphasis added).

32. Harry Jaffa, *A New Birth of Freedom: Abraham Lincoln and the Coming of the Civil War* (Lanham, MD: Rowman & Littlefield, 2000), 237–38.

33. Paludan, "Review Essay of *A New Birth of Freedom*," 65.

34. In his essay "Discourse on the Origin and the Foundations of Inequality among Men," written nearly a century before Darwin published *On the Origin of Species*, Jean-Jacques Rousseau subtly suggested experimental cross-breeding between humans and orangutans, "in which the crudest observers could satisfy themselves on the question" of whether men and apes are related biologically. He was fully aware that public morality would probably forbid such experiments, writing, "it must also be regarded as impracticable because what is but an assumption would have to have been demonstrated as true before the test to confirm the fact could be tried in innocence." That is, human beings would need to prove the assumption that men and apes are biological kin to one another before they would be willing to attempt to procreate with apes "in innocence." See Victor Gourevitch, ed., *Rousseau: The Discourses and Other Early Political Writings* (New York: Cambridge University Press, 2004), 208.

35. Paludan, "Review Essay of *A New Birth of Freedom*," 65.

36. Lincoln, *Collected Works*, II:406.

37. Paludan, "Review Essay of *A New Birth of Freedom*," 66.

38. Thomas Jefferson, letter to Henry Lee, May 8, 1825, in *Jefferson: Writings*, ed. Merrill D. Peterson (New York: Library of America, 1984), 1501.

39. Philip Shaw Paludan, *The Presidency of Abraham Lincoln* (Lawrence: University Press of Kansas, 1994), 230 (emphasis added).

40. Philip Shaw Paludan, *"A People's Contest": The Union and Civil War, 1861–1865* (Lawrence: University of Kansas Press, 1988), 341.

41. Leo Strauss, "Address in the General Seminar of the Graduate Faculty of Political and Social Science of the New School for Social Research," February 26, 1941, published in *Interpretation: A Journal of Political Philosophy* 26, no. 3 (spring 1999): 364. See also Leo Strauss, *Natural Right and History* (Chicago: University of Chicago Press, 1965 [1950]), 9–80.

42. Lincoln, *Collected Works*, I:115.

43. Charles R. Kesler and Clinton Rossiter, eds., *The Federalist Papers* (New York: Signet Classic, 2003), 314.

44. See Paul A. Rahe, *Republics Ancient and Modern: New Modes and Orders in Early Modern Political Thought* (Chapel Hill: University of North Carolina Press, 1994), II:3–18.

45. To my knowledge, the two most valiant attempts to defend the position that all thoughts are relative to time, and therefore there is no universal and unchanging truth, are found in the essays and books of Friedrich Nietzsche and Martin Heidegger.

46. Barry Schwartz, "Postmodernity and Historical Reputation: Abraham Lincoln in the Late Twentieth-Century American Memory," *Social Forces* 77, no. 1 (September 1998): 63–103.

5

DO STATES POSSESS
A CONSTITUTIONAL RIGHT
OF SECESSION?

The Founders, who feared federal consolidation of power, saw secession as the ultimate brake on federal abuse and usurpation. However, President Abraham Lincoln, through nothing less than brutal military force, settled that issue. He acted unconstitutionally and with ruthless contempt for the founding principles.

—Walter Williams, "Parting Company," August 7, 2002

It might seem, at first thought, to be of little difference whether the present movement at the South be called "secession" or "rebellion." The movers, however, well understand the difference. . . . They invented an ingenious sophism, which, if conceded, was followed by perfectly logical steps, through all the incidents, to the complete destruction of the Union. The sophism itself is that any State of the Union may, consistently with the national Constitution, and therefore lawfully, and peacefully, withdraw from the Union, without the consent of the Union, or of any other State.

—Abraham Lincoln,
address to Congress in special session, July 4, 1861

The harshest criticisms of Abraham Lincoln hinge on the insistence that each state possessed a constitutional right to secede from the Union under the original Constitution of 1787; therefore, Lincoln was wrong to oppose the eleven states that chose to form a separate confederacy. By refusing to acknowledge the legal right of secession and by resorting to violence in order to maintain the Union, critics insist, Lincoln conducted an unconstitutional and unjust war that effectively obliterated the constitutional principle of federalism and the delicate balance between national power and states' rights that safeguarded individual liberty prior to his presidency.

Walter Williams, an award-winning economist and distinguished scholar and public intellectual known by many Americans for his syndicated writings and his frequent appearances on national radio and television programs (occasionally he guest-hosts the *Rush Limbaugh Show*), writes angrily,

> The War between the States settled by force whether states could secede. Once it was established that states cannot secede, the federal government, abetted by a Supreme Court unwilling to hold it to its constitutional restraints, was able to run amok over states' rights, so much so that the protections of the Ninth and Tenth Amendments mean little or nothing today.[1]

Joe Sobran, another popular syndicated columnist who for many years was a senior editor at *National Review* magazine, wrote in a 2001 column that Lincoln "launched a bloody war against the South, violating the Constitution he'd sworn to uphold."[2]

"From the very beginning," Thomas DiLorenzo insists in *The Real Lincoln*, "the right of secession was viewed by Americans as the last check on the potential abuse of power by the central government." DiLorenzo agrees with Williams that Lincoln's denial of the right to secession betrayed not only the true meaning of the Constitution but the very principles of liberty that the Founders sought to establish:

> In the eyes of the American founding fathers, the most fundamental principle of political philosophy was the right of secession. . . . The United States were founded by secessionists and began with a document, the Declaration, that justified the secession of the American states. That is the language of the Declaration. When it mentions equality, it is the equality of the people of the several states.[3]

Kevin Gutzman restates this argument in his 2007 *The Politically Incorrect Guide to the Constitution*, in which he assumes that many Americans prior to the Civil War had acknowledged the existence of a state's right to secede because "logically, it had to exist, because without such a right the American colonies/states could not have seceded from the British Empire."[4]

In his recent *When in the Course of Human Events: Arguing the Case for Southern Secession*, Charles Adams adds,

The right of secession was so deeply rooted in the early history of the nation that hardly any region did not at one time assert or recognize that right. Thus Lincoln's assertion that secession had no basis in law makes no sense. It is possible that Lincoln simply convinced himself that no right to secede existed. . . . Yet he had been active in law, politics, and debates throughout his life. I submit that it was more than just stubbornness that determined his anti-secessionism. He knew that secession had solid credentials and that once he permitted discussion and debate, he would lose. Logic, history, constitutional law, and even his beloved Declaration of Independence were all against him. He had to close his mind.[5]

From Adams's point of view, Lincoln's opposition to secession was nothing less than opposition to limited government and free society. According to Adams, Lincoln did not save the free union formed by the Founders. He destroyed it. And he did so knowingly and willingly.

Thomas Woods sums up these views defending secession in his popular *The Politically Incorrect Guide to American History*:

The question that no text book bothers to raise is whether the Southern states possessed the legal right to secede. They did. . . . The Constitution is silent on the question of secession. And the states never delegated to the federal government any power to suppress secession. Therefore, secession remained a reserved right of the states.[6]

In many ways, Lincoln's legacy hinges on the question of whether states did in fact possess a constitutional right of secession. If they did, then virtually everything Lincoln did as president during the Civil War was illegal at best, immoral at worst. If Lincoln had no legal power and no constitutional duty to maintain the Union against secessionist movements, then Lincoln might well deserve the title "war criminal" (which many Lincoln critics today have suggested) and should be viewed with contempt. For differing reasons, there remains in America a wide base of sympathy for the cause of secession, ranging from a general suspicion of governmental power coupled with a view of rugged individualism on the Right, to a view on the Left that "tolerance" and "diversity" require that individuals be left alone to pursue whatever "lifestyle" they please. From these points of view, Lincoln's iconic status is ambiguous at best.

But if states did not possess a constitutional right of secession, then Lincoln might be vindicated not only on constitutional but on moral grounds, as well as on the grounds of the social compact theory of the Founding. Perhaps

Lincoln is the iconic American. In order to answer these questions, I will examine Lincoln's arguments against secession. I then turn to the most prominent defender of secession in American history, John C. Calhoun, and allow him to make his case so that the reader can better judge what to make of Lincoln with regard to the question of secession.

LINCOLN ON SECESSION

Immediately after Lincoln was elected president in November 1860, but four months before he was sworn into office, secession movements spread throughout the South, with South Carolina taking the lead. By the time Lincoln delivered his inaugural address on March 4, 1861, seven states had already passed ordinances of secession and elected a provisional Confederate government under the authority of a new Confederate Constitution. These seven Southern states claimed to secede not because of any injury caused directly by the Lincoln administration—he was not yet president— but because of various perceived threats to their liberties and interests. It was a preventative measure from their point of view, a "preventative secession," in their case, rather than a "preventative war," about which we hear so much today. Eventually, four more states joined the original seven, raising the total to the eleven states that would make up the short-lived Confederate States of America (CSA).

Lincoln never acknowledged (at least not intentionally) the political sovereignty of the CSA because he did not believe any state possessed a constitutional right of secession. (I say "not intentionally" because when Lincoln declared a "blockade" of Southern ports, he quickly learned that "blockade" was a legal term of art that, according to international law, applied to belligerent nations. If Lincoln did not want to acknowledge the independence and sovereignty of the CSA, he should have simply ordered the ports to be "closed" rather than ordering a "blockade.") From Lincoln's point of view, the Union was unbroken, although he understood that there was significant discontent throughout the South and that a sizable number of Southern citizens had gathered to draft and ratify ordinances and resolutions declaring secession, all of which Lincoln believed had no constitutional, legal, or otherwise binding authority. When Southern cannons fired on April 12, 1861, upon Fort Sumter in the harbor of Charleston, South Carolina, Lincoln interpreted the act as a rebellious assault against the U.S. government and called up a force of seventy-five thousand volunteer troops to squelch the revolt. In the days, weeks, and months that followed, Lincoln took many extraordinary measures, including appropriating money from the Treasury without the approval of Congress (which was not in session when the war began), suspending the writ of habeas corpus, and other actions that would almost certainly be deemed unconstitutional during any normal time of peace, in order to suppress the rebellion and restore the constitutional union. The Civil War had begun.

Prior to his inauguration as president, Lincoln reflected deeply on the question of secession, and his thoughts crystallized first in his inaugural address and then in his July 4, 1861, message to Congress in special session. Lincoln took a circuitous train route from Illinois to Washington, D.C., during which he made many short speeches from the rear platform of the train. Along the way, Lincoln asked on more than one occasion why a state could secede but not a county. The implication of Lincoln's question is clear: if the purpose of secession is to protect a minority from an oppressive majority, which, as I discuss below, is exactly the argument formulated by the Southern architect of session, John C. Calhoun, then any argument for a state to secede legally and peacefully from the Union must be an argument for counties to secede from states. And any argument for counties to secede from states must be an argument for towns to secede from counties, neighborhoods from towns, families from neighborhoods. The ultimate and irreducible minority is the individual citizen. Again, if the purpose of secession is to protect a minority against the majority, why may not an individual citizen secede whenever he is displeased by the laws or policies under which he lives? And after individuals become convinced that they have a legal right to secede, that each individual has the legal right to reject the outcome of any election with which he happens to disagree, does not civil society under law become impossible? In principle, secession implies that no law can be truly binding, that anyone who dislikes a law has the right to declare himself or herself exempt from its reach. This is why Lincoln argued in his first inaugural address that "the central idea of secession is the essence of anarchy."[7] A state of anarchy, or a state of lawlessness, is characterized by the rule of might, or brute force. Lincoln understood clearly that secession represents nothing less than a movement away from civil society back toward the state of nature and anarchy, a movement away from freedom under law toward slavery without law.

Lincoln consistently maintained that the people of the Southern states, like all people, possessed a natural right of revolution but not a legal right of secession, a distinction that was, and continues to be, blurred or ignored by many Lincoln critics. "All profess to be content in the Union, if all constitutional rights can be maintained," Lincoln rightly observed in his first inaugural address. "Is it true, then, that any right, plainly written in the Constitution, has been denied?" America was born out of revolution, and if

Southerners had been injured seriously and were being governed without their consent, they had no less a natural right of revolution than the Americans of 1776 had. But how had Lincoln injured the South? What part of the Constitution had he ignored or violated? He was not even president when South Carolina became the first state to declare secession from the Union! The South had no answer. The seceding states could not justify their actions by recourse to the natural right of revolution. In the weeks, months, and years before his inauguration as president, Lincoln was merely private citizen Lincoln with no more of a voice in the actions of government than any other citizen. Private citizen Lincoln had done nothing to injure the people of the Southern states, and on the sensitive point of slavery, he had stated repeatedly, and he repeated again in his first inaugural address, "I have no purpose, directly or indirectly, to interfere with the institution of slavery in the States where it exists" because "I have no lawful right to do so, and I have no inclination to do so."[8]

From Lincoln's point of view, the Union of the Constitution is perpetual. "I hold that in contemplation of universal law, and of the Constitution," Lincoln announced in his first inaugural address, "the Union of these States is perpetual." "Perpetuity is implied, if not expressed, in the fundamental law of all national governments," Lincoln continued, because "no government proper ever had a provision in its organic law for its own termination. Continue to execute all the express provisions of our national Constitution, and the Union will endure forever—it being impossible to destroy it, except by some action not provided for in the instrument itself."[9] The Constitution contains no provision for its own demise. Only two conditions might bring about the end of the constitutional union: One is if some Americans violate the Constitution itself and infringe on the rights of others causing others to exercise their natural right to replace the Constitution and establish a new government (an act authorized not by the written law of the Constitution but by the natural law). The second is if some external power, such as an invading army, destroys the authority of the Constitution and prevents its provisions from being put into practice.

"The Union," Lincoln maintained, "is much older than the Constitution."[10] The Constitution itself supports Lincoln's argument. The preamble announces that among the purposes of ordaining the Constitution is the effort to "form a more perfect Union," clearly indicating that a union of some kind existed prior to the Constitution. In Article VII, the framers dated the Constitution by two references: to the seventeenth day of September in the year 1787, and "of the Independence of the United States of America the Twelfth." If September 1787 was the twelfth year of independence, then independence began in 1776. The Constitution, in other words, recognizes the Declaration of Independence of 1776 as the origin of the Union, which the Constitution seeks to make "more perfect."

According to Lincoln, the First Continental Congress's adoption of the 1774 Articles of Association represented Americans' first contemplation of themselves as a *people*, as *Americans* instead of British subjects. Concluding with the words "we do solemnly bind ourselves and our constituents, under the ties aforesaid, to adhere to this association," the Articles of Association marked the Continental Congress as the beginning of the American union, although there were ambiguity and differences of opinion among Americans at this early date regarding the status of their sovereignty. The Union, Lincoln continued, was then "matured and continued by the Declaration of Independence in 1776."

In *Lincoln Unmasked*, DiLorenzo dismisses Lincoln's argument that the Union preceded the states as an "absurd assertion" and "falsehood."[11] The idea that the American union was born with the Declaration of Independence, according to DiLorenzo, was simply part of "Lincoln's big lie."[12] Yet, both Thomas Jefferson and James Madison, the primary author of the Declaration and the Father of the Constitution, respectively, referred to the Declaration as "the fundamental act of Union."[13] Still, DiLorenzo does not believe Jefferson and Madison, at least not on this occasion. Asserting the "absurdity of Lincoln's claim in his First Inaugural address that the states were not sovereign," DiLorenzo insists "they certainly were."

> [State sovereignty] was understood by the founding fathers and by statesmen for decades thereafter. Neither President Jefferson nor his successor, President Madison, believed that they had any authority to use military force to compel a state to abide by their political dictates. In fact, it's impossible to believe that the thought even would have entered their minds.[14]

Perhaps it is impossible for DiLorenzo to believe that Jefferson would ever entertain the thought of using "military force to compel a state to abide by" his political dictate, but it was quite possible for Jefferson himself to think such thoughts. In fact, Jefferson did just that as president in attempting to enforce compliance with his embargo policies. As Leonard Levy describes it in *Jefferson and Civil Liberties*,

> The embargo, begun as a means of coercing and starving England and France into respect for American rights, rapidly became an instrument of coercion against American citizens. To avoid foreign war, Jefferson made

domestic war. . . . Jefferson inclined to attaint and blockade a whole lo-
cality, because some of its citizens dared to speak against his embargo
policies. . . . [President Jefferson], shortly after accepting the doctrine that
the ends justify the means, ordered out the regular army as a normal enforcement agency, without the formality of public proclamation, and
without lawful authority. He permitted his Attorney General to experiment with a treason prosecution as another means of enforcement. He
deliberately and lawlessly ordered collectors of the customs to ignore a
decision by a Supreme Court justice who ruled that the President had
acted without authority. He recommended a new enforcement act that
subverted the Bill of Rights and possessed little semblance of constitutionality. The gentle libertarian philosopher, who never forgot the painful
criticism that he had been a timid and indecisive war governor of Virginia, had become a presidential autocrat.[15]

One need not defend Jefferson's actions in enforcing the embargo—I happen to think they were constitutionally and morally questionable—to recognize that DiLorenzo simply skips over evidence not to his advantage as
he attempts to conjure a distinction between Lincoln on the one hand and
Jefferson and Madison on the other.

Despite Lincoln's appeal at the end of his inaugural to the patriotism of
his fellow citizens in the South, as well as to the "better angels of our nature," secessionists refused to back down, and within a few weeks of the
Southern attack on Fort Sumter, the country was at war. It is hard to imagine today, but in Lincoln's time (when government was much smaller and
did much less than it does now) an entire session of Congress might last only
a few months, or even only a few weeks. The Thirty-seventh Congress,
which had been elected in November 1860, was not slated to convene until more than a year later in December 1861. With the bombing of Fort
Sumter in April 1861, Lincoln had little choice but to begin fighting the
Civil War without approval from, or consultation with, Congress. Exercising his power under Article II, Section 3 of the Constitution, he called for
Congress to convene in a special session scheduled for July 4, 1861, in order
to ask for congressional approval for his emergency actions (which Congress
promptly granted) and to request additional funding for the war effort. In
preparation for the special session, Lincoln drafted a message that contained
the fullest articulation of his thinking on the question of secession.

In the first several pages of his message, Lincoln recounted the events
the bombardment of Fort Sumter had triggered and detailed the actions he
had taken in response before he turned to the secession issue. Secession,
Lincoln argued, ultimately represents a rejection of constitutional govern-

ment and government by free election. He characterized American constitutionalism as that process through which political disputes are decided by ballots instead of bullets:

> Our popular government has often been called an experiment. Two points in it our people have already settled—the successful establishing and the successful administering of it. One still remains—its successful maintenance against a formidable internal attempt to overthrow it. It is now for them to demonstrate to the world, that those who can fairly carry an election, can also suppress a rebellion; that ballots are the rightful and peaceful successors of bullets; and that when ballots have fairly and constitutionally decided, there can be no successful appeal back to bullets; that there can be no successful appeal except to ballots themselves, at succeeding elections. Such will be a great lesson of peace; teaching men that what they cannot take by an election, neither can they take it by a war; teaching all the folly of being the beginners of a war.[16]

Lincoln here described free government operating by majority rule at the ballot box. But majority rule presupposes the equal rights of all those who will compose the majority and minority. The rights of some can never be the legitimate object of political dispute; they cannot be put up for vote in an election because they are the very ground of free elections. Free government results from a voluntary compact between each individual and the whole and between the whole and each individual, and the purpose of government will be to protect the equal rights of all who have agreed to the compact, whether they belong to the majority or a minority. With the guarantee that their rights will be secure regardless of the outcome of an election, the recourse for a losing minority is the next election in which they can try to become the new majority. But the losers of an election must accept its results and wait to try again. The Southern argument for secession was based precisely on a refusal to accept the result of a free, legal, and legitimate election.

Now contested, Lincoln explained, was "the position that secession is consistent with the Constitution—is lawful, and peaceful." But he quickly showed the injustice of secession as the United States, as one union, had accepted certain debts and responsibilities:

> The nation purchased, with money, the countries out of which several of these States were formed. Is it just that they shall go off without leave, and without refunding? The nation paid very large sums, to relieve Florida of the aboriginal tribes. Is it just that she shall now be off without consent,

or without making any return? The nation is now in debt for money applied to the benefit of these so-called seceding States, in common with the rest. Is it just, either that creditors shall go unpaid, or the remaining States pay the whole? A part of the present national debt was contracted to pay the old debts of Texas. Is it just that she shall leave, and pay no part of this herself?

Lincoln also reminded Americans that they presented themselves as a union bound together by a government when they sought loans from foreign countries:

Again, if one State may secede, so may another; and when all shall have seceded, none is left to pay the debts. Is this quite just to creditors? Did we notify them of this sage view of ours when we borrowed their money? If we now recognize this doctrine by allowing the seceders to go in peace, it is difficult to see what we can do if others choose to go, or to extort terms upon which they will promise to remain.[17]

Lincoln then inquired about the national constitution the Confederates had already ratified and whether they had incorporated secession as a legal feature of their constitution:

The seceders insist that our Constitution admits of secession. They have assumed to make a national constitution of their own, in which, of necessity, they have either discarded or retained the right of secession, as, they insist, it exists in ours. If they have discarded it, they thereby admit that, on principle, it ought not to be in ours. If they have retained it, by their own construction of ours they show that to be consistent they must secede from one another, whenever they shall find it the easiest way of settling their debts, or effecting any other selfish or unjust object. The principle itself is one of disintegration, and upon which no government can possibly endure.[18]

Lincoln here repeated a prediction that he had offered in his first inaugural address:

If a minority, in such case, will secede rather than acquiesce, they make a precedent which, in turn, will divide and ruin them; for a minority of their own will secede from them, whenever a majority refuses to be controlled by such minority. For instance, why may not any portion of a new confederacy, a year or two hence, arbitrarily secede again, precisely as portions of the present Union now claim to secede from it.[19]

DiLorenzo thinks this was preposterous. "Lincoln theorized that allowing the Southern states to secede might cause a rash of copycat secessions," he comments, "but this never happened, either in the United States or anywhere else."[20] In fact, what Lincoln argued in speech, the Confederacy proved in practice: By 1864, leading Georgians, including Confederate vice president Alexander Stephens and Georgia governor Joseph E. Brown, both of whom vehemently opposed conscription, the suspension of habeas corpus, and the general centralization of confederate governmental power, were leading a movement for Georgia to secede from the confederacy![21] Had the CSA endured any longer than it actually did, it is highly likely that the Confederacy would have been dissolved by multiple internal secessions.

In principle, secession stands opposed to the very idea of government. A government possesses the power to govern, to command, to rule. To say that a state (or any other group) possesses the right of secession is to say that the government over it is not truly a government, that those who want to secede can ignore its commands and rules. In principle, the difference between government and secession truly is the difference between government and anarchy, as Lincoln argued. If secession is right, then government is impossible. If government is impossible, only anarchy (or despotism) remains. But Lincoln believed government—good government, at least—was both desirable and possible. And he believed he was conserving the principled arguments of the Founders regarding the ends and means of government.

POLITICAL ENDS: THE FOUNDERS' ARGUMENT

The first and most important thing to understand about the American Founders' political project is that America was founded upon an idea. While most countries throughout history trace their origins and their claim to rule to some ethnic or sectarian religious tradition, the American Founders proposed to form a new political society upon an abstract idea: that all men are born free and equal and that the purpose of any legitimate government is to protect the equal natural rights of all the people who live under it.

The American Founders held that any reasoning human being, at any time and in any place, could comprehend the truth of human equality because it is a principle rooted in human nature. By nature, every human being possesses equal rights; every human being is born equally free. There is no hierarchy of dominion among humans by nature, no natural principle of who rules and who is ruled. As Jefferson once wrote, "The mass of mankind has not been born with saddles on their backs, nor a favored few booted and spurred, ready to ride them legitimately, by the grace of God."[22] This is the simple meaning of the famous line from the Declaration of Independence, "We hold these truths to be self evident, that all men are created equal."

The political implications of this idea are radical. It challenges every kind of political rule based on artificial hierarchy, be it the divine right of kings or the rule of a "master" class over an "inferior" class of people. It also means that for a particular government whose authority derives from universal human nature, one need not belong to any particular class, tribe, or religion to be an equal citizen. Citizenship, in principle, is open to anyone who recognizes that the natural source of his own rights is at once the source of the rights of all others and that the protection he desires for his own rights he must extend to his fellow citizens, regardless of rank or station. Nothing is so common in America, yet so uncommon in human history, as seeing people who slaughtered one another in their Old World settings—Greeks and Turks, Protestants and Catholics, Palestinian Arabs and Jews—living in America as equal fellow citizens, and possibly even as friends. In America, religious and ethnic differences are meant to be removed from the political process and to have no bearing on the protection of law because rights are understood to belong equally to every man and woman, regardless of religious beliefs, skin color, or cultural heritage. The timeless and universal idea of human equality is the central idea from which the precepts of American government and citizenship flow. It was the ultimate cause and justification for American independence.

Acting on the principle of human equality and equal natural rights, the American Founders formed a government, or a "social compact" as they often called it, the end or purpose of which was to protect those rights:

- The Declaration of Independence, proclaiming that all human beings possess by nature certain "unalienable rights," including the rights to "life, liberty, and the pursuit of happiness" among others, asserts "that to secure these rights, governments are instituted among men."
- Later, the Declaration states that the end or goal of government is "to effect" the "safety and happiness" of the people.
- James Madison echoes this in *Federalist* 43, writing "that the safety and happiness of society are the objects at which all political institutions aim."
- The Constitution's preamble states the following ends of American government: "We the people of the United States, in order to form a

more perfect union, establish justice, insure domestic tranquility, provide for the common defense, promote the general welfare, and secure the blessings of liberty to ourselves and our posterity, do ordain and establish this Constitution for the United States of America."

- In *Federalist* 51, Madison writes, "Justice is the end of government. It is the end of civil society. It ever has been, and ever will be pursued, until it be obtained, or until liberty be lost in the pursuit."

There is a logic to these different ends; they are aspects of one sovereign purpose. By understanding those ends and that purpose, the connection between the Declaration of Independence and the Constitution becomes intelligible as the means (the Constitution) relates to the ends (the Declaration). As I mentioned earlier, in its very first sentence, the Constitution points to the Declaration: the Constitution is established in order to "secure the blessings of liberty," and what is a blessing other than a gift from God? The liberty that the Constitution is designed to protect is not government granted but God given. Thus, the Constitution recognizes that human beings have been "endowed by their Creator with certain unalienable rights," among which is the right to liberty, as stated in the Declaration. In a draft speech, Lincoln summed up the relationship between the Declaration and Constitution in biblical terms:

> The assertion of that principle [that all men are created equal and possess equal natural rights], at that time, was the word, "fitly spoken" which has proved an "apple of gold" to us. The Union, and the Constitution, are the picture of silver, subsequently framed around it. The picture was made, not to conceal or destroy the apple, but to adorn and preserve it. The picture was made for the apple—not the apple for the picture.[23]

The first and most basic purpose of government is to secure the "safety" of the citizens. This means securing their rights to life and liberty. Government must protect citizens from foreign enemies, as well as from fellow citizens who threaten their rights. The first instance requires strong national defense and a prudent foreign policy; the second requires effective criminal laws that justly punish those citizens who violate the rights of others.

Securing the safety of the people is a necessary condition to fulfill the other purposes of government. Only when the lives, liberties, and properties of citizens are secure against foreign and domestic dangers will the people enjoy the "domestic tranquility" needed to "establish justice." And the Founders understood not only justice but all the moral virtues to be essential ingredients of the citizenry's "general welfare." As Jefferson once remarked, man is "inherently independent of all but moral law."[24] The "moral law" is the source of the rights, duties, and happiness of man. The Founders understood the principles of free government within this framework of moral law. As the Virginia Declaration of Rights proclaims, the blessings of liberty depend on "a firm adherence to justice, moderation, temperance, frugality, and virtue."[25]

In the Founders' view, a government that succeeds in securing a safe, free, tranquil, and moral society will have succeeded in establishing, as far as human design is capable, the conditions for achieving the ultimate purpose of government, the "happiness of society." These noble ends, to a large extent, inform the means most proper to legitimate and good government.

POLITICAL MEANS: THE FOUNDERS' ARGUMENT

In *The Politically Incorrect Guide to the Constitution*, historian Kevin Gutzman denies the relevance of the Declaration of Independence to the American Founding:

> And what did the Declaration declare? That the colonies were independent states. Politicians and historians have made a habit of fixating on the second paragraph of the Declaration, which includes a restatement of Richard Bland's account of the origin and just powers of government (including the statement "We hold these truths to be self-evident"). They say that America was founded on that. But it wasn't.[26]

On July 6, 1776, John Hancock, in his capacity as president of the Continental Congress, ordered the transmission of the newly ratified Declaration of Independence to the American people. Accompanying the Declaration was a letter by Hancock in which he announced to all Americans, "The important consequences to the American states from this Declaration of Independence, *considered as the ground and foundation of a future government*, will naturally suggest the propriety of proclaiming it in such a manner, that the people may be universally informed of it."[27] The "ground and foundation" of American government, according to Hancock and the Continental Congress that he represented, contrary to Gutzman's argument, are to be formed by the principles of the Declaration of Independence, principles rooted in and springing from the self-evident truth that all men are created equal.

But that still leaves an important question: if all men possess equal rights by nature, what means should be employed to protect those rights? Again, the Founders looked to human nature for an answer. James Madison famously asked in *Federalist* 51, "What is government itself but the greatest of all reflections on human nature? If men were angels, no government would be necessary."[28] If men were angels, that is, if men were wholly good and wholly reasonable, there would be no need for government because every man would naturally respect the rights of others without government or law. But men are not angels. In addition to his reason, man possesses self-ish passions and appetites; sometimes men follow these passions and violate the rights of others. Thus, there is a need for some way to restrain the baser and often destructive elements of human nature. Government meets this need.

The same human nature that indicates the need for government also indicates the need that the government's foundation be legitimate, that it be based on the consent of the governed. Traditionally, most governments in human history have operated without this consent. Pharaohs, kings, and emperors have claimed special dispensation from God that supposedly authorized them to rule over other men without their sanction. In America, these traditions were rejected.[29] The preamble of the Massachusetts Constitution of 1780 expresses the idea of government by consent in these terms: "The body-politic is formed by a voluntary association of individuals: It is a social compact, by which the whole people covenants with each citizen, and each citizen with the whole people, that all shall be governed by certain laws for the common good."[30] Free government is government founded on a "social compact," where each citizen agrees with the whole, and the whole agrees with each citizen, to be governed by laws directed toward the common good of the people, which means laws that protect the equal rights of each citizen to promote the happiness of all.

Government by consent is foremost a moral principle. It is *wrong* for one man to rule another without the other's consent. And just as no person who does not wish to be a slave should enslave another, so governments should not rule without the consent of the governed. This is what George Washington meant in his first inaugural address when he said that "the foundation of our national policy will be laid in the pure and immutable principles of private morality."[31] The principles of private morality are immutable because they derive from human nature, which is immutable, and human nature is at once the cause of government and the standard by which all governments are to be judged. The needs of human nature make government necessary. The capacities of human nature make government possible. And where there is good government, human nature will flourish.

From the simple observation that human beings are not angels, it follows that absolute, or unlimited, government is unsuitable for human beings.

The only form of government appropriate for beings of limited wisdom and limited goodness is government of limited power. When government becomes too large and too powerful, government represents a threat to, rather than a protector of, the rights and happiness of the people. This underlies Madison's famous statement in *Federalist* 51:

> If angels were to govern men, neither external nor internal controls on government would be necessary. In framing a government which is to be administered by men over men, the great difficulty lies in this: You must first enable the government to control the governed; and in the next place, oblige it to control itself.[32]

To limit the powers of the government, the Founders defined and distributed those powers in a written constitution. Among its features, the Constitution separates political power between three coordinated branches of the national government—a bicameral legislative branch with staggered elections and different lengths of office, an executive branch chosen indirectly by the Electoral College, and an independent judicial branch equipped with the power to strike down unconstitutional laws—and gives to each branch significant power to check abuses or usurpations of power by the others. This "separation of powers" is intended to make it difficult for any one branch to dominate the whole government. As James Madison wrote in *Federalist* 47, "The accumulation of all powers, legislative, executive, and judiciary, in the same hands . . . may justly be pronounced the very definition of tyranny."[33] The Constitution aims to keep the separate powers in separate "hands," making it difficult to combine and exercise political power for tyrannical purposes. Further, the Constitution provides a fairly specific list of what government can and cannot do. Article I, Section 8 of the Constitution, for example, enumerates the powers of the legislative branch, while the next section, Article I, Section 9, places restrictions on its powers.

The Constitution also separates power between the national government and state and local governments, something often referred to as "federalism." The proper objects of the national government's power are few, pertaining mainly to those problems or duties that are national in scope. The bulk of legislative and regulatory power, what the Founders called the "police powers" of regulating the health, safety, and morals of the people, remains with the states. But one cannot read the Constitution and fail to notice that it *does establish* a national government, one that is more than a mere confederacy of states, even though some secessionists, such as Kevin

Gutzman, continue to insist that "there was nothing in the Declaration of Independence, the Articles of Confederation, or the ratification process of the Constitution that created a national (rather than federal) government."[34] Article I, Section 10, for example, places important restrictions on powers states might otherwise exercise. The third paragraph of that section in particular commands that "no state shall, without the consent of Congress . . . enter into any agreement or compact with another state." In other words, states may enter into an "agreement" or a "compact" with other states, but only with the consent of Congress. Some states may find it useful, economically, socially, or otherwise, to make certain agreements with other states—for example, neighboring states might make agreements with others regarding the use of a common river or mineral rights for adjacent lands—but the requirement that Congress consent to such agreements ensures that they are not designed to injure the common good or the integrity of the Union. Any agreement between individual states must be authorized by a constitutional majority of Americans as represented in Congress. The first paragraph of Article I, Section 10 is even more prohibitory: "No state shall enter into any treaty, alliance, or confederation."[35] Further, Article IV, Section 4 of the Constitution authorizes the national government to "guarantee to every state in the union a republican form of government," meaning that the national government has the constitutional power to oppose any monarchical or other nonrepublican form of government that one or several of the states might attempt to implement.

Timothy Sandefur has taken up these questions in a recent essay. Sandefur is interesting because he is a libertarian lawyer and constitutional scholar, but he parts ways with his fellow libertarians when they attempt to defend the idea that the Constitution merely establishes a confederation and that states possess a constitutional right of secession. Sandefur has emphasized, for example, that many anti-Federalists opposed the Constitution *precisely because* they understood that, in certain respects, the states would be subordinated to government by the Union's Constitution:

> "Cincinnatus," for instance, complained that "such is the anxiety manifested by the framers of the proposed constitution, for the utter extinction of the state sovereignties, that they were not content with taking from them every attribute of sovereignty, but would not leave them even the name.—Therefore, in the very commencement they prescribe this remarkable declaration—*We the People of the United States.*" The "Federal Farmer" wrote that "when the people [of each state] shall adopt the proposed [constitution] . . . it will be adopted not by the people of New Hampshire, Massachusetts, &c., but by the people of the United

States. . . ." Robert Yates opposed ratification of the Constitution precisely
on these grounds: he admitted that "if it is ratified, [it] will not be a compact entered into by the States, in their corporate capacities, but an agreement of the people of the United States as one great body politic. . . . It
is to be observed, it is not a union of states or bodies corporate; had this
been the case the existence of the state governments might have been secured. But it is a union of the people of the United States considered as
one body, who are to ratify this constitution, if it is adopted."[36]

That is, not only did the supporters of the Constitution of 1787 understand
that it would form a national government proper and that states would fall
under the jurisdiction of that national government, at least to some extent,
but even the most vehement opponents of the Constitution agreed!

Under the Constitution and the "more perfect union" formed by it,
therefore, states are governed to a significant extent by the national government. While the Constitution reserves a large realm of political power for
the states, it is difficult to imagine how a state might have the constitutional
authority to change the nature of the Union by seceding when it does not
even have the authority to institute any form of government it desires for
its own internal governance. Further, to grant the national government certain (albeit limited) constitutional powers over the states, while simultaneously authorizing states to secede any time they dislike the exercise of those
powers, would effectively nullify the powers of the national government. In
other words, if states possess a legal right to secede, then there can be no
national government in the strict sense of the word "government": the national government, the source of national law, would have no power to enforce the Constitution against those who disagreed with or disliked some of
its laws. As Lincoln remarked in his first inaugural address, if states possessed
a legal right of secession under the Constitution, then the Union of the
Constitution was not "more perfect" but less perfect than the Articles of
Confederation *and Perpetual Union*.[37]

Perhaps most importantly, from the Founders' point of view, the ultimate means of checking abusive governmental power lay in the natural
right of revolution. As the Declaration of Independence explains, "When
a long train of abuses and usurpations, pursuing invariably the same object,
evinces a design to reduce them under absolute despotism, it is their right,
it is their duty, to throw off such government, and to provide new guards
for their future security." "To throw off" a government means to get rid of
it, and if a government resists a just attempt to dissolve it, armed revolution
by the people may be required. Indeed, this is precisely how the Americans
of 1776 understood their own Revolutionary War. This is also what Madi-

son meant when he wrote in *Federalist* 51 that while "auxiliary precautions," such as a written constitution with separation of powers and checks and balances are important, in the end, "a dependence on the people is, no doubt, the primary control on the government." All free societies and all just governments rest on the ground of revolution, a direct inference from the principle of natural human equality, that no man may justly rule over another absent his consent.

Regarding slavery, the Founders understood that the black slaves whom they held in bondage could equally have claimed the same natural right of revolution to which Americans appealed in their 1776 war against the British Crown. In light of their own principles, justice ultimately required nothing less than "the eventual total extirpation of slavery from the United States," as John Adams wrote in a letter late in his life.[38] If slaves had risen in revolution against the government that enslaved them, the principles of the American Founding would have justified their cause. If slavery could be eliminated from the United States peacefully and gradually, that too would be justified by the principles of the Founding. The principles of the Founding could *not* justify—without stretching their meaning beyond recognition—the view that chattel slavery was good, that it should be championed and allowed to spread wherever possible, and that no one had the right to judge or criticize it.

While this view of slavery as a positive good was virtually unheard of in the era of the American Founding, by the eve of the Civil War, American public opinion, and Southern opinion in particular, had changed, abandoning the position that slavery was wrong and embracing slavery as a positive good. This change of opinion required a rethinking of the foundation of government. If it was right for some men to rule others without their consent, if it was right for whites to enslave blacks, for example, then there could be no natural or God-given right to revolution. The last thing Southern apologists for slavery wanted to teach the slaves toiling in their fields was that they too possessed the natural right of revolution. Instead, a new science of politics was required, one that incorporated a science of race and racial hierarchy and would secure limited government and freedom for whites, while justifying slavery (total government) for blacks. That new science of politics and race came from the mind of John C. Calhoun, who in many ways was the intellectual father of the 1860–1861 secession movement, even though he had died ten years earlier. When push came to shove, and leading politicos in South Carolina, Georgia, and other Southern slave states faced the issue of secession after Lincoln's election, they drew upon Calhoun's political science to defend their decision. The question of whether states possessed a right of secession, then, ultimately boils down to the question, who was right, Lincoln or Calhoun? If Calhoun was correct, then Lincoln must have been wrong. Vindicating Lincoln, therefore, necessarily entails refuting Calhoun, a task that is neither simple nor quick and requires an understanding of the intellectual framework of Calhoun's political science, which provided a large degree of internal consistency to his theories and gave them wide popular appeal.

CALHOUN: NEW ENDS, NEW MEANS

In his *Politically Incorrect Guide to the Constitution*, Gutzman rightly acknowledges that on the eve of the Civil War, secessionists were "following Calhoun's teaching" as they denounced Lincoln and attempted to depart from and disrupt the Union that Lincoln had just been elected to preside over as chief executive.[39] The statement that "Calhoun's teaching" was widely influential is not at all controversial, but what, precisely, Calhoun taught *is*.

South Carolina's John C. Calhoun was a public intellectual of the highest order. For an entire generation, Calhoun was at or near the center of political controversy, holding virtually every office of political power except the presidency, including the vice presidency, the secretaryships of war and state, and long service in both the U.S. House of Representatives and Senate. He was no simple politician. He offered philosophic reflections on the politics of his day and beyond, writing treatises on human government and human nature. He was renowned for his public oratory, rivaled perhaps only by Daniel Webster in his ability to persuade minds and move souls through the power of speech. In these and other ways, Calhoun displayed excellences that were, and remain, highly uncommon. He was a remarkable man and a uniquely gifted American politician.

These facts matter because Calhoun was among the first, and certainly the most prominent, American thinkers to offer a theory of constitutional government based not on the principles of the American Founding but on an explicit rejection of them. Although Calhoun did not live to witness the Civil War (he died in 1850), Southern secessionists in 1860 and 1861 championed his political theory because it provided them with an argument that defended slavery and limited government simultaneously, assuring advocates of slavery that the institution was not a problem to be solved but a morally right and constitutionally legitimate institution to be preserved and expanded. This is precisely the political science of secession with which Lincoln had to wrestle as a newly elected president faced with the prospect of the Union's dissolution.

Calhoun's political science begins with a science of race and concludes with a constitutional theory of the "concurrent majority," which offers an absolute veto to every part of a political whole and defends secession as a way of protecting each part against the injurious designs of the whole. In practice, Calhoun's concurrent majority implies that every state possesses a constitutional right to secede from the Union of the United States. Calhoun's concurrent majority was a function of his scientific racism: he proposed it as a constitutional solution to the problem of limiting governmental power precisely because he rejected the Founders' principles of natural rights, including the natural right of revolution, as the foundation of government.

Calhoun correctly identified the Founding proposition "that all men are created equal" as the cause of the growing sectional agitation over the question of slavery and whether it should be allowed to spread into the federal territories. Unless arrested, Calhoun predicted, the conflict over slavery would sooner or later destroy the United States. The cause of the conflict, in Calhoun's mind, had nothing to do with the injustice of black slavery because he did not believe black slavery to be unjust. Rather, slavery had become a source of controversy only because many Americans, having been misled into believing that human equality was true, had wrongly concluded that slavery was immoral. Calhoun called this "the most false and dangerous of all political errors" disguised as a "hypothetical truism."[40] His wholesale rejection of the Founders' idea of human equality formed the backbone of Calhoun's political theory. In an 1848 speech before the U.S. Senate, he offered perhaps his most pointed and succinct critique of equality, which he began by attacking the Massachusetts Constitution and its assertion that "all men are born free and equal":

> Taking the proposition literally, there is not a word of truth in it. It begins with "all men are born," which is utterly untrue. Men are not born. Infants are born. They grow to be men. It concludes with asserting that they are born "free and equal," which is not less false. They are not born free. While infants they are incapable of freedom, being destitute alike of the capacity of thinking and acting, without which there can be no freedom. . . . They grow to all the freedom of which the condition in which they were born permits, by growing to be men. Nor is it less false that they are born "equal." They are not so in any sense in which it can be regarded; and thus, as I have asserted, there is not a word of truth in the whole proposition, as expressed and generally understood.[41]

Calhoun's literalness would be almost laughable were his attacks on the central principle of the American Revolution not undertaken with deadly seriousness. Certainly, no one in the Founding generation, or in Calhoun's generation, understood the proposition that all men are born free and equal as Calhoun purported. Who would deny that human beings come into the world as babies, not fully grown men? Who would deny that babies are not free in the sense that they are utterly dependent for their survival upon their parents or any other adults who might care for them? The statement that "all men are born free and equal" clearly refers to human nature, which all human beings share and which is rooted in the generation by which the human species perpetuates itself. But this distinction between the human and nonhuman species is exactly what Calhoun wanted to deny, or at least minimize. Instead, Calhoun emphasized that however one understands the origin and development of human beings, whether one appeals to evolutionary science or to biblical creation, all humans come into the world in a state of inequality and hierarchy, not a state of equality.

"If we trace it back" from the Massachusetts Constitution, Calhoun continued in his speech, "we shall find the proposition differently expressed in the Declaration of Independence," which "asserts that 'all men are created equal'" and which is "not less erroneous." "All men are not created," Calhoun reminded his audience, "according to the Bible, only two, a man and a woman, ever were, and of these one was pronounced subordinate to the other. All others have come into the world by being born, and in no sense, as I have shown, either free or equal."[42]

Calhoun rightly traced the philosophic origins of the various expressions of natural human equality and natural right in the formative documents of the American Founding to "certain writers on government who had attained much celebrity in the early settlement of these states, and with whose writings all the prominent actors in our revolution were familiar," the most prominent being John Locke and Algernon Sidney. For Calhoun, these "state of nature" theorists were the real culprits, and he labeled their respective philosophies "a great misnomer" that led to "dangerous errors" because "that cannot be called a state of nature which is so opposed to the constitution of man as to be inconsistent with the existence of his race and the development of the high faculties, mental and moral, with which he is endowed by his Creator."[43] According to Calhoun, the so-called state of nature Locke and Sidney described was nothing less than a myth, a figment of their imaginations, yet educated people who read them came to believe that the unreal "state of nature" was in fact real, that it described the true natural state of man as a state of equality.

The question for Calhoun, if men are not equal, was how much power government should have over the lives of the people who live under it and how much liberty the people should be granted. For Calhoun, the answer was a continuum running closely along racial lines. More advanced races that possess greater capacity for living freely and peacefully and taking care of themselves require less governmental power over them than races that are less advanced:

> The quantum of power on the part of the government, and of liberty on that of individuals, instead of being equal in all cases, must necessarily be very unequal among different people, according to their different conditions. For just in proportion as a people are ignorant, stupid, debased, corrupt, exposed to violence within and danger from without, the power necessary for government to possess . . . becomes greater and greater, and individual liberty less and less, until the lowest condition is reached, when absolute and despotic power becomes necessary on the part of government, and individual liberty extinct. So, on the contrary, just as a people rise in the scale of intelligence, virtue, and patriotism . . . the power necessary for government becomes less and less, and individual liberty greater and greater.

By focusing on the "quantum" of power that particular governments must exercise, and by measuring the liberty a people enjoy as an inverse function of that power, Calhoun rejected the idea that all human beings might possess any kind of equal claim or right to freedom:

> Instead, then, of all men having the same right to liberty and equality, as is claimed by those who hold that they are all born free and equal, liberty is the noble and highest reward bestowed on mental and moral development, combined with favorable circumstances. Instead, then, of liberty and equality being born with man; instead of all men and all classes and descriptions being equally entitled to them, they are prizes to be won.[44]

The American Founders would have agreed with the general point that not all people are suited for free self-government. They argued strenuously that as free society requires limited government, so limited government requires moral virtue and knowledge on the part of the people. John Adams, for example, repeatedly warned that "virtue is the only foundation of republics," while Samuel Adams remarked that "neither the wisest constitution nor the wisest laws will secure the liberty and happiness of a people whose manners are universally corrupt."[45] Thomas Jefferson was even more direct when he famously remarked, "If a nation expects to be ignorant and free in a state of civilization, it expects what never was and never will be."[46] Not only did the Founders argue that freedom requires many virtues, but they consistently maintained that those who would use freedom tyrannically have no right to freedom. Yet, they never argued that the virtues necessary for freedom were the sole possession of a select racial group; nor did they deny that less civilized people are educable and capable of moral and political improvement. For Calhoun, however, the line that separates civilized from uncivilized people is a racial line that seemingly cannot be crossed.

The question still remains of the relative position of whites and blacks (as well as other races) on Calhoun's scale of extensive freedom and limited government on one end and extensive government and limited freedom on the other. How do we know where to place whites or blacks on the scale? Calhoun provided an answer when he argued that liberty and equality "are prizes to be won." The races that possess rights to liberty and equality, in other words, are those that have *won* them. Races that have demonstrated their "fitness" (Calhoun's word) to live freely deserve to live freely; races that have not demonstrated a fitness for freedom, races that have been unable to throw off the shackles of slavery and to live freely, do not deserve liberty. In this way, Calhoun argued from the ground of empirical science: blacks were obviously not fit for freedom because they were not living freely, and whites obviously were fit for freedom because they were in fact living freely.

Unfortunately for America, Calhoun lamented, the idea of human equality had such "a strong hold on the mind of Mr. Jefferson" that it had caused him "to take an utterly false view of the subordinate relation of the black to the white race in the South."[47] Therein lay the source of the conflict over slavery, a conflict that would not be resolved until Jefferson's "utterly false view" was corrected and discussions regarding slavery became informed by the "subordinate relation of the black to the white race." Where Lincoln argued on one occasion that "the principles of Jefferson are the definitions and axioms of free society" and on another occasion celebrated Jefferson as "the most distinguished politician of our history," Calhoun denounced Jefferson's principles as "the most false and dangerous of all political errors."[48]

Rejecting natural human equality and natural rights, therefore rejecting nature as a normative standard of right, Calhoun was left with historical evolution, or historicism, as the only standard of right. In Calhoun's political thought, the way things are is the best indicator of the way they ought to be. Calhoun was not consistent on this decisive point—he did think certain historical-political developments were wrong (such as the antislavery movement), which raises serious problems for the coherency of his overall theoretical framework. But on the subject of slavery, Calhoun left no doubt that he believed the relation between the white and black races in the slave South was just as it ought to be. Black slavery in America was a product of historical and evolutionary forces and to suggest that slavery was wrong because of some abstract and false idea of human equality was both erroneous, because it denied the reality of historical evolution, and dangerous, because it treated black slaves, who were unfit for freedom, as if they were fit:

> The attempt to carry into practice this, the most dangerous of all political errors, and to bestow on all, without regard to their fitness either to acquire or maintain liberty, that unbounded and individual liberty supposed to belong to man in the hypothetical and misnamed state of nature, has done more to retard the cause of liberty and civilization, and is doing more at present, than all other causes combined.

Deepening in his conviction that slavery was a "positive good," Calhoun increasingly supported measures that would aid the institution's spread. In December 1837, for example, Calhoun strongly encouraged the U.S. Senate to pass several resolutions declaring that Congress possessed no power to abolish slavery in Washington, D.C., or in any territory and, further, that Congress could not even consider the morality of slavery when deciding to acquire new territory.[49]

Until Calhoun, few Americans doubted that the Union of the United States was principally formed on July 4, 1776, when the "one people" of America officially voiced their choice "to dissolve the political bands which have connected them with another, and to assume among the powers of the earth, the separate and equal station to which the laws of nature and of nature's God entitle[d] them." But Calhoun considered the chief principle of 1776, the self-evident truth that all men are created equal, to be the "most false and dangerous of all political errors," and he therefore refused to identify the principled origin of the Union with the Declaration of Independence. But if Calhoun was right, if slavery was right and the principle of human equality really had "done more to retard the cause of liberty and civilization . . . than all other causes combined," what is the true principle for understanding the ends and means of government? Calhoun suggested that answering this question required a new science of politics and constitutional government based on a new understanding of human nature. It is not surprising that in formulating his new political science, Calhoun identified the locus of the American union in the Constitution rather than the Declaration as he attempted to sever all logical and principled connections between the two. Calhoun understood that if he could persuade Americans to divorce the Constitution from the principles of the Declaration, he could strengthen his argument that human equality in no way should inform the laws or policies of the United States.

The most theoretical development of Calhoun's new political science is found in his *Disquisition on Government*, written late in his life and published only after his death in 1850. Here, eschewing the "state of nature" thesis and the principle of equal natural rights, Calhoun instead constructs his new political science upon the foundation of three "incontestable" facts: first, humans are social beings; second, human society is impossible without government of some kind; and, third, man is "so constituted, that his direct or individual affections are stronger than his sympathetic or social feelings."[50] Man, in other words, is a paradox: on one hand, human beings need to live with other human beings in society and under government; on the other hand, man is self-centered and cares more for his own well-being than for that of those with whom he lives, leading to conflicts and making society and government problematic. Man's selfishness causes conflicts in society, which is why government is necessary, but government has within itself "a strong tendency to disorder and abuse of its power" because of the very human selfishness that makes government necessary.

The problem of human government is that men administer it, and the same nature of man that compels him to care more for himself than for his neighbors compels those who control government to use it for their own interests at the expense of the interests of others. According to Calhoun, the only kind of government that can resist the natural selfishness of man is one whose internal structure (what Calhoun calls its "organism") resists the abuse of power. This "organism" of government consists of two elements, suffrage and the concurrent majority. The first step in building a government that checks the ability of rulers to oppress the ruled is the implementation of suffrage: "The responsibility of the rulers to the ruled, through the right of suffrage, is the indispensable and primary principle in the *foundation* of a constitutional government." But Calhoun is quick to point out the limitations of representative government, or government by consent, because

> the right of suffrage, of itself, can do no more than give complete control to those who elect, over the conduct of those they have elected. . . . The sum total, then, of its effects, when most successful, is, to make those elected, the true and faithful representatives of those who elected them.[51]

The problem with suffrage is that it only "changes the seat of power"; it does not counteract the natural tendency of those who control government to use and abuse it for their own advantage. If suffrage simply acts to amplify the selfish nature of men to selfish majorities of men, what principle or rule can counteract this problem, asks Calhoun? "This demands the most serious consideration; for *of all the questions* embraced in the science of government, it involves a principle, the most important, and the least understood; and when understood, the most difficult of application in practice." The solution is to "give to each division or interest, through its appropriate organ, either a *concurrent voice* in making and executing the laws, or a *veto* on their execution."[52] For Calhoun, only a *concurrent majority*, one in which every significant interest group in the community has an absolute veto over the actions and policies of government, is truly a *constitutional majority*, and he contrasts that with what he calls a mere numerical, or absolute, majority. The problem with rule by numerical majority is that while it is a majority of the community, it nonetheless represents only a part of the community, yet it is treated as if it stands for the whole, as if the interests of the majority represent the sum total of all of the community's interests.

Calhoun describes what he calls the "conservative principles" of numerical majorities versus concurrent majorities: Numerical majorities are necessarily driven by *force* as the antagonism between majority and minority interests—the majority will try to maintain its majority status while a minority will try to become the majority—will be ceaseless and increasingly violent. In a concurrent majority, however, the driving principle is *compromise*. Compromise, according to Calhoun, necessarily results from a concurrent majority because if each interest group is equipped with an absolute veto over government policy, then only those policies agreeable to all interest groups will be advanced. Policies that divide the nation into sections (such as policies limiting the spread of slavery) will never be put before a concurrent majority government because they will have no chance of success.

For Calhoun, the concurrent majority does more than encourage compromise in politics, however: it actually changes and improves human nature. Human nature evolves, but the political science of the concurrent majority offers human beings, for first time, the ability to direct their own evolution. Generations of people living under a concurrent majority will habituate themselves to compromise and placing the interests of their fellow citizens over their own interests: "Concession would cease to be considered a sacrifice—it would become a free-will offering on the altar of the country, and lose the name of compromise."[53] In his assumption that human nature is malleable and evolutionary, Calhoun draws upon a philosophic critique of human nature reaching back at least to eighteenth-century European political philosophy.

Almost a century before Calhoun penned his *Disquisition*, the French political philosopher Jean-Jacques Rousseau challenged Locke and other "state of nature" theorists in his essay "Discourse on the Origin and the Foundations of Inequality among Men" (commonly referred to as Rousseau's "Second Discourse"). Rousseau's critique of Locke's state of nature anticipated Calhoun's rejection of Locke in certain ways, but while Calhoun insisted that man by his very nature exists in a political state, Rousseau argued that anyone who believed that man is political by nature had not discovered the true nature of man. Rousseau criticized Locke in particular for not being radical enough in his attempt to reveal human nature: "The philosophers who have examined the foundations of society have all felt the necessity of going back as far as the state of nature, but none of them has reached it." "They spoke of savage man," Rousseau explained, but they "depicted civil man." Locke and other state of nature theorists depicted natural man as possessing reason and "continually speaking of need, greed, oppression, desires, and pride," thereby transferring "to the state of nature ideas they had taken from civil society."[54]

Rousseau argued that natural man is neither political nor rational, that man by nature is not altogether unlike the lower-order beasts. But if man is similar to beasts in being neither rational nor political by nature, is there any principle of moral or political right according to which human beings might live their lives? Rousseau wanted to anchor right in nature, but according to his own theoretical account, natural right could not be rational because human nature was not rational.

Rousseau's solution was to replace reason with will as the source of right. Man may not be rational by nature, Rousseau posited, but he is undeniably willful. Right is not *discovered* by human reason; rather, right is *created* by human will. Rousseau did not present his political philosophy as a crude doctrine of political power where some simple or single act of might makes right, to be sure, because he did not see all expressions of will as equal. If all human beings possess will (but not reason) by nature, then the most moral will is the most common will of the people, which Rousseau termed the "general will." The morality of the general will springs from its universality; its generality accounts for its intrinsic goodness. Will expressed by all is morally superior to will expressed only by some. For Rousseau, therefore, all legitimate political authority arises from, and is informed by, the general will. The generality or universality of the general will confers political legitimacy on law and government. In the politics of Rousseau, any constitution or law that reflects the general will of the people cannot be wrong or unjust because there is no standard of right above the general will; that is, there is no expression of human will more general than the general will. Carried to its logical conclusion, the doctrine of the general will means that the will of the people is not judged by the will of God; rather, the will of God is judged by (or synonymous with) the general will of the people. "The most general will," Rousseau argued in an essay titled "Political Economy," "is also the most just," because "the voice of the people is indeed the voice of God."[55]

Rousseau's arguments regarding political legitimacy formed the intellectual framework Calhoun adopted with this difference: Calhoun believed that he had solved the problem that earlier thinkers such as Rousseau could not, that his theory of the concurrent majority was the first to provide an adequate mechanism, or "organism," that allowed for an accurate and true expression of the authentic general will of the people. In his *Disquisition*, Calhoun's concurrent majority represented the pure expression of the most general will of the people at any given time because the concurrent majority is the least partial will. Echoing Rousseau, Calhoun argued that the voice of the people, after being filtered and distilled through the concurrent majority, becomes nothing less than "the voice of God."[56]

Ironically, DiLorenzo argues that it was Lincoln, not Calhoun, who was the true disciple of Rousseau: "Rousseau was one of the founders of modern nationalism," DiLorenzo writes, "with Lincoln following in his footsteps."[57] I agree that Rousseau was one of the founders of modern nationalism. There is a principled connection between Rousseau and later thinkers, especially Hegel, for whom "the state" became the highest moral and political authority. But DiLorenzo never explains these principles or connections. Nor does he attempt to demonstrate the influence of Rousseau on Lincoln's political thought. If he tried, he would find it a tough row to hoe. In his insistence that nature supplies an unchanging, objective, rational standard of right, Lincoln's political thought has much more in common with classical political philosophy than it does with the historicist threads of Rousseau's theory.

As I have explained, Calhoun follows Rousseau in his attempt to legitimize law in the most general will, the concurrent majority. But DiLorenzo shows no evidence of understanding this. Instead, DiLorenzo denounces "Lincoln cultists," who "are quick to assassinate the character of . . . Calhoun," while he praises scholars who defend Calhoun as people who have "obviously spent a considerable amount of time educating [themselves] about these men and their political positions and priorities."[58] In other words, critics of Calhoun suffer from inadequate education, while those who defend Calhoun are, in DiLorenzo's words, "transparent truth seeker[s]." But has DiLorenzo "spent

a considerable amount of time" educating himself about Lincoln and Calhoun
and the origins of their politics? If so, it is unclear why he would associate Lincoln with Rousseau while failing to see the clear connection between Calhoun's concurrent majority and Rousseau's theory of the "general will."

When Calhoun applied his general theory to the United States under
the Constitution, he envisioned a concurrent majority comprising the
states, each of which formed a minority interest group within the larger
union, and therefore each state should possess a veto over all national policy proposals. With each state armed with the veto power, sectional agitation (over slavery or any other subject) would be avoided in its entirety because any policy that favored one state or one section at the expense of
another would be vetoed by any state that found it objectionable. But if a
concurrent majority of the United States was to work in practice, each
state's veto must be given teeth; each state must possess the power to make
its veto effective and ensure that some combination of other states would
not ignore it. Calhoun found the teeth he was looking for in the right of
secession. If a state's right to veto national policy were ever violated, each
state would retain the legal right to secede from the United States. If a combination of states conspired to pass laws over the veto of one or more states,
secession would quickly result, raising the specter of anarchy. Not unlike
modern theories of "mutually assured destruction," the mere threat of secession would prevent actual secession by precluding any sectional injury
that might prompt such an action. No state would attempt to injure or benefit at the expense of another state because any such action would prompt
secession, which in turn would be detrimental to all the states.

Here, Calhoun's attempt to alter decisively the nature of the union
formed by the Constitution becomes clear: the Constitution no longer
formed a national government in the true meaning of the term because, in
Calhoun's final analysis, it lacked authority over individual states. The Constitution could not be the "supreme law of the land" as indicated by Article VI because the Constitution could not be binding on states that possessed a constitutional right to secede from the union it formed. In
Calhoun's formulation, the "union" of the United States was really no
union at all; rather, it was a temporary confederacy or a kind of forum in
which states could come together for the purposes of deliberating and passing public policies for the mutual benefit of all but which any number of
states could dissolve at any point.

At the same time, Calhoun understood that his political science must
sever all connections between the Declaration of Independence and the
Constitution because his racial science could not admit that blacks possessed

a natural right of revolution. Calhoun, in other words, had to reject the political science of the Constitution itself because that political science rested upon the principles of the Declaration. In *Federalist* 40, for example, James Madison raised the question of what authority the Constitutional Convention had to design and propose a new constitution, an act not legally authorized by the Articles of Confederation. In answering the question, Madison quoted the Declaration, arguing that there are times when "informal and unauthorized propositions" can rightfully be made by "patriotic and respectable citizens" because it is the "precious right of the people to 'abolish or alter their governments as to them shall seem most likely to effect their safety and happiness.'"[59] If a people possess a natural right to abolish their government through revolution, in other words, they must also possess a natural right to alter it.

Madison returned to the Declaration in *Federalist* 43 (which happens to be the central number of the *Federalist's* eighty-five papers). Article VII of the proposed Constitution stated that the ratification of only nine of the thirteen states "shall be sufficient for the establishment of this Constitution between the states so ratifying the same." Thus, Madison addressed a delicate question: "On what principle the Confederation, which stands in the solemn form of a compact among the States, can be superseded without the unanimous consent of the parties to it?" The Articles of Confederation did not provide for its own replacement upon the ratification of a new constitution by nine (or any other number of) states.[60] Instead, the authority for adopting the new Constitution, Madison wrote, derived from "the absolute necessity of the case," "the great principle of self-preservation," and, above all, "the transcendent law of nature and of nature's God, which declares that the safety and happiness of society are the objects at which all political institutions aim, and to which all such institutions must be sacrificed."[61]

According to the father of the Constitution writing in the *Federalist*, Americans' very authority to propose and ratify the Constitution sprang from the "transcendent law of nature and of nature's God" enshrined in the Declaration. This is precisely why Lincoln, in his Gettysburg Address, famously dated the beginning of America to "four score and seven years" before 1863: America began, in other words, in 1776 with the Declaration of Independence. But Calhoun could not, and would not, accept a politics informed by the natural law of the Declaration. In his book subtitled *Arguing the Case for Southern Secession*, Charles Adams adopts Calhoun's theory and ridicules the Gettysburg Address, suggesting that Lincoln instead should have opened with, "Three score and fourteen years ago" and dated the beginning of the Union to 1789, the year the Constitution went into legal effect. "Yet today," Adams laments, "that gross ignorance [of Lincoln's Gettysburg Address] is chiseled in stone as if it were some great truth like scripture, instead of a willful misstatement."[62]

Whatever powers might be reserved to the states under Calhoun's concurrent majority, and whatever protections for state interests might be employed, no power and no protection was to be extended to the rights of black slaves. This much is undeniable in Calhoun's theory: the legal right of secession that he defended belonged to states; it was not a natural right belonging to individuals. The legal right of secession emerged from the constitutional contract between the states; therefore, each state could exercise its legal and constitutional right to leave the constitutional union anytime it pleased. But that right belonged, for example, to the state of South Carolina, not to the slaves toiling in South Carolina's fields. For Calhoun, the slave had no natural rights because there was no such thing as a natural right, especially of revolution, and any suggestion that slaves did possess natural rights was a "false and dangerous error." According to Calhoun's political science, South Carolina might legally depart from the Union, but the slave in South Carolina could never be justified in any illegal act in order to secure his own freedom. Lincoln was absolutely right to see that the sophisticated "science" of race and politics offered by Calhoun and repeated by others was merely a cover for slavery: "Turn it whatever way you will," Lincoln commented in an 1858 speech in Chicago, "whether it comes from the mouth of a King [as] an excuse for enslaving the people of his country, or from the mouth of men of one race as a reason for enslaving the men of another race, it is all the same old serpent" that says, "You work and I eat."[63]

In an essay titled "John C. Calhoun Was Right," Clyde Wilson praises Calhoun as "one of the great anti-consolidationist thinkers of the nineteenth century."[64] He trumpets Calhoun's warnings against "centralization" and "consolidation" as especially relevant in today's political climate of big government. I agree with Wilson that the application of Calhoun's theory of the concurrent majority would go far in preventing political consolidation and that any government by a concurrent majority would be very limited in its scope, power, and operations. But government by concurrent majority would have also ensured that South Carolina and other Southern states would have been virtually unopposed as they practiced slavery, the ultimate negation of limited government.

The political theory of the concurrent majority flowed from Calhoun's denial of natural human equality and supported a regime that desired to limit the government's power over the white class, while that same white class exercised virtually unlimited power over the black slave class. I believe this is what historian Richard Hofstadter meant in describing Calhoun as "The Marx of the Master Class."[65] Calhoun argued vigorously for the protection of minority interests against the larger and possibly consolidated power of the majority, but why did he not include black slaves among the minorities who needed the protection of the concurrent majority? The contradiction in Calhoun's concurrent majority theory—that it sought to protect some minorities (whites in Southern states) against a majority (whites in America) in order that some other minority (black slaves) could be oppressed without interference—is revealed most clearly by that fact that every Southern state that acted upon Calhoun's theory decided for secession by a simple majority vote: not one seceding state would allow a dissenting (pro-Union) minority to veto the policy of secession. If a Southerner in 1861 was among the minority pro-Union voices in any seceding slave state, his minority interests were ignored and trampled upon, the very thing the concurrent majority was intended to prevent.

None of this, however, stops Mark Graber from recommending that Americans should have adopted Calhoun's concurrent majority as their central constitutional principle and abandoned the Constitution of 1787, which he believes was the underlying cause of the Civil War. "By privileging sectional appeals and inflating support for sectional candidates, the Constitution aggravated the antagonisms responsible for the Civil War."[66] Graber has especially harsh words for the Constitution's Electoral College, which "permitted a free-state party to capture the White House by gaining bare majorities in most free states" and no majorities in slave states. "By mandating rules that promoted sectional extremism and inhibited cooperation between sectional moderates, [the Constitution is] as much to blame for the secession crisis as the Wilmot Proviso, the Kansas-Nebraska Act, *Dred Scott*, and Lecompton."[67] "No interpretative schism would have arisen," Graber concludes, had Americans followed Calhoun rather than Lincoln and "had the Constitution . . . constitutionalized Calhoun's concurrent majority." Indeed. And no political movement to end slavery might have been successful. In his attempt to vindicate the principles of Calhoun at the expense of Lincoln's, Graber's Union would have been a Union of perpetual slavery.

MADISON AND HAMILTON OPPOSE SECESSION

As the secession crisis deepened in the months after his election, Lincoln on several occasions pointed out the contradictions and self-destructive character of Calhoun's theory of secession. But Lincoln had more than logic on his side. He also had the arguments and examples of the two most prominent constitutional theorists in American history: Alexander Hamilton and James Madison.

In *Federalist* 22, Hamilton anticipated Calhoun's argument for government by concurrent majority and secession. In principle, Calhoun's theory of the concurrent majority is nothing more than the principle that disputes should be decided by a super, rather than a simple, majority. Hamilton understood no less than Calhoun did that requiring a supermajority for the purpose of deciding national policy would effectively empower a minority to block or dictate national policy, and therefore sectional policies or policies injurious to the common good of the Union were unlikely to be passed: "When the concurrence of a large number is required by the constitution to the doing of any national act, we are apt to rest satisfied that all is safe, because nothing improper will be likely to be done." But Hamilton thought more comprehensively than did Calhoun, warning that "we forget how much good may be prevented, and how much ill may be produced, by the power of hindering the doing what may be necessary, and of keeping affairs in the same unfavorable posture in which they may happen to stand at particular periods."[68]

Foremost in Hamilton's mind was the influence foreign powers might exert on American politics and government. In a republic, Hamilton warned,

> persons elevated from the mass of the community, by the suffrages of their fellow-citizens, to stations of great pre-eminence and power, may find compensations for betraying their trust, which to any but minds animated and guided by superior virtue, may appear to exceed the proportion of interest they have in the common stock, and to over-balance the obligations of duty. Hence it is that history furnishes us with so many mortifying examples of the prevalence of foreign corruption in republican governments.[69]

Not only are republics more susceptible to foreign corruption in general, but the problem was especially acute in the case of the early United States, a small and relatively weak republic in a world dominated by powerful and hostile monarchies. Any foreign power looking to influence American politics would find a supermajority political process to its advantage because it would need to corrupt fewer Americans to achieve success.[70] A truly national government, one that not only represented the interests of the nation but was at the same time binding on the nation, was therefore indispensable, argued Hamilton. He pointed, for example, to the lack of a national judiciary under the Articles of Confederation and the obstacle this created in forming treaties with other nations.[71] Absent a sovereign and authoritative national government, national legislation and treaties made with foreign nations were "liable to the infractions of thirteen different Legislatures, and as many different courts of final jurisdiction, acting under the authority of those Legislatures," placing "the faith, the reputation, the peace of the whole union . . . at the mercy of the prejudices, the passions, and the interests of every member of which it is composed." "Is it possible," Hamilton asked rhetorically, "that foreign nations can either respect or confide in such a government?"

The only way the proposed Constitution of 1787 could remedy these defects, Hamilton argued, was to abolish once and for all any notion of "state sovereignty." States are not sovereign; *the people* of the United States are sovereign. And while individual states retain certain legal powers under the Constitution, the issue of "states' rights" is not a pretext for interfering with or preventing a legitimate and constitutional exercise of national power. The argument of secession, running from Calhoun to his modern apologists, rests on the assumption that states are the fundamental source of sovereignty and legitimacy in the American constitutional order, that the Constitution possesses no power and no legitimacy other than that given to it by the states, and that, therefore, as the states are the sources of authority for the Constitution, they have the authority to withdraw from the Union any time they choose.

Yet, Hamilton argued in the *Federalist* that the greatest defect of the Articles of Confederation was that a *lesser* source of authority, the *states*, not *the people*, had ratified them. As Hamilton pointed out, the Articles of Confederation possessed no more authority than any ordinary article of state legislation: "Owing its ratification to the law of a State, it has been contended, that the same authority might repeal the law by which it was ratified." This had led some "respectable advocates" to suggest "that *a party to a compact* has a right to revoke that *compact*," in other words, that a state has a right to secede, "however gross a heresy it may be." This problem, explained Hamilton, "proves the necessity of laying the foundations of our national government deeper than in the mere sanction of delegated authority." States, according to Hamilton, possess mere "delegated authority" because they have only the limited powers granted to them by the people, who retain full and original sovereign power. "The fabric of American Empire ought to rest on the solid basis of THE CONSENT OF THE PEOPLE. The streams of national power ought to flow immediately from that pure original fountain of all legitimate authority."[72] It is "the people" who will ratify the Constitution because it is the people, not the states, who are

ultimately sovereign, the "pure original fountain of all legitimate authority."
Any rights possessed by states are rights the people have delegated, and any
change in the character of the national union and its constitutional charter,
therefore, requires their consent and authority. According to the *Federalist*,
a state has no power under the Constitution to decide by itself to change
the Union by seceding.

Thanks to Aaron Burr's bullet, Hamilton did not live to see the development of Calhoun's concurrent majority theory, but Madison did. In the
last years of his life (he died in 1836), Madison was consumed with refuting Calhoun's arguments for nullification and secession. Madison attacked
Calhoun's theory most effectively by charging that Calhoun had failed to
understand the natural foundation of true political sovereignty. "The main
pillar of nullification," Madison wrote in response to Calhoun's arguments,
"is the assumption that sovereignty is a unit, at once indivisible and unalienable; that the states therefore individually retain it entire as they originally held it, and, consequently that no portion of it can belong to the
United States."

> But is not the Constitution itself necessarily the offspring of a sovereign
> authority? . . . And where does the sovereignty which makes such a
> Constitution reside? It resides not in a single state but in the people of
> each of the several states, uniting with those of the others in express and
> solemn compact which forms the Constitution. To the extent of that
> compact or Constitution, therefore, the people of the several states must
> be a sovereign as they are a united people.[73]

Rejecting Calhoun's argument that all political sovereignty resides in states,
Madison argued that the Constitution created divided, or dual, sovereignty
between the national and state governments, all of which the original sovereignty of the people authorized. The people of a state, Madison argued,
were sovereign over matters reserved for state government, but the united
people of the several states were the only legitimate sovereign over the U.S.
government. In other words, no single state was sovereign over or possessed
the power to alter the constitutional union of states:

> [The Constitution] was formed by the States—that is by the people in
> each of the States, acting in their highest sovereign capacity; and formed,
> consequently, by the same authority which formed the State Constitu-
> tions. Being thus derived from the same source as the Constitutions of
> the States, it has within each State, the same authority as the Constitu-
> tion of the State, and is as much a Constitution, in the strict sense of the

term, within its prescribed sphere, as the Constitutions of the States are within their respective spheres, *but with this obvious & essential difference,* that being a compact among the States in their highest sovereign capacity, and constituting the people thereof one people for certain purposes, [the U.S. Constitution] *cannot be altered or annulled at the will of the States individually,* as the Constitution of a State may be at its individual will.[74]

Madison was well aware that many, including Calhoun himself, viewed the doctrines set forth in his own Virginia Resolutions and Jefferson's Kentucky Resolutions (1798–1799) as providing the first principled defense for state sovereignty and secession. Jefferson's argument in the Kentucky Resolutions clearly defended the right of a state to nullify federal laws it believes are unconstitutional:

> Where powers are assumed [by the national government] which have not been delegated, a nullification of the act is the rightful remedy: that every State has a natural right in cases not within the compact, to nullify of their own authority all assumptions of power by others within their limits.[75]

But the language of the Kentucky Resolutions was typical of Jefferson in the 1780s and 1790s, when he was more interested in inciting political unrest than in maintaining the rule of law. During this period, Jefferson penned some of his most memorable statements regarding revolution: "The tree of liberty must be refreshed from time to time with the blood of patriots and tyrants. It is its natural manure," and "I hold that a little rebellion, now and then, is a good thing, and as necessary in the political world as storms are in the physical world."[76] During the same period, Jefferson almost gushed with enthusiasm for the French Revolution.

But after his election to the presidency in 1800, he never again spoke that way. The election of 1800 taught Jefferson that under a well-designed constitution, free elections might provide better security for individual rights, along with political stability, than endless, violent revolution, so long as the natural right of revolution provides the political horizon within which free elections are conducted.[77] Without the threat of revolution, those who control the power of government might have little incentive to obey the outcomes of free and lawful elections, but without free elections under the protection of law, it is difficult if not impossible to transform revolutionaries into founders and thereby prevent a revolution from devouring itself (such as the French Revolution). In his inaugural address, Jefferson stated that "a jealous care of the right of election by the people" is a "mild and safe corrective of abuses which are lopped by the sword of revolution where peaceable remedies are unprovided."[78] Elections by the people, in other words, are a "mild and safe corrective" and therefore provide "peaceable remedies" for abuses, but where peaceable remedies are not available—where the results of free elections are ignored or rejected—then abuses might need to be "lopped by the sword of revolution." In the same sentence, Jefferson, contrary to Calhoun, describes "absolute acquiescence in the decisions of the majority" as the "vital principle of republics" and argues that there is no other appeal except "to force, the vital principle and immediate parent of despotism."[79]

Madison denied that his own Virginia Resolutions sanctioned the theories of nullification and secession that Calhoun was advancing. In an 1830 correspondence with Edward Everett, Madison wrote, "In favor of the nullifying claim of the states, individually, it appears, as you observe, that the proceedings of the Legislature in Virginia in '98 and '99 against the Alien and Sedition Acts, are much dwelt upon." But Madison quickly pointed out that these were "erroneous constructions" offered by "distinguished individuals," such as Calhoun, who had "misconceived the intention of those proceedings."[80] "This brings us to the expedient lately advanced," Madison continued,

> which claims for a single state a right to appeal against an exercise of power by the government of the United States decided by the states to be unconstitutional . . . [with] the decision of the state to have the effect of nullifying the act of the Government of the United States.

Madison rejected this theory of nullification in favor of majoritarian constitutionalism, one characterized by majority rule, minority rights, and free elections:

> How far this structure of the Government of the United States is adequate and safe for its objects, time alone can absolutely determine. Experience seems to have shown that whatever may grow out of future stages of our national career, there is, as yet, a sufficient control, in the popular will, over the executive and legislative departments of the government. When the Alien and Sedition Laws were passed in contravention to the opinions and feelings of the community, the first elections that ensued put an end to them.[81]

Here, Madison echoes an argument he made almost a half-century earlier in *Federalist* 58, where he raised the basic question of majority rule, of whether it is best to make most political decisions by a simple majority or a supermajority, which is, in principle, a concurrent majority—a concurrent majority is nothing but a supermajority system in which a small minority can block any measure proposed by the majority. "That some advantages might have resulted from such a precaution," Madison commented, "cannot be denied." Among the benefits of a concurrent majority system, government would do little because a minority could easily stop the majority, making such a system an effective model for limiting the powers of government. "But," Madison cautioned, "these considerations are outweighed by the inconveniences in the opposite scale."

> In all cases where justice or the general good might require new laws to be passed, or active measures to be pursued, the fundamental principle of free government would be reversed. It would be no longer the majority that would rule: the power would be transferred to the minority. . . . Lastly, *it would facilitate and foster the baneful practice of secessions*; a practice which has shown itself even in States where a majority only is required; a practice subversive of all the principles of order and regular government; a practice which leads more directly to public convulsions, and the ruin of popular governments, than any other which has yet been displayed among us.[82]

Madison, in other words, wanted more than mere *limited* government; he wanted *good* government, a government limited in its scope that also possesses the energy necessary to execute its limited purposes well and to facilitate the public good and protect individual rights, especially in moments of grave danger.

Calhoun had failed to understand sovereignty, Madison argued, which originated not in states but in individuals. "Let us consult the Theory," Madison wrote in an 1835 essay titled "Sovereignty,"

> which contemplates a certain number of individuals as meeting and agreeing to form one political society, in order that the rights, the safety, and the interest of each may be under the safeguard of the whole. The first supposition is that each individual being previously independent of the others, the compact which is to make them one society must result from the *free* consent of every individual.[83]

The natural freedom and independence of each individual is transformed into political sovereignty by voluntary "compact," and it was by virtue of their compact that the citizens of the several colonies declared their independence from Great Britain and their union with each other, adopted the

Articles of Confederation, and later replaced those articles with the "more perfect union" established by the Constitution.[84] Madison's supposition that each individual had been independent prior to the compact means that no relationship of governing or being governed had existed between them. That is to say, in the state of nature, or by nature, each individual is equal in authority to every other, with no one having greater claim to the obedience of another than another has claim to obedience from him. Only by virtue of each person's recognition of this equality with those with whom he contracts can legitimate civil society be formed.

The compact theory describes how *legitimate* political authority can arise among men, as well as why such authority is consistent with human nature. Of course, authority can, and often does, arise in many ways other than through compact. Throughout history, conquest has been the most common. But only the social compact guarantees that the rulers will rule in the interest of the ruled. For Madison and the Founders, no less than for Lincoln, national or political sovereignty is an abstraction from the original sovereignty each individual possesses by nature. National or political sovereignty, therefore, precedes the formation of government because the social compact, as a voluntary agreement of free individuals who consent to form civil government, precedes positive law.

While unanimous consent between the whole of society and each of its members is the only foundation for legitimate political sovereignty, unanimous consent is impossible for the operations of government. Thus, Madison continued,

> Whatever be the hypothesis of the origin of the *lex majoris partis*, it is evident that it operates as a plenary substitute of the will of the majority of the society for the will of the whole society; and that the sovereignty of the society as vested and exercisable by the majority, may do anything that could be *rightfully* done by the unanimous concurrence of the members; the reserved rights of individuals in becoming parties to the original compact being beyond the legitimate reach of sovereignty, wherever vested or however viewed.[85]

Majority rule is a necessary consequence of compact because a government, no less than an individual, if it is to preserve itself (or those for whom it acts), must be capable of being moved by a single will. That will is the will of the majority, so long as that will is rightful and does not violate what Madison called the "reserved rights of individuals," those unalienable rights with which all men are endowed by their Creator. As Jefferson explained in his first inaugural address, "The will of the majority is in all cases to prevail, but that will to be rightful must be reasonable, that the minority possess their equal rights which equal law must protect."[86]

Only within the context of natural rights is a government of majority rule and minority rights possible because it is only within that context that members of any minority are understood to possess the same rights, requiring the same protection, as those in the majority. A government built upon the consent of the governed, operating through majority will and protecting the equal rights of all citizens, is the only truly sovereign government according to the principles of natural rights and natural justice.

In his first inaugural, Lincoln summed up the political science of Madison and Hamilton when he said,

> A majority, held in restraint by constitutional checks, and limitations, and always changing easily, with deliberate changes of popular opinions and sentiments, is the only true sovereign of a free people. Whoever rejects it, does, of necessity, fly to anarchy or to despotism. Unanimity is impossible; the rule of a minority, as a permanent arrangement, is wholly inadmissible; so that, rejecting the majority principle, anarchy, or despotism in some form, is all that is left.[87]

In his demand that secession be a legal right, combined with his defense of slavery as a morally correct institution, Calhoun rejected not only "the majority principle" but the principles of natural rights and consent that legitimize a regime of majority rule and minority rights. And as Calhoun rejected them, so too did Southerners in 1860 and 1861 who followed Calhoun's teaching on secession, and so too do Calhoun's many defenders today.

CONFUSING SECESSION AND REVOLUTION

Many of the critics' attacks on Lincoln are bound up with a defense of Calhoun. From the point of view of Lincoln critics, if Calhoun can be vindicated, then Lincoln must be wrong. Clyde Wilson, whose defense of Calhoun I have mentioned above, complains when Lincoln is quoted as an authority on the meaning of the Union and when select racist remarks from Confederates are presented as evidence that Confederates were overturning, not upholding, the principles of the Founding.[88] In particular, Wilson likes to quote Jefferson Davis, who insisted repeatedly on government by consent of the governed, as counterevidence that it was Davis and the Confederates, not Lincoln, who were preserving the principle of consent. It is true that Davis justified the separation of the Confederate states from the Union by clear references to the Declaration of Independence. Consider the following from Davis's inaugural address as he was sworn into office as the first president of the Confederacy, which Wilson presents as proof positive that Davis was continuing the Declaration's political legacy:

> Our present position has been achieved in a manner unprecedented in the history of nations. It illustrates the American idea that government rests upon the consent of the governed, and that it is the right of the people to alter or abolish a government whenever it becomes destructive of the ends for which it was established.[89]

Davis clearly thought that government without consent is wrong, and Wilson seems to agree. But neither Davis nor Wilson bothers to ask why. Why is it wrong for some men to govern others without their consent? Why is it right for a people to alter or abolish a government that becomes destructive of the ends for which it was established? The Founders' answer to both questions was the principle that all men are created equal and possess equal natural rights, a principle Jefferson Davis positively denied. Thus, however much some Confederates might have quoted select language from the Declaration and other Founding documents, they could not justify Confederate secession by the natural rights principles of the American Revolution, which is why there was, and remains, much confusion about secession versus revolution.

Defenders of secession, then and now, stubbornly refuse to acknowledge the difference between *secession* (a legal separation) and *revolution* (an illegal separation, or, more accurately, a violation of unjust human law sanctioned by natural law). This leads some critics to accuse Lincoln of being caught in a contradiction because he opposed Southern secession in 1861 but, allegedly, he had defended secession in his earlier political career. "The right of secession is a technical form of the right to self-government," Clyde Wilson asserts, "which is its own justification." He seems almost delighted when he points out that "[n]obody put it better than Lincoln in his other true statement (1848): 'Any people anywhere, being inclined and having the power, have the right to rise up and shake off the existing government and form a new one that suits them better. This is a most valuable, a most sacred right—a right which we hope and believe is to liberate the world.'"[90] Lincoln did indeed speak those words while voicing his concerns about the Mexican War in a speech before the House of Representatives in 1848. But Wilson fails to quote what Lincoln said next. The right that is "most valuable," according to Lincoln, is a "most sacred" right—implying it is a God-given right, not a legal one—which Lincoln then identified as the right to "revolutionize." After invoking America's "own revolution," Lincoln goes on to explain that the "sacred" right to "revolutionize" cannot be a right granted by positive law or by government because "[i]t is a quality of revolutions not to go by old lines, or old laws, but to break up both, and make new ones."[91] The sacred right of revolution, in other words, is not the same as a legal right of secession and therefore Lincoln's 1848 speech defending revolution did not contradict his later opposition to Southern secession.

Lincoln offered a similar argument in a set of resolutions that he drafted for an 1852 "Kossuth meeting" in Springfield, Illinois, celebrating the Hungarian revolutionary and political exile, Louis Kossuth. The first of the resolutions stated: "That it is the right of any people, sufficiently numerous for national independence, to throw off, to revolutionize, their existing form of government, and to establish such other in its stead as they may choose." In the seventh resolution, Lincoln identified the right "to revolutionize" with "the cause of civil and religious liberty."[92] Ultimately, Lincoln argued, "the more sacred principles of the laws of nature," not positive laws, justify revolution and distinguish it from secession.

Defenders of secession, then and now, also confuse means with ends. As Lincoln proved, secession cannot stand as an organizing principle of law, but even if one grants the premise of the secession argument, secession remains a *means* of political governance, not the *end* of government, and means are subordinate to ends. The legitimate end, or goal, of any decent government is the protection of the rights of those living under it. Defenders of the Confederacy find themselves in the awkward position of insisting that the North should have affirmed secession as a means, while the South denied the ends of legitimate government as it held more than four million human beings in slavery.

In his first book-length attack on Lincoln, *The Real Lincoln*, DiLorenzo titles the longest chapter "The Myth of Secession as Treason." In this, his most concentrated defense of Calhounian principles, DiLorenzo offers historical evidence purportedly proving that "secession was *the* principle of the American Revolution, and there would be nothing so un-American as opposing the right of secession."[93] In *When in the Course of Human Events*, Charles Adams argues along similar lines and therefore finds it perplexing that "in America, of all places, secession was called treason." America was founded in an act of secession, Adams maintains; thus, "Lincoln's adamant stance against it makes no sense."[94] But DiLorenzo's and Adams's examples fail to prove what they think they do. In some instances, these authors take historical quotations grossly out of context and impute to them a meaning they did not originally possess. In other cases, they refuse to acknowledge the difference between a legal right of secession and a natural right of revolution, which prevents them from understanding the texts they claim to read; they imagine secession where documents are clearly appealing to revolution.

DiLorenzo's most glaring mistake is his account of the Declaration of Independence. The overwhelming fact of the American Founding is that the Founding generation believed in natural rights, a fact DiLorenzo either must ignore or deny. DiLorenzo writes,

> The Jeffersonian dictum that governments derive their just powers from the consent of the governed and that whenever a government becomes destructive of the rights of life, liberty, and property, citizens have a right to secede from that government and form a new one, was the basis of America's two wars of secession: 1776 and 1861.[95]

Like DiLorenzo, Adams also insists repeatedly that the "fundamental right of self-determination as expressed in the Declaration of Independence" is identified with "the consent of the governed" and offered support for Southern secessionists. "The guiding principle of the Declaration of Independence," Adams informs his readers, is "that governments derive their just powers from the 'consent of the governed.'"[96] Perhaps most revealing about these passages and the books in which they are found is what the authors leave out.

Like Clyde Wilson and Jefferson Davis, Thomas DiLorenzo and Charles Adams never ask *why* governments ought to secure the consent of the governed. The answer given in the Declaration is that "all men are created equal." This DiLorenzo and Adams cannot and will not admit. Without a shred of historical evidence, DiLorenzo merely repeats the assertion first made by Jefferson Davis, that "when [the Declaration] mentions equality, it is the equality of the people of the several states." In other words, when the Founders wrote, "We hold these truths to be self evident, that all men are created equal," they did not mean what they wrote, that *all men are created equal*; rather, they meant that New York was equal in some way to South Carolina. The equality mentioned in the Declaration really refers, according to DiLorenzo, to an equality among and limited to *states*. Adams supports DiLorenzo's view, arguing that "the term *all men* [in the Declaration] meant all white men . . . and it really meant *white guys*, as white women weren't much better off." Thus, Adams concludes, "the declaration that Lincoln refers to in his [Gettysburg] Address, of four score and seven years ago, was not conceived in liberty nor was it dedicated to the proposition that all men were created equal." One can imagine Adams throwing up his hands in exasperation as he concludes, "So much for logic and reality."[97] What DiLorenzo, Adams, and other Calhoun apologists fail to understand is that by redefining human equality as state equality, they undermine the entire argument for government by consent of the governed: if it is merely states that are equal to other states, then why is it wrong for one man to rule another without the other's consent? Why would it be wrong for a state to rule over its citizens without their consent?

Unlike DiLorenzo and Adams (and Jefferson Davis and Calhoun), Lincoln understood well the various attempts in his own day to redefine equality in order to justify the unjust treatment of certain groups and the terribly unjust consequences that might follow. Among anti-immigrant nativists, or "Know-Nothings," it was popular to argue that the proposition that all men are created equal did not include immigrants, especially Catholics. In an 1855 letter to his friend Joshua Speed, Lincoln commented,

> Our progress in degeneracy appears to me to be pretty rapid. As a nation we began by declaring that *"all men are created equal."* We now practically read it "all men are created equal, *except negroes."* When the Know-Nothings get control, it will read, "all men are created equal, except negroes, *and foreigners, and Catholics."* When it comes to this I should prefer emigrating to some country where they make no pretense of loving liberty—to Russia, for instance, where despotism can be taken pure, and without the base alloy of hypocrisy.[98]

Yet, in the hands of Jefferson Davis and Thomas DiLorenzo, the Declaration would read, "We hold these truths to be self-evident, that all states are equal," abandoning the principle that had justified government by consent from the time of the American Revolution.

According to the Declaration, "governments are instituted among men, deriving their just powers from the consent of the governed," but DiLorenzo never considers the distinction the Declaration implies between the *just* powers of government and the *unjust*. Consent is necessary, but not sufficient, for legitimate government. A majority mob that consents to tyrannize a minority is no less a tyranny simply because it is consensual tyranny. The people have a natural right to consent to the government under which they live, but only if they consent to a government that exercises "just powers." The distinction between just and unjust governments is one between governments that secure the natural rights of the governed and those that do not.

DiLorenzo invokes the rights to life, liberty, and property to justify what he calls the "two wars of secession: 1776 and 1861." But what kind of rights are these? Where do they come from? Lincoln and the Founders argued that rights originate in the natural liberty shared by all human beings; rights first and foremost are natural rights that belong to all human beings. When a government violates natural rights, an oppressed people can appeal to the natural law to justify the destruction of that government. This is the natural right of revolution. But DiLorenzo cannot embrace the natural law of the Declaration of Independence any more than could John C. Calhoun or anyone else seeking to defend secession in order to protect slavery. The best DiLorenzo can offer is to repeat Jefferson's principles of government by consent and the rights to life, liberty, and property, while ignoring the principle of natural human equality, the foundational principle underlying all of Jefferson's politics.

When DiLorenzo asserts that the Declaration of Independence justified two wars of secession, one in 1776 and another in 1861, he is seconded by Adams, who scorns the idea that human equality is a self-evident truth, arguing instead that "for Americans, the right of self-determination was self-evident." "The Declaration of Independence," Adams continues, "set forth general principles of secession."[99] But immediately readers are struck by an irresolvable contradiction: The American revolutionaries of 1776 understood themselves as lawbreakers—they were openly violating the laws of Britain because they believed those laws were unjust by the standard of the natural law. Every signer of the Declaration, including John Hancock, who famously offered his signature in large script so that King George III could read his name without spectacles, understood that he risked execution for treason if caught by the British. The Confederate secessionists of 1861, however, claimed to be following the law of the Constitution. According to DiLorenzo himself, they did not think of themselves as lawbreakers. They were not rebels, and they were not guilty of treason, an argument DiLorenzo makes explicit right in the title of his chapter, "The Myth of Secession as Treason." If the Declaration of Independence supports legal secession, as DiLorenzo and Adams maintain, then how could it justify both the revolutionaries' attempt to separate from Britain by *breaking* English law and the Confederates' attempt to separate from the Union by *following* American law?

This confusion is amplified when DiLorenzo insists that the "Declaration of Independence was, first and foremost, a declaration of secession from the British government of King George III," then asserts that the "Declaration of Independence was the cornerstone of the states' rights doctrine embraced by the Southern secessionists of 1861 and was seen as the most important defense against the tyranny of centralized governmental power."[100] In a remarkable speech given in March 1861, Confederate vice president Alexander Stephens defended what he and other Confederates believed to be the true "cornerstone" of the Confederacy: the "foundations [of the Confederate government] are laid, *its cornerstone rests*, upon the great truth that the negro is not equal to the white man; that slavery—subordination to the superior race—is his natural and normal condition."[101] According to Stephens, the "prevailing ideas entertained by [Jefferson] and most of the leading statesmen at the time of the formation of the old Constitution, were that the enslavement of the African was in violation of the laws of nature; that it was wrong in principle, socially, morally, and politically." Stephens understood clearly that these conclusions necessarily followed from the natural rights principles of the Declaration. "Those ideas, however, were fundamentally wrong," Stephens argued, because "they rested upon the assumption of the equality of races. This was an error. It was a sandy foundation, and the government built upon it fell when the 'storm came and the wind blew.'" DiLorenzo might believe that the Declaration was the "cornerstone . . . embraced by the Southern secessionists of 1861," but the Confederate vice president argued exactly the opposite, that Southern secession was a rejection of the principles of the Declaration.

Consider also the problem that arises when DiLorenzo argues that secession was a perfectly legal right exercised not only by the Confederates in 1861 but also by the Revolutionaries in 1776. Can one imagine anything more preposterous than the suggestion that the British subjects living in North America under the authority of *King* George III possessed a *legal right of secession*? Why had monarchy survived as long as it had in Europe if Europeans living under various kings had possessed a legal right of secession all along?

DiLorenzo's refusal to distinguish revolution from secession causes him to misread the documents from the Founding he chooses to examine. Where the Founders referred to or described the natural right of revolution, DiLorenzo sees a legal right of secession. For example, DiLorenzo stresses the official acts of Virginia, New York, and Rhode Island ratifying the Constitution. According to DiLorenzo, "These three states declared in their ordinances of ratification that, being sovereign states, *they reserved the right to secede from the Union*."[102] He then quotes from only one of the state ratifications, that of Virginia: "The powers granted under the Constitution being derived from the People of the United States may be resumed by them whensoever the same shall be perverted to their injury or oppression."

Adams also cites the Virginia, New York, and Rhode Island ratification documents, repeating the assertion that all three states reserved the legal right to secede from the Union. And, like DiLorenzo, Adams quotes the same section of the Virginia ratification act.[103] In a 2002 syndicated column titled "Parting Company," Walter Williams quotes from all three state ratification documents (Virginia, New York, and Rhode Island), concluding that "states have a right to take back powers delegated to the federal government—in a word the right to secede from the Union."[104]

In *The Politically Incorrect Guide to American History*, Thomas Woods repeats the same assertion: "So concerned were Virginians about the possibility that the new Union would infringe upon their rights of self-government that upon ratification of the Constitution, Virginia declared that it reserved the right to secede from the Union."[105] Woods does not provide the language used by Virginia to ratify the Constitution, but he assures his readers that "New York and Rhode Island would include similar clauses in their own acts of ratification" (Woods does not provide these "similar clauses" either). Later in his book, Woods reminds readers that "another argument in support of the right of secession involves the states of Virginia, New York, and Rhode Island." "Readers may recall that those states included a clause in their ratifications of the Constitution that permitted them to withdraw from the Union if the new government should become oppressive," although it is unclear how readers might "recall" what Virginia, New York, and Rhode Island stated in their ratifying documents when Woods provides no text from those documents.[106] Yet, Woods is certain that "it was on this basis," the basis of reserving the right of secession, "that they acceded to the Union." And "since the Constitution is also based on the principle of equality—all the states are equal in dignity and rights, and no state can have more rights than another—the right of secession cited by these three states must extend equally to all the states."[107] While offering no evidence that *one* state reserved the right of secession, Woods concludes that *all* the states reserved that right when ratifying the Constitution.

In another "politically incorrect" book, *The Politically Incorrect Guide to the Constitution*, Kevin Gutzman asserts categorically that the "southern states had every right to secede in 1860–61." His main evidence is a repetition of the assertions of DiLorenzo, Adams, and Woods (though he substitutes Maryland for New York): "In fact, Virginia, Maryland, and Rhode Island had ratified the Constitution on the explicit understanding that they could withdraw from it."[108] Like Woods, Gutzman does not offer his readers an opportunity to read the language from any of those states' ratification documents. The readers, apparently, should simply trust the authors.

But what did Virginia, New York, Rhode Island, and other states actually put in their respective ratification documents? Upon reading them, the first thing that struck me was the fact that the words "secede" and "secession" appear nowhere in the documents that DiLorenzo, Adams, Williams, Woods, and Gutzman cite as clearly affirming the right of secession. The language that DiLorenzo, Adams, and Williams quote from Virginia's ratification of the Constitution explicitly states that the powers granted to the Constitution are "derived from the People of the United States," clearly indicating that it is "the People of the United States" who may resume those powers "whensoever the same shall be perverted to their injury or oppression." It is a statement, in other words, about a rightful power possessed by the people, independently of the government under which they live. It refers to a *natural* right, then, certainly not a *legal* right. Further, it says nothing about whether a *state* possesses a *legal right of secession*. From these few words of the Virginians ratifying the Constitution, however, DiLorenzo, Adams, and Williams conclude that the state of Virginia reserved the legal right to secede from the Constitution.

If they had taken time to read a bit further, they would have discovered that their own interpretation—that Virginia was talking about legal rights, not natural rights, and secession, not revolution—becomes all the more implausible. The same Virginia ratification convention from which they quote, in addition to ratifying the Constitution of 1787, also recommended a "Declaration or Bill of Rights" to accompany it. Virginia's proposed Declaration of Rights begins with a three-step premise that offers a succinct summary of the natural rights, social compact theory of government:

> First, That there are certain natural rights of which men, when they form a social compact cannot deprive or divest their posterity, among which are the enjoyment of life and liberty, with the means of acquiring, possessing and protecting property, and pursuing and obtaining happiness and safety.
>
> Second, That all power is naturally vested in and consequently derived from the people; that Magistrates, therefore, are their trustees and agents and at all times amenable to them.
>
> Third, That Government ought to be instituted for the common benefit, protection and security of the People; and that the doctrine of nonresistance against arbitrary power and oppression is absurd [*sic*] slavish, and destructive of the good and happiness of mankind.[109]

This is anything but a statement of a state's legal right (i.e., a right granted by government or positive law) to secede from the government of the Union.

Rather, its entire premise rests on the assertion that human beings possess "certain *natural* rights," and it concludes that it is "absurd" and "slavish" for a people not to resist "arbitrary power and oppression." The "good and happiness of mankind" requires nothing less than active resistance against tyrannical government, that is, *illegal* active resistance against tyrannical government. Can this mean anything other than revolution, which the Declaration of Independence considers to be both a natural right and a natural duty?

Neither DiLorenzo nor Woods nor Gutzman quotes from the ratifying documents of New York and Rhode Island, but when I turn to those documents, I find no mention or implication of secession. Instead, I find repeated statements of natural rights. Consider the following from New York's ratification convention:

> That all Power is originally vested in and consequently derived from the People, and that Government is instituted by them for their common Interest Protection and Security.
> That the enjoyment of Life, Liberty and the pursuit of Happiness are essential rights which every Government ought to respect and preserve.
> That the Powers of Government may be reassumed by the People, whensoever it shall become necessary to their Happiness.[110]

"All power" is derived not from states but from "the People," and it is "the People" who may resume that power "whensoever it shall become necessary to their Happiness." Consider also the insistence of Calhoun and his many libertarian followers that states possess ultimate sovereignty. According to the New York ratifying documents, life, liberty, and the pursuit of happiness are "essential rights" that "*every* Government ought to respect and preserve." Sovereignty ultimately resides neither in the national nor the state governments but in *the people* because it is *the people* alone who possess natural rights, and they alone who retain the natural right to overthrow *any* government, national or state, which "evinces a design to reduce them under absolute despotism," in the language of the Declaration.

The natural rights principles of the social compact stated by Rhode Island's ratifying convention are even more explicit:

> 1st That there are certain natural rights, of which men when they form a social compact, cannot deprive or divest their posterity, among which are the enjoyment of Life and Liberty, with the means of acquiring, possessing and protecting Property, and pursuing and obtaining happiness and safety.
> 2nd That all power is naturally vested in, and consequently derived from the People; that magistrates therefore are their trustees and agents, and at all times amenable to them.

3rd That the powers of government may be reassumed by the people, whensoever it shall become necessary to their happiness.[111]

As I have mentioned, Gutzman asserts that Maryland (along with Virginia and Rhode Island) "ratified the Constitution on the explicit understanding that they could withdraw from it." But the ratification document offered by Maryland in support of the U.S. Constitution consists of only one sentence, "We the Delegates of the people of the State of Maryland . . . in the Name and on the behalf of the People of this State assent to and ratify the said Constitution," followed by the signatures of the Maryland ratification convention's delegates.[112] Perhaps Gutzman refers to the final report issued by the convention as found in Jonathan Elliott's *The Debates in the Several State Conventions on the Adoption of the Federal Constitution*.[113] (It is difficult to know what Gutzman refers to because he offers no quotations and no citations.) The Maryland report includes a list of proposed constitutional amendments considered by a special committee within the convention, most of which concerned specific policies aimed at preventing federal judges from being on state payrolls while the federal government was paying them to decide federal cases and other matters relating to the use of the state militia. One proposed amendment read,

> That it be declared, that all persons intrusted with the legislative or executive powers of government are trustees and servants of the public; and, as such, accountable for their conduct. Wherefore, whenever the ends of government are perverted, and public liberty manifestly endangered, and all other means of redress are ineffectual, the people may, and of right ought to, reform the old or establish a new government.

The proposed Maryland amendment then concluded with language similar to that used by the Virginians: "The doctrine of non-resistance against arbitrary power and oppression is absurd, slavish, and destructive of the good and happiness of mankind." The Maryland delegates' argument that when government endangers public liberty and "all other means of address" have been exhausted, "the people may and of right ought to reform the old or establish a new government" simply restates the Declaration's acknowledgement of the natural right of revolution—"whenever any form of government becomes destructive of these ends, it is the Right of the People to alter or to abolish it." As the Maryland amendment makes clear, it is a right that "the people" possess; it is not a legal right derived from the government (indeed, it is a right to get rid of the government and establish a new one) or that belongs to a state. Thus, the proposed amendment that some in Maryland's ratification convention offered did not in any way support a state's legal right to secede from the Union. Besides, the amendment itself did not pass! It was defeated in special committee and formed no part of Maryland's official ratification of the U.S. Constitution.

Calhoun well understood (as his modern defenders surely must) that if admitted, the natural right of revolution affirmed by the Founding generation and articulated in many of the state ratification documents, among other places, could not be denied to black slaves. Calhoun chose instead to deny the natural right of revolution by denying all natural rights. Calhoun differs from his modern libertarian defenders in that he openly rejected the natural right principle of revolution in favor of a legal right of secession, while the modern defenders of Calhoun and secession whose arguments I have been analyzing prefer to blur the distinction between the two.

NEW ENGLAND SECESSIONISTS

The centerpiece of the historical evidence DiLorenzo cites is the New England Federalists' attempt to secede, beginning in 1804 and culminating in the failed Hartford Convention of 1814. While the Hartford Convention ultimately decided not to exercise the right of secession and form an independent New England confederacy, DiLorenzo claims that that choice was merely prudential. "No one questioned the *right* of the New England states to secede," he writes, citing several New England secessionists as evidence.[114]

DiLorenzo's inclusion of John Quincy Adams among New England's secessionists perhaps best reveals the lack of basic historical research in his work, and Woods follows DiLorenzo's lead. There was no stronger opponent of the New England secessionism than John Quincy Adams.[115] In his discussion of the New England secessionists, DiLorenzo cites several short letters by Timothy Pickering and other New England separatists that are reproduced in a book titled *Documents Related to New-England Federalism, 1800–1815*, edited by Henry Adams (grandson of John Quincy Adams). The central and longest document contained in the book, stretching more than half of the volume's total pages, is an essay in which John Quincy Adams exposed in exacting detail the New England secessionists' treasonous intentions and explained why he opposed them.[116] John Quincy Adams clearly questioned "the *right* of the New England states to secede," and he did so in the very book that DiLorenzo cites. But DiLorenzo never mentions John Quincy Adams's essay.

John Quincy Adams's retelling of why he left the Federalist Party, the party of his father, John Adams, best reveals his view of the New England secessionists during this period. As the British and French were at war, the

British Crown issued "orders in council" affirming its right to "impress" or capture British sailors who had deserted the Royal Navy, "wherever found," and commanding the British navy to do so. This order authorized the British navy to stop American ships at sea and search them for missing British seamen. It quickly became common practice for the British to "impress" sailors who were in fact American, not British, and to seize American ships in European ports. On June 22, 1807, the British gunship *Leopard* followed the American frigate *Chesapeake* out to sea from the Norfolk port and fired upon her, damaging the ship, wounding sixteen of her crew, and killing three. A British lieutenant then boarded the *Chesapeake* and proceeded to "impress" four of the crew, at least three of whom were Americans. Of the four impressed seamen, one was hanged by a British naval court-martial, one died in confinement, and the other two were not returned to the *Chesapeake* until five years later.[117]

This event triggered Jefferson's embargo, enacted in December 1807, which prohibited all trade with Britain and France and prohibited American trading vessels from leaving American ports without special permission. The embargo was a tremendous economic burden whose effects were felt most directly in the shipping Northeast with ripples of higher costs and lower supplies of goods affecting the rest of the country. But as John Quincy Adams remarked in defense of the embargo, "That measure, by retaining at home the vessels and property of the citizens of Massachusetts, at least saved them to their owners. Had it not been adopted, they would have fallen into the hands of British captors, and the owners would never have seen it more."[118]

Before Jefferson imposed the embargo, John Quincy Adams and many other Americans were outraged by the actions of the British, and "numerous meetings had been held of the people, at which resolutions had been adopted expressive of their abhorrence of the deed." Adams urged his fellow Massachusetts Federalists to produce their own resolutions condemning the unjust actions of the British navy. To his astonishment and great disappointment, the leading Massachusetts Federalists refused to call any such meeting and refused to condemn the British "impressment" policy. As Adams learned shortly after, the same Federalist leaders were actively conspiring with the British governor of Nova Scotia to establish British rule in New England, extending as far south as New York. "This," wrote Adams, "was the cause . . . which alienated me from that day and for ever from the councils of the Federal party."[119]

DiLorenzo's suggestion that the New England secessionists at the Hartford Convention were exercising a constitutional right, the purpose of which was to provide a check on centralized or oppressive governmental power, could not be farther from the truth. Although the Hartford Convention ultimately chose not to attempt secession, the most ardent secessionists at Hartford aimed to plant on American soil British monarchical rule, the exact centralized and oppressive government against which the Americans of 1776 had revolted. As John Quincy Adams explained, "The Hartford Convention was the omega of that of which the projected confederacy of 1804 was the alpha." In his 1839 speech titled "The Jubilee of the Constitution," John Quincy Adams explained his opposition to nullification and secession in these clear terms: "The right of a State to nullify an act of Congress is too absurd for argument, and too odious for discussion . . . the right of a state to secede from the Union is equally disowned by the principles of the Declaration of Independence."[120]

In the end, the problem for Thomas DiLorenzo, Charles Adams, Thomas Woods, Kevin Gutzman, Walter Williams, Joe Sobran, Clyde Wilson, and other libertarian defenders of Calhoun and secession is simple: Americans in general approve of the revolution of 1776. Few Americans today would deny (although some might) that the Americans of that time rightly fought for their independence from Britain. Modern Calhounites want to borrow from the nobility that surrounds the American Revolution by equating the Southerners who attempted to "withdraw" from the American union in 1861 with the Americans who "withdrew" from the British Empire. But those who sought to disrupt the Union in 1861 rejected the natural right principles by which the Americans justified their revolution in 1776. Southern disunionists openly avowed secession rather than revolution precisely because they rejected the idea of a natural right of revolution. Thus, today's defenders of Calhoun and secession struggle as they try in vain to fit the Confederacy into the principled political framework of the American Founding. It will not fit because states do not possess a constitutional right of secession, while human beings do possess a natural right of revolution. Calhoun was wrong. Lincoln was right.

NOTES

1. Walter Williams, foreword to Thomas J. DiLorenzo, *The Real Lincoln: A New Look at Abraham Lincoln, His Agenda, and an Unnecessary War* (Roseville, CA: Prima Publishing, 2002), xii.

2. Joe Sobran, "The Imaginary Abe," August 2001, www.sobran.com/replyJaffa .shtml (accessed July 1, 2007).

3. DiLorenzo, *The Real Lincoln*, 85–86, 92.

4. Kevin R. C. Gutzman, *The Politically Incorrect Guide to the Constitution* (Washington, DC: Regnery Publishing, 2007), 122.

5. Charles Adams, *When in the Course of Human Events: Arguing the Case for Southern Secession* (Lanham, MD: Rowman & Littlefield, 2000), 15–16.

6. Thomas E. Woods Jr., *The Politically Incorrect Guide to American History* (Washington, DC: Regnery Publishing, 2004), 62–63.

7. Roy P. Basler, ed., *The Collected Works of Abraham Lincoln* (New Brunswick, NJ: Rutgers University Press, 1953), IV:263. Cited hereafter as Lincoln, *Collected Works*.

8. Lincoln, *Collected Works*, IV:268.

9. Lincoln, *Collected Works*, IV:264.

10. Lincoln, *Collected Works*, IV:265.

11. Thomas DiLorenzo, *Lincoln Unmasked: What You're Not Supposed to Know about Dishonest Abe* (New York: Crown Forum, 2006), 62.

12. DiLorenzo, *Lincoln Unmasked*, 86–91.

13. Thomas Jefferson, report from the minutes of the Board of Visitors, University of Virginia, March 4, 1825, in *Jefferson: Writings*, ed. Merrill D. Peterson (New York: Library of America, 1984), 479.

14. DiLorenzo, *Lincoln Unmasked*, 65.

15. Leonard Levy, *Jefferson and Civil Liberties: The Darker Side* (New York: Quadrangle, 1973 [1963]), 105–106, 125.

16. Lincoln, *Collected Works*, IV:439.

17. Lincoln, *Collected Works*, IV:436.

18. Lincoln, *Collected Works*, IV:436.

19. Lincoln, *Collected Works*, IV:267.

20. DiLorenzo, *The Real Lincoln*, 274.

21. Thomas J. Pressly, *Americans Interpret Their Civil War* (New York: The Free Press, 1962 [1954]), 107.

22. Jefferson, *Jefferson: Writings*, 1517.

23. Lincoln, *Collected Works*, IV:168–69.

24. Jefferson, *Jefferson: Writings*, 1426.

25. Virginia Declaration of Rights, June 12, 1776, Founding.com, www.founding.com/library/lbody.cfm?id=476&parent=475 (accessed June 10, 2006).

26. Gutzman, *The Politically Incorrect Guide to the Constitution*, 11.

27. Letters of Delegates to Congress: Vol. 4, May 16, 1776–August 15, 1776, available on the website of the American Memory project of the Library of Congress, http://memory.loc.gov/cgi-bin/query/r?ammem/hlaw:@field(DOCID+@lit(dg004313)) (accessed January 8, 2007), (emphasis added).

28. Charles R. Kesler and Clinton Rossiter, eds., *The Federalist Papers* (New York: Signet Classic, 2003), 319.

29. Jefferson, *Jefferson: Writings*, 1202.

30. Massachusetts Constitution, 1789, Founding.com, www.founding.com/library/lbody.cfm?id=478&parent=475 (accessed June 10, 2006).

31. George Washington, First Inaugural Address, in *Washington: Writings* (New York: Library of America, 1997), 732.

32. Kesler and Rossiter, *The Federalist Papers*, 319.

33. Kesler and Rossiter, *The Federalist Papers*, 298.

34. Gutzman, *The Politically Incorrect Guide to the Constitution*, 29.

35. See John Quincy Adams, "Reply to the Appeal of the Massachusetts Federalists," in *Documents Related to New England Federalism, 1800–1815*, ed. Henry Adams (Boston: Little, Brown, & Co., 1905), 255–56.

36. Timothy Sandefur, "How Libertarians Ought to Think about the U.S. Civil War," *Reason Papers* 28 (2006): 61–83.

37. Lincoln, *Collected Works*, IV:265.

38. John Adams to Evans, June 8, 1819, in *Selected Writings of John and John Quincy Adams*, ed. Adrienne Koch and William Peden (New York: Knopf, 1946), 209.

39. Gutzman, *The Politically Incorrect Guide to the Constitution*, 121.

40. John C. Calhoun, "Speech on the Oregon Bill," in *Union and Liberty: The Political Philosophy of John C. Calhoun*, ed. Ross M. Lence (Indianapolis: Liberty Fund, 1992), 565. Cited hereafter as Lence, *Union and Liberty: The Political Philosophy of John C. Calhoun*.

41. Lence, *Union and Liberty: The Political Philosophy of John C. Calhoun*, 565–66.

42. Lence, *Union and Liberty: The Political Philosophy of John C. Calhoun*, 566.

43. Lence, *Union and Liberty: The Political Philosophy of John C. Calhoun*, 567.

44. Lence, *Union and Liberty: The Political Philosophy of John C. Calhoun*, 568–69.

45. See Matthew Spalding, ed., *The Founders' Almanac* (Washington, DC: Heritage Foundation, 2001), 211–12.

46. For contemporary evidence that founding and perpetuating self-government is difficult and not universally suited to all people, one need only observe the tremendous challenges the Iraqis face as they struggle to found a constitutional regime following the removal of Saddam Hussein.

47. Lence, *Union and Liberty: The Political Philosophy of John C. Calhoun*, 569.

48. Lincoln, *Collected Works*, II:249, III:372.

49. *Congressional Globe*, 25th Cong., 2nd sess., 55, cited in Mark Graber, *Dred Scott and the Problem of Constitutional Evil* (New York: Cambridge University Press, 2006), 137.

50. Lence, *Union and Liberty: The Political Philosophy of John C. Calhoun*, 5–6.

51. Lence, *Union and Liberty: The Political Philosophy of John C. Calhoun*, 13.

52. Lence, *Union and Liberty: The Political Philosophy of John C. Calhoun*, 21 (emphasis added).

53. Lence, *Union and Liberty: The Political Philosophy of John C. Calhoun*, 52.

54. See Victor Gourevitch, ed., *Rousseau: The Discourses and Other Early Political Writings* (New York: Cambridge University Press, 2004), 132.

55. See Victor Gourevitch, ed., *Rousseau: The Social Compact and Other Later Political Writings* (New York: Cambridge University Press, 2004), 8.

56. Lence, *Union and Liberty: The Political Philosophy of John C. Calhoun*, 31.

57. DiLorenzo, *Lincoln Unmasked*, 158.

58. DiLorenzo, *Lincoln Unmasked*, 172.

59. Kesler and Rossiter, *The Federalist Papers*, 249. The quotation from the Declaration provided by Madison is not fully accurate, as the Declaration stated that "whenever any Form of Government becomes destructive of these ends, it is the Right of the People to alter or to abolish it, and to institute new Government, laying its foundation on such principles and organizing its powers in such form, as to them shall seem most likely to effect their Safety and Happiness."

60. Under the Articles of Confederation, ordinary legislation required the approval of nine of the thirteen states (see Arts. IX, X, and XI of the Articles of Confederation). Article XIII declared that "the Articles of this Confederation shall be inviolably observed by every State, and the Union shall be perpetual," authorizing the states only to alter or amend, not replace, the Articles of Confederation by confirmation of "the legislatures of every state." In terms of positive law, in other words, the Articles did not confer any legal power upon the states to adopt a new constitution, but they did command that every state observe them and that the union under the authority of the Articles be perpetual.

61. Kesler and Rossiter, *The Federalist Papers*, 276.

62. Adams, *When in the Course of Human Events*, 194.

63. Lincoln, *Collected Works*, II:500.

64. Mike Tuggle, *Confederates in the Boardroom: The New Science of Organisations* (New York: Traveller Press, 2003), ix–xiv. See also Clyde Wilson, "John C. Calhoun Was Right," October 23, 2003, LewRockwell.com, www.lewrockwell.com/wilson/wilson15.html (accessed July 14, 2007).

65. Richard Hofstadter, *The American Political Tradition and the Men Who Made It* (New York: Vintage Books, 1974 [1948]), ch. 4.

66. Graber, *Dred Scott and the Problem of Constitutional Evil*, 166.

67. Graber, *Dred Scott and the Problem of Constitutional Evil*, 167–68.

68. Kesler and Rossiter, *The Federalist Papers*, 144.

69. Kesler and Rossiter, *The Federalist Papers*, 145.

70. Kesler and Rossiter, *The Federalist Papers*, 145.

71. Kesler and Rossiter, *The Federalist Papers*, 146.

72. Kesler and Rossiter, *The Federalist Papers*, 148.

73. Marvin Meyers, ed., *The Mind of the Founder: Sources of the Political Thought of James Madison* (Hanover, NH: University Press of New England, 1981), 436–37.

74. Jack Rakove, ed., *Madison: Writings* (New York: Library of America, 1999), 842 (emphasis added).

75. Jefferson, *Jefferson: Writings*, 449–56.

76. Jefferson, letter to Madison, January 30, 1787; letter to William Smith, November 3, 1787, in Jefferson, *Jefferson: Writings*, 882, 911.

77. See Harry Jaffa, *A New Birth of Freedom: Abraham Lincoln and the Coming of the Civil War* (Lanham, MD: Rowman & Littlefield, 2000), ch. 1. See also John

Zvesper, *From Bullets to Ballots: The Election of 1800 and the First Peaceful Transfer of Political Power* (Claremont, CA: Claremont Institute, 2000).

78. Jefferson, First Inaugural Address, March 4, 1801, in Jefferson, *Jefferson: Writings*, 494-95.

79. Jefferson, *Jefferson: Writings*, 495.

80. Saul Padover, ed., *The Complete Madison: His Basic Writings* (New York: Harper and Bros., 1953), 159.

81. Padover, *The Complete Madison*, 155.

82. Kesler and Rossiter, *The Federalist Papers*, 359 (emphasis added).

83. James Madison, "Sovereignty," in *Writings of James Madison*, Gaillard Hunt, ed. (New York: Putnam, 1900–1910), IX:570.

84. See Kesler and Rossiter, *The Federalist Papers*, no. 40.

85. Madison, *Writings of James Madison*, IX, 571.

86. Jefferson, *Jefferson: Writings*, 492–93.

87. Lincoln, *Collected Works*, IV:268.

88. Clyde Wilson, "DiLorenzo and His Critics," June 18, 2002, LewRockwell .com, www.lewrockwell.com/orig/wilson7.html (accessed July 1, 2007).

89. Quoted in Wilson, "DiLorenzo and His Critics."

90. Wilson, "DiLorenzo and His Critics."

91. Lincoln, *Collected Works*, I:438.

92. Lincoln, *Collected Works*, II:115–16. See also Thomas J. Pressly, "Bullets and Ballots: Lincoln and the 'Right of Revolution,'" *The American Historical Review* 67, no. 3 (April 1962): 647–62.

93. DiLorenzo, *The Real Lincoln*, 101.

94. Adams, *When in the Course of Human Events*, 14.

95. DiLorenzo, *The Real Lincoln*, 86.

96. Adams, *When in the Course of Human Events*, 125, 167.

97. Adams, *When in the Course of Human Events*, 196.

98. Lincoln, *Collected Works*, II:323.

99. Adams, *When in the Course of Human Events*, 14.

100. DiLorenzo, *The Real Lincoln*, 85–86.

101. Alexander H. Stephens, "Cornerstone Speech," March 21, 1861, in *Alexander H. Stephens in Public and Private with Letters and Speeches* (Philadelphia: National Publishing, 1866), 721 (emphasis added).

102. DiLorenzo, *The Real Lincoln*, 91 (emphasis added).

103. Adams, *When in the Course of Human Events*, 15.

104. Walter Williams, "Parting Company," August 7, 2002, WorldNetDaily.com, www.worldnetdaily.com/news/article.asp?ARTICLE_ID=28529 (accessed June 10, 2007).

105. Woods, *The Politically Incorrect Guide to American History*, 18.

106. Woods, *The Politically Incorrect Guide to American History*, 62.

107. Woods, *The Politically Incorrect Guide to American History*, 62–63.

108. Gutzman, *The Politically Incorrect Guide to the Constitution*, 122, 132.

109. *Documentary History of the Constitution of the United States of America, 1786–1870: Derived from the Records, Manuscripts, and Rolls Deposited in the Bureau of Rolls and Library of the Department of State* (Washington DC: State Department, 1894), II:377.

110. *Documentary History of the Constitution*, II:190–91.

111. *Documentary History of the Constitution*, II:311.

112. *Documentary History of the Constitution*, II:121–22.

113. Jonathan Elliot, *The Debates in the Several State Conventions on the Adoption of the Federal Constitution, as Recommended by the General Convention at Philadelphia, in 1787* (Philadelphia: J. B. Lippincott & Co., 1836–1859), II:547–56.

114. DiLorenzo, *The Real Lincoln*, 98. Charles Adams also cites the Hartford Convention. See Adams, *When in the Course of Human Events*, 15.

115. DiLorenzo, *The Real Lincoln*, 94; Woods, *The Politically Incorrect Guide to American History*, 65.

116. Adams, *Documents Related to New England Federalism*, 107–329.

117. Adams, *Documents Related to New England Federalism*, 180.

118. Adams, *Documents Related to New England Federalism*, 247. This is not to deny that Jefferson's embargo raised serious constitutional questions and generated significant political backlash. The best that can be said is that Jefferson's administration used heavy-handed tactics to enforce the embargo. Leonard Levy argues persuasively in *Jefferson and Civil Liberties* that American civil liberties were violated as Jefferson adopted "measures of an arbitrary and military nature for enforcement against the American people." See Levy, *Jefferson and Civil Liberties: The Darker Side*, 124.

119. Adams, *Documents Related to New England Federalism*, 181.

120. John Quincy Adams, *The Jubilee of the Constitution: A Discourse Delivered at the Request of the New York Historical Society* (New York: Samuel Colman, 1839), 68.

6

WAS THE CIVIL WAR CAUSED
BY SLAVERY OR ECONOMICS?

Union means so many millions [of dollars] a year lost to the
South; secession means the loss of the same millions to the
North. The love of money is the root of this as of many, many
other evils. . . . The quarrel between the North and South [in
the American Civil War] is, as it stands, solely a fiscal quarrel.

—Charles Dickens, *All the Year Round*, December 28, 1861

History books have misled today's Americans to believe the
war was fought to free slaves.

—Walter Williams, "The Civil War Wasn't about Slavery,"
December 2, 1998

The whole movement [leading to the American Civil War]
was and is based on the slave question.

—Karl Marx, "The North American Civil War,"
October 20, 1861

You think slavery is right and ought to be extended; while we
think it is wrong and ought to be restricted. That I suppose is
the rub. It certainly is the only substantial difference between us.

—Abraham Lincoln, letter to Alexander Stephens,
December 22, 1860

Without question, a sectional divide over economic policy existed in
the United States during the first half of the nineteenth century.

205

The question of tariffs (duties laid on imports) formed the center of most economic disputes, with related questions of paper money, banks, and internal improvements adding fuel to the fights over economic policy. Tariffs tended to favor Northern manufacturing states by raising the costs of imported goods and thereby encouraging the consumption of goods produced domestically in the North. Northern manufacturers could pass additional production costs imposed by tariffs on to consumers, but Southern agrarian states viewed tariffs an unfair economic burden. The South depended primarily on exports for income, competing in a more global economy. They were the consumers who would bear the brunt of higher prices paid for the goods produced in the North, unable to pass off higher costs to someone else.

These economic facts are important because they arise in any serious discussion of the causes of the Civil War. Were the disputes over economic policy of such intensity that they caused brothers from the North and South to take up arms against each other? This view has had many prominent defenders as evidenced by the 1861 quotation from Charles Dickens in one of the epigraphs above. In the years following the Civil War, both the president and vice president of the Confederacy went to great lengths to downplay and virtually deny the role of slavery in causing the war and to emphasize the antebellum sectionalism resulting from economic disputes as the real cause.[1] Abraham Lincoln, of course, was in the grave by that time and could not respond.

The growing ranks of libertarian Lincoln critics, who see little if any distinction between moral, political, and economic questions, have given new life to the Southern postwar account of the Civil War. They collapse all disputes into economic battles for at least two reasons: first, many libertarians are economists or have an interest in economics and tend to identify economic variables more easily; and second, by emphasizing economics over political and moral concerns, they can argue that Lincoln waged a bloody war merely to satisfy his greed for money and power. They seem to understand, as Jefferson Davis and Alexander Stephens did, that if the Civil War was waged over slavery, Lincoln might deserve vindication, but if he waged war merely for economic gain, he should be vilified.

SIMPLIFIED HISTORY

By emphasizing the economic causes of the Civil War, some libertarians fail to pay adequate attention to other important causes for the growing antebellum rift between North and South. "The North was attempting to use the powers of the state to plunder the South," writes libertarian Thomas DiLorenzo. "The South was acting defensively" because "the North was the political mugger, whereas the South was the victim of the mugging, with slaves diabolically used as political pawns."[2] Charles Adams chimes in with support by quoting approvingly from John C. Calhoun:

> The North has adopted a system of revenue and disbursements in which an undue proportion of the burden of taxation has been imposed upon the South, and an undue proportion of its proceeds appropriated to the North. . . . The South, as the great exporting portion of the Union, has in reality paid vastly more than her due proportion of the revenue.

This leads Adams to conclude that "the war between the states was caused by the forces that have caused wars throughout history—economic and imperialistic forces behind a rather flimsy façade of freeing slaves."[3]

This simple economic view of the sectionalism that caused the Civil War is compelling but difficult to square with historical facts. Even a task as basic as identifying the opposing sides turns out to be more complicated than libertarians let on. DiLorenzo, for example, insists that "Southerners from Jefferson to Calhoun to Jefferson Davis championed states' rights in defense of liberty." But it is historically untrue that the South represented a monolithic and unbroken tradition of "states' rights" from the Founding through the Civil War.

Going back to the Constitutional Convention of 1787, Southerners were nationalists whenever they believed that constitutional provisions and uniform national laws would offer more protection for their interests in slavery than diverse local policies; witness, for instance, their demand to include protection for the international slave trade and the right of slave owners to recover runaway slaves in the Constitution and later the federal Fugitive Slave Act.[4] When Southerners possessed unrivaled control of the national government, many tended to favor national power. For example, when New Englanders questioned the constitutionality of Thomas Jefferson's purchase of Louisiana, John Taylor, who would later argue vigorously for states' rights and strict limits on the power of the national government, eschewed any such concern in favor of broad national power in 1803.[5]

As Joel Silbey has argued, as late as the early 1850s, party divisions and loyalty were more important politically in many instances than sectional interests. Southern Whigs, writes Silbey, were "reluctant to cast aside their party allegiance to work with members of the opposite party in their section against whom they had fought so long, [and] they preferred to continue to work with Whigs from the North and West rather than with Southern Democrats." Rather than arguing over simple sectional divisions based on economics as DiLorenzo describes, "political leaders disagreed as to whether or not they should take heed of sectional influences rather than party influences," and therefore "the whole political scene from the mid 1840s onward [was] complex and conflict-ridden with much hesitation, exhortation, and articulate disagreement, all of which affected the growth and importance of sectional influences in American politics."[6]

But DiLorenzo insists repeatedly that a shared political philosophy united the most important Southerners, writing that "after Jefferson's death in 1825, his states' rights tradition was carried on effectively for a quarter of a century most forcefully by John C. Calhoun." DiLorenzo mistakes the date of Jefferson's death; he died on July 4, 1826 (the fiftieth anniversary of the Declaration of Independence). More importantly, however, Calhoun explicitly rejected Jefferson's principles as the "most false and dangerous of all political errors."[7] Calhoun did indeed want to defend states' rights, but his was an understanding of states' rights divorced from the natural rights of Jefferson. Whatever legacy Calhoun carried on "effectively" and "forcefully," it was not Jefferson's legacy. Further, Calhoun, who in his later years became the Democratic champion of the Southern view of states' rights and secession and who was the great opponent of tariffs during and after the nullification crisis of 1832 and 1833 (in response to the Tariff of Abominations), was one of the architects of the earlier tariff of 1816. Following the War of 1812, Calhoun was a strident nationalist and promoter of both tariffs and internal improvement plans, and he openly celebrated the economics of Alexander Hamilton. In this Calhoun was joined by none other than Henry Clay, who had been a pro-agrarian critic of banks, tariffs, and internal improvements before the War of 1812, but who, like Calhoun, had been horrified by the near defeat of the Americans by the British and became a staunch supporter of what he would later call the "American System." The young Calhoun and Clay were opposed by none other than Daniel Webster, the New England Whig who later became one of the preeminent national political figures of the nineteenth century. Perhaps the greatest proponent of the greatest internal improvement plan of all, a transcontinental railroad system, was Stephen Douglas, a *Democrat*. These facts merely suggest that identifying who was on which side of the issue of national power versus state power during the period from 1800 through the 1850s is a complicated historical question, one that DiLorenzo glosses over too easily.

TARIFF OF ABOMINATIONS

Libertarians who insist that economics was the single most important cause of the war point as their single most important piece of evidence to the

1828 tariff, a tariff so oppressively high that it has lived in infamy as the "Tariff of Abominations." The 1828 tariff, libertarians argue, proves that the North was engaged in systematic economic oppression of the South long before the Civil War began. But is this true?

According to a simple libertarian view of American economic history, repeated by Thomas DiLorenzo, Charles Adams, Walter Williams, Thomas Woods, and others, the Tariff of Abominations, which raised tariffs on a number of imported goods from 30 to 50 percent, initiated an unrelenting conflict between the North, which wanted to raise tariffs, and the South, which wanted tariffs lowered.[8] In this simplified version of history, the 1828 Tariff of Abominations led to the 1832–1833 nullification crisis, during which South Carolina passed an "ordinance of nullification" declaring the 1828 tariff (and a subsequent tariff passed in 1832) as unconstitutional and void within the jurisdiction of South Carolina. But even in the nullification crisis, we see the blurring of the sectional lines between the North and South, as well as of the political lines between Democrats and Whigs. Responding to South Carolina's 1832 Ordinance of Nullification, President Andrew Jackson, a Democrat born in South Carolina and a longtime resident of Tennessee who was generally sympathetic to the South, threatened to send in federal troops to force South Carolina to comply, arguing that South Carolina was on "the brink of insurrection and treason" for attempting to nullify a federal law. The Whig leader, Henry Clay, resolved the crisis by proposing a compromise to lower tariff rates.

In 1824, John Quincy Adams, a New Englander, won a very close race for the presidency against Democratic rival Andrew Jackson (who claimed he had been cheated out of the office). Also in 1824, a modest raise in tariff rates had passed in Congress. This increase was unpopular in South Carolina and other Southern states, but it was supported by western and New England states. Southern Democrats, including Calhoun, began scheming ways to defeat Adams in the next election (1828) and get Andrew Jackson elected.

In order to appease their own constituents, Southerners like Calhoun had to oppose any tariff hikes. At the same time, Jacksonian Democrats needed to appear friendly to western and New England states that favored tariffs. The Democratic solution was to propose a tariff so ridiculously high that New England senators would kill it in Congress. The result was the Tariff of Abominations. Had the New Englanders defeated the tariff in Congress as planned, it would have been the party of John Quincy Adams that opposed the tariff and, by that act, appeared hostile to the manufacturing interests of New England. The Jacksonian Democrats, by claiming to have sponsored and supported the increased tariff, would have seemed its real supporters and the real friend of manufacturing (even though they disliked the tariff and had intentionally designed it to fail) and could thereby have hoped to attract some northern and western electoral votes in the upcoming presidential election. In *The Tariff History of the United States*, F. W. Taussig explains the Democratic strategy behind the "abominable" tariff of 1828:

> The Jackson men of all shades, the protectionists from the North and the free-traders from the South, were to unite in preventing any amendments [to the Tariff of Abominations]; that bill, and no other, was to be voted on. When the final vote came, the Southern men were to turn around and vote against their own measure. The New England men, and the [John Quincy] Adams men in general, would be unable to swallow it, and would also vote against it. Combined, they would prevent its passage, even though the Jackson [Democrats] from the North voted for it. The result expected was that no tariff bill at all would be passed during the session, which was the object of the Southern wing of the opposition. On the other hand, the obloquy of defeating it would be cast on the Adams party, which was the object of the Jacksonians of the North. The tariff bill would be defeated, and yet the Jackson men would be able to parade as the true "friends of domestic industry."[9]

A fiction writer could not invent a more duplicitous political conspiracy than the politics behind the Tariff of Abominations. Unfortunately for Calhoun and his fellow Democrats, their plan backfired. New England senators were able to amend the tariff bill enough to make it tolerable, and the bill passed.

Calhoun, who participated in the political intrigue and whose name could easily have been attached to the greatest increase in tariff rates in American history, scrambled to think of a way to reassure South Carolinians of his antitariff credentials. After promoting the tariff of 1816 and early internal improvement plans, Calhoun had earned a reputation in some Southern quarters as an ally of Hamiltonian-Clay economic policies. Had he been identified as a sponsor of the 1828 Tariff of Abominations, he surely would have lost all credibility as a friend of South Carolina's growing opposition to tariffs. Thus, Calhoun looked to offer South Carolina some way they could resist the new tariff with which Calhoun's own party had just saddled them. His answer came several months later as he sat down and penned his "Exposition," arguing that each state retained the legal right under the Constitution to "nullify" any act of Congress that it might deem unconstitutional, assuring his fellow South Carolinians that they had a constitutional right to resist the law Calhoun himself and his coconspirators had foisted upon them.

DiLorenzo offers his readers not even a hint of the political maneu-vering behind the 1828 tariff, resorting instead to his simple, sectional in-terpretation:

> The economic nationalists in Congress, led again by Lincoln's political idol, Henry Clay, succeeded in increasing the tariff rate even further, to an average of almost 50 percent in 1828. This "Tariff of Abominations" was loudly denounced throughout the South, especially in South Car-olina, home of the port of Charleston.[10]

Woods also glosses over the politics behind the tariff, praising Calhoun for his proposal that "an aggrieved state [could] hold a special nullification con-vention, much like the ratifying conventions held by the states to ratify the Constitution, and there decide whether to nullify the law in question." "This is how it was practiced in the great standoff between South Carolina and Andrew Jackson," Woods continues, "when South Carolina nullified [the Tariff of Abominations]."[11]

Whatever conclusion might be drawn about Calhoun based on his ac-tions in 1828, one fact is indisputably clear: the Tariff of Abominations was far from a simple attempt by Northern states to benefit at the expense of the South by way of an oppressive tariff. Rather, as one biographer of Cal-houn puts it, "The famous Tariff of Abominations . . . resulted not from a conspiracy of one section against another, but from an irresponsible bit of political chicanery in which all the sections shared."[12] Calhoun and his fel-low Democrats were hoisted by their own petard.

We should also recall that the tariff involved more than merely eco-nomic questions. In the late 1820s and early 1830s, as both abolitionism and the positive good theory of slavery emerged, controversies over the tariff were sometimes tied to slavery. In every year of the Jackson administration, federal revenues exceeded federal expenditures, and Congress was able to pay down the federal debt.[13] In fact, during Jackson's presidency, the federal gov-ernment was debt free and ran budget surpluses for the first and only time in American history. As the national debt was retired, it was widely assumed that the federal government might enjoy a financial windfall with surplus revenues beyond what was required to fund the operations of the federal government. What might the federal government do with this surplus money? For the first time, compensated emancipation, voluntary policies according to which slave owners could free their slaves with the promise of compensation provided by federal monies, became a real possibility.

Looking forward, some Southerners saw that such policies, while they might provide just compensation to individual slave owners for freeing their slaves, would transform Southern life, which, in growing degrees, identified the honor of white Southerners in contrast to the inferior position of black slaves. From this point of view, the tariff, which was the main source of revenues for the federal government, pointed to concerns larger than mere economics; it called into question the preservation of the Southern way of life. As one Southerner explained in a series of newspaper articles, "It would be suicidal for Carolinians [and other Southerners] to consider the protective tariff simply as a constitutional question. If Congress could pass such a tariff to promote the general welfare, what was to stop it from abolishing slavery for the same reason?"[14] I do not mean to suggest that fear of widespread compensated emancipation financed by the federal government alone fueled Southern opposition to the Tariff of Abominations. I mention it simply to demonstrate how deeply slavery was entangled with many seemingly unrelated questions of national policy, such as the tariff, and how seemingly economic questions were bound up with the moral question of slavery.

Looking at the intervening years between the Tariff of Abominations and the ensuing nullification crisis and the outbreak of the Civil War, it becomes especially difficult to identify the sectional agitation and ultimate cause of the war with the tariff and other economic policies. As Taussig explains,

> In the years between 1832 and 1860 there was great vacillation in the tariff policy of the United States; there were also great fluctuations in the course of trade and industry. A low tariff was succeeded by a high tariff, which in turn was succeeded by another low tariff. Periods of undue inflation and of great demoralization, or prosperity and of depression, followed each other. The changes in the rates of duty and the fluctuations in industrial history have often been thought to be closely connected. Protectionists have ascribed prosperity to high tariffs, depression to low tariffs; free traders have reversed the inference.[15]

Northern and Southern interests were both brought to bear on the politics of the tariff, reflected by the "great vacillation" in tariff rates during the 1830s through the 1850s. This was hardly symptomatic of one section of the nation tyrannizing another with oppressive economic measures, and this would hardly be the cause of brothers and cousins taking up arms and waging war against each other. DiLorenzo even acknowledges that Whigs had "failed to deliver protectionist tariffs . . . during the 1833–1853 period, and the party imploded," as well as that "on the eve of the War between the States, [the tariff] was at the lowest level it would be during the nineteenth century," contradicting his own thesis that the South seceded due to oppressive tariff rates used to benefit the North at the expense of the South.[16]

One of the popular fictions among Confederate apologists is that the Morrill tariff allegedly passed by Lincoln and his fellow Republicans in Congress, which raised the tariff considerably, was the final straw for Southerners. This is the story told by economist Walter Williams: "Shortly after Lincoln's election, Congress passed the highly protectionist Morrill tariff. That's when the South seceded, setting up a new government."[17] In fact, the Morrill tariff passed the House of Representatives in May 1860 (six months before Lincoln was elected president), but it did not pass the Senate until February 1861 (after Lincoln's election but before his inauguration). Democratic president James Buchanan signed the Morrill tariff into law on March 2, 1861, two days *before* Lincoln's inauguration. If Southerners did not like the Morrill tariff, their dispute was with *Democrat* Buchanan, not *Republican* Lincoln.

In the 1860 elections, Republicans gained five seats in the Senate, but they were still one seat short of a majority (and Republicans would only have had a plurality in the House, controlling 106 of the 237 seats). Had Southern senators been present in the Senate, they might have prevented the Morrill tariff from passing Congress and reaching the desk of any president. But senators from at least seven Southern states had abandoned their Senate seats before the tariff was taken up for a vote in the Senate, which points to another historical fact that Williams misses. The South did not begin its attempted secession *after* the Morrill tariff passed Congress or was signed into law by President Buchanan. South Carolina led the secession movement by adopting its secession resolution as early as December 1860, three months *before* the Morrill tariff became law. Whatever justifications Southern states might have offered during the 1860–1861 "secession winter," before the Morrill tariff had become law and before Lincoln had taken the oath of office, they could not have included opposition to Lincoln and the Republicans for imposing a new tariff hike.

In the face of historical facts, the claim that economic policies caused the Civil War becomes questionable. Yet, many libertarians remain firm in their conviction that economics, far more than slavery, explains the Civil War and that Lincoln in particular was far more interested in advancing "Whig economics" than in striking a blow against slavery.

ECONOMIC DETERMINISM

In one of the epigraphs at the beginning of this chapter, I quote Karl Marx's observation in 1861 that the Civil War "was and is based on the slave question." Marx took great interest in the American Civil War, writing a series of essays as the war proceeded. Throughout, Marx was surprised at how much the European, and especially the British, press downplayed the role of slavery in the conflict. Charles Dickens, also quoted in an epigraph above, summed up the British press's general view of the Civil War as "solely a fiscal quarrel" over money and economic policies, such as the tariff. If anyone had an interest in promoting an economic interpretation of the Civil War, it would have been the father of economic determinism, Karl Marx. Yet, Marx scolded the British press for its narrow focus on economics and its refusal to discuss the escalating fights over slavery preceding the Civil War. Criticizing the *London Times*, the *Economist,* the *Examiner,* the *Saturday Review*, and other influential newspapers and journals of his day, Marx summed up their positions:

> In essence the extenuating arguments read: The war between the North and South is a tariff war. The war is, further, not for any principle, does not touch the question of slavery and in fact turns on Northern lust for sovereignty. Finally, even if justice is on the side of the North, does it not remain a vain endeavour to want to subjugate eight million Anglo-Saxons by force![18]

Marx then proceeded "point by point [to] probe the plea of the English press," offering a blistering critique of both the British press and the Southern cause in the Civil War that is compelling even to those who may not hold the same theoretical views that Marx did. How, then, do libertarians account for Marx's analysis?

In a 2001 article published in *Liberty* magazine, "The Economic Causes of the Civil War," libertarian Donald Miller quotes the sentence in which Marx writes, "The war between the North and South is a tariff war," to support Miller's own argument that tariffs were the real cause of the war.[19] But Marx was not presenting his own view when he wrote those words; he was describing the views of what he believed were incompetent and dishonest journalists! In *When in the Course of Human Events*, libertarian Charles Adams quotes the same passage from Marx, though he at least acknowledges that Marx was not stating his own opinion but was instead describing the opinions presented by the British press. Still, Adams nowhere indicates that Marx *disagreed* with this opinion, leaving readers to think that both the British press and Marx viewed the Civil War simply as a tariff war.[20]

It is ironic that many libertarians identify themselves as "public choice" or "political" economists, yet tend to reduce all political questions to economic issues. In *The Real Lincoln*, for example, DiLorenzo characterizes virtually everything Lincoln said regarding slavery as, ultimately, a function of his economic agenda. In the final analysis, he contends, the only important fact is that as a young politician, Lincoln had been a Whig and had supported the economic policies of Henry Clay's "American System," including a tariff, internal improvements, and a national bank. At the core of the "real" Lincoln was an unqualified commitment to "mercantilism" not much different from socialism. Lincoln, according to DiLorenzo, would stop at nothing to impose the "Whig economic system" upon America, and any opinion he voiced regarding slavery was merely instrumental in advancing his economic agenda. Lincoln's "cause," in DiLorenzo's words, was "centralized government and the pursuit of empire."[21] According to DiLorenzo, Lincoln said this "over and over again," although he does not trouble himself to produce a shred of evidence to support his assertion.[22]

In his more recent *Lincoln Unmasked*, DiLorenzo suspects there is nothing less than a conspiracy to cover Lincoln's not-so-admirable economic motives:

> Searching through the modern literature of the [Civil War], one finds relatively little mention of economic issues despite the fact that North and South were consumed for the previous half century by conflicts over tariffs, banking, internal improvements, land policy, and other economic issues. . . . There is a conspiracy of silence over the issue, which should pique the curiosity of any student of American history.[23]

DiLorenzo never attempts to understand Lincoln's arguments and principles as Lincoln presented them. Instead, he looks at Lincoln through the lens of *economic determinism*, the theory that economic interests compel and inform all human experience. From this point of view, economic interests explain Lincoln's rhetoric and deeds far better than moral principles because moral principles merely reflect economic interests. Insofar as they believe that economic interests determine human thought and action, libertarians like DiLorenzo stand on essentially the same intellectual ground as earlier generations of Marxist and quasi-Marxist scholars.

When the famed historian Charles Beard turned to study the Civil War, he was interested almost exclusively in the competing economic interests that divided the North and South. Beard paid almost no attention to slavery as a moral issue.[24] "The institution of slavery as a question of ethics," he wrote, "was not the fundamental issue in the years preceding the bombardment of Fort Sumter."[25] Although Beard rejected the label of "Marxist," he made his affinity with Marx clear when he described his own research method as "economic determinism," an idea central to Marx's theory.[26] It comes as no surprise that what little attention Beard did give to slavery, he paid almost exclusively in terms of economics because economic oppression, according to him, was the only source of "real" conflict that led to war. For Beard, the economic conflict preceding the Civil War consisted primarily of Northern "capitalists" oppressing the South. Beard's critique of capitalism was strikingly similar to that offered a half-century earlier by George Fitzhugh, one of the most outspoken defenders of slavery. Thomas Pressly explains Beard's account of the Civil War this way:

> So infused with hostility to Northern "capitalism" was Beard's interpretation of the Civil War era that its over-all implications could be construed as pro-Confederate in several important respects. His view that the ethical issue involved in Negro slavery was not a fundamental factor of the irrepressible conflict, and his description of the aims of the North almost solely in terms of economic benefits, were positions that were squarely in agreement with the contentions of Confederate sympathizers beginning with Jefferson Davis. Beard's criticism of Northern "capitalism" was so unrelieved and this theme so dominated his pages that the Southern planters very nearly became the heroes of the narrative, and Beard very nearly became the ally of John C. Calhoun.[27]

Beard did not expressly describe himself as a Confederate sympathizer; rather, he understood himself as providing an "objective" analysis by getting to the "real" underlying economic motives for the war. "[Beard's] interpretation," according to Pressly, "was presumably neither pro-Northern nor pro-Southern, but economic; it said in effect that all previous explanations of the causes and nature of the Civil War were unrealistic since they did not recognize the crucial role of economic forces."[28] Like Beard, modern libertarians never proclaim themselves as sympathizers of the Confederacy or its policies regarding slavery. Like Beard, they claim merely to present the "real" economic causes for the increasing sectional conflicts of the 1850s and 1860s.

Mark Thornton and Robert Ekelund Jr. offer another libertarian economic analysis of the Civil War in *Tariffs, Blockades, and Inflation: The Economics of the Civil War.*[29] At the outset, they announce their economic methodology: "Economics is necessary to understand the cause, course, and consequences of the Civil War . . . [because] economics is a means of explaining and understanding history."[30] They acknowledge the existence and power of "ideologies," but while "ideology is important, we must know the economic interest behind the ideologies."[31] Hence, an ideology of economic determinism, *their* ideology, explains all other ideologies.

But what precisely are economic interests? Many economists bandy about the phrase as a synonym for "happiness," as if the pursuit of economic interests were identical to the pursuit of happiness. The premise seems to be that human happiness amounts to nothing more than the satisfaction of human appetites. If Aristotle is right that happiness is the highest human good, that all human actions aim at happiness, then from the libertarian point of view, what is good for an individual is anything an individual finds pleasurable. A purely economic view of human beings, in other words, contains within it a latent moral relativism that equates all human appetites and renders impossible the search for an objectively true or right way for human beings to live.

Informing the libertarian *homo economicus* view of man assumed by Thornton and Ekelund is a crude hedonism not unlike that developed by the English philosopher Thomas Hobbes. As Hobbes wrote, the fundamental drive—*the* fundamental interest behind all "ideologies"—is all men's desire for their own "conservation" or preservation, which is necessary if one is to enjoy the pleasurable sensations of what Hobbes calls "delectation." This is why, Hobbes argued, all men by nature seek peace in place of war: to escape the painful passion of fear of violent death, while seeking "such things as are necessary for a commodious living."[32]

"Commodious" things are suitable, handy, useful; traditionally, they have been considered means for higher ends. Aristotle, for example, understood health, wealth, and friends as goods in themselves but, at the same time, as means to a higher end, the life of pure virtue. For Hobbes, as for the libertarian economists whose writings I am reviewing, the "commodiousness" of useful commodities—the pleasurable sensations they create in the body and mind—are ends in themselves and do not point to anything higher. For Hobbes and the economists, it is difficult, if not impossible, to separate the good from the pleasurable; they are the same. Hobbes's hedonism is rooted in the mechanical processes of what he calls "sensation," the physical pressure of external objects pressing on the sensory organs of the body, the effects of which are then transmitted to the mind to form "the thoughts of man." The universe of beings, including human beings, "is nothing but bodies and their aimless motions." In the Hobbesian, mechanistic perspective of the human condition, morality is unmoored; there is no *right* to which one ought to subordinate one's *pleasure* because whatever is pleasurable *is* right. As Hobbes puts it, "There is no such *finis ultimus* [ultimate aim] nor *summum bonum* [greatest good] as is spoken of in the books of the old moral philosophers. . . . Happiness is a continual progress of the desire, from one to another." The "general inclination of all mankind," Hobbes writes, is a "perpetual and restless desire of power after power that ceases only in death."[33]

When economists such as Thornton and Ekelund assert that "economic interests" account for all human "ideologies," they must answer two questions: Is their theory of economic determinism *caused by* their peculiar economic interests? And do they claim their theory to be *true*? Thornton and Ekelund are suspicious of any professed "ideologies," which they believe are merely veils for economic interests; ideologies are, in effect, illusions that conceal the true economic source of human thought. But, on their own ground, why should we not be suspicious of the beliefs they offer? They do not say.[34] When Thornton and Ekelund and other economic libertarians assume economic interests are the cause for our political and moral opinions, they implicitly deny the metaphysical freedom of the human mind, the source of human freedom. This is why Francis Fukuyama wryly dubbed libertarians as the "*Wall Street Journal* school of deterministic materialism."[35]

Ignoring much of the complicated history of the period, Thornton and Ekelund measure the economic policies of the antebellum and Civil War era against the standard of "complete free and unencumbered trade between countries and regions." Aware that relations between nations and regions are sometimes strained, occasionally exploding in violent war, they discuss war only in terms of its harm to free market exchange. "War is always and everywhere bad for the economy," they announce.[36] Clearly, any moral or political justification for the Civil War will fall short because, like any other war, it was bad for the economy.

Thornton and Ekelund confidently assert that "the war itself had little to do with the positive developments in the postwar economy and that its actual impact was to retard economic growth and to cause important distortions that harmed both black and white rural populations."[37] In the end, "economic theory, then, would suggest that the American Civil War was a destructive rather than constructive event."[38] For Thornton and Ekelund, ending slavery and preserving the Union were of little consequence.[39] But a decisive effect of the Civil War, according to them, was its hindrance of science and technological innovation. "All of the basic national science institutions had already been started prior to the conflict, [but] the war stopped most of the military and science exploration teams that had begun their work during the 1850s." In other words, the developers of war-waging military technology would have made much more progress if they had not been distracted by the waging of a war!

Thornton and Ekelund also remind us of the inflationary effect of paper money: when government produces large amounts of paper money in a short period, there is more money in the economy chasing the same number of goods than was available before the increase in the money supply, resulting in inflation. Thus, another charge leveled against Lincoln, especially in his capacity as president, was that he preferred paper money over specie, or gold-backed money. I do not challenge the authors' theoretical account of paper money and its economic effects, but they pay little attention to the relationship between politics and money. Over the course of the war, the federal government printed $450 million in greenbacks and also sold various notes and bonds, some of which were redeemable in twenty years.[40] Whatever might be said about the economic consequences of these policies, politically they were of significant importance because Americans now had a vested interest in making sure the United States succeeded in its war efforts because the U.S. government backed all paper money.

> The American System of the wartime Republican Party thus marshaled the resources of the nation to help save the Union. The Whig concept of enterprise assisted by government action received the mantle of patriotism. In the hothouse of war, prosperity and military victory walked hand in hand. The nature of the assistance provided did help the entrepreneurs who were already forging the modern economy of the prewar years. What was good for the General Motors of the day was linked inexorably to the good of the nation.[41]

Even Thornton and Ekelund admit that for the Union, "battlefield losses were associated with declines in value while victories meant higher values for the greenback." Another irony appearing in their book is the fact that the Confederacy printed money far more aggressively during the Civil War than Lincoln's government. The Union financed only 16 percent of its overall war expenses with printed currency, relying on loans and taxes, forms of financing much less inflationary than currency, to pay the remainder. The Confederacy, on the other hand, relied on printed money to cover more than 60 percent of its war expenses. As a result, the Union minimized currency-caused inflation, while the Confederacy suffered such enormous and unprecedented inflation that on the eve of the war's conclusion, it stood on the brink of complete economic failure.[42]

In *Lincoln Unmasked*, DiLorenzo cites a recent essay by economics professors Robert McGuire and T. Norman Van Cott, who attempt to demonstrate the Confederate Constitution's superiority in terms of economic free trade, which made it a more pro-freedom document than the U.S. Constitution Lincoln defended.[43] In "The Confederate Constitution, Tariffs, and the Laffer Relationship," McGuire and Van Cott draw on the famous "Laffer curve" established by economist Arthur Laffer, which presents a parabolic relationship between rates of taxation and government revenues. According to the Laffer curve, government revenue will be zero at taxation rates of 0 percent and 100 percent. In the first instance, the government seeks no revenue; in the second, all revenue-producing activity ceases because of the tax's completely confiscatory nature, leaving no economic base from which the government can collect revenue. Somewhere in between these poles lies an optimal tax rate that generates the maximum government revenue and beyond which revenue-producing activity will decline, eroding the base of revenues available for taxation. Therefore, all varying levels of expected government revenue, falling between the maximum revenue level of taxation and zero, can be derived from two levels of taxation, one lying on the left side of the Laffer curve and the other on the right, but both producing the same total government revenue. For example, under a hypothetical Laffer curve, government could expect to generate the same amount of revenue from a tax rate of either 5 percent or 95 percent. While the former is a much lower rate of taxation, economic growth is encouraged, and taxes will be levied on a large tax base; the latter rate, while much higher, discourages economic growth and shrinks the taxable economy.

Identifying the tariff as a form of taxation, McGuire and Van Cott compare the U.S. and Confederate constitutions against the Laffer curve standard. In particular, they demonstrate that tariffs designed for the purpose of collecting revenue only, those not intended to protect domestic industry, fall on the left, or lower side, of the curve; protectionist tariffs, which go beyond revenue purposes and attempt to aid domestic industry by raising the prices of imported goods substantially, necessarily fall on the right, or upper, side of the curve. The U.S. Constitution permitted protectionist tariffs, the first enacted in 1816 (supported by Calhoun, among others) and followed by the Tariff of Abominations of 1828.[44] The Confederate Constitution, on the other hand, contained the following clause, found in Article I, Section 8, Clause 1:

> The Congress shall have the power . . . to lay and collect taxes, duties, imposts and excises, *for revenue necessary* to pay the debts, provide for the common defense, and carry on the Government of the Confederate States; but no bounties shall be granted from the treasury; *nor shall any duties or taxes on importations from foreign nations be laid to promote or foster any branch of industry*, and all duties, imposts, and excises shall be uniform throughout the Confederate States (emphasis added).

By prohibiting protective tariffs and allowing only those levied for revenue purposes, the Confederate Constitution ensured that tariffs could not be so high as to fall on the right, or upper, side of the Laffer curve. Thus, the Confederate Constitution, McGuire and Van Cott suggest, is characterized more by freedom and free trade than the U.S. Constitution.

This is a sound analysis as far as economic theory goes, but we ought not to lose sight of another important feature of the Confederate Constitution: its perpetual protection for slavery. Unlike the authors of the U.S. Constitution, who were too embarrassed to mention slavery by name in their document, the architects of the Confederate Constitution refer to slavery explicitly throughout. Consider a few such places, beginning with Article I, Section 9, Clause 4, which prohibited the Confederate government from restricting slavery in any way: "No bill of attainder, ex post facto law, or law denying or impairing the right of property in negro slaves shall be passed." Article IV, Section 2 also prohibited states from interfering with slavery:

> The citizens of each State shall be entitled to all the privileges and immunities of citizens in the several States; and shall have the right of transit and sojourn in any State of this Confederacy, with their slaves and other property; and the right of property in said slaves shall not be thereby impaired.

So much for states' rights!

Perhaps the most menacing provision of the Confederate Constitution was the explicit protection Article IV, Section 3, Clause 3 offered to slavery in all future territories conquered or acquired by the Confederacy:

> The Confederate States may acquire new territory; and Congress shall have power to legislate and provide governments for the inhabitants of all territory belonging to the Confederate States, lying without the limits of the several States; and may permit them, at such times, and in such manner as it may by law provide, to form States to be admitted into the Confederacy. In all such territory the institution of negro slavery, as it now exists in the Confederate States, shall be recognized and protected by Congress and by the Territorial government; and the inhabitants of the several Confederate States and Territories shall have the right to take to such Territory any slaves lawfully held by them in any of the States or Territories of the Confederate States.[45]

This provision ensured the perpetuation of slavery as long and as far as the Confederate States could extend its political reach, and more than a few Confederates had their eyes fixed on Cuba and Central and South America as objects of future conquest. That a society featuring chattel slavery cannot be described as "free" seems to be lost on McGuire, Van Cott, and DiLorenzo in large measure because they insist on identifying freedom within the narrow framework of theoretical economics and its emphasis on free trade: where there is *free trade* there is, by definition, *freedom*. Where there are obstacles to free trade, such as protective tariffs, there is proportionately less freedom. "The Confederate Constitution, Tariffs, and the Laffer Relationship" leads to the conclusion that the Confederate Constitution, complete with its strict endorsement of and perpetual protection for slavery, was a freer one than the U.S. Constitution fathered by James Madison.

But Lincoln never for a moment believed that one could separate the grave injustice of slavery from discussions of freedom. The abolitionist ex-slave Frederick Douglass once described the U.S. Constitution as a "glorious liberty document."[46] Unlike the Confederate Constitution, the U.S. Constitution freely permitted states to abolish slavery. If the day ever came when slavery was eliminated voluntarily throughout the United States, not one word of the U.S. Constitution would need to be changed, whereas slavery could never lawfully be abolished under the Confederate Constitution. Both Douglass and Lincoln would probably be shocked to learn that modern academics use theoretical economics to argue that the Confederate Constitution offered greater protection for freedom than the U.S. Constitution.

While DiLorenzo offers no analysis of the slavery provisions of the Confederate Constitution, he is confident that slavery would not have lasted long under that document. He argues that the influence of Enlightenment philosophy, "the waning support for laws that artificially propped up slavery," and "the advance of the industrial revolution in the South . . . would have made slavery more and more uneconomical compared to capital-intense agriculture and manufacturing," which in turn "would probably have led to the institution's demise long before the end of the century."[47] But each of DiLorenzo's premises is problematic. First, the latest iterations of European philosophy during the antebellum period were to be found in the writings of G. W. F. Hegel and Charles Darwin, whose teachings, when transported to the United States, were often interpreted as justifications for, not arguments against, black slavery. Second, "support for laws that artificially propped up slavery" was waxing, not waning, as Lincoln demonstrated in his 1857 speech on *Dred Scott v. Sandford*. Third, serious questions have been raised about the assumed economic superiority of free labor over slave labor, beginning with Kenneth Stampp's observation that "critics of slavery who argue that the institution was an economic burden to the master were using the weakest weapon in their arsenal."[48] Robert Fogel and a generation of cliometricians have demonstrated that "the growing mountains of evidence [have] finally made it obvious that the profitability of slavery was increasing, not declining, on the eve of the Civil War."[49] Given the profitability of slavery, there is reason to believe that it might have lasted far longer than many economists believe. Further, neither Abraham Lincoln nor anyone else could know in 1861 what slavery's fate was to be. But Lincoln did know that slavery, and slavery alone, had become the most polarizing subject in American politics.

LINCOLN AND POLITICAL ECONOMY

Some libertarians object more deeply to Lincoln's Whig economics, a form of political economics. Lincoln adopted an older view, one that dates back at least to Aristotle, which understands economics in terms of politics. Lincoln believed that political justice is real, not an illusion, and therefore that all questions of economics and other public policies should bend to the demands of what is just or right.

Some libertarian economists are so consumed with what one might call the theory of pure market economics, or purely theoretical economics, that they ignore the basic premise of political economy. That all economics is political means that economics serves politics. Stated differently, politics commands economics in a way that economics does not command politics. This is because moral questions of right and wrong, justice and injustice, are not the proper subject of economics; they are the subject of politics. Economics is concerned with means; politics is concerned with ends (as well as means).

In certain circumstances, a particular mode of economic acquisition or a particular thing to be acquired may be unjust or injurious either to individuals or to the common good of the political community. Trafficking in and owning human beings is an example. Confronted with an institution like slavery, politics should order the economy, or at least the injurious part of it, so that the freedom within it is consistent with natural and civil justice and does not undermine the conditions necessary for a free and decent society. We do this when we pass laws regulating drugs, prostitution, and other forms of economic exchange that we deem injurious to the public morality and the common good.

Other times, for example, threats to national security from enemy nations require that economic policies be subordinated to national defense measures. This was especially true in early American history, when the nation was a budding and weak republic surrounded by a world of monarchs and imperial powers whose very legitimacy the republican principles of America threatened and who therefore had a great interest in seeing America fail. In what turns out to be more than a slight irony, one of the clearest and succinctest explanations of political economy, as well as one of the strongest defenses of the tariff and internal improvement policies, was offered by an early American whom libertarians claim as their own free market champion: John C. Calhoun.

In his younger years, while serving as a member of the U.S. House of Representatives from South Carolina—when he still believed in the natural rights foundation of constitutional government—Calhoun held political and economic views markedly different from what his later reputation tells. He was an ardent nationalist and among the congressional "hawks" during the War of 1812. Immediately after the war, he supported economic policies identified by all sides as "Hamiltonian," including tariff policies to help pay off American war debts and protect developing American industries.[50] So persuasive was Calhoun's defense of tariffs and protection that in 1843 a group of young Illinois Whigs, in a campaign circular they had prepared for the citizens of Illinois explaining the importance of a protective tariff, cited Calhoun as one of their main authorities, quoting at length from his 1816 speech on the tariff. The chief author of the campaign circular was a young Whig politician named Abraham Lincoln.

In 1816, terrified by the reality that the United States had no navy and had barely survived the War of 1812, Calhoun took up the work of advancing in Congress a proposed tariff, one that would pay down the war debt while simultaneously protecting certain American industries and strengthening the American military. In his April 4, 1816, speech to Congress, he spoke about the preeminent concern for all economic policy, national security:

> The security of the country mainly depends on its spirit and its means; and the latter principally on its moneyed resources. Modified as the industry of this country now is, combined with our peculiar situation and want of a naval ascendancy, whenever we have the misfortune to be involved in a war with a nation dominant on the ocean—and it is almost with such at present we can be—the moneyed resources of the country to a great extent must fail.[51]

In Calhoun's mind, at least his mind in 1816, sound economic and national security policies are intrinsically intertwined:

We cannot be indifferent to dangers from abroad, unless, indeed, the House [of Representatives] is prepared to indulge in the phantom of eternal peace, which seems to possess the dream of some of its members. Could such a state exist, no foresight or fortitude would be necessary to conduct the affairs of the republic; but as it is the mere illusion of the imagination, as every people that ever has or ever will exist, are subject to the vicissitudes of peace and war, it must ever be considered as the plain dictate of wisdom, in peace to prepare for war.[52]

To drive home the importance of economic and military self-sufficiency, Calhoun emphasized the question of war-making production:

It is admitted by the most strenuous advocates, on the other side, that no country ought to be dependent on another for its means of defense; that at least, our musket and bayonet, our cannon and ball, ought to be of domestic manufacture. But what is more necessary to the defense of a country than its currency and finance? Circumstanced as our country is, can these withstand the shock of war? Behold the effect of the late war on them.[53]

Just as America should not depend on foreign powers for its "musket and bayonet" and its "cannon and ball," so America should not depend on foreign powers for its necessities and the conveniences of life, at least not while the nation was a young republic struggling merely for survival against monarchical and nonrepublican enemies who viewed America's success as a threat to their own political rule. Under the protection of what Calhoun called "the fostering care of government," American manufactures would surely grow "to certain perfection . . . and we will no longer experience these evils." Indeed, self-sufficiency, what Aristotle identified as a necessary condition of the best regime, ought to be the aim of American political-economic policies, according to the young Calhoun.

In his speech, Calhoun acknowledged earlier economic "blunders," alluding to the extreme nature of Jefferson's embargo. But the central mistake of American economic policy prior to the late war was one not of excess but of deficiency: "The taxes were not laid sufficiently early, or to as great an extent as they ought to have been." According to Calhoun in 1816, American legislators' main mistake was that they had taxed too little and too late!

In the end, Calhoun concluded, the "liberty and union of this country are inseparably united." The chord that united liberty and union was entwined around policies that encouraged the economic growth and independence of the young and vulnerable nation. For Calhoun in 1816, the most "terrible danger" America faced was the threat of disunion, a sure consequence of severe economic depression or failure. Disunion: "This single word comprehends the sum of our political dangers, and it is against it we ought to be perpetually guarded." In this most remarkable reversal of political opinion, here the future father of nullification, interposition, and secession, the leading mind who would later fuel the fires of *disunion* in protest against tariffs and internal improvements, sounded the alarm in 1816 that the greatest threat to American union was the want of internal improvements and a protective tariff and that the greatest threat to American liberty was disunion! Whatever might be said of Calhoun's later positions on these critical subjects, the Calhoun of 1816 provided a defense perhaps unequaled in his day of political economics and the Whig economics later championed by Lincoln.

None of this is to deny that some criticism can be leveled against Lincoln's economic policies. In his earlier years, Lincoln did not understand the total economic influence of various economic policies. He was so devoted to Henry Clay and his "American System" that he did not think through all of its economic problems. But economics was never Lincoln's major point of interest. In his masterful biography of Lincoln, Lord Charnwood points out that "the chief questions which agitated the Illinois Legislature [during Lincoln's early political career] were economic, and so at first were the issues between Whigs and Democrats in Federal policy." "Though he threw himself into these affairs with youthful fervor," Charnwood writes, "[Lincoln] would appear never to have had much grasp of such matters."[54]

Lincoln failed to understand, for example, that any tax or tariff laid on any particular goods raises not merely their direct costs for those who purchase them but the overall transaction costs for the entire economy. The economy as a whole absorbs an artificial increase in the prices of some goods, directly or indirectly raising costs for all citizens. For example, Lincoln wrote in 1843,

> By the tariff system, the whole revenue is paid by the consumers of foreign goods, and those chiefly, the luxuries, and not the necessities of life. By this system, the man who contents himself to live upon the products of his own country, *pays nothing at all*. And surely, that country is extensive enough, and its products abundant and varied enough, to answer all the real wants of its people. In short, by this system, the burthen of revenue falls almost entirely on the wealthy and luxurious few, while the substantial and laboring many who live at home, and upon home products, *go entirely free*.[55]

In the end, argued Lincoln, only "those whose pride, whose abundance of means, prompt them to spurn the manufactures of our own country, and to strut in British cloaks, and coats, and pantaloons, may have to pay a few cents more on the yard for the cloth that makes them." Lincoln then added the sarcastic jest, "A terrible evil, truly, to the Illinois farmer, who never wore, nor never expects to wear, a single yard of British goods in his whole life." His joke, however, indicates Lincoln's probable lack of understanding that when tariffs are high, domestic producers have a powerful incentive to raise the prices of their goods, thus costing Americans money. As noted by Gabor Boritt, who has produced the most exhaustive treatment of Lincoln's Whig economics, Lincoln here "carried his point too far," misrepresenting the overall economic effects caused by increased tariffs or taxes. "Instead of making a broad, long-term case for economic development," writes Boritt, "for purposes of electioneering he had fallen back to simplistic, short-term demonstrations of the democratic virtues of Whig policies. This was not Lincoln at his best."[56]

DiLorenzo rightly criticizes economic mistakes Lincoln made in some of his early speeches on the Independent Treasury System and other economic matters, and he also points out some of Lincoln's rhetorical excesses in those speeches (in 1839, for example, Lincoln said that "all [would] suffer more or less, and very many [would] lose every thing that renders life desirable" if the money supply were backed by gold or silver).[57] DiLorenzo is at his best when describing the theoretical principles of market economics and the harmful economic effects of government regulation. I agree with him, for example, in his following general analysis:

> Protectionism is an indirect subsidy to politically influential businesses that comes at the expense of consumers (who pay higher prices) and potential competitors. Because government never has the resources to subsidize all businesses, so-called internal improvement subsidies could never have amounted to anything but selective subsidies to politically favored businesses. And a nationalized banking system . . . has always been used as a means of printing money (and thereby creating inflation) to pay for even more selective special-interest subsidies.[58]

It is fair for DiLorenzo and other economists to provide an economic critique of Lincoln's defense of internal improvements and other items on the Whig economic agenda, including a national bank and paper money policies. But they should balance those critiques with a discussion of the constitutional, political, moral, and other issues that influenced Lincoln's thought and action, rather than simply collapsing them all together under the umbrella of economics. As Charnwood acknowledges, "It is only when constitutional or moral issues [such as the extension of slavery] emerge that his politics become interesting."[59] Lincoln seemed to be of a similar opinion. "We, the old Whigs," Lincoln wrote in an 1859 letter, "have been entirely beaten out on the tariff question." Lincoln believed that Whig economic policies could not help win elections unless the absence of those policies "shall have demonstrated the necessity for [them], in the minds of men heretofore opposed to [them]."[60]

An economist today might argue that because the economic effects of protectionism are always more harmful than helpful, the absence of protectionist economic policies would never "have demonstrated the necessity" for them and that Lincoln was wrong to think otherwise. But DiLorenzo never mentions Lincoln's own concession that many Whig economic ideas had been defeated politically and placed on the political back burner as slavery took center stage in the arena of national politics. As the 1850s progressed, Whigs and eventually the newly formed Republican Party became less confident that economic policies such as a national bank, tariffs, and internal improvements would help them win elections and they turned instead to the growing sectional controversy over the spread of slavery into federal territories. In an 1860 speech in Connecticut, Lincoln explained that by the time the Republican Party had been organized in 1854, "this question of Slavery was more important than any other." Indeed, "no other national question," not the tariff or any other economic question, "can even get a hearing just at present."[61]

SOUTHERNERS OPPOSE CALIFORNIA, THEN DOUGLAS

In the antebellum period, two events reveal most clearly the passions and discord slavery sparked, unmatched by any other public policy question, and the grip that racism had come to have on the American mind, especially in the South. The first was the fight in 1849–1850 over the admission of California to the Union; the second was the breakup of the 1860 Democratic Party convention.[62]

In 1848, the discovery of gold in California generated an unprecedented rush to the West. By the time Congress convened in 1849, the people of California had skipped over the usual process of territorial organization and were asking for entry into the Union, complete with their own proposed state constitution. The trouble was that Californians wanted to be admitted as a free state, prohibiting slavery within their jurisdiction. This the South would not accept.

It was not that Southerners were clamoring to take their slaves to the Golden State—common opinion held that slavery could never flourish in the desert climes of California. The question of California arose as Congress was still fighting over the Wilmot Proviso and its prohibition against slavery in any new territory gained from Mexico. Southerners were most angered by the moral condemnation of slavery California's constitutional prohibition implied. So strong was their conviction that slavery was a positive good and so fanatical were they to have the rest of the country accept the institution as such that Southerners in Congress opposed the admission of California with its proposed state constitution prohibiting slavery. As Lincoln later recounted, "There California stood, kept *out* of the Union because she would not let slavery *into* her borders."[63]

While they protested California's refusal to accept slavery in the winter of 1849 and 1850, Southerners were busy organizing secession meetings throughout the slave states, resolved that if Congress did not offer unqualified protection for slavery, they would prefer to depart from the Union. In response, Ohio congressman Columbus Delano exploded in anger, threatening "to establish a cordon of free states that shall surround you; and then we will light up the fires of liberty on every side until they melt your present chains and render all your people free."[64] President Zachary Taylor, a Southerner, gave Delano's sentiments teeth when he threatened to use military force against any state attempting to secede, an act Taylor considered treasonous.[65] In all of the fighting over California, which nearly resulted in secession and civil war as early as 1850, slavery alone, not tariffs, banks, internal improvements, or any other economic issue, formed the pivotal point of dispute.[66]

California was finally admitted to the Union with the Compromise of 1850, which would never have passed except for the deaths of the most strident defender of slavery in Congress, John C. Calhoun, and one of the most strident defenders of the Union, Zachary Taylor. The compromise measures were split into separate bills and successfully shepherded through Congress by Stephen Douglas, turning him into a national political celebrity almost overnight (which is one reason he was able to secure the Kansas-Nebraska Act and repeal the Missouri Compromise four years later in 1854). The Compromise of 1850 featured a number of Northern concessions to slavery, including a new and tougher fugitive slave law, under the terms of which a fee of $10 would be paid to a federal commissioner who declared an alleged runaway slave to be the property of a slave owner claiming him, but the commissioner would receive payment of only $5 if he found the alleged slave to be a free man.[67] Perhaps the most odious part of the 1850 fugitive slave law, from the antislavery point of view, was that it effectively transformed all Northerners into slave catchers. The law required all "marshals and deputy marshals" in free states to assist in capturing alleged runaway slaves. If they failed in this duty, they could be fined $1,000 and sued "for the full value of the service or labor of said fugitive in the State, Territory, or District whence [the slave had] escaped."[68] Further, the new fugitive slave law prohibited private citizens from aiding runaway slaves in any way. Any citizen who helped a runaway slave escape capture would be subject to a fine of $1,000 and up to six months in prison.

A decade later, in April 1860, the Democratic Party held its national convention in Charleston, South Carolina. At one of the longest and certainly most boisterous of American party conventions, Democrats were split between those who supported Stephen Douglas and his doctrine of "popular sovereignty," which included the right of the people of a territory to exclude slavery, and those who championed the position announced by the Supreme Court in the *Dred Scott* case, which held that it was unconstitutional to prohibit slavery from federal territories because slave owners possessed a constitutional right to their slave property and could take that property where they pleased.

The Democratic Party, the only truly national political party on the eve of the Civil War, could not reconcile these differences. The climax of the meeting came with the speech of Alabama's "fire eater," William Yancey. Ignoring all questions of tariffs, banks, and internal improvements, Yancey spoke to a whooping and excited crowd, telling them that Northern Democrats' fundamental error was their acceptance of the view that slavery was evil. Had Northern Democrats defended slavery as a good and benign institution all along, he explained, the party would be united; because they had not, the blame for the Democratic schism lay with the North, not the South, according to Yancey.

Twelve years earlier, during the 1848 Democratic convention, with the controversy over California just coming into view, Yancey had led a failed movement for Southern delegates to walk out of the convention unless the party adopted a platform declaring that neither Congress nor a territorial legislature could exclude slavery from a territory. Twelve years later, at the 1860 convention, however, he was successful. When the convention failed to adopt a platform that offered federal police protection for slavery throughout all U.S. territories, delegates from the entire lower South walked out, with Yancey and his fellow Alabamans leading the way. Historian David Potter captures the significance of what happened in Charleston: "The Democratic convention of 1860 . . . ended with a schism which not only destroyed the last remaining party with a nationwide constituency, but also foreshadowed with remarkable accuracy the schism that appeared in the Union itself less than a year later."[69] Mark Graber suggests Southern Democrats were not "astute" enough to know that "maintaining a sectional balance of power was more crucial to securing their constitutional understandings," that they could have won political alliances with Northern Democrats, which would have been the most effective security for Southern interests, if only they had compromised on slavery in the territories.[70] But Graber fails to recognize how obsessed many Southerners had become with slavery by 1860, interpreting the slightest suggestion that slavery was wrong as a great insult to Southern pride and honor. In fact, there was no cause for the disruption of the 1860 Democratic convention *other than slavery*. The two wings of Democrats ended up holding separate conventions in 1860 and nominating two Democratic candidates for the presidency, Stephen Douglas and John Breckinridge. In the general election later that November, both Democratic candidates appeared on the ballot, splitting the Democratic vote and contributing to the election of the Republican candidate, Abraham Lincoln. The delegates' walking out of the 1860 Democratic convention was the first real act of secession: as historian Don Fehrenbacher has noted, any Democrat who would not accept Stephen Douglas as the Democratic nominee would never accept Abraham Lincoln as the Republican president of the United States.[71]

Lincoln critics today who want to equate the cause of the Confederacy with the cause of limited government and economic freedom must answer an embarrassing question: why did Southern Democrats oppose Stephen Douglas for the presidential nomination in 1860?[72] The answer: they did so not out of a desire for limited government but out of a stubborn insistence that *all* Democrats affirm slavery as a good thing and allow it to spread without limits. In his last debate with Douglas at Alton, Illinois, Lincoln had clearly demonstrated that if one accepted Douglas's popular sovereignty principle—that by "unfriendly legislation . . . slavery may be driven from the territories"—then the logical conclusion furnished "an argument by which abolitionists may deny the obligation to return fugitives, and claim his fugitive [slave]." "I defy any man," Lincoln said, "to make an argument that will justify unfriendly legislation to deprive a slaveholder of his right to hold his slave in a territory, that will not equally, in all its length, breadth and thickness, furnish an argument for nullifying the fugitive slave law." "Why," Lincoln famously concluded, "there is not such an Abolitionist in the nation as Douglas, after all."[73] Douglas was amused that Lincoln had labeled him an abolitionist, but the Southern mind followed Lincoln's political logic perfectly and did not find it funny.

Pro-slavery Southerners became persuaded that Douglas's "popular sovereignty" might be used to obstruct rather than aid the advance of slavery, which is precisely why Southern Democrats opposed Douglas at the 1860 convention. They had become students of Lincoln far more than Douglas suspected.

With the clarity offered by hindsight, it seems ridiculous for Southerners to have rejected Douglas, who was firmly committed to Manifest Destiny expansionism. As president, he would have supported the Southern demand for the acquisition of Cuba and probably the rest of Latin America as well. The 1860 Democratic platform, upon which Douglas was nominated, stated that "the Democratic Party [is] in favor of the acquisition of the Island of Cuba on such terms as shall be honorable to ourselves and just to Spain."[74] Throughout Cuba and South America, slavery could have expanded, almost certainly with Douglas's active support. The spread of slavery to distant lands was a logical extension of Douglas's oft professed belief that America was "made by white men for the benefit of white men and their posterity for ever" and his repeated insistence that he was "in favor of confining citizenship to white men, men of European birth and descent, instead of conferring it upon negroes, Indians, and other inferior races."[75] These acquired lands most likely would have added slave states to the Union, and they certainly would have added Democratic states, thereby bolstering the power of Democrats in Congress to pass any policies demanded by the Democratic slave interests of the South.

Had the South supported Douglas and remained united in the Democratic Party, and had the Democratic Party presented a united platform dedicated to the Union but also recognizing the sectional interests of the South, it is unlikely Lincoln could have been elected over Douglas. But Southerners rebelled against Douglas for no other reason than their zealous attachment to slavery. The South would not support those who did not share their enthusiasm for the spread of that institution, those, like Douglas, who did not believe that the Constitution required it. The South rejected Douglas and seceded from the Democratic convention because of its demand that in every U.S. territory then or thereafter acquired, slavery be guaranteed and given federal police protection. Douglas rejected this because it stood opposed to his doctrine of popular sovereignty. Contrary to Lincoln critics who want to argue that Southerners were merely trying to protect states' rights and limited government against the intrusive government of Republicans like Lincoln, the Southern demand for federal slave protection represented a demand for an unprecedented expansion of federal power.

DiLorenzo complains that Northern "Yankees never shied away from using the coercive powers of government to compel others to be remade in their image."[76] But he ignores altogether similar attempts by the South. From the 1850 fugitive slave law, which legally turned all free citizens into slave catchers, to the Southern Democrats' 1860 demand for a federal slave code in the territories, Southerners, too, were quite willing to use the power of the national government to "compel others to be remade in their image."

The Southern threats of secession, both in the controversy over California and at the 1860 Democratic convention, as well as their unprecedented demand for federal protection for slavery, would have been unimaginable had the Southern mind not become convinced that slavery was right and worth defending. No one summarized more clearly the new view of blacks as an inferior race that should, for their own good, be enslaved than Confederate vice president Alexander Stephens in 1861:

> The prevailing ideas entertained by [Thomas Jefferson] and most of the leading statesmen at the time of the formation of the old constitution, were that the enslavement of the African was in violation of the laws of nature; that it was wrong in principle, socially, morally, and politically. . . . Our new [Confederate] government is founded upon exactly the opposite idea; its foundations are laid, its cornerstone rests, upon the great truth that the negro is not equal to the white man; that slavery—subordination to the superior race—is his natural and normal condition. This, our new government, is the first, in the history of the world, based upon this great physical, philosophical, and moral truth.[77]

Powerful intellectual forces that rejected the natural right principles of the Founding were shaping the American mind and rendering it increasingly difficult for intelligent (and not so intelligent) Americans to comprehend, much less agree with, those principles. "It is now no child's play to save the principles of Jefferson from total overthrow in this country," Lincoln remarked in an 1859 letter. The challenge, as Lincoln understood it in the 1850s and 1860s, was more than reasoning properly about basic political principles of right; it was recovering the very foundation upon which such reasoning could be exercised:

> One would start with great confidence that he could convince any sane child that the simpler propositions of Euclid are true; but, nevertheless, he would fail, utterly, with one who should deny the definitions and axioms. The principles of Jefferson are the definitions and axioms of free society. And yet they are denied, and evaded, with no small show of success. One dashingly calls them "glittering generalities"; another bluntly calls them "self evident lies"; and still others insidiously argue that they apply only to "superior races."[78]

Lincoln understood that while these expressions of disagreement with the principle of equality might differ in form, they were all identical in object: "supplanting the principles of free government, and restoring those of classification, caste, and legitimacy." Those who denounced the principles of the Founding, Lincoln argued, "would delight [in] a convocation of crowned heads, plotting against the people. They are the van-guard—the miners, and sappers—of returning despotism. We must repulse them, or they will subjugate us." As Lincoln pointed out in his 1857 speech on *Dred Scott,*

> Our Declaration of Independence [used to be] held sacred by all, and thought to include all; but now, to aid in making the bondage of the negro universal and eternal, it is assailed, and sneered at, and construed, and hawked at, and torn, till, if its framers could rise from their graves, they could not at all recognize it. All the powers of earth seem rapidly combining against him. Mammon is after him; ambition follows, and philosophy follows, and the theology of the day is fast joining the cry.[79]

PRO-SLAVERY CHRISTIAN THEOLOGY

Corresponding to the rise of the "positive good" theory of slavery was a transformation in American Christian theology, increasingly influenced by modern European, particularly German, philosophy. The German philosopher Hegel posed an especially difficult problem for theologians by arguing that all knowledge, including theological knowledge, is historical or evolutionary knowledge. According to Eldon Eisenach, "By 1900, churchmen had been integrating German historical scholarship and German philosophy into American religion and moral philosophy for more than sixty years." Hegelian historicism, in particular, "was initially responsible for transforming American theology." "In so doing," Eisenach writes, "the older millennial/national themes of American Protestantism became increasingly merged into theories of social evolution. Hegel was the framework within which 'Darwinism' was incorporated into religious thought, and German historicism was the means by which God's spirit was charted in both church and society."[80] In the antebellum South, religious thought incorporated the ideas of Hegel and Darwin to provide a potent defense of slavery that was well received by many Southern whites.

In the religious and political thought of James Henley Thornwell, for example, we see the combination of strict biblical interpretation with Hegelianism and Darwinism that Eisenach describes, used effectively for the purpose of defending slavery. Thornwell, who was widely known throughout the South as the "Calhoun of the Church," was a prominent Presbyterian preacher in South Carolina and an influential professor at, and later president of, South Carolina College. According to historian of religion Mark Noll, Thornwell had a reputation as "the Southern apologist with the greatest intellectual integrity and the most consistently forceful exposition of orthodox Christian faith."[81] In an 1861 sermon, "A Southern Christian View of Slavery," Thornwell opened his defense of slavery by placing it beyond the concerns of true Christians:

> In the first place, we would have it distinctly understood that, in our ecclesiastical capacity, we are neither the friends nor the foes of slavery, that is to say, we have no commission either to propagate or abolish it. The policy of its existence or nonexistence is a question which exclusively belongs to the state. We have no right, as a church, to enjoin it as a duty or to condemn it as a sin.[82]

True Christians, according to Thornwell, should concern themselves almost exclusively with spiritual matters, not moral or political concerns such as slavery. Echoing certain medieval Christian doctrines, Thornwell had earlier maintained that the church and the state are in almost completely separate orbits, each having very little influence or bearing on the other. (As the secession crisis approached, however, Thornwell abandoned his theory of the separation of church and state and pledged the support of the church to the secessionist movement. When South Carolinians met in 1860 to consider secession from the Union, the meeting opened with a prayer by Thornwell.)[83] If, on rare occasions, Christians do venture into politics, Thornwell maintained, their only guide for political or moral judgment is holy scripture. The only question regarding slavery for the church, therefore, was whether or not slavery was a sin according to scripture. "In answering this question," Thornwell reminded his pious followers, "let it be distinctly borne in mind that the only rule of judgment is the written word of God."

> The Church knows nothing of the intuitions of reason or the deductions of philosophy, except those reproduced in the Sacred Canon. She has a positive constitution in the Holy Scriptures and has no right to utter a single syllable upon any subject except as the Lord puts words in her mouth. She is founded, in other words, upon express revelation.[84]

Christians should not try to reason, Thornwell argued, because the question of how Christians viewed slavery must be asked within the narrow confines of revelation: "Do the Scriptures directly or indirectly condemn slavery as a sin? If they do not, the dispute is ended, for the Church, without forfeiting her character, dares not go beyond them."[85] When Thornwell opened his Bible, he found no explicit prohibition or condemnation of slavery. Rather, in both the Old and the New Testaments, slavery is to be regulated, and slaves are to be treated kindly by their masters.[86] Thornwell and other leading Southern theologians found it instructive that the Bible contains no clear, categorical condemnation or prohibition of slavery, suggesting that slavery existed because God willed it to exist. "Slavery is no new thing. It has not only existed for ages in the world but it has existed, under every dispensation of the covenant of grace, in the Church of God." Thus, Thornwell insisted, "if men had drawn their conclusions upon this subject [of slavery] only from the Bible, it would no more have entered any human head to denounce slavery as a sin than to denounce monarchy, aristocracy, or poverty." Instead of reading the Bible, however, some "men have listened to what they falsely considered as primitive intuitions, or necessary deductions from primitive cognitions, and then have gone to the Bible to confirm the crotchets of their vain philosophy."

Thornwell also addressed the question of whether the Bible's Golden Rule and other "general denunciations of tyranny and oppression" require Christians to conclude that slavery is sinful. He answered with a resounding no, reasoning that "no principle is clearer than that a case positively excepted cannot be included under a general rule." Thus, while the Bible supplies a general Golden Rule instructing human beings to treat others as they wish to be treated, the same Bible also "expressly mention[s] and treat[s] [slavery] as a lawful relation." According to Thornwell, only two conclusions can be drawn from this seeming paradox: either "scripture is to be interpreted as inconsistent with itself," or "slavery is by necessary implication excepted" from the scope of the Golden Rule.[87] In other words, the Golden Rule does require human beings to treat others as they want to be treated, but it does not apply to the way slaves are to be treated because slavery is "expressly" protected as a lawful institution within the Bible and therefore exempt from the Bible's Golden Rule. Far from considering slaveholding to be un-Christian, Thornwell assured his fellow Southerners that it was precisely the Southern defense of slavery that best represented true Christianity. "We stand upon the foundation of the prophets and apostles, Jesus Christ himself being the chief cornerstone," he exclaimed.

Interestingly, Thornwell also urged Southern Christians to embrace the idea of slavery as a Christianizing institution and reminded them of their duty to Christianize slaves. He opposed those who assumed the slave had no soul. Even the "meanest slave," he argued, "has in him a soul of priceless value," a soul that should be saved and not neglected by the slave owner. But Thornwell was also quick to point out that the Christian salvation of the souls of slaves in no way suggested that slaves should be freed or treated as anything other than slaves. "Our design in giving [slaves] the

Gospel," Thornwell argued, "is not to civilize them, not to change their social condition, not to exalt them into citizens or freemen—it is to save
them."[88] A Christian's highest duty toward his slave was to turn the slave
into a pious Christian, but there was no duty to set the slave free. Thornwell was widely influential because his message came at just the right time,
when Southern Christians most needed assurance that they could be good
Christians and good slave owners at the same time, that being a good Christian in no way threatened the Southern way of life built upon slave labor.

Near the end of his sermon, Thornwell turned to the question of natural rights and whether slaves possessed rights equal to their masters. In his
discussion of rights, a subject not textually supported by the Bible, Thornwell's historicism emerges: "As to the endless declamations about human
rights, we have only to say that human rights are not a fixed but a fluctuat-
ing quantity. Their sum is not the same in any two nations on the globe.
The rights of Englishmen are one thing, the rights of Frenchmen another."
Rights, according to Thornwell, are not rooted in an unchanging nature
but rather change with history. Taking the difference of rights among different peoples as his premise, Thornwell implied that it was historically
right for some people to possess more or fewer or different rights than others. By establishing an evolutionary hierarchy among different races,
Thornwell then built an argument strikingly similar to Calhoun's:

> The education of the species consists in its ascent along [a] line. As you
> go up, the number of rights increases . . . [and] as you come down the
> line, rights are diminished. . . . Now, when it is said that slavery is in-
> consistent with human rights, we crave to understand what point in this
> line is the slave conceived to occupy. There are, no doubt, many rights
> which belong to other men—to Englishmen, to Frenchmen, to his Mas-
> ter, for example—which are denied to [the slave]. But is he fit to pos-
> sess them? Has God qualified the Negro slave to meet the responsibili-
> ties which their possession necessarily implies? His place in the
> [evolutionary] scale is determined by his competency to fulfill his duties.
> . . . Before slavery can be charged with doing him injustice, it must be
> shown that the minimum which falls to his lot at the bottom of the line
> is out of proportion to his culture and his capacity—a thing which can
> never be done by abstract speculation.

Thornwell clearly rejected the idea of immutable, natural rights in favor of
historical rights. Rights, according to Thornwell, are "not a fixed but a fluc-
tuating quantity." "The truth is," he argued, "the education of the human race
for liberty and virtue is a vast providential scheme, and God assigns to every
man, by a wise and holy degree, the precise place he is to occupy in the great

school of humanity." "[Rights] are distributed into classes according to their competency and progress. For God is in history."[89] Rights, in other words, increase as a "race" of men advances in history, the "great school of humanity."

Thornwell echoed Hegel when he wrote that "God is in history." Hegel had concluded *The Philosophy of History* by arguing that "the history of the world, with all the changing scenes which its annals present, is this process of development and the realization of Spirit . . . the justification of God in History."[90] According to Hegel, God is *in*, not outside of, history; God is not an eternal being independent of time but a product of time. The unfolding of history is the unfolding of God, and the knowledge gained by the new science of evolutionary history is the first genuine knowledge of God's will. Divine right, in other words, is evolutionary right. Thornwell used Hegelian historicism to argue that if evolution had placed some men in slavery, then it was God's will that slaves they should remain, at least until God or historical evolution indicated otherwise. Thornwell had no patience for "abstract speculation"; he would not entertain what Lincoln referred to as an "abstract truth applicable to all men and all time." Thornwell dismissed the idea of "abstract truth" as "crotchets of vain philosophy." Instead, he argued that one must look to actual conditions here and now to determine what God intended for various races of men. When Thornwell asked whether slaves were fit to possess rights, whether "God qualified him to meet the responsibilities which their possession necessarily implies," his question was rhetorical: to him it was obvious that God intended for blacks to be slaves because they were in fact living as such. Had God intended for slaves to be free, then they would be free in fact; their own slavery was proof that God and historical evolution, which was but one of God's instruments, intended for blacks to be slaves. Any disagreement based on abstract principles of natural right, therefore, was sinful pride because it assumed to know better than God the "vast providential scheme" by which "God assigns [a position] to every man."

Consider also the theology of the prominent Alabaman pastor, the Rev. Dr. Fred A. Ross. In *Slavery Ordained of God*, an 1857 collection of his speeches (most delivered before general assemblies as he traveled through New York and other parts of New England), Ross not only argued that slavery is a social good sanctioned by the Bible but condemned anyone who disagreed as being impious.[91] Ross praised the "powerful intellects in the South, following the mere light of a healthy good sense, guided by the common grace of God, [who] reached the very truth of this great matter—namely, that the relation of the master and slave is not sin." Ross argued further that slavery

> is a connection between the highest and lowest races of man, revealing
> influences which may be, and will be, most benevolent for the ultimate

good of the master and the slave—conservative of the Union, by preserving the South from all forms of Northern fanaticism, and thereby being a great balance-wheel in the working of the tremendous machinery of our experiment of self-government. This seen result of slavery was found to be in absolute harmony with the word of God.[92]

Assuming "there is no right and wrong in the nature of things," Ross looked with suspicion on those "anti-slavery men who have left the light of the Bible, and wandered into the darkness until they have reached the blackness of the darkness of infidelity." That infidelity consisted above all in the "theory" that "right and wrong are eternal facts; that they exist per se in the nature of things; that they are ultimate truths above God; that He must study, and does study, to know them as really as man." "Now, sir, this theory is atheism," Ross emphasizes, because "if right and wrong are like mathematical truths—fixed facts—then I may find them out as I find out mathematical truths, without instruction from God."[93] Any belief in immutable, rational, natural principles of right and wrong, according to Ross, "is atheism." Far from being "fixed facts," Ross insisted, right and wrong "are results brought into being, mere contingencies, made to exist solely by the will of God." Ross used incest and polygamy to demonstrate his argument that nothing is intrinsically right or wrong. Citing the book of Genesis in the Old Testament and assuming that Cain and Abel had incestuous relations with their sisters in order to propagate the human race—according to the biblical account, there was no mankind at that time other than the children of Adam and Eve—Ross asks, "Was [incest] wrong in the nature of things?" When someone in the audience responded, "Certainly," Ross denied it:

> What an absurdity, to suppose that God could not provide for the propagation of the human race from one pair, without requiring them to sin! Adam's sons and daughters must have married, had they remained in innocence. [But according to the audience member who thinks incest is sinful], they must then have sinned in Eden, from the very necessity of the command upon the race: "Be fruitful, and multiply, and replenish the earth." What pure nonsense![94]

Ross emphasized that "there is not a word [in the Bible] forbidding [incestuous] marriage, until God gave the law (Leviticus 18) prohibiting marriage in certain degrees of consanguinity."

> That law made, then, such marriage sin. But God gave no such law in the family of Adam; because he made, himself, the marriage of brother and sister the way, and the only way, for the increase of the human race.

> He commanded them thus to marry. They would have sinned had they
> not thus married; for they would have transgressed his law.

According to Ross's strict interpretation of the Bible, incest is not intrinsically wrong, a wrong in nature that can be discovered by reason; rather, incest *becomes* wrong only after God declares it to be sinful. Using the same
biblical analysis, Ross argues that the same is true in the case of polygamy:
"God made no law against polygamy, in the beginning. Therefore it was no
sin for a man to have more wives than one."[95] It is not until the New Testament, Ross explains, that God "now forbids polygamy," but he is clear that
"polygamy now is sin—not because it is in itself sin, but because God forbids it." The transition from the Old to the New Testament, for Ross, represents the process of how "the transition from the lower to the higher
table-land of our progress upward is made." After the New Testament, Ross
argues, "we sin, then, if we marry the sister, and other near of kin; and we
sin if we marry, at the same time, more wives than one, *not because there is
sin in the thing itself* . . . but because in so doing we transgress God's law."

More importantly than incest or polygamy, however, "the subject of
slavery, in this view of right and wrong, is seen in the very light of heaven."

> God sanctioned slavery then, and sanctions it now. He made it right,
> they know, then and now. Having thus taken the last puff of wind out
> of the sails of the anti-slavery phantom ship, turn to the twenty-first
> chapter of Exodus. God, in these verses, gave the Israelites his command
> how they should buy and hold the Hebrew servant—how, under certain
> conditions, he went free—how, under other circumstances, he might be
> held to service forever with his wife and her children. There it is.[96]

Ross also pointed out that "God in the New Testament made no law prohibiting the relation of master and slave."

> The precepts in Colossians 4 and 1 Timothy 6 and other places, show,
> unanswerably, that God has really sanctioned the relation of master and
> slave as those of husband and wife, and parent and child. . . . He sanc-
> tioned [slavery] under the Old Testament and the New, and ordains it
> now while he sees it best to continue it, and he now, as heretofore, pro-
> claims the duty of the master and the slave.

Convinced that nothing is wrong except that which God has declared sinful, and convinced that God has never declared slavery to be such, Ross
made clear his understanding of the two sides in the fight over slavery:

> These two theories of Right and Wrong—these two ideas of human
> liberty—the right, in the nature of things, or the right as made by

God—the liberty of the individual man, of Atheism, of Red Republicanism, of the Devil—or the liberty of man, in the family, in the State,
the liberty from God—these two theories now make the conflict of the
world. This anti-slavery battle is only part of the great struggle: God will
be victorious—and we, in his might.[97]

From Ross's theological point of view, Lincoln's principled opposition to slavery represented nothing less than "atheism," "Red Republicanism," and "the
Devil" because Lincoln believed in immutable principles of natural right.

Throughout his speeches and correspondence, Ross often cited man's
"natural history," in addition to the Bible, as the proper moral guide for
Christians. For example, he wrote in a letter,

> I agree with you, sir, that the second paragraph of the Declaration of In-
> dependence contains five affirmations, declared to be self-evident truths,
> which, if truths, do sustain you and all abolitionists in every thing you
> say as to the right of the negro to liberty; and not only to liberty—to
> equality, political and social. But I disagree with you as to their truth,
> and I say that not one of said affirmations is a self-evident truth, or a
> truth at all. On the contrary, that each one is contrary to the Bible; that
> each one, separately, is denied; and that all five, collectively, are denied
> and upset by the Bible, *by the natural history of man,* and by Providence,
> in every age of the world.

As there is no intrinsic right or wrong, as nothing is eternally right or
eternally wrong, as God's will changes in time, history becomes a guide for
Christians to discern God's will. For Ross, interpreting God's will in light
of evolutionary history "vindicates God from unintelligible abstractions,"
foremost the "abstraction" that all men are created equal and possess equal
rights by nature.[98] For the purposes of American government and politics,
the meaning of rights and who has them evolves with history, as does God's
will. Ross was emphatic on this point: "Life, liberty, and the pursuit of happiness *never were* the inalienable right of the individual man." To argue otherwise, as the American Founders and as Abraham Lincoln did, is to "find
fault with God, ye anti-slavery men, if you dare."[99]

The theological defense of slavery evidenced in Ross's arguments
made its way into legal arguments as well. The 1858 California Supreme
Court case *In Re Archy* (discussed in chapter 3) raised the question of
whether a Mississippi slave owner could bring his slave property with him
to California when California's constitution prohibited slavery. The attorney representing the slave owner argued that the California Constitution
was wrong to prohibit slavery because slavery was justified by "its origin in
the laws of nature." "Slavery derives its force and dignity from the same

principles of right and reason, the same views of the nature and constitution of man, and the same sanction of Divine revelation as those from which the science of morality is deduced," the lawyer argued. Slavery was also beneficial, he concluded, because "[its] effect is the moral and physical improvement of the slave himself."[100]

SLAVERY, RACE, AND THE SOUTHERN MIND

Although Lincoln opposed the theological arguments justifying slavery, he learned from Southern theologians to be cautious when invoking God as a justification for political right. In 1862, as the Civil War grew in intensity, Lincoln reflected on this problem with perspicuity:

> The will of God prevails. In great contests each party claims to act in accordance with the will of God. Both *may* be, and one *must* be wrong. God can not be *for*, and *against* the same thing at the same time. In the present civil war it is quite possible that God's purpose is something different from the purpose of either party.[101]

Russell Kirk approvingly cites this passage from Lincoln, explaining, "Man's order, Lincoln was saying, is subordinate to a providential order."[102] The problem or challenge, however, is in *understanding* the "providential order" to which "man's order is subordinate," especially in light of competing claims over what the "providential order" means. Should "man's order" be subject to the "providential order" as understood by Thornwell and by Ross? Whose theology is the correct foundation for politics? Who will decide? And what principle will be appealed to in order to solve theological-political disputes? Lincoln believed the best star and compass available to man as he navigates the complicated and turbulent waters of politics is the abstract and theoretical principle of human equality comprehended by reason, yet Kirk praises Lincoln precisely because Lincoln was, in Kirk's words, "not a man of theoretic dogmas in politics." But without the abstract principle of natural right, it is unclear how, on Kirk's own ground, Lincoln could exercise practical judgment and choose a course of action he believed to be most right in the face of the many passionate theological, political, and moral claims that surrounded him in his darkest days in the White House.

Unlike Kirk, Lincoln was quite willing to examine the political claims of theology in light of "theoretic" principles of equality and self-government. In a surviving fragment, for example, Lincoln responded to Ross's arguments, exposing how the new theological apologies for slavery were really thinly veiled attempts to serve the interests of slave owners: "Suppose it is true," Lincoln reflected, "that the negro is inferior to the white, in the gifts of nature; is it not the exact reverse [of] justice that the white should, for that reason, take from the negro, any part of the little which has been given him?" "*Give to him that is needy* is the Christian rule of charity; but *Take from him that is needy* is the rule of slavery.*" Lincoln proceeded to dismantle the pro-slavery theological arguments presented by Ross, Thornwell, and others:

> The sum of pro-slavery theology seems to be this: "Slavery is not universally *right*, nor yet universally *wrong*: it is better for *some* people to be slaves; and in such cases it is the Will of God that they be such."
>
> Certainly there is no contending against the Will of God; but still there is some difficulty in ascertaining, and applying it, to particular cases. For instance, we will suppose the Rev. Dr. Ross has a slave named Sambo, and the question is, "Is it the will of God that Sambo shall remain a slave, or be set free?" The Almighty gives no audible answer to the question, and his revelation—the Bible—gives none—or, at most, none but such as admits of a squabble, as to its meaning. No one thinks of asking Sambo's opinion on it. So, at last, it comes to this, that *Dr. Ross* is to decide the question. And while he considers it, he sits in the shade with gloves on his hands, and subsists on the bread that Sambo is earning in the burning sun. If he decides that God wills Sambo continue a slave, he thereby retains his own comfortable position; but if he decides that God wills Sambo to be free, he thereby has to walk out of the shade, throw off his gloves; and delve for his own bread. Will Dr. Ross be actuated by that perfect impartiality, which has ever been considered favorable to correct decisions?

Lincoln concluded by pointing out the ultimate irony of the argument that slavery was a *positive good*:

> But slavery is good for some people!!! As a good thing, slavery is strikingly peculiar in this, that it is the only good thing which no man ever seeks the good of *for himself.* Nonsense! Wolves devouring lambs, not because it is good for their own greedy maws, but because it is good for the lambs!!![103]

In his 1860 speech at the Cooper Institute in New York City, Lincoln concluded by raising the question, what will satisfy pro-slavery Southerners? It will not be enough, Lincoln argued, for Republicans merely to leave Southerners alone.

> We must not only let them alone, but we must, somehow, convince them that we do let them alone. This, we know by experience, is no

easy task. We have been so trying to convince them from the very beginning of our organization, but with no success. In all our platforms and speeches we have constantly protested our purpose to let them alone; but this has had no tendency to convince them. Alike unavailing to convince them, is the fact that they have never detected a man of us in any attempt to disturb them.[104]

What else might Republicans do to appease the South? One thing only, argued Lincoln: "Cease to call slavery *wrong*, and join them in calling it *right*."

And this must be done thoroughly—done in *acts* as well as in *words*. Silence will not be tolerated—we must place ourselves avowedly with them. Senator Douglas's new sedition law must be enacted and enforced, suppressing all declarations that slavery is wrong, whether made in politics, in presses, in pulpits, or in private. We must arrest and return their fugitive slaves with greedy pleasure. We must pull down our Free State constitutions. The whole atmosphere must be disinfected from all taint of opposition to slavery, before they will cease to believe that all their troubles proceed from us.[105]

In a slender, but powerful, book, *Apostles of Disunion,* historian Charles Dew reviews the speeches of "secession commissioners" as they traveled throughout the South during the "secession winter" of 1860 and 1861 trying to persuade their fellow Southerners to leave the Union.[106] In this critical moment, with nothing less than the fate of the United States and constitutional government at stake, what arguments were they advancing to justify secession? Most were not talking about states' rights or old squabbles over tariffs or other economic policies. They were talking about slavery.

As Judge William Harris from Mississippi argued before the Georgia legislature, blacks were "an ignorant, inferior, barbarian race, incapable of self government, and not . . . entitled to be associated with the white man." Perhaps the greatest fear, argued Georgian Henry Benning before the Virginia secession convention, was that "our women" would suffer "horrors we cannot contemplate in imagination." As Dew comments, "There was not an adult present who could not imagine exactly what Benning was talking about." Other secession commissioners were even more direct. Leroy Pope Walker, Alabama's commissioner deployed to Tennessee (and subsequently the first Confederate secretary of war), predicted that if the South did not secede immediately, everything it valued would be lost: "first our property," then "our liberties," and finally the greatest Southern treasure of all, "the sacred purity of our daughters." The wives and daughters of the South would be lost to "pollution and violation to gratify the lust of half-civilized Africans."[107]

When the time came for Southern secession, it was chosen out of a concern to preserve slavery, a concern fueled by fears of black equality and black and white amalgamation. Consider Mississippi's official declaration of secession, styled "A Declaration of the Immediate Causes Which Induce and Justify the Secession of the State of Mississippi from the Federal Union":

> Our position is thoroughly identified with the institution of slavery—the greatest material interest of the world. Its labor supplies the product which constitutes by far the largest and most important portions of commerce of the earth. These products are peculiar to the climate verging on the tropical regions, and by an imperious law of nature, none but the black race can bear exposure to the tropical sun. These products have become necessities of the world, and a blow at slavery is a blow at commerce and civilization. That blow has been long aimed at the institution, and was at the point of reaching its consummation. There was no choice left us but submission to the mandates of abolition, or dissolution of the Union, whose principles had been subverted to work out our ruin.[108]

The turning of the tide toward disunion and civil war rested squarely on the question of race and slavery, and the moving force within the South was a powerful fear that blacks would come to be viewed as equal human beings with the same rights as whites.

Late in the Civil War, as the South found itself in dire straits and victory seemed increasingly elusive, the prospect of arming slaves and enlisting them to fight for the Confederacy was raised as a last-ditch measure. Eventually, in March 1865, out of sheer desperation and panic, the Confederate Congress passed a bill authorizing the arming of black slaves and training them to fight; it turned out to be too little, too late, as Confederate forces would surrender to the Union a mere one month later. But even in their darkest hour, Confederates clung with zeal to their professed belief in the inferiority of blacks.

Hearing that the Confederate Congress was considering enlisting slaves, one Alabama newspaper lamented,

> We are forced by necessity of condition to take a step which is revolting to every sentiment of pride, and to every principle that governed our [Confederate] institutions before the war, [yet] it is better for us to use the negroes for our defense than that the Yankees should use them against us.

Some Southerners would not relent on the question of arming slaves—and the equality it implied, if not required—even in the face of defeat. The *Charleston Mercury* editorialized that if slaves were armed, "the poor man [would be] reduced to the level of the nigger. His wife and daughter are to be hustled on the street by black wenches, their equals. Swaggering buck niggers are to ogle and elbow them." Inside the Confederate Congress, the president pro tem of the Confederate Senate, Robert Hunter, expressed skepticism about enlisting slaves in the army, asking "What did we go to war for, if not to protect our property?" Georgian Howell Cobb acknowledged that "if slaves will make good soldiers [then] our whole theory of slavery is wrong. The day you make soldiers out of them is the beginning of the end of [our Confederacy]." When the most celebrated of all Southern generals, Robert E. Lee, supported the idea of training and enlisting slaves, coupled with the proposal of freeing them after they had served, South Carolina's *Mercury* erupted in anger, "*We want no Confederate Government without our institutions* [i.e. slavery]." The newspaper chided Lee as "author of this scheme of nigger soldiers and emancipation" and as a "disbeliever in slavery," and it questioned whether Lee was "a good Southerner; that is, whether he [was] satisfied with the justice and beneficence of negro slavery."[109] This is the ugly truth of America during the Civil War, so ugly it is hard for some Americans today to imagine, but true nonetheless.

LINCOLN'S POLITICAL THEOLOGY

With erudition and beauty, Lincoln demonstrated in his first and second inaugural addresses, with the Gettysburg Address situated between them, that slavery was the main cause for the Civil War. But even these great monuments of American political rhetoric are not without their detractors. In *Abraham Lincoln: A Constitutional Biography*, George Anastaplo takes issue with Lincoln's most famous utterances on the Civil War and slavery.

The title of his book's central chapter, "The Poetry of Abraham Lincoln" perhaps best states Anastaplo's thesis. He argues that poetry, as opposed to rational argument, was central to Lincoln's thought and speech, and therefore Lincoln's legacy has had profoundly undesirable effects on American politics. Anastaplo is concerned that Americans have made too much of Lincoln, explaining, "I would prefer to see more made of the American regime, and less of Abraham Lincoln."[110] This is because, in Anastaplo's opinion, "an undue emphasis upon particular personages, as distinguished from the principles of the regime, may make the American Republic precarious in the way that republican Rome was when it depended as much as it did on someone such as Marcus Brutus to reverse the decline into Caesarism." But America is not Rome. Rome did not find its justification in self-evident truths rooted in human nature. Further, no one was more conscious of the dangers of modern Caesarism than Lincoln, who spoke directly to the problem of Caesarism in his 1838 Lyceum speech:

> Many great and good men sufficiently qualified for any task they should undertake, may ever be found, whose ambition would aspire to nothing beyond a seat in Congress, a gubernatorial or a presidential chair; but such belong not to the family of the lion, or the tribe of the eagle. What! think you these places would satisfy an Alexander, a Caesar, or a Napoleon? Never! Towering genius disdains a beaten path. . . . It scorns to tread in the footsteps of any predecessor, however illustrious. It thirsts and burns for distinction; and, if possible, it will have it, whether at the expense of emancipating slaves, or enslaving freemen.[111]

In some instances, however, Anastaplo praises Lincoln and argues that at certain critical moments he exercised his political and poetic skills in the service of constitutionalism and in defense of natural right. So, why does Anastaplo seek to lower Lincoln's status in the American mind?

Anastaplo's chapter on the Gettysburg Address provides part of the answer. That chapter moves from Lincoln's Lyceum speech to the Gettysburg Address. In his analysis of the earlier Lyceum speech, Anastaplo directs the reader's attention to Lincoln's emphasis on reason as providing the "critical support for the regime." In that speech, Lincoln argued against the dangers of the "mobocratic spirit" that was growing in parts of America, as evidenced by increasingly frequent mob violence against abolitionists and other critics of slavery, and explained that "passion has helped us, but can do so no more." Passion, Lincoln argued, "will in the future be our enemy. Reason, cold, calculating, unimpassioned reason, must furnish all the materials for our future support and defense. Let those materials be molded into general intelligence, sound morality, and, in particular, a reverence for the Constitution and laws."[112] This reverence for the laws, Lincoln urged, should become the "political religion" of the nation.

When Anastaplo turns to the Gettysburg Address, however, he finds something very different. Instead of an appeal to "cold, calculating, unimpassioned reason," he reads a speech dripping with religiosity and religious sentiments. In his treatment of Lincoln's two last major speeches, the Gettysburg Address and the second inaugural, Anastaplo focuses almost exclusively on their religious connotations and orientation. These utterances by Lincoln, writes Anastaplo, are "biblical," "prophetic," and "messianic." As Anastaplo notes, the Gettysburg Address is like a prayer, opening with an invocation of the paternal ("Four score and seven years ago, our Fathers brought forth on this continent") and concluding with a vision of the ever after ("that government of the people, by the people, for the people, shall not perish from the earth"). The second inaugural almost reads like a passage from the Old Testament, as Lincoln interprets the suffering of the Civil War as a divine punishment for the sin of slavery:

> Fondly do we hope—fervently do we pray—that this mighty scourge of war may speedily pass away. Yet, if God wills that it continue, until all the wealth piled by the bond-man's two hundred and fifty years of un-requited toil shall be sunk, and until every drop of blood drawn with the lash, shall be paid by another drawn with the sword, as was said three thousand years ago, so still it must be said "the judgments of the Lord, are true and righteous altogether."[113]

Lincoln's appeal to the religious is highly problematic, Anastaplo insists, because religion is related to, if not identical with, emotion, passion, and unreason; he describes it as "mystical." Anastaplo's account of Lincoln's more religious-sounding speeches, in fact, is strikingly similar to those offered by earlier historical revisionists who charged Lincoln with "emotionalism."[114] The problem, according to Anastaplo, is that Lincoln, in effect, refounded America on principles far more religious and far less rational than those of Jefferson and the Founders. Anastaplo agrees with Garry Wills, whose *Lincoln at Gettysburg: The Words That Remade America* (1992) won the Pulitzer Prize and the National Book Award. According to Wills, Lincoln at Gettysburg "performed one of the most daring acts of open-air sleight-of-hand ever witnessed by the unsuspecting." "Everyone in the vast throng of thousands," he asserts, "was having his or her intellectual pocket picked" by Lincoln, who had cleverly "substituted" a new constitutional understanding "for the one they brought with them."[115] According to Wills, modern America owes far more to the "values created by the Gettysburg Address" and far less to the principles of the Founders, which both Wills and Anastaplo see as largely incongruent to, if not incompatible with, one another. But while Wills seems willing to celebrate Lincoln's veiled transformation of the American regime, Anastaplo has serious reservations.

According to Anastaplo, the Founders had "presented divinity in the image of the political," as the divine was subordinate to, or understood in light of, the rational principles of the regime. But Lincoln reversed this and presented the "political in the image of divinity." According to Anastaplo, Lincoln's rhetorical politics appeals far too much to the supernatural and ignores far too greatly nature and reason.

Toward the end of his Gettysburg Address chapter, Anastaplo writes, "The passions aroused by the terrible fratricidal struggle proved to be such as to permit, perhaps even to compel, the public identification of the entire experience with the Passion."[116] Anastaplo then argues that Lincoln "helped turn serious American thought away from . . . classical political philosophy," while the "divine takes the place in Lincoln's thought of nature."[117] This is a problem because it is nature, not the divine, "upon which classical political thought rests." Anastaplo goes on to write that

> whatever the political usefulness or the ultimate sincerity of such sentiments, they do seem somehow more impassioned, somewhat less urbane, than those which one associates with classical political philosophy or for that matter the Declaration of Independence. . . . Thus philosophy—the essentially Socratic understanding—seems, by the end of Lincoln's life, not to have the status one finds assigned to it in classical political thought.

Anastaplo seems to agree that the Declaration's rational principles are the ground of rational constitutionalism. But as *the* American poet, Lincoln renders rational constitutionalism, as well as Socratic rationalism, difficult, if not impossible, by elevating the divine in his political poetry. Anastaplo suggests that antebellum America provided much richer intellectual ground for reasoning than postbellum America because Lincoln denigrated the status of reason and nature. Anastaplo even suggests, in a vague and cautious way, that the religious and irrational emphasis of Lincoln's rhetoric somehow caused the rise of pragmatism and progressivism in the United States.[118] This is why Anastaplo wants to demote Lincoln and argues against his defenders and celebrators. This is also why his book on Lincoln is not an ordinary biography, but a *constitutional biography*, emphasizing that Lincoln was a product of the American constitutional regime, not vice versa.

Anastaplo's problem lies in his failure to understand the principles of the Declaration of Independence and the Constitution in their fullness; in particular, he fails to see the firm moral ground upon which reason and revelation intersect and the American constitutional order was constructed. From the Founders' point of view, passion can never be eliminated from the human soul: they believed human nature to be unchanging because they believed that human beings always have been, and always will be, a combination of passion and reason. The Founders would see any attempt to remake human beings into singularly rational, unimpassioned creatures as both impossible and tyrannical.

This is perhaps best demonstrated by contrasting the American Revolution with the French. Unlike the French, the Americans possessed a decidedly moderate, or reasonable, opinion of human reason. They understood that human reason is capable of discerning certain truths, including self-evident moral and political truths, that inhere in nature. But they also understood that there are limits to human reason, that it is neither omniscient nor omnipotent, and it is therefore a mistake to assume that human reason (or the claims of certain human beings on behalf of reason) should rule with absolute and unrestrained authority. This is precisely why the Americans thought a constitutional government of limited powers was best suited for human beings with limited powers of reason.

Perhaps the most important principled difference between the American Revolution versus that of the French is the understanding of reason's capacity in light of the claims of revelation: The French assumed that reason alone could and should rule human affairs without restraint or interference from religion. Thus, the French tried desperately to drive religion from French society, famously renaming the cathedral at Notre Dame the "Temple of Reason" and abandoning the Christian calendar in favor of a secular one.

The Americans, however, inaugurated a regime of religious liberty where religious inquiry and worship were not only free, but were encouraged, to flourish. Religious liberty is a necessary political corollary to the rational recognition of the limits of human reason, a recognition that religion or revelation might provide answers that reason alone cannot discern. The Founders understood that the complete political rule of reason, unchecked and unhindered by the claims of revelation, leads to tyrannical fanaticism no less than the complete political rule of revelation unchecked and unhindered by the claims of reason. The wisdom of the Founders is nowhere more evident than in their reasonable assessment of reason and reasonable respect for the claims of revelation. Lincoln recognized that wisdom as early as 1838, proudly announcing that "we find ourselves under the government of a system of political institutions conducing more essentially to the ends of civil and religious liberty than any of which the history of former times tells us."[119]

The Founders understood that reason is no less the voice of God than sacred scripture. Lincoln shared this opinion. Lincoln's appeal to the divine, therefore, was no different than those made by the Founders. (One need only think of Washington's first inaugural, in which he offered thanks to "that Almighty Being who rules over the universe" and asked "that his benediction may consecrate the liberties and happiness of the people of the United States.") Both Lincoln and the Founders assumed that the fundamental distinction between morality and immorality, whether discovered in the pages of scripture or discerned through unassisted reason, is real and binding on all human beings. Like the Founders, Lincoln also understood the limitations of reason, that reason cannot answer every human question, which means certain appeals to revelation might be reasonable precisely because reason cannot prove otherwise.

Edward Erler, a political scientist and Lincoln scholar, compares Lincoln's first and second inaugural addresses and offers a compelling argument regarding the depth of Lincoln's understanding of reason and revelation and the philosophic statesmanship that flowed from it:

> The First Inaugural begins with custom ("In compliance with a custom as old as the government itself . . . ") and ends with nature (" . . . the better angels of our nature."); the Second Inaugural begins with a "second coming" ("At this second appearing to take the oath . . . ") and ends with peace among nations (" . . . a lasting peace, among ourselves, and with all nations."). Thus the First Inaugural represents an appeal to reason, whereas the Second Inaugural represents an appeal to revelation. . . . It is obvious, however, that the "somber theology" of the Second Inaugural has none of the optimism of the First Inaugural. The two speeches represent a move from comedy, as it were, to tragedy.[120]

The movement from comedy to tragedy that Erler rightly discerns in Lincoln's rhetoric reflects the human failure to solve the problem of slavery through reason or speech, or *logos*. Instead, the solution required blood.

In his first inaugural address, delivered after seven states had declared secession from the Union but before the bombing of Fort Sumter or any fighting had erupted between North and South, Lincoln concluded by stating, "I am loath to close." Lincoln did not want to stop talking because he prayed that as long as there was talk, there was some hope that reason might triumph, that cool and peaceful minds might be open to persuasion by rational discussion. Thus, Lincoln pleaded, "We are not enemies, but friends. We must not be enemies." Friends want what is good for one another; they talk to and help one another to discover what that is. Enemies, however, seek each other's destruction.

Lincoln recognized as well as anyone that "passion may have strained" friendships between North and South, but he insisted that "it must not break our bonds of affection," and he hoped that the "mystic chords of memory, stretching from every battle-field, and patriot grave, to every living heart and hearthstone, all over this broad land, will yet swell the chorus of the Union, when again touched, as surely they will be, by the better angels of our nature."[121] The first inaugural address ends with optimism because the country, however deeply divided, was still at peace; therefore, there was still a chance for North and South to keep talking. There was still a chance to regain the "rulership of reason," to borrow the words of Leo Strauss.[122] There was still a chance, however remote, that Americans would be touched "by the better angels of [their] nature." The distinction in Lincoln's rhetoric between the "better angels" that formed the "chorus of the Union" versus the "passion" that was dividing Americans corresponds to Aristotle's distinction between the two parts of the human soul, reason and passion.[123] By preserving the Union, Americans could demonstrate that reason still ultimately ruled the passions pushing toward disunion and conflict, however powerful at the moment. Preserving the American union would mean preserving the superiority of reason over passion, speech over force, right over might. Unionism at least provided the opportunity to negotiate and debate peacefully and to devise laws acceptable to most. Thus, Lincoln asked earlier in his first inaugural, "Can aliens make treaties easier than friends can make laws? Can treaties be more faithfully enforced between aliens, than laws can among friends?" A united America would be an America in which speech, that is, reasoned and reasonable discussion, about the most divisive problems might solve them.

But Americans were not touched by the better angels of their nature. Instead, the war came.

When Lincoln stood to deliver his second inaugural address, there was little cause for optimism, as there had been four years earlier. Between Lincoln's inaugural addresses, America had suffered almost unimaginable losses in a horrific, bloody war—a brother's war. In this moment of terrible sorrow, Lincoln's purpose was "to bind up the nation's wounds," not to incite more fighting and deepen those wounds by pointing the finger of blame at one side of the conflict. The Civil War took on many dimensions of a war of religion as churches and theologians, in both the North and South, claimed that their respective causes were the causes of God.[124] In his second inaugural address, Lincoln, almost alone among his contemporaries, discerned the hand of Providence not as a weapon to be used to strike the enemy but as a call to all Americans to come together and sin no more. As historian Mark Noll explains,

> If . . . we set the address in its own times rather than consider its importance for the Meaning of America, we find it defines a major historical puzzle concerning the character of theology. The puzzle is posed by that fact that none of America's respected religious leaders—as defined by contemporaries or later scholars—mustered the theological power so economically expressed in Lincoln's Second Inaugural. None probed so profoundly the ways of God or the response of humans to the divine constitution of the world. None penetrated as deeply into the nature of

providence. And none described the fate of humanity before God with the humility or sagacity of the president.[125]

Among the second inaugural's most striking features is Lincoln's refusal to claim all moral high ground for the North. He would not demonize the South. While Lincoln did say that everyone knew that slavery "was, somehow, the cause of the war" and that "one [side] would *make* war rather than let the nation survive; and the other would *accept* war rather than let it perish," he also emphasized that "both parties deprecated war" and that "neither party expected for the war, the magnitude, or the duration, which it ha[d] already attained."[126] Neither North nor South could have anticipated how great the war would prove to be, and therefore it would not be altogether fair to blame one side for all the suffering and damage it had caused. Most theologians of the day, almost to a man, interpreted the evils of the war as a consequence of the evils of the enemy and argued that therefore God would sanction punishing the enemy as a kind of divine retribution.

But Lincoln was far more cautious in claiming to know the will of God, reflecting his own understanding of the limitations of reason. The war and all the suffering that came with it, Lincoln indicated, might well be punishment from God for the sins of both the North and the South. Thus, Lincoln placed the ultimate cause of the war not in the hands of one side but in those of an inscrutable God. In many ways, the beauty of Lincoln's second inaugural is unparalleled in the history of American political oration, so I ask the reader's forgiveness when I quote the following passage in full:

> Both read the same Bible, and pray to the same God; and each invokes His aid against the other. It may seem strange that any men should dare to ask a just God's assistance in wringing their bread from the sweat of other men's faces; but let us judge not that we be not judged. The prayers of both could not be answered; that of neither has been answered fully. The Almighty has His own purposes. "Woe unto the world because of offences! For it must needs be that offences come; but woe to that man by whom the offence cometh!" If we shall suppose that American Slavery is one of those offences which, in the providence of God, must needs come, but which, having continued through His appointed time, He now wills to remove, and that He gives to both North and South, this terrible war, as the woe due to those by whom the offence came, shall we discern therein any departure from those divine attributes which the believers in a Living God always ascribe to Him? Fondly do we hope— fervently do we pray—that this mighty scourge of war may speedily pass away. Yet, if God wills that it continue, until all the wealth piled by the bond-man's two hundred and fifty years of unrequited toil shall be sunk,

and until every drop of blood drawn with the lash, shall be paid by another drawn with the sword, as was said three thousand years ago, so still it must be said "the judgments of the Lord, are true and righteous altogether."[127]

For some critics, however, Lincoln's appeal to the Divine showed either a sign of lunacy or was merely designed to ease his guilty conscience. In *When in the Course of Human Events*, Charles Adams asserts that the second inaugural address, with all of its religious allusions, was a sign of "Lincoln's Jehovah complex," which gave the Civil War a "psychopathic Calvinistic fatalism." "Not even the maddest of religious fanatics ever uttered words to equal Lincoln's Second Inaugural Address," Adams exclaims, suggesting that Lincoln was most likely desperately attempting "to shift the blame and remove his own guilt, and he was quite willing to resort to reasoning more characteristic of a psychotic mind than a healthy mind." In his second inaugural, Adams asserts, Lincoln "was guilt-ridden and was close to becoming mentally ill at this time," evidenced in no small part by the fact that Lincoln claimed that he "saw God as the primary force behind the war, thus granting himself absolution and exculpating his actions in driving the nation into war and refusing to promote peace when the opportunity was always there."[128] Only a madman, in other words, might believe that God intervenes in human affairs and punishes men for their sins!

Lincoln concluded the second inaugural with what has become one of the most famous perorations in history:

> With malice toward none; with charity for all; with firmness in the right, as God gives us to see the right, let us strive on to finish the work we are in; to bind up the nation's wounds; to care for him who shall have borne the battle, and for his widow, and his orphan—to do all which may achieve and cherish a just, and a lasting peace, among ourselves, and with all nations.[129]

Lincoln said that Americans should care for *all* who had "borne the battle," meaning soldiers of the South no less than those of the North, as well as the widows and orphans they had left behind. Had Lincoln devoted his second inaugural address, delivered near the end of the Civil War, to placing blame with the South, he might have fueled a new wave of violence by Northerners seeking vengeance. Instead, Lincoln called for charity and generosity, poetically deflecting the animosity between the North and South and calling the attention of both to a mysterious God whose ways are difficult to discern but whose justice is perfect. In so doing, Lincoln highlighted the great gulf that separates all mankind from God and thus encourages humility and reconciliation in place of revenge. Lincoln wanted the war to end and knew it never would so long as Americans viewed one another as enemies. Americans must, once again, become friends. The foundation for this renewed American civic friendship would be a deeper understanding of America's first principle, human equality, an understanding made more profound by the painful lessons taught to those who disavowed or disobeyed the "father of all moral principles." The renewed friendship among all Americans, Northern and Southern, white and black, that might be possible after the Civil War represented, in the immortal words of the Gettysburg Address, "a new birth of freedom."

Anastaplo correctly detects a strong poetic presence in Lincoln's later rhetoric, but he is wrong if he agrees with H. L. Mencken, who dismissed the Gettysburg Address as "poetry not logic; beauty, not sense."[130] Lincoln's philosophic poetry, especially in the second inaugural, but also in the first inaugural and the Gettysburg Address, was the mark of deep reflection on human nature, evidence that Lincoln possessed a profound understanding of human capacity and human excellence, as well as human limitations. This quality, perhaps above all else, accounts for Lincoln's unique role in helping Americans understand what and who they are. As Mark Noll has explained, "The contrast between the learned religious thinkers and Lincoln in how they interpreted the war poses the great theological puzzle of the Civil War." Lincoln, who was "a layman with no standing in a church and no formal training as a theologian," nevertheless "propounded a thick, complex view of God's rule over the world and a morally nuanced picture of America's destiny," while the country's most celebrated theologians, by contrast, "presented thin, simple views of God's providence and a morally juvenile view of the nation and its fate."

> The theologians talked as if God had accomplished all that had been done, yet they assumed that humans could control their own destinies. Lincoln urged his fellow citizens to seize the opportunities of the moment but did not assume they could control their own fate. For the theologians there was little mystery in how God dealt with the world; for Lincoln there was awesome mystery. . . . For the theologians, the end of the war only tightened the bond between God and his American chosen people; for Lincoln the course of the war injected doubt about whether America was the people of God.[131]

The "thick, complex" view of God Lincoln offered makes perfect sense given the horrific injustice of slavery and the horrific suffering required to end it. There was a time when Lincoln's presidential speeches were etched in the American mind. Americans knew those speeches precisely because they understood, with Lincoln, that slavery stood at the center of the great conflict of the Civil War. We, today, cannot understand those speeches unless we understand once again that the Civil War tested whether America would live up to its own noble principles, however difficult that might be.

NOTES

1. See Jefferson Davis, *The Rise and Fall of the Confederate Government* (New York: D. Appleton & Co., 1881), and Alexander Stephens, *A Constitutional View of the Late War between the States* (Philadelphia: National Publishing Co., 1868).

2. Thomas DiLorenzo, *Lincoln Unmasked: What You're Not Supposed to Know about Dishonest Abe* (New York: Crown Forum, 2006), 177.

3. Charles Adams, *When in the Course of Human Events: Arguing the Case for Southern Secession* (Lanham, MD: Rowman & Littlefield, 2000), 80, 82.

4. Max Farrand, *The Records of the Federal Convention of 1787* (New Haven, CT: Yale University Press, 1911), II:453–4, III:254.

5. C. William Hill, "Contrasting Themes in the Political Theories of Jefferson, Calhoun, and John Taylor of Caroline," *Publius* 6, no. 3 (summer 1976), 73–91.

6. Joel H. Silbey, *The Shrine of Party: Congressional Voting Behavior 1841–1852* (Westport, CT: Greenwood Press, 1981 [1967]), 7–9.

7. See chapter 5.

8. DiLorenzo, *Lincoln Unmasked*, 170–72; Adams, *When in the Course of Human Events*, 90; Walter Williams, "The Civil War Wasn't about Slavery," December 2, 1998, *Jewish World Review*, www.jewishworldreview.com/cols/williams120298.asp (accessed June 10, 2006); Thomas E. Woods Jr., *The Politically Incorrect Guide to American History* (Washington, DC: Regnery Publishing, 2004), 37–40.

9. F. W. Taussig, *The Tariff History of the United States* (New York: G. P. Putnam's Sons, 1892), 88–89.

10. DiLorenzo, *Lincoln Unmasked*, 117.

11. Woods, *The Politically Incorrect Guide to American History*, 38.

12. Irving H. Bartlett, *John C. Calhoun: A Biography* (New York: W. W. Norton & Co., 1993), 145.

13. Bray Hammond, *Banks and Politics in America: From the Revolution to the Civil War* (Princeton, NJ: Princeton University Press, 1985 [1957]), 451.

14. Bartlett, *John C. Calhoun: A Biography*, 143.

15. Taussig, *The Tariff History of the United States*, 109.

16. DiLorenzo, *Lincoln Unmasked*, 119, 136.

17. Williams, "The Civil War Wasn't about Slavery."

18. Karl Marx, "The North American Civil War," October 25, 1861, Marxists Internet Archive, www.marxists.org/archive/marx/works/1861/10/25.htm (accessed July 10, 2007).

19. Donald Miller, "The Economic Causes of the Civil War," September 7, 2001, LewRockwell.com, www.lewrockwell.com/orig2/miller1.html (accessed July 15, 2007).

20. Adams, *When in the Course of Human Events*, 79.

21. Thomas DiLorenzo, *The Real Lincoln: A New Look at Abraham Lincoln, His Agenda, and an Unnecessary War* (Roseville, CA: Prima Publishing, 2002), 263–64.

22. Quotation taken from DiLorenzo, *The Real Lincoln*, 263. See also chapter 8, "Reconstructing America: Lincoln's Political Legacy," and chapter 9, "The Great Centralizer: Lincoln's Economic Legacy."

23. DiLorenzo, *Lincoln Unmasked*, 115.

24. Charles A. Beard and Mary R. Beard, *The Rise of American Civilization* (New York: Macmillan Co., 1927).

25. Beard and Beard, *The Rise of American Civilization*, II, 40.

26. Charles A. Beard, *An Economic Interpretation of the Constitution of the United States* (New Brunswick, NJ: Transaction Publishers, 2003 [1913]), 7, 15.

27. Thomas J. Pressly, *Americans Interpret Their Civil War* (New York: The Free Press, 1962 [1954]), 242.

28. Pressly, *Americans Interpret Their Civil War*, 243–44.

29. Mark Thornton and Robert B. Ekelund Jr., *Tariffs, Blockades, and Inflation: The Economics of the Civil War* (Wilmington, DE: SR Books, 2004). In *Lincoln Unmasked*, DiLorenzo cites Thornton and Ekelund at p. 16.

30. Thornton and Ekelund, *Tariffs, Blockades, and Inflation*, xv.

31. Thornton and Ekelund, *Tariffs, Blockades, and Inflation*, xxviii.

32. See C. B. Macpherson, ed., *Thomas Hobbes: Leviathan* (New York: Penguin Books, 1968), part I, chapters 11–13.

33. Macpherson, *Thomas Hobbes: Leviathan*, 160–61.

34. For an intelligent discussion of the contradiction inherent in any materialistic interpretation of the human mind, see Phillip E. Johnson, *Reason in the Balance: The Case against Naturalism in Science, Law, and Education* (Downers Grove, IL: InterVarsity Press, 1995).

35. Francis Fukuyama, "The End of History?" *The National Interest* (summer 1989), www.wesjones.com/eoh.htm#source (accessed January 8, 2007).

36. Thornton and Ekelund, *Tariffs, Blockades, and Inflation*, xxix.

37. Thornton and Ekelund, *Tariffs, Blockades, and Inflation*, 81.

38. Thornton and Ekelund, *Tariffs, Blockades, and Inflation*, 83.

39. Thornton and Ekelund, *Tariffs, Blockades, and Inflation*, 88–89.

40. Philip Shaw Paludan, *The Presidency of Abraham Lincoln* (Lawrence: University of Kansas Press, 1994), 110.

41. Philip Shaw Paludan, *"A People's Contest": The Union and Civil War, 1861–1865* (Lawrence: University of Kansas Press, 1996), 149, 150.

42. Thornton and Ekelund, *Tariffs, Blockades, and Inflation*, 69, 75.

43. DiLorenzo, *Lincoln Unmasked*, 127. See also Robert A. McGuire and T. Norman Van Cott, "The Confederate Constitution, Tariffs, and the Laffer Relationship," *Economic Inquiry* 40, no. 3 (July 2002), 427–38.

44. In time, John C. Calhoun challenged the view that the U.S. Constitution permitted protectionist tariffs, notably in his responses to the 1828 tariff as he switched from his earlier defense of the tariff. As McGuire and Van Cott point out, however, no less an authority than James Madison rejected Calhoun's interpretation: "In two separate correspondences, one in 1828 and another in 1832, Madison disputed Calhoun's idea about what transpired at the 1787 Philadelphia convention with respect to protective or prohibitory tariffs. Such tariffs, argued Madison, were never meant to be unconstitutional. Madison's challenge of Calhoun's view . . . appears to be supported by events at Philadelphia. The New Jersey Plan for organizing a federal form of government, which was introduced to the Philadelphia convention on 15 June, stated that Congress is 'authorized to pass acts *for raising revenue*, by levying duties on all goods or merchandise of foreign growth or manufacture, imported into any part of the United States.' The New Jersey Plan was supplanted four days later by the national-oriented Virginia Plan, which contained no 'for raising revenue' clause, when the convention voted on 19 June to report the Virginia Plan, without alteration." McGuire and Van Cott, "Confederate Constitution, Tariffs, and the Laffer Relationship," 431.

45. "Constitution of the Confederate States of America, March 11, 1861" The Avalon Project at Yale Law School, www.yale.edu/lawweb/avalon/csa/csa.htm (accessed January 2, 2007).

46. Frederick Douglass, "What to the Slave Is the Fourth of July?" July 5, 1852, TeachingAmericanHistory.org, www.teachingamericanhistory.org/library/index.asp?document=162 (accessed August 22, 2007).

47. DiLorenzo, *The Real Lincoln*, 277.

48. Quoted in Robert W. Fogel, *The Slavery Debates: A Retrospective 1952–1990* (Baton Rouge: Louisiana State University Press, 2003), 9.

49. Fogel, *The Slavery Debates*, 27.

50. William Meigs, *The Life of John Cadwell Calhoun* (New York: Perseus Books, 1970), 176–77.

51. John C. Calhoun, speech on the 1816 Tariff Bill, in *Union and Liberty: The Political Philosophy of John C. Calhoun*, ed. Ross M. Lence (Indianapolis: Liberty Fund, 1992), 301. Cited hereafter as Lence, *Union and Liberty: The Political Philosophy of John C. Calhoun*.

52. Lence, *Union and Liberty: The Political Philosophy of John C. Calhoun*, 302.

53. Lence, *Union and Liberty: The Political Philosophy of John C. Calhoun*, 303.

54. Lord Charnwood, *Abraham Lincoln* (Lanham, MD: Madison Books, 1996 [1946]), 55.

55. Roy P. Basler, ed., *The Collected Works of Abraham Lincoln* (New Brunswick, NJ: Rutgers University Press, 1953), I:311, 313 (emphasis added). Cited hereafter as Lincoln, *Collected Works*.

56. Gabor S. Boritt, *Lincoln and the Economics of the American Dream* (Urbana: University of Illinois Press, 1994), 95.

57. DiLorenzo, *Lincoln Unmasked*, 134. See also Lincoln, *Collected Works*, I:163.

58. DiLorenzo, *The Real Lincoln*, 59.

59. Charnwood, *Abraham Lincoln*, 55.

60. Lincoln, *Collected Works*, III:487.

61. Lincoln, *Collected Works*, IV:14.

62. If the discovery of gold in California in 1848 and the disruption of the Democratic Convention of 1860 form the poles in the antebellum conflict over slavery, as I contend they do, it is interesting to note that the Kansas-Nebraska Act, with Douglas's vaunted "popular sovereignty" doctrine, occurs in 1854, precisely midway between 1848 and 1860.

63. Lincoln, *Collected Works*, II:253.

64. David M. Potter, *The Impending Crisis, 1848–1861* (New York: Harper & Row, 1976), 68.

65. We will never know whether Taylor was really willing to use force to maintain the Union because he died in the summer of 1850. See my discussion of Taylor in chapter 2.

66. Potter, *The Impending Crisis*, chapters 4 and 5.

67. Douglas defended this provision by arguing that the federal commissioner should be paid more if he decided against the accused runaway slave and returned him to the slave owner because there would be more paperwork involved than if he merely decided for the accused and let him go as a free man.

68. "The Fugitive Slave Act of 1850," The Avalon Project of Yale Law School, www.yale.edu/lawweb/avalon/fugitive.htm#five (accessed January 2, 2007).

69. Potter, *The Impending Crisis*, 407.

70. Mark Graber, *Dred Scott and the Problem of Constitutional Evil* (New York: Cambridge University Press, 2006), 170 .

71. Don E. Fehrenbacher, *The South and Three Sectional Crises* (Baton Rouge: Louisiana State University Press, 1980).

72. See Robert W. Johannsen, *The Frontier, the Union, and Stephen A. Douglas* (Chicago: University of Illinois Press, 1989), especially chapter 8, "Douglas at Charleston," 146–64.

73. Lincoln, *Collected Works*, III:318.

74. Donald B. Johnson and Kirk H. Porter, eds., *National Party Platforms: 1840–1972* (Urbana: University of Illinois Press, 1973), 31.

75. Lincoln, *Collected Works*, III:9.

76. DiLorenzo, *Lincoln Unmasked*, 37.

77. Alexander H. Stephens, "Cornerstone Speech," March 21, 1861, in *Alexander H. Stephens in Public and Private with Letters and Speeches* (Philadelphia: National Publishing, 1866), 721–22.

78. Lincoln, *Collected Works*, III:375.

79. Lincoln, *Collected Works*, II:404.

80. Quoted in John Marini, "Theology, Metaphysics, and Positivism: The Origins of the Social Sciences and the Transformation of the American University," in *Challenges to the American Founding: Slavery, Historicism, and Progressivism in the Nineteenth Century*, ed. Ronald J. Pestritto and Thomas G. West (Lanham, MD: Lexington Books, 2005), 166, 188.

81. Mark A. Noll, *The Civil War as a Theological Crisis* (Chapel Hill: University of North Carolina Press, 2006), 429. See also H. Shelton Smith, "The Church and the Social Order in the Old South as Interpreted by James H. Thornwell," *Church History* 7, no. 2. (June 1938): 115.

82. James Henley Thornwell, "A Southern Christian View of Slavery," December 4, 1861, in *The Annals of America* (Chicago: Encyclopaedia Britannica Inc., 1968), IX:298–303.

83. Smith, "The Church and the Social Order in the Old South as Interpreted by James H. Thornwell," 124.

84. Thornwell, "A Southern Christian View of Slavery," 298.

85. Thornwell, "A Southern Christian View of Slavery," 299.

86. See, e.g., Exodus 21:2–12 and 21:20–21, Leviticus 25:39–46, Luke 12:41–48, Ephesians 6:5–9, and 1 Timothy 6:1–2.

87. Thornwell, "A Southern Christian View of Slavery," 300.

88. Smith, "The Church and the Social Order in the Old South as Interpreted by James H. Thornwell," 121.

89. Thornwell, "A Southern Christian View of Slavery," 302.

90. Georg W. F. Hegel, *The Philosophy of History*, trans. J. Sibree (New York: Prometheus Books, 1991), 457.

91. Rev. Fred A. Ross, DD, *Slavery Ordained of God* (Philadelphia: J. B. Lippincott & Co., 1857).

92. Ross, *Slavery Ordained of God*, 36.

93. Ross, *Slavery Ordained of God*, 39.

94. Ross, *Slavery Ordained of God*, 43.

95. Ross, *Slavery Ordained of God*, 45.

96. Ross, *Slavery Ordained of God*, 60–61.

97. Ross, *Slavery Ordained of God*, 52.

98. Ross, *Slavery Ordained of God*, 44.

99. Ross, *Slavery Ordained of God*, 48, 62–63.

100. *In Re Archy*, 9 Cal. 147 (1858).

101. Lincoln, *Collected Works*, V:403–404.

102. Russell Kirk, *The Roots of American Order* (Washington, DC: Regnery Gateway, 1991 [1974]), 456.

103. Lincoln, *Collected Works*, III:204–205.

104. Lincoln, *Collected Works*, III:547.

105. Lincoln, *Collected Works*, III:548.

106. Charles B. Dew, *Apostles of Disunion: Southern Secession Commissioners and the Causes of the Civil War* (Charlottesville: University Press of Virginia, 2001).

107. Dew, *Apostles of Disunion*, 79–81.

108. "Confederate States of America: Mississippi Secession," The Avalon Project at Yale Law School, www.yale.edu/lawweb/avalon/csa/missec.htm (accessed January 2, 2007).

109. Quotations are taken from Jay Winik, *April 1865: The Month That Saved America* (New York: HarperCollins, 2001), 50–59.

110. George Anastaplo, *Abraham Lincoln: A Constitutional Biography* (Lanham, MD: Rowman & Littlefield, 1999), 150.

111. Lincoln, *Collected Works*, I:114.

112. Lincoln, *Collected Works*, I:115.

113. Lincoln, *Collected Works*, VIII:333.

114. See chapter 4.

115. Garry Wills, *Lincoln at Gettysburg: The Words That Remade America* (New York: Simon & Schuster, 1992), 38–39.

116. Anastaplo, *Abraham Lincoln: A Constitutional Biography*, 241.

117. Anastaplo, *Abraham Lincoln: A Constitutional Biography*, 347.

118. Anastaplo, *Abraham Lincoln: A Constitutional Biography*, 350.

119. Lincoln, *Collected Works*, I:108.

120. Edward Erler, "*Marbury v. Madison* and the Progressive Transformation of Judicial Power," in *The Progressive Revolution in Politics and Political Science: Transforming the American Regime*, ed. John Marini and Ken Masugi (Lanham, MD: Rowman & Littlefield, 2005), 216–17. See also Lucas E. Morel, *Lincoln's Sacred Effort: Defining Religion's Role in American Self-Government* (Lanham, MD: Lexington Books, 2000), 163–222.

121. Lincoln, *Collected Works*, IV:271.

122. See chapter 4.

123. Joe Sachs, trans., *Aristotle: Nicomachean Ethics* (Newburyport, MA: Focus Publishing, 2002), 1–36.

124. Noll, *The Civil War as a Theological Crisis.*

125. Mark A. Noll, *America's God: From Jonathan Edwards to Abraham Lincoln* (New York: Oxford University Press, 2002), 426.

126. Lincoln, *Collected Works*, VIII:332.

127. Lincoln, *Collected Works*, VIII:333.

128. Adams, *When in the Course of Human Events*, 205–207.

129. Lincoln, *Collected Works*, VIII:333.

130. H. L. Mencken, "Abraham Lincoln," in *The Vintage Mencken*, ed. Alistair Cooke (New York: Vintage Books, 1955), 79.

131. Noll, *America's God*, 434.

7

WAS LINCOLN'S GOAL TO PRESERVE THE UNION OR END SLAVERY?

> The right of self-determination, what Lincoln called "government of the people," is empty chatter when a larger power wants to hold on to its territories. The North went to war to preserve the Union, and that was the reason for the war. It was what Lincoln was fighting for. As with all secession wars throughout history, it was a fight for land and resources. Moral issues are not really motivating factors.
>
> —Charles Adams, *When in the Course of Human Events: Arguing the Case for Southern Secession*

> My paramount object in this struggle is to save the Union, and is not either to save or destroy slavery. If I could save the Union without freeing any slave I would do it, and if I could save it by freeing some and leaving others alone I would also do that.
>
> —Abraham Lincoln, letter to Horace Greeley, August 22, 1862

Statesmanship is the art of reconciling the particulars here and now, as far as they can be, with the unchanging principles of right. How that is to be done is always unclear because the particulars change, there is always dispute over what is right, and human reason does not, because it cannot, understand these things perfectly. Uncertainty, therefore, looms over statesmanship like a cloud, making it difficult sometimes to discern who is, and who is not, a statesman, what a statesman is to do, and how a statesman ought to think.

My purpose is to vindicate Abraham Lincoln by vindicating his statesmanship, but I cannot do that by merely asserting that he was a statesman. Rather, I must try to demonstrate the terrible challenges he faced, as well as the awful conclusions that would have followed any decision he made, and to explain why reason dictated that Lincoln decide just as he did, however fateful the consequences. As president, Lincoln's immediate purpose was to put down a rebellion and preserve the Union. But his love of the Union and its animating principle inspired in him a hatred of slavery. For Lincoln, saving the Union and destroying slavery were intrinsically bound together, in principle, and never for a moment did Lincoln separate them. But he understood that prudence and the particular challenges of the Civil War demanded at times that more attention be focused on the Union than on slavery, that the Union must survive if slavery were to be destroyed, an understanding becoming of statesmanship.

LINCOLN'S INAUGURATION: UNPRECEDENTED CHALLENGE

As Lincoln prepared to leave his home in Springfield, Illinois, and make his way to Washington, D.C., for his inauguration as president, the unprecedented challenge he confronted weighed heavily upon him. To his friends and fellow citizens of Springfield, he spoke the following:

> No one, not in my situation, can appreciate my feelings of sadness at this parting. To this place, and the kindness of these people, I owe every thing. Here I have lived a quarter of a century, and have passed from a young to an old man. Here my children have been born, and one is buried. I now leave, not knowing when, or whether ever, I may return, with a task before me greater than that which rested upon Washington. Without the assistance of that Divine Being, who ever attended him, I cannot succeed. With that assistance I cannot fail. Trusting in Him, who can go with me, and remain with you and be every where for good, let us confidently hope that all will yet be well. To His care commending you, as I hope in your prayers you will commend me, I bid you an affectionate farewell.[1]

When Lincoln was sworn in to office, seven Southern states had already passed ordinances of secession. A provisional Confederate Constitution had been ratified, and a Confederate government had already been elected. Maintaining that secession was unconstitutional and believing that only a small portion of Southerners supported an independent Confederacy, Lincoln intended to preserve the integrity of the Union, which required the seven seceded states to dissolve their Confederate government and return to the government under the U.S. Constitution.

How this might be accomplished was far from clear. While seven of the fifteen slave states claimed secession as an accomplished fact, the majority of slave states—Delaware, Maryland, Virginia, Kentucky, Missouri, North Carolina, Tennessee, and Arkansas—remained in the Union. Lincoln knew that public opinion in those states was divided between unionist and secession sentiments. He also knew that any movement on his part to employ aggressive means against the seceded states would surely drive the remaining slave states to join the Confederacy.

Further complicating the political landscape of Lincoln's inauguration, Lincoln was uncertain, if war ever became necessary to preserve the Union, how much support there would be among Northerners to wage it. Some Americans would fight for the Union only if slavery was abolished; others would fight for the Union only if slavery was preserved. The immediate crisis Lincoln confronted was a crisis of the Union; his challenge was to combine the opposing forces within the nation for the common purpose of preserving the Union and the principles upon which it was built. In this critical moment, Lincoln had no models and no precedents to follow. He had to rely on his prudence, the highest art of the statesman.

In a meeting with his cabinet on April 9, 1861, Confederate president Jefferson Davis made the historic decision to take Fort Sumter, which sat in the harbor of Charleston, South Carolina. The next day, April 10, Confederate general P. G. T. Beauregard received orders to demand the immediate evacuation of Union troops from Fort Sumter; if the demand was ignored, Beauregard was to reduce the fort to rubble. Just before the morning twilight on April 12, 1861, the first Confederate cannon shell streaked over Charleston Harbor. With the bombardment of Fort Sumter, the Civil War began.

Lincoln's election was perfectly legal and perfectly in accordance with the Constitution.[2] At issue was not the 1860 presidential election's legitimacy but its outcome. Discontented Southerners preferred to attempt to secede from the Union over accepting Lincoln's election as president of the United States. But to what lengths was the South willing to go in order to establish its independence? In his inaugural address, Lincoln made it clear that the real choice of action lay with the South:

> In *your* hands, my dissatisfied fellow countrymen, and not in mine, is the momentous issue of civil war. The government will not assail you. You

can have no conflict, without being yourselves the aggressors. You have no oath registered in Heaven to destroy the government, while I shall have the most solemn one to "preserve, protect and defend" it.[3]

Some have insisted that the Lincoln administration tricked the South into attacking Fort Sumter, that mixed messages sent to Jefferson Davis assured him that Sumter would be evacuated on the one hand, while signaling naval preparations to defend the fort on the other. But as David Potter explains, it made little difference: "If a peaceable evacuation of Fort Sumter had somehow been arranged, Lincoln would only have redoubled his efforts to hold Fort Pickens, and the Davis government was as determined to have one as the other." The positions of Lincoln and Davis were irreconcilable, because each was based on a different understanding of the Union and states' rights:

> Lincoln was prepared to accept war rather than acknowledge the dissolu-
> tion of a Federal Union which in Davis's eyes had ceased to exist; Davis,
> in turn, was ready to make war for the territorial integrity of a Southern
> Confederacy which in Lincoln's eyes had never begun to exist.[4]

Lincoln viewed the attack on Fort Sumter as an attack on the federal government of the United States, which represented nothing less than an attempt to overthrow the American experiment in self-government. This was the central argument he delivered to Congress during a special session on July 4, 1861, convened by Lincoln for the purpose of examining the crisis of the Union and working with Congress to formulate the best response:

> It is thus seen that the assault upon, and reduction of, Fort Sumter, was,
> in no sense, a matter of self defense on the part of the assailants. . . . In
> this act, discarding all else, they have forced upon the country, the dis-
> tinct issue: "Immediate dissolution or blood."
>   And this issue embraces more than the fate of these United States. It
> presents to the whole family of man the question, whether a constitutional
> republic, or democracy—a government of the people, by the same peo-
> ple—can, or cannot, maintain its territorial integrity against its own do-
> mestic foes. It presents the question, whether discontented individuals, too
> few in numbers to control administration, according to organic law, in any
> case, can always, upon the pretences made in this case, or on any other pre-
> tences, or arbitrarily, without any pretence, break up their government, and
> thus practically put an end to free government upon the earth.[5]

Confederate apologists such as Charles Adams, Thomas DiLorenzo, Walter Williams, Thomas Woods, and others who defend the right of secession and the Southern view of the Union typically ignore the questions Lincoln raised: "Is there, in all republics, this inherent and fatal weakness?" "Must a government, of necessity, be too strong for the liberties of its own people, or too weak to maintain its own existence?" But Lincoln's questions get to the heart of the problem and show the impossibility of admitting secession as a basis for any government.

Recall the election of Thomas Jefferson in 1800, perhaps the most hotly contested election between two hostile rival parties in American history, in which the losing minority accepted the election results and allowed the winning majority to exercise the powers of government, looking to the next election as the proper forum to challenge the majority. In his first inaugural address, Jefferson had announced that "the will of the majority is in all cases to prevail, but that will to be rightful must be reasonable, that the minority possess their equal rights which equal law must protect."[6] Minority rights, in other words, limit majority rule. In a free society based on natural rights, the majority may not do anything it pleases; it may do only those things that do not injure the rights of the minority. There must be an agreement between, and universal opinion among, all the people, those in the majority and those in the minority, that each individual possesses equal rights "which equal law must protect." As Jefferson said, "Every difference of opinion is not a difference of principle. We have called by different names brethren of the same principle. We are all republicans—we are federalists." Fully aware of the many disputes that divided Republicans and Federalists, Jefferson emphasized the principle shared by all Americans, belief in equal natural rights. So long as Americans remained unified in their defense of equality, they could easily tolerate those few "who would wish to dissolve this Union or to change its republican form," allowing them to "stand undisturbed as monuments of the safety with which error of opinion may be tolerated where reason is left free to combat it."

Jefferson was clear, however, that minds seeking the dissolution of the Union represented "error of opinion." He also made it clear that toleration of such erroneous opinions was possible so long as "reason is left free to combat it." But a free society, a society of free elections in which all those who live under the laws participate in making them and share equally in their protection, is the necessary condition for reason to combat error, and it was this understanding of free society that the seceding states of the South were rejecting. In their denial of the outcome of a legal and free election, not to mention their placing gag rules against antislavery speech, refusal to deliver abolitionist mail, and other efforts to silence any criticism of slavery, Southern secessionists disarmed reason of its natural weapons, free speech and persuasion. It is not unreasonable to conclude from Jefferson's inaugural address that, where not left free to combat error of opinion, reason may require the assistance of force.

A union of free, self-governing citizens settles its disputes through elections, a process that necessarily divides the Union into a majority and one or more minorities. The minority is to accept the majority that wins an election as the rightful electoral victor, so long as the rights of the minority are in no way injured or violated. If a free political union has any meaning at all, it must mean that election results are binding upon the losers no less than the winners. The only alternative is to allow the losers of each election to secede from the Union responsible for the election, which means each successive election is a successive step in dissolution. A government formed on the principle of secession is no government at all; it is self-destructive by design. Lincoln did not believe, however, that the United States was designed to self-destruct; he believed it was his responsibility, and the responsibility of the Union government, to demonstrate

> that those who can fairly carry an election, can also suppress a rebellion; that ballots are the rightful and peaceful successors of bullets; and that when ballots have fairly and constitutionally decided, there can be no successful appeal back to bullets; that there can be no successful appeal except to ballots themselves, at succeeding elections.[7]

Immediately after the bombardment of Fort Sumter, Lincoln requested seventy-five thousand men to serve the cause of putting down the rebels who had attacked the government of the United States. His overarching goal was the preservation of the Union under the Constitution, but that goal that was inseparable from preserving free elections.

A UNION WORTH SAVING

Lincoln wanted to preserve the Union because he believed the law of the Constitution to be perpetual:

> I hold, that in contemplation of universal law, and of the Constitution, the Union of these States is perpetual. Perpetuity is implied, if not expressed, in the fundamental law of all national governments. It is safe to assert that no government proper ever had a Provision in its organic law for its own termination. Continue to execute all the express provisions of our national Constitution, and the Union will endure forever—it being impossible to destroy it, except by some action not provided for in the instrument itself.[8]

Lincoln also sought to preserve the Union because he wanted to preserve free elections, the peaceful political process by which citizens with equal rights divide into changing majorities and minorities to solve political disputes, while always recognizing and protecting their mutual equal rights, whether they belong to the political majority or minority, and always following the rules and order established by the Constitution. But even with these purposes in mind, we have not yet discussed the whole of Lincoln's purpose in the Civil War.

Lincoln wanted to preserve the constitutional union of free elections not merely because it was *a* union but because he believed it was a *good* union.

Of the many letters Lincoln wrote, among the most famous was his letter of August 22, 1863, to Horace Greeley, the antislavery editor of the *New York Tribune*, the most widely read newspaper in the United States at that time. This letter is often held up as evidence that Lincoln subordinated morality to expedience, that the moral question of slavery occupied a lower place in Lincoln's mind than the political question of the Union. Russell Kirk, for example, writes that "the act for which [Lincoln] is most celebrated, the Emancipation Proclamation, he undertook as a measure of military expediency, not as a moral judgment. If he could have preserved the Union, short of war, by tolerating slavery, he would have done so, he said."[9]

Lincoln's letter was a response to an editorial in which Greeley had expressed great disappointment that the president had supposedly been "strangely and disastrously remiss . . . with regard to the emancipating provisions of the new Confiscation Act," then pleaded, "On the face of this wide earth, Mr. President, there is not one disinterested, determined, intelligent champion of the Union cause who does not feel that all attempts to put down the Rebellion and at the same time uphold its inciting cause are preposterous and futile." The "inciting cause" to which Greeley referred was, of course, slavery, and Greeley, like so many of the abolitionists, insisted that Lincoln turn the Civil War into an open war on that "peculiar institution" of the South. Here is Lincoln's response:

> I would save the Union. I would save it the shortest way under the Constitution. The sooner the national authority can be restored; the nearer the Union will be "the Union as it was." If there be those who would not save the Union, unless they could at the same time *save* slavery, I do not agree with them. If there be those who would not save the Union unless they could at the same time *destroy* slavery, I do not agree with them. My paramount object in this struggle *is* to save the Union, and is *not* either to save or to destroy slavery. If I could save the Union without freeing *any* slave I would do it, and if I could save it by freeing *all* the slaves I would do it; and if I could save it by freeing some and leaving

> others alone I would also do that. What I do about slavery, and the col-
> ored race, I do because I believe it helps to save the Union; and what I
> forbear, I forbear because I do *not* believe it would help to save the
> Union. I shall do *less* whenever I shall believe what I am doing hurts the
> cause, and I shall do *more* whenever I shall believe doing more will help
> the cause. I shall try to correct errors when shown to be errors; and I shall
> adopt new views so fast as they shall appear to be true views.[10]

I have no reason to doubt that in the immediate crisis of the Civil War, as
the death tolls of Americans grew daily, Lincoln would have adopted the
quickest and surest measures to save the Union, even if those measures did
not include abolishing slavery. If Lincoln could stop the slaughter and restore the Union without touching slavery, why should he not have done so?
Had he been able to bring the war to a speedy end, slavery would once
again be a problem to solve through the peaceful political processes under
the Constitution. Slavery would remain an evil institution, and all the dif-
ficulties that attended earlier attempts to eradicate it would remain as well,
but these were lesser evils than the bloody carnage happening daily on the
fields of battle. This is perhaps the most difficult lesson of statesmanship to
learn: sometimes the choice confronting a statesman is not between good
and evil but between two evils, and sometimes it may be difficult to determine which is the lesser of the evils. Further, Lincoln had no lawful authority to engage in an antislavery crusade, as Greeley desired, and the
American people would not have supported one. Thus, Lincoln rightly told
Greeley that he would do with regard to slavery whatever "help[ed] to save
the Union."

Citing the nationalism and centralization occurring in places such as
Italy, Germany, and Japan in the nineteenth century, Thomas Woods, for
example, argues that Lincoln merely represented the "spirit of nationalism"
of his age, and he cites Lincoln's letter to Greeley as proof that Lincoln
cared much more about American nationalism and unification than he did
about slavery.[11] But Woods should remember that in his official capacity as
president, Lincoln possessed no more power than that delegated to him by
the Constitution; he was not authorized to interfere with slavery in the
states merely because he or others disliked it, a point he made clear in his
first inaugural address. Nonetheless, to ensure that no one misunderstood
his personal beliefs, Lincoln clarified at the end of his letter the distinction
between what he was empowered to do as president and what his personal
hopes were: "I have here stated my purpose according to my view of *official* duty; and I intend no modification of my oft-expressed *personal* wish
that all men every where could be free."

When Lincoln wrote to Greeley, he knew his letter would be printed and read by millions of Americans in the North and the border slave states, many of whom were all for preserving the Union, but some of whom cared little about slavery. Thus, Lincoln calculated his rhetoric to appeal to the lowest and largest common denominator among his audience, emphasizing the need to save the Union. He needed the support of the largest portion of Americans possible. Had he implied that only those who sought the end of slavery should enlist in saving the Union, had he identified the cause to save the Union with abolitionism, he would have not only alienated all those who cared more for Union than the plight of black slaves but violated the constitutional authority of his office, injuring both the cause of Union and the cause of freedom.[12]

A month prior to writing Greeley, however, Lincoln had already announced to his cabinet his intention to issue an emancipation proclamation sometime during the fall of 1862. Thus, when he wrote to Greeley, the cause of saving the Union and the cause of ending slavery had already become one in Lincoln's view. A cynical mind might conclude that his public rhetoric during this period was duplicitous, that he intentionally deceived the American people by not laying all his cards on the table and stating clearly his intention to issue an emancipation proclamation, striking at slavery as part of his overall strategy for restoring the Union. But we must ask ourselves what the likely outcome would have been had Lincoln been less cautious in his speech and more revealing of all his tactics. Lincoln understood that to identify the cause of the war as simply a war against slavery would have alienated Northern support and thereby injured, perhaps mortally, the Union cause. Union victory might well have become impossible. The result would have been an independent and sovereign Confederate States of America with a constitution that offered strict and perpetual protection for slavery, making life for millions of black slaves a perpetual hell on earth. Could justice be ascribed to any speech or action that led to such an unjust and wrong result?

THE EMANCIPATION PROCLAMATION

Nowhere is the connection between preserving the constitutional union and ending slavery more apparent than in Lincoln's Emancipation Proclamation, the full historical account of which may be found in Allen C. Guelzo's authoritative *Lincoln's Emancipation Proclamation: The End of Slavery in America*.[13] But there remains much controversy regarding the proclamation. While

Lincoln himself believed that the Emancipation Proclamation was "the central act of [his] administration, and the great event of the nineteenth century," Lincoln critic Walter Williams, for example, ridicules it as "little more than a political gimmick."[14]

Any thoughtful discussion of the Emancipation Proclamation must begin with the establishment of two important, but often overlooked, facts. First, slavery was entirely a product of state, not federal, law. Officers of the federal government, from the president down, had no lawful authority under the Constitution to interfere with or adjust the slave laws of various slave states. As Guelzo writes,

> The Constitution and constitutional law had erected a firewall between federal and state spheres of sovereignty, and in an era before the Fourteenth Amendment, it was the states, not the federal government, that determined what the range of civil rights in any state might be. The Constitution left it to the states to determine women's legal standing and voting rights (Lincoln had once advocated women's suffrage in Illinois), whether communities ought to be taxed to provide free public education, whether banks should be allowed to incorporate, what were the exact terms of citizenship, and, in this case, whether blacks could be enslaved.[15]

Not only did each state decide for itself whether to allow chattel slavery or not, but each slave state also placed in its statutory code requirements that had to be met if a slave was to be legally set free, or "manumitted."

In most slave states, it was illegal for a slave owner simply to allow a slave to walk away as a free man. Certain conditions, which varied from state to state, had to be met before a slave owner could legally manumit a slave, including, in some cases, establishing a security bond that would help pay for the education and support of a freed slave and ensure that he would not become a burden on the community. Many state codes also provided stiff penalties for slave owners who attempted to free slaves without meeting the legal manumission requirements. In principle, the manumission laws aimed to ensure that slaves would possess some minimum level of education and skill, as well as some minimal amount of personal property, before they were freed, equipping them to be productive citizens who would not turn to crime or otherwise become dependent on others for their well-being. But as Lincoln remarked in his 1857 speech on *Dred Scott v. Sandford*, manumission had been transformed into a system designed to keep slaves in bondage, as the legal requirements for manumission had grown increasingly steep in the nineteenth century, prohibiting many who might otherwise have manumitted their slaves from doing so. This change in manumission policies corresponded to the growing view that slavery was a positive good. In Lincoln's America, slave-state laws and public opinion conspired to ensure that anyone born a slave would likely die a slave.

The second fact that highlights the significance of the Emancipation Proclamation is that Lincoln, while fervently opposed to slavery throughout his life, was *not* an abolitionist. Abolitionists viewed slavery as a great sin, perhaps the greatest sin, and in their zeal against slavery, many abolitionists believed that no cost was too high and no burden was too heavy if it meant ending slavery. Abolitionists cared little about the consequences of their antislavery crusade and even less about the restraints and parameters represented by the law and the Constitution. Lincoln took a different approach. He developed his policies regarding slavery, like all other public policy questions he took up, with a view to the lawful structure of the Constitution. Unlike some abolitionists, Lincoln *did* care about consequences and the Constitution's legal authority. While the antebellum Union was imperfect, and while the ugly stain of slavery was manifest throughout the South, America under the Constitution had nonetheless achieved an unprecedented degree of freedom and representative government. Unlike abolitionists such as Garrison, according to whom the Constitution was nothing but an agreement with hell because it offered certain protections to slavery, Lincoln wanted to preserve this constitutional system, working within the laws to bring about the end of that institution:

> If Lincoln's differences with the abolitionists could be put on paper in the form of a comparative table, the two columns would go on for quite a way. Where the abolitionists built their argument on the demand of evangelical religion for repentance, Lincoln preferred gradualism and compensation for emancipated slaves. Where they preached from passion and choice, he worked from reason and prudence; where they called for immediatism without regard for consequences, it was precisely the consequences of slavery and its extension which kindled Lincoln's opposition in the 1850s. And where they brushed aside the Constitution, Lincoln would proceed against slavery no farther than the Constitution allowed.[16]

As Lincoln understood, but abolitionists refused to accept, the supreme price paid for adherence to the Constitution was *delay*. "God will settle it, and settle it right," Lincoln reportedly said in 1854, "but for the present it is our duty to wait."

If abolitionists stood on one side of Lincoln, on the other stood the defenders of slavery, defenders of the proposition that blacks were naturally

inferior to whites, that the enslavement of inferior races accorded with natural law, and that the Constitution ought to protect the spread of slavery
forever. When a bill was introduced in Congress, for example, authorizing
the president to receive runaway blacks into the army, Willard Saulsbury of
Delaware immediately objected to the "attempt to elevate the miserable
nigger, not only to political rights, but to put him in your Army."[17] Lincoln
stood opposed to both extremes of abolitionism and pro-slavery fanaticism,
unwavering in his insistence on the evil of slavery but equally adamant that
its elimination must be constitutional. In Lincoln's mind, the Emancipation
Proclamation fit the bill.

On September 22, 1862, when the Civil War had already become far
more bloody than Lincoln or anyone else had thought it would be, Lincoln
issued his preliminary Emancipation Proclamation, stating in the first paragraph that "the war will be prosecuted for the object of practically restoring
the constitutional relation between the United States, and each of the states,
and the people thereof, in which states that relation is, or may be suspended,
or disturbed." The purpose of this preliminary Emancipation Proclamation
was to offer the Southern states then in rebellion an ultimatum: they could
return to the Union or forfeit their slaves. The choice was theirs. Lincoln
gave them one hundred days, until January 1, 1863, to decide:

> That on the first day of January in the year of our Lord, one thousand
> eight hundred and sixty-three, all persons held as slaves within any state,
> or designated part of a state, the people whereof shall then be in rebel-
> lion against the United States, shall be then, thenceforward, and forever
> free; and the executive government of the United States, including the
> military and naval authority thereof, will recognize and maintain the free-
> dom of such persons, and will do no act or acts to repress such persons,
> or any of them, in any efforts they may make for their actual freedom.[18]

Any state wishing to avoid the liberating arm of the proclamation needed
only to send representatives "in good faith" to be present in Congress. Those
states not represented in Congress would be considered in rebellion, and on
January 1, all slaves in those states (or parts thereof) would be declared
"thenceforward, and forever free." This meant, however, that the Emancipation Proclamation would have no immediate effect for slaves in the loyal slave
states—Maryland, Delaware, Kentucky, and Missouri—that had remained in
the Union. Slaves in the western part of Virginia, which refused to join the
rest of Virginia in secession, as well as slaves in certain parts of Louisiana,
which were not in rebellion because they were under Union army control,
would also be excluded from the proclamation's liberating sweep.

These facts prompted the *London Times*, in October 1862, to ridicule Lincoln's preliminary proclamation, lamenting that "where he has no power Mr. Lincoln will set the Negroes free," while "where he retains power he will consider them as slaves. This is more like a Chinaman beating his two swords together to frighten his enemy than like an earnest man pressing forward his cause." Another London paper, the *Spectator*, mocked, "The principle is not that a human being cannot justly own another, but that he cannot own him unless he is loyal to the United States."

The view that Lincoln declared slaves free only where he had no power to make them free, while leaving untouched those slaves in the Union whom it was in his power to free, has formed the most popular account of the Emancipation Proclamation. Richard Hofstadter, in his widely read *The American Political Tradition and the Men Who Made It*, bitterly complains that the Emancipation Proclamation "contained no indictment of slavery," "expressly omitted the loyal slave states from its terms," and "it did not in fact free any slaves." "The Emancipation Proclamation," Hofstadter famously concludes, "had all the moral grandeur of a bill of lading."[19] Lerone Bennett adopts and expands Hofstadter's characterization of the Emancipation Proclamation at length in his 2000 *Forced into Glory: Abraham Lincoln's White Dream*, and DiLorenzo then repeats it in *The Real Lincoln*.[20]

DiLorenzo writes that Lincoln "was not particularly supportive of emancipation" because he viewed emancipation "only as a tool to be used in achieving his real objective: the consolidation of state power, something that many had dreaded from the time of the Founding."[21] Persuaded that Lincoln had little concern for emancipation, DiLorenzo criticizes him for failing to end slavery peacefully, or at least without war, as some European and other countries had. DiLorenzo argues that Lincoln could not have waged the Civil War to end slavery because war was not necessary to do so (as evidenced by Britain and France, for example). Had Lincoln been the statesman he was purported to be, he would have found a way to solve the problem of slavery without war. Thus, DiLorenzo, in a chapter titled "Why Not Peaceful Emancipation?" writes derisively,

> The man whom historians would later describe as one of the master politicians of all time failed to use his legendary political skills and his rhetorical gifts to do what every other country of the world where slavery once existed had done: end it peacefully, without resorting to warfare. That would have been the course taken by a genuine statesman.[22]

In sum, the charge amounts to this: if Lincoln, as president of the United States, had acted as Europeans had, America could have avoided the Civil

War. But Lincoln was an American president, limited in his authority and his powers by the Constitution, while many Americans within slave states refused to consider getting rid of slavery even when the federal government offered to compensate them.

Raising the question of why Lincoln did not end slavery peacefully points not only to the great challenge America faced in solving that problem but to the more general challenge of founding and sustaining free government. The social compact rests upon two essential conditions: first, government must offer the equal protection of equal rights to all individuals living under it, and second, government must operate with and by the consent of the governed. In theory, these are easily combined: the governed consent to policies that will protect all those who live under the government. But what appears easy in theory can be incredibly difficult in practice. Clearly, if a people refuse to consent to the protection of the equal rights of all, there are only two options: they can either maintain consent and forgo the equal protection of rights or forgo consent and rule dictatorially for the equal protection of all.

America had achieved an unprecedented realm of government by consent, yet the entire population of slaves was being ruled without their consent. From the time of the Founding through the 1830s, it was expected that this problem would be solved by changing public opinion, by persuading those who gave their consent that they ought to consent to abolish slavery, thereby satisfying the moral requirements of the social compact. This movement in fact characterized America's early history as a majority of the original states either had eliminated slavery or were in the process of doing so by the beginning of the nineteenth century. But ending slavery throughout the United States depended on forming a national consensus that slavery was wrong and ought to be abolished. In the years preceding the Civil War, public opinion had changed drastically, especially in the South but in the North as well, as more and more Americans became persuaded that slavery was not a moral wrong to right but a good institution to protect and allow to spread. This is why Lincoln labored so long to remind Americans of their own Founding principles and to remind them why slavery was wrong and ought to be restricted, if not abolished, as soon as the public peace allowed it.

We must also remember the first fact I mentioned above, that slavery was entirely a function of state, not national, law. Intrinsic to the compromises reached in the formation of the Constitution, the federal government, including the president, was powerless to interfere with slavery as it existed in any state. Slavery in South Carolina, for example, could be abolished only by the people of South Carolina. In his first inaugural address, delivered more than a month before the South fired upon Fort Sumter, Lincoln stated clearly the limitations on his power imposed by the Constitution: "I have no purpose, directly or indirectly, to interfere with the institution of slavery in the States where it exists. I believe I have no lawful right to do so, and I have no inclination to do so."[23] Neither Lincoln nor anyone else in the federal government had any authority to interfere with slavery as it existed within the states. This is why Lincoln indicated that he would not oppose the Corwin Amendment. This was a last-ditch effort proposed by Congress during the final days of the Buchanan administration, attempting to mollify Southerners by expressly prohibiting Congress from interfering "with the domestic institutions [of any state], including that of persons held to labor or service by the laws of said state." Lincoln understood that such an amendment would merely reiterate the principle of federalism already secured by the Constitution: with or without the Corwin Amendment, the national government had no jurisdiction over slavery in South Carolina or any other state.

The only constitutional way to abolish slavery in states without their consent would have been to amend the Constitution to prohibit the institution. According to Article V of the Constitution, an amendment must be ratified by no fewer than three-fourths of the states; in practical terms, this means that a three-fourths majority of free states might have abolished slavery via constitutional amendment against the wishes of the one-quarter minority of slave states. This explains why some Southerners were adamant that slavery be allowed to spread into new territories and states, so that the balance between slave and free states remained more or less even. Had slavery been prohibited from spreading into the territories under the authority of policies such as the Missouri Compromise and the proposed Wilmot Proviso, and had the number of free states continued to grow while the number of slave states remained the same, the day might have come in an America when free states outnumbered slave states by a three-quarter majority, rendering the South incapable of stopping a constitutional amendment to abolish slavery nationally. But any such scheme was in no way possible in 1861. Creating a supermajority of free states required prohibiting the spread of slavery, which Lincoln and the Republicans had been unable to accomplish against Democratic resistance since the Kansas-Nebraska Act of 1854.

What Lincoln could do, and, in fact, did do both during his lone term in Congress and as president, was propose compensation from the federal government for those states that abolished slavery of their own accord. Over the course of the Civil War, Lincoln made repeated, at times almost desperate, attempts to convince slave states to abolish slavery, while offering them financial compensation for the loss of their slave property. Delaware, for example, was a border state with fewer than eighteen hundred slaves, most of whom were concentrated in one county. Lincoln met with George Fisher, Delaware's lone congressman in the House who also happened to be antislavery (though he was not a Republican), and later sent him various proposals for compensated emancipation to present to the Delaware legislature. But Delaware would not take Lincoln's offer. While many Delaware unionists looked "upon slavery as a curse," they looked "upon freedom possessed by a negro . . . as a greater curse," so deep did their hatred for blacks run.[24] Lincoln made additional attempts to encourage Congress to provide offers to border states for the gradual elimination of slavery with compensation for slave owners. But in the end, all offers of compensated emancipation were rejected. While DiLorenzo chalks this up to a failure of Lincoln's statesmanship, a far more plausible explanation is that Southern slave states were simply unwilling, at any cost and in the face of any argument, to concede equality of rights to the black slaves among them. The social compact would, of necessity, be fulfilled by other means.

The critics of Lincoln's Emancipation Proclamation fail to see the consummate prudence—the practical wisdom of knowing the best course of action in a particular situation, which in some instances may entail choosing the greatest good, while in others necessity might require determining the lesser evil—combined with a deep reverence for the Constitution that guided Lincoln's thoughts and actions with regard to slavery. Guelzo demonstrates clearly the indomitable prudence that guided Lincoln toward the goal of emancipation from the moment he took the oath of office as president: "Lincoln understood emancipation not as the satisfaction of a 'spirit' overriding the law, nor as the moment of fusion between the Constitution and absolute moral theory, but as a goal to be achieved through prudential means, so that worthwhile consequences might result."[25]

Early in the war, some of Lincoln's officers took it upon themselves to inaugurate policies of "contraband" regarding slaves: the Union army could confiscate slaves owned by rebel citizens. In Missouri, a border slave state that had remained in the Union, one of Lincoln's renegade generals, John C. Fremont, declared emancipation for all slaves throughout the state as a decree of martial law. These policies Lincoln resisted; in the case of Fremont, Lincoln ultimately dismissed him from command. Aside from the political jeopardy in which these actions placed the Union cause—the border slave states would have joined the Confederacy in a heartbeat if they thought the Lincoln administration had any designs to exercise unconstitutional power over their domestic institutions—Lincoln objected to these efforts on the two grounds that guided all his thoughts on emancipation. First, in some cases, such as Fremont's declaration of martial law throughout the state of Missouri, there was clearly no constitutional authority for such actions. Missouri was not in rebellion; therefore, the federal government had only those powers over Missouri outlined in the Constitution, which certainly did not include the wholesale confiscation of private property. Second, these measures against slavery lacked any kind of permanence: "None of them had any promise that they would stick."[26] Radicals in Congress, for example, kept advocating polices of "confiscation"—and Lincoln signed some—that authorized the Union army to "confiscate" slaves of Southern rebels, but this still did not solve the problem for good. Lincoln well understood that slaves confiscated as "contraband" during wartime, an action justified only as a wartime emergency measure, would legally have to be returned to their owners once the war concluded.

Lincoln reflected deeply on the idea that during times of war or armed rebellion, the executive branch possesses broadly defined "war powers," including the power to confiscate enemy property. As the war proceeded and the Union lost important battles, the president's "war powers" were at the front of his mind. Lincoln understood that while these constitutional powers are vague, they are nonetheless constitutional. At the same time, he believed he could not rightly use any "indispensable means" unless it was truly "indispensable" for saving the Union and protecting the Constitution, which his constitutional oath bound him to do. In late 1862, after the Civil War had dragged on for a year and a half, Lincoln believed the time had come when nothing short of emancipating slaves within rebellious states would save the Union cause.

Statesmanship, or the political exercise of prudence, often requires new or different means in response to changing conditions in the pursuit of a given end. For Lincoln, the challenge was to reach for the natural law standard of the Declaration of Independence, that is, offering equal protection for equal natural rights, while never straying beyond the legal limits the Constitution set forth. When viewed in light of the struggle to save the Union and the Union's Constitution, Lincoln's actions regarding slavery were perfectly consistent. Always opposed to the institution in principle, he took immediate action against it only when he believed the Constitution authorized him to do so. But where Lincoln believed that as president he could pursue moral ends only through constitutional means, some modern critics see moral dithering on his part.

Lerone Bennett, for example, seethes with frustration as he denounces Lincoln for overruling the unconstitutional emancipation policy of Fremont and other generals who attempted to "confiscate" slave property by taking slaves away from their owners without legal authority:

> Lincoln said in 1864 that "so long as I have been here I have not willingly planted a thorn in any man's bosom." He meant, of course, any *White man's* bosom. For he entered the White House putting thorns into the bosoms of Black men, women, and children, and he never, so long as he lived there, stopped. If you're running a tab, you can add the fugitive slaves he personally ordered returned to slavery and the tens of thousands returned to slavery by generals and aides under his command. To this long and mournful procession, one can also add . . . the 115,000 Missouri Blacks who were condemned to four additional years of slavery when Lincoln revoked Fremont's emancipation proclamation, the 926,000 persons in Georgia, Florida, and South Carolina who were condemned to three additional years of slavery when Lincoln revoked the Hunter emancipation proclamation, and the half-million or so condemned to two more years of slavery by *his own* Emancipation Proclamation.[27]

DiLorenzo seconds Bennett's opinion, siding with abolitionists who were outraged when Lincoln dismissed Fremont from his command. DiLorenzo quotes approvingly from abolitionist Ben Wade of Ohio, who wrote "in bitter execration" that "the President don't [*sic*] object to General Fremont's taking the life of the owners of slaves, when found in rebellion, but to confiscate their property and emancipate their slaves he thinks monstrous." Exactly right: as president and commander in chief, Lincoln had the constitutional right and duty to put down those who chose to make war against the U.S. government, which at times would include "taking the life of the owners of slaves," but Lincoln and his subordinates, including Fremont, had no constitutional authority to interfere with the property or lives of the citizens of Missouri, who had chosen to remain loyal to the United States.

DiLorenzo joins Wade and the abolitionists in believing that Lincoln should have allowed Fremont to free slaves in Missouri under the guise of martial law, even though martial law was in no way warranted. (Ironically, some libertarians, like DiLorenzo, Williams, Adams, and others, accuse Lincoln of *violating* the Constitution with his wartime measures, such as the suspension of habeas corpus, while they simultaneously criticize him for being *too dedicated* to the Constitution to allow Fremont and other generals to free slaves without the sanction of law.) Like the abolitionists, DiLorenzo laments the fact that Lincoln exempted slave-holding sections of the country from the scope of the Emancipation Proclamation. His analysis would be more balanced and persuasive if he attempted to explain Lincoln's constitutional reasons for limiting the proclamation's reach. Instead, DiLorenzo writes dismissively, "Lincoln, one of the nation's preeminent lawyers, was careful to craft the proclamation in a way that would guarantee that it would not emancipate any slaves."[28]

Two events propelled and justified Lincoln's decision to issue the Emancipation Proclamation: the border slave states' persistent refusal to consider the federal government's proposals for compensated emancipation and Lincoln's trip to Harrison's Landing, where he inspected General George McClellan's Army of the Potomac.

Convinced that border states would never consent to emancipate their slaves, and equally convinced that McClellan's army would not fight aggressively—evidence surfaced suggesting that McClellan may have been entertaining prospects of leading a military coup against the Union government—Lincoln came to think "that a change of policy in the conduct of the war was necessary." Necessity had forced his hand to reach for the weapon he had until then refused to use, emancipation by an executive military order. Waiting for a battlefield victory so that the proclamation would not appear a desperate measure, Lincoln issued the preliminary Emancipation Proclamation immediately following the Union victory at Antietam in September 1862. After offering the rebel states one hundred days to rejoin the Union, Lincoln then issued the final Emancipation Proclamation on January 1, 1863, declaring,

> Now, therefore I, Abraham Lincoln, President of the United States, by virtue of the power in me vested as Commander-in-Chief, of the Army and Navy of the United States in time of actual armed rebellion against authority and government of the United States, and as a fit and necessary war measure for suppressing said rebellion, do, on this first day of January, in the year of our Lord one thousand eight hundred and sixty three, and in accordance with my purpose so to do publicly proclaimed for the full period of one hundred days, from the day first above mentioned, order and designate as the States and parts of States wherein the people thereof respectively, are this day in rebellion against the United States.[29]

Lincoln proceeded to identify the states and parts of states then in rebellion that were included in the Emancipation Proclamation's scope, declaring that

> by virtue of the power, and for the purpose aforesaid, I do order and declare that all persons held as slaves within said designated States, and parts of States, are, and henceforward shall be free; and that the Executive government of the United States, including the military and naval authorities thereof, will recognize and maintain the freedom of said persons.

Lincoln concluded by enjoining "upon the people so declared to be free to abstain from all violence, unless in necessary self-defence; and I recommend to them that, in all cases when allowed, they labor faithfully for reasonable wages." For any slave from a state listed in the Emancipation Proclamation who could make his way to the Union army, "such persons of suitable condition, will be received into the armed service of the United States to garrison forts, positions, stations, and other places, and to man vessels of all sorts in said service."[30]

Lincoln understood that, absent extraordinary conditions of national emergency, one that threatened the existence of the constitutional union itself, a president did not possess the constitutional authority to interfere with citizens' slave property. But those who chose to make war upon the government of the Constitution forfeited the Constitution's protection of civil rights. The Emancipation Proclamation was justified by the war powers of a president attempting to save the Union, and nothing else: "And upon this act, sincerely believed to be an act of justice, warranted by the Constitution, upon military necessity, I invoke the considerate judgment of mankind, and the gracious favor of Almighty God."

THE THIRTEENTH AMENDMENT

When the final proclamation was ordered, Lincoln identified ten states then in rebellion, exempting certain counties and parishes in Virginia and Louisiana (the Louisiana parishes under Union army control and the western Virginia counties that opposed Virginia's secession and formed the new state of West Virginia). Lincoln's treasury secretary, Salmon Chase, argued against these exemptions, urging Lincoln to extend the proclamation to all of Virginia and Louisiana. Lincoln replied to Chase in these terms:

> The original Proclamation has no constitutional or legal justification except as a military measure. The exemptions were made because the military necessity did not apply to the exempted localities. . . . If I take the step [you suggest] must I not do so, without the argument of military necessity, and so, with out any argument, except the one that I think the measure politically expedient and morally right? Would I thus not give up all footing upon constitution or law? Would I not thus be in the boundless field of absolutism? Could this pass unnoticed or unresisted? Could it fail to be perceived that without any further stretch, I might do the same in Delaware, Maryland, Kentucky, Tennessee, and Missouri; and even change any law in any state?[31]

Lincoln's reliance on military necessity to justify the Emancipation Proclamation appalled many abolitionists. Freeing slaves for strategic military reasons, rather than for purposes of morality or righteousness, was "the most God insulting doctrine ever proclaimed," Parker Pillsbury exclaimed. Lydia Maria Child lamented "this entire absence of a moral sense on the subject," warning that "even should slaves be merely as a war necessity[,] everything must go wrong if there is no heart or conscience on the subject."[32]

President Lincoln, however, sought to win the war, save the Union, and place slavery in the most perilous position possible, but not at the expense of violating the Constitution and destroying the rule of law. Thus, Lincoln assured the loyal "middle states" that the war was being waged not by him, personally, against the sin of slavery but rather by America in defense of constitutional government and freedom. Lincoln's Emancipation Proclamation is perhaps the foremost American example of how prudence and principle, strategic calculation and moral understanding, can be united in a public policy that respects the people's Constitution and instructs the people at the same time.

The causes of Union and freedom were intrinsically bound together in Lincoln's mind long before the Civil War. But after the Emancipation Proclamation, the connection between preserving the Union and abolishing slavery became manifestly clear not only to all Americans but to all nations as well. The Emancipation Proclamation transformed the Union army into the largest liberating force on the planet, leaving in its wake a path of freed men wherever it marched. At the same time, it offered new hope, causing thousands of slaves to abandon their plantation homes and seek the protection of the Union army. It also changed the way foreign governments viewed the war and the South: an alliance with the South now became an alliance with slavery, while an alliance with the North became an alliance with freedom, dooming any hope the Confederacy might have had of inducing aid from European powers.

Even after issuing the proclamation, however, Lincoln knew that freedom was not yet secure in America. The Emancipation Proclamation could be subject to judicial scrutiny, and the Supreme Court that had decided the *Dred Scott* case might all too willingly strike down the act Lincoln considered his greatest achievement as president. Further, the Emancipation Proclamation found legitimacy solely as an executive order issued during a wartime emergency; a future president could easily repeal it. As Guelzo writes, "It was precisely his constitutionalism that never allowed any rest to his anxieties that a presidential proclamation based on the concept of war powers might not survive a postwar challenge in the civil courts."

Lincoln thus sought to place the question of slavery beyond the reach of future courts and presidents, to entrench freedom in firm ground that would resist the corrosive effects of whatever pro-slavery forces survived the war. The solution was the Thirteenth Amendment, Lincoln's brainchild, which would forever prohibit slavery throughout the United States but never would have seen the light of day had it not been for Lincoln's determined resolve to see it pass through Congress to be submitted to the states for ratification.

> [Lincoln did not] agree with Henry David Thoreau's dictum that "there is no such thing as accomplishing a righteous reform by the use of expediency." What Thoreau sneered at as "expediency" was for Lincoln prudence, and the kind of prudence that regarded constitutional means as being fully as sacred as abolitionist ends. Prudence drove Lincoln to seek emancipation, not through a righteous imposition that ignored the Constitution as a "covenant with Hell" but through a legislative solution.[33]

The Thirteenth Amendment, which reads, "Neither slavery nor involuntary servitude, except as a punishment for crime whereof the party shall have been duly convicted, shall exist within the United States, or any place subject to their jurisdiction," settled once and for all the question of whether the Constitution was a pro-slave or pro-freedom document. It was now a pro-freedom document. While the Constitution does not require the president's signature for a constitutional amendment to be sent to the states for ratification, Lincoln signed the Thirteenth Amendment anyway, using his full name, which he rarely did. Shortly after, Lincoln addressed a crowd outside the White House, declaring that he "thought all would bear him witness that he had never shrunk from doing all that he could to eradicate slavery." Lincoln openly expressed concerns that the Supreme Court or future governments might question "whether the [Emancipation] Proclamation was legally valid," as well as its legal effect "upon the children of slaves born hereafter." But, Lincoln said confidently, a constitutional amendment "is a King's cure for all the evils. . . . It winds the whole thing up."[34]

SAVING THE UNION AND ENDING SLAVERY

In his 1854 speech on the Kansas-Nebraska Act, Lincoln made clear why the American union, unique among the nations of the world, was especially worthy of preservation and protection:

> Our republican robe is soiled, and trailed in the dust. Let us repurify it. Let us turn and wash it white, in the spirit, if not the blood, of the Rev-

olution. Let us turn slavery from its claims of "moral right," back upon its existing legal rights, and its arguments of "necessity." Let us return it to the position our fathers gave it; and there let it rest in peace. Let us re-adopt the Declaration of Independence, and with it, the practices, and policy, which harmonize with it. . . . If we do this, we shall not only have saved the Union; but we shall have so saved it, as to make, and to keep it, *forever worthy of the saving.*[35]

When Lincoln spoke of saving the Union, it was a good Union he wanted to save. But the American mind was becoming corrupted; Americans were abandoning the good principle with which they had started their experiment in freedom in 1776. If Americans could return to those principles, if they could once again stand united in their conviction that all men are created equal and in the view that slavery, which might be tolerated out of necessity for a period, was nonetheless an evil to extirpate as soon as possible, then America would be "forever worthy of the saving."

But if America degenerated to the point at which its citizens no longer viewed slavery as an evil, Lincoln doubtless would have believed the nation was no longer worth saving. Lincoln would use every opportunity afforded him to remind Americans of the noble principles of their own Founding, perhaps most memorably in his address at Gettysburg.

Few scholars writing about Lincoln today understand as Lincoln did that the goodness of America stands or falls with the American dedication to the principle of human equality. Thus, DiLorenzo, for example, denies that the American constitutional union is good because of the principle of equality because he denies that the Union is based on equality: "The word 'equality' does not appear in the Constitution, so Lincoln's insistence that this was the principal feature of the federal government really was revolutionary."[36] An America that finds its sheet anchor in the principle of equality for its laws and culture, however imperfectly they may reflect it, is an America capable of moral improvement and excellence. An America that abandons equality, however, an America dedicated to the proposition that it is right for some men to rule others without their consent, is an America not worth preserving.

If Lincoln is quoted selectively, or if excerpts are taken out of their proper context, only then can some critics assert that Lincoln was a "reluctant emancipator" who subordinated the moral fight against slavery to the amoral political fight for union and national interest. But when all the elements of Lincoln's thoughts are brought together, as Lincoln understood them himself, we find, in the words of Harry Jaffa,

the indissoluble unity of Lincoln's three permanent and unchanging goals: preserving the right of free elections, preserving the Union, and placing slavery in the course of ultimate extinction. These three ends were distinguishable in Lincoln's mind only as different aspects of one sovereign purpose, represented by the principles of the Declaration of Independence.[37]

As Jaffa notes, "The comprehensive reasoning underlying these apparent differences was not grasped by many of Lincoln's contemporaries, and has not been grasped by historians," but that makes Lincoln's "comprehensive reasoning" no less true.

Did Lincoln fight the Civil War to preserve the Union or to end slavery? The dichotomy is false. Lincoln understood that the Union represented the finest example of constitutional government by consent of the governed in human history. The Constitution represented government of majority rule and minority rights, a government under which political disputes were solved through free elections. Though elections were binding on losers no less than winners, losers could always look forward to the next to gain an electoral majority and become winners. And free elections, to be genuinely free, must be open to everyone governed, including those held against their wills as slaves. Saving the Union of the Constitution, preserving free elections, and placing slavery in the course of ultimate extinction were the goals for which Lincoln fought the Civil War. Unifying and justifying all of them is the principle that all men are created equal.

NOTES

1. Roy P. Basler, ed., *The Collected Works of Abraham Lincoln* (New Brunswick, NJ: Rutgers University Press, 1953), IV:190. Cited hereafter as Lincoln, *Collected Works*.

2. Much is often made of the fact that Lincoln failed to receive a majority of the popular vote, although he did win a majority of the electoral votes. Usually omitted, however, is the fact that in ten of the eleven states that would later comprise the Confederacy, Lincoln's name was not allowed to appear on the ballot.

3. Lincoln, *Collected Works*, IV:271.

4. David M. Potter, *The Impending Crisis, 1848–1861* (New York: Harper & Row, 1976), 581.

5. Lincoln, *Collected Works*, IV:425–26.

6. Thomas Jefferson, First Inaugural Address, in *Jefferson: Writings*, ed. Merrill D. Peterson (New York: Library of America, 1984), 492–93.

7. Lincoln, *Collected Works*, IV:439.

8. Lincoln, *Collected Works*, IV:264.

9. Russell Kirk, *The Roots of American Order* (Washington, DC: Regnery Gateway, 1991 [1974]), 455.

10. Greeley's editorial and Lincoln's letter of August 22 in response are both quoted in Lincoln, *Collected Works*, V:388–89.

11. Thomas E. Woods Jr., *The Politically Incorrect Guide to American History* (Washington, DC: Regnery Publishing, 2004), 67–68.

12. Philip S. Paludan, "Lincoln and the Greeley Letter," in *Lincoln Reshapes the Presidency*, ed. Charles M. Hubbard (Macon, GA: Mercer University Press, 2003), 83.

13. Allen C. Guelzo, *Lincoln's Emancipation Proclamation: The End of Slavery in America* (New York: Simon & Schuster, 2004).

14. Abraham Lincoln, comment to Francis Carpenter, in *The Life and Public Services of Abraham Lincoln, 16th President of the United States*, ed. Henry J. Raymond (New York: Derby and Miller Publishers, 1865), 764; Thomas DiLorenzo, *The Real Lincoln: A New Look at Abraham Lincoln, His Agenda, and an Unnecessary War* (Roseville, CA: Prima Publishing, 2002), x.

15. Guelzo, *Lincoln's Emancipation Proclamation*, 21.

16. Guelzo, *Lincoln's Emancipation Proclamation*, 26.

17. Guelzo, *Lincoln's Emancipation Proclamation*, 113.

18. Lincoln, *Collected Works*, V:434.

19. Richard Hofstadter, *The American Political Tradition and the Men Who Made It* (New York: Vintage Books, 1973 [1948]), 169.

20. Lerone Bennett Jr., *Forced into Glory: Abraham Lincoln's White Dream* (Chicago: Johnson Publishing Co., 2000), 6–7, 15–21, 27–30, 532–37.

21. DiLorenzo, *The Real Lincoln*, 53.

22. DiLorenzo, *The Real Lincoln*, 52.

23. Lincoln, *Collected Works*, IV:263.

24. Guelzo, *Lincoln's Emancipation Proclamation*, 57–58, 92.

25. Guelzo, *Lincoln's Emancipation Proclamation*, 5.

26. Guelzo, *Lincoln's Emancipation Proclamation*, 54.

27. Bennett, *Forced into Glory*, 347–48.

28. DiLorenzo, *The Real Lincoln*, 36.

29. Lincoln, *Collected Works*, VI:29.

30. Lincoln, *Collected Works*, VI:30.

31. Lincoln, *Collected Works*, VI:428–29.

32. Quoted in Philip Shaw Paludan, *"A People's Contest": The Union and Civil War, 1861–1865* (Lawrence: University of Kansas Press, 1996), 224.

33. Guelzo, *Lincoln's Emancipation Proclamation*, 201.

34. Quoted in Guelzo, *Lincoln's Emancipation Proclamation*, 232.

35. Lincoln, *Collected Works*, II:276 (emphasis added).

36. DiLorenzo, *The Real Lincoln*, 163.

37. Harry Jaffa, *A New Birth of Freedom: Abraham Lincoln and the Coming of the Civil War* (Lanham, MD: Rowman & Littlefield, 2000), 250.

8

WAS LINCOLN THE FATHER OF BIG GOVERNMENT?

From Lord Acton to Murray Rothbard, the leading classical liberals have embraced the cause of the Confederacy. Lincoln, in their view, was a faithful votary of Leviathan. By a bloody crusade that cost vast numbers of lives, he crushed those who dared resist centralizing power.

— David Gordon, "The Indefensible Abe," 2001

Abraham Lincoln opened the door to the kind of unconstrained, despotic, arrogant government we have today, something the framers of the Constitution could not have possibly imagined.

— Walter Williams, "The Civil War Wasn't about Slavery," December 2, 1998

The Lincoln Myth is the ideological cornerstone of big government in America.

— Thomas DiLorenzo, *The Real Lincoln*

As the patriots of Seventy-Six did to the support of the Declaration of Independence, so to the support of the Constitution and Laws, let every American pledge his life, his property, and his sacred honor.

— Abraham Lincoln, speech to the Young Men's Lyceum of Springfield, Illinois, January 27, 1838

A strange alliance between conservative defenders of the Confederate cause and libertarians is producing the fastest-growing body of scholarship on

Abraham Lincoln today. I say "strange" because, at first glance, libertarians, who are committed to the idea of individual liberty, free markets, and limited government, would seem to have little in common with a regime that rested upon the "cornerstone" of slavery.[1]

Uniting these somewhat disparate libertarian Lincoln critics is a view that "big government," a term referring to high rates of taxation, the redistribution of wealth, intrusive government policies, and large government bureaucracies, threatens individual freedom and economic growth. They also share something else in common: they believe that big government began with Abraham Lincoln. Historian Herman Belz perhaps best summarizes the libertarian case against Lincoln:

> [Lincoln] has been described as tearing down the inherited structure of government and building by dictatorial means a new Union based on the dogma of equality, or, less threateningly, as rejecting the limited government, natural rights Unionism of the Founders in favor of an organic nationalism that anticipated twentieth-century statism.[2]

But are libertarians right about Lincoln and big government? I believe they are mistaken, and badly so. In order to explain myself, however, I must venture to explain the principled origins of big government and contrast them with Lincoln's political and economic principles. This chapter veers farther from Lincoln than any other in this book, but that is because the principles used to justify big government were far removed from the principles of Lincoln.

WAS THE SOUTH DEFENDING LIMITED GOVERNMENT?

At the core of the mutual hostility toward Lincoln shared by libertarians and modern Confederates is a simple three-step argument. The major premise is that the Confederate South was fighting for limited government, trying to protect the states' rights from an overbearing national government. The minor premise is that Lincoln opposed the Confederacy by opposing secession. The conclusion, therefore, is that Lincoln opposed limited government. And by so opposing the rights of states, which served as powerful checks against an intrusive national government, Lincoln effectively paved the way for the big government we have today. The argument is internally consistent, if the major premise is true. But when the major premise is shown to be false, the argument crumbles.

It is certainly true that in speeches and essays, letters and newspaper columns, many Confederates employed the term "states' rights" in defending their decision to secede. But what is it they wanted to do with their states' rights? The Confederate understanding of states' rights had no connection to individual, natural rights, evidenced foremost by the fact that Confederates seceded so that they would be left free to perpetuate slavery, itself the grossest example of unlimited government of one people over another.

Chapter 6 examines the libertarian claim that the 1861 Confederate Constitution, despite its strict and perpetual protection for slavery, was a more pro-freedom constitution than the one James Madison and others designed in 1787. Thomas DiLorenzo expands on that claim to argue that, had the South been allowed to secede, not only would the Confederate Constitution have prevented the development of big government in the Confederacy, but it would have helped to ensure limited government in what remained of the United States as well:

> The Confederate Constitution explicitly outlawed protectionist tariffs and internal improvement subsidies and eliminated the general welfare clause of the U.S. Constitution. . . . This would have made for a much smaller government with a traditionally minimal role in economic policy affairs, and that would have been more conducive to economic growth than the Northern mercantilist state. The elimination of the general welfare clause was momentous, for thousands of special-interest expenditure items have been inserted into the federal budget over the years under the most specious and bizarre reasoning with regard to how they supposedly serve the "general welfare." This would have been avoided with the Confederate Constitution.

DiLorenzo continues in his celebration of the Confederate Constitution, predicting the felicitous effects it would have had on the Confederacy's northern neighbor, the United States:

> With a smaller and more efficient government just to its south, with its thriving free-trade ports and no cumbersome bureaucracy meddling in every industry's affairs, the U.S. government would have been forced to compete by sticking closer to the original intent of the U.S. Constitution as designed by the founding fathers. The Leviathan state would have been indefinitely delayed, if it came into creation at all, especially if involvement in World War I could have been avoided.[3]

There is a certain economic logic to DiLorenzo's argument, but he fails to acknowledge that the South was *not* defending limited self-government against an oppressive federal government. The South did not attempt to secede from the Union in 1860 and 1861 in order to defend republicanism, equal protection of equal rights, and government by consent within its own boundaries. As I demonstrate in chapter 6, it seceded to secure the Southern way of life, a way of life that revolved in many ways around the institution of human slavery, even though Lincoln posed no threat to that way of life. Neither he nor the federal government during his administration ever threatened republican self-rule. The main antislavery policy Lincoln advocated after 1854 was the restoration of the Missouri Compromise, which would only have prevented slavery from spreading to territories where it did not yet exist. Restoring the Missouri Compromise would not have affected slavery in South Carolina or any other Southern state; contrary to the demands of fanatical abolitionists, Lincoln strongly opposed any unconstitutional attempt to interfere with slavery in the states where slavery was lawful.

Consider also the fate of free speech throughout the South during the antebellum period. Leading American political thinkers dating back to the Founding openly and strongly endorsed what they believed was an intrinsic connection between republicanism, free speech, and justice. "The right of freely examining public characters and measures, and of free communication among the people thereon," argued James Madison, "has ever been justly deemed the only effectual guardian of every other right."[4] Without free speech and the free examination of ideas, it would be impossible for Americans to establish "good government from reflection and choice," in terms used in the first paper of the *Federalist*; they would instead depend "for their political constitutions on accident and force."[5] In a republic that protected free speech, unjust or immoral institutions like slavery would be under constant scrutiny, and, the Founders hoped and prayed, citizens persuaded through speech of slavery's injustice would someday eliminate it.

Prior to the sectional crisis of 1860, however, many Southern state governments were violating the leading republican principle of free speech in order to stop the free examination and discussion of slavery. "Free speech is considered as treason against slavery," one (rare) Southern abolitionist observed. Southerners employed the famous "Gag Rule" in the 1830s and 1840s to silence opposition to slavery in Congress; postmasters refused to deliver antislavery literature in Southern states; most slave states classified public speech against slavery as a criminal offense; and anyone speaking publicly against slavery might find himself the object of public ridicule and perhaps mob violence. As Katherine Hessler sums it up in a 1998 essay in the *Boston University Public Interest Law Journal*, "The South preferred to jeopardize the civil rights of Northern citizens rather than have the work of abolitionists jeopardize slavery in the South."[6]

The Civil War erupted because the South refused to accept the results of the 1860 presidential election, although it had been conducted in strict conformity with the rules of the Constitution. The cause of the Confederacy was not the cause of limited government or states' rights. Slavery represented the ultimate rejection of limited government. Allowing slavery to spread without restriction, as Southerners demanded at the 1860 Democratic convention, was not spreading limited government; it was spreading despotism. Yet, the South demanded not only that slavery be allowed to spread but that its spread be protected by an unprecedented expansion of federal power.

PROGRESSIVISM AND BIG GOVERNMENT

The libertarian critique of Lincoln is gaining public influence due to concern on the part of many Americans about the seemingly unrestrained growth of our government. Many Americans want to know how government became so big in order to understand better how to scale it back. Libertarian Lincoln critics offer a simple answer: big government in America began with Lincoln. And many Americans believe it.

U.S. Senator Barack Obama, a liberal Democrat from Illinois, for example, writes that Lincoln's "basic insight" was "that the resources and power of the national government can facilitate, rather than supplant, a vibrant free market." Senator Obama goes on to suggest that while Lincoln's "insight" was true, that markets do need government regulation, it was not until "the stock market crash of 1929 and the subsequent Depression that the government's vital role in regulating the marketplace became fully apparent." The Great Depression of the 1930s, according to Obama, offered the first genuine opportunity to implement Lincoln's political and economic strategy when "F.D.R. engineered a series of government interventions that arrested further economic contraction."[7] According to Obama, Lincoln first envisioned the principles of New Deal liberalism, while Franklin Roosevelt put them into practice.

But the principles that informed Roosevelt's New Deal policies, principles that liberals cheer and libertarians jeer at, stand in direct opposition to the principles that guided Lincoln's politics. In fact, there is an inverse relation between them: FDR's progressive principles rose in popularity and political prominence in proportion to the decline and fall of the natural right principles of Lincoln and the American Founders.

It is true that Lincoln demanded an increase in governmental power, coupled with increases in revenue, in order to prosecute the Civil War. But

Lincoln understood that the economic policies necessary to fund the war were all temporary: they were emergency measures that would end with the emergency's resolution. In 1861, we had our first income tax; by 1863, we had a progressive income tax; but by 1872 the income tax was gone. In 1865, we had a huge budget deficit and a mammoth $2.7 billion national debt. But then we had twenty-eight continuous years of budget surpluses. Fifty years after the Civil War, the national debt had been more than halved to $1.1 billion. These are not the legacies of a president who wanted to replace limited constitutional government with a large welfare state. Lincoln never wavered in his commitment to the principles of limited constitutional government; rather, his policies resulted from the fact that he was fighting a war to save limited constitutional government.

Limited constitutional government results from an understanding that the ends of government are limited primarily to securing the natural rights of individual citizens and fostering the general moral and political conditions necessary for free society. The ends of limited government, in other words, are rooted in unchanging human nature. Toward the end of the nineteenth century, an intellectual movement calling itself "progressivism" began, which later became the basis of what we today call "liberalism." While the label "progressivism" lumped together many different individuals and differing and competing schools of thought, they were united in their emphatic rejection of the natural right principles of the American Founding. As Thomas West and Douglas Jeffrey sum it up,

> At the beginning of the Progressive Era in the late nineteenth century, many educated Americans began to turn away from the natural rights theory of the American Founding. Their thought was greatly influenced by the doctrines of relativism and historicism—the denial of objective truth and the doctrine that "values" change over time. This rejection occurred on both the political right and political left. . . . The rejection of the idea of natural rights required a new understanding of the purpose of government and its relationship with the people. This new understanding became the basis of modern liberalism and its redefinition of equality and rights.[8]

Following European thinkers such as G. W. F. Hegel, Charles Darwin, and Karl Marx, American progressives such as Woodrow Wilson, Theodore Roosevelt, John Dewey, and Herbert Croly disavowed the Declaration's "laws of nature and of Nature's God" in favor of history, or what academicians call "historicism." According to historicism, all ideas and all beings evolve constantly. Not even the principles of right or truth remain the same over time; they change because all ideas are historical and progressive. Progressives denied the principles of the Founding precisely because those principles were understood to be timeless and immutable, not historical and progressive.

As the influential progressive intellectual John Dewey explained in his essay "The Future of Liberalism," the principles of the Declaration of Independence "formed part of a philosophy in which the ideas of individuality and freedom were asserted to be absolute and eternal truths, good for all times and places."[9] This was fundamentally wrong, argued Dewey, because "this absolutism" ignored "temporal relativity." Progressivism, in contrast, "is committed to the idea of historic relativity." "It knows that the content of the individual and freedom change with time," he wrote. Denying that human nature is immutable, that it is a self-evident truth that all men inherently possess equal rights to life, liberty, and the pursuit of happiness and that the purpose of government is to secure those natural rights, Dewey asserted that progressivism "knows that an individual is nothing fixed, given ready-made." Human nature "is something achieved" by the operations of "economic, legal, and political institutions." The purpose of government, in Dewey's progressive view, becomes an "experimental procedure," an open-ended exercise of political power, directed by the expertise of the bureaucratic class, in the attempt to achieve "social justice," the meaning of which changes as society changes.

Intellectual progressivism gave rise to a political movement, modern liberalism, which has had tremendous influence on American politics and the American way of life. Woodrow Wilson, for example, a founder and leading proponent of progressivism, was the first president in American history to criticize openly the Constitution in a fundamental way. He objected that the Constitution was built upon outdated ideas that human nature doesn't change, and therefore neither does the purpose of government. As Wilson wrote, "Governments [and rights] have their natural evolution and are one thing in one age, another in another age." The natural rights theory of the American Founding, as well as the Constitution constructed upon it, is problematic in that it assumes certain political principles are true always and everywhere and fails to take into account the historical relativity of all principles. As Wilson wrote in *Constitutional Government*,

> The government of the United States was constructed upon the Whig theory of political dynamics, which was an unconscious copy of the Newtonian theory of the universe. In our day, whenever we discuss the structure or development of a thing, whether the thing is in nature or

society, we consciously or unconsciously follow Mr. Darwin. But before Darwin they followed Mr. Newton.[10]

The Constitution was an eighteenth-century document, but America faced nineteenth-century and, eventually, twentieth-century problems that the Founders could not have anticipated. Therefore, according to progressives, a government adequate to meet the exigencies of the eighteenth century would not be adequate to meet those of later times. Moreover, the Constitution was not merely an obstacle to progressive politics: rooted in principles that claimed to be nonhistorical, to be true, simply, without reference to time, it represented an unscientific, if not superstitious, "worldview." This is why, at the end of his first book, *Congressional Government*, Wilson compared the Constitution to "political witchcraft."[11] In the name of progressive social science and its political corollary, progressive "social justice," the Constitution had to be overcome.

Indeed, modern liberalism throughout the last century has sought nothing less than to replace limited constitutional government by consent with an unlimited bureaucratic "state" whose purpose is open-ended and whose powers are therefore unlimited (at least in principle). One solution progressives invented to circumvent the original Constitution was to redefine it as a "living constitution," one whose meaning changes as judges and bureaucrats think necessary. Only a "living constitution," as opposed to the original Constitution and its strict limitations on governmental power, is compatible with the progressive project of building big government.

In 1903, progressive political scientist Charles Merriam published *A History of American Political Theories*, which tracked the decline and rejection of the principles of the American Founding. According to Merriam,

> The individualistic ideas of the "natural right" school of political theory, endorsed in the [American] Revolution, are [now] discredited and repudiated. The notion that political society and government are based upon a contract between independent individuals and that such a contract is the sole source of political obligation, is regarded as no longer tenable. . . . In the refusal to accept the contract theory as the basis for government, practically all the political scientists of note agree. The old explanation no longer seems sufficient, and is with practical unanimity discarded. The doctrines of natural law and natural rights have met a similar fate.[12]

Echoing John C. Calhoun, Merriam wrote that "the earlier explanation and philosophy [of the Founders] was not only false but dangerous and misleading." Our rights come not from nature but from government, in other words, and to think otherwise, as the Founders did, is "dangerous and misleading." Merriam fully understood the theory of the Founding, explaining,

> The [Founding] Fathers believed that in the original state of nature all men enjoy perfect liberty, that they surrender a part of this liberty in order that a government may be organized, and that therefore the stronger the government the less the liberty remaining to the individual. Liberty is, in short, the natural and inherent right of all men; government the necessary limitation of the liberty.

But "Calhoun and his school repudiated this idea, and maintained that liberty is not the natural right of all men, but only the reward of the races or individuals properly qualified for its possession." Somewhat embarrassed that Calhoun and other historicists of the antebellum era used historical right to justify slavery, Merriam wrote that the "mistaken application of the idea [to slavery] had the effect of delaying recognition of the truth in what had already been said until the controversy over slavery was at an end."[13] It was not that slavery was *wrong*—the principles of natural right invoked by Lincoln to condemn slavery were illusions, according to Merriam—but, rather, slavery was destined for the dustbins of history as proven by history itself, and therefore Calhoun was not as astute a historicist as he might have been. Further, slavery so divided the American people that the modern progressive state could not be built until the dispute over that institution had been resolved, and Calhoun helped to agitate, rather than end, the controversy.

As the progressives rejected natural rights, so they rejected the view that the ends or powers of government should be limited. According to Merriam, "the ultimate end of the state" is nothing less than "the perfection of humanity, the civilization of the world; the perfect development of the human reason and its attainment to universal command over individualism."[14] Thus, Merriam wrote, "it is denied that any limit can be set to governmental activity."

If rights come from government, and if the purpose of government is the perfection of humanity, then limiting government is tantamount to limiting rights and hindering the perfection of man. Rather, "each function [of government] must rest on its own utilitarian basis," that is, government may do anything that is "useful," while the "specific determination" of what is and is not useful "belongs to the domain of government." This represents a complete reversal of the Founders' understanding of government: instead serving as an agent of the people, drawing its purpose and power from, and always accountable to, them, in the new progressive view, government is accountable only to itself because government is home to progressive intellectuals and experts.

PROGRESSIVES CELEBRATE LINCOLN

Although they rejected, and in some instances scorned, the natural rights constitutionalism of the Founders, most Progressives championed Abraham Lincoln. But they did not celebrate him for his principles, which were the same natural rights principles of the Founders. In fact, progressives wrote and spoke little about Lincoln's principles. Some even suggested that Lincoln had none, which was precisely why he was so nimble in politics: he was not burdened by any unchanging, clumsy principles. In his account of Lincoln, for example, Woodrow Wilson virtually reads natural rights right out of Lincoln's politics. In his book on Wilson's political thought, Ronald Pestritto explains how Wilson understood Lincoln:

> It is hardly debatable that Lincoln relied heavily on natural-rights theory in his own statesmanship. . . . Yet Wilson praised Lincoln for precisely the opposite quality—for eschewing abstract theory and being guided instead by the circumstances of the time. Wilson simply denied that Lincoln was guided by theoretical principles: "What commends Mr. Lincoln's studiousness to me is that the result of it was he did not have any theories at all. . . . Lincoln was one of those delightful students who do not seek to tie you up in the meshes of any theory." Lincoln was repeatedly held up by Wilson as a model Burkean statesman—one who never tried to draw on abstract notions of equality and liberty but instead embraced the practical model of evolutionary change.[15]

In *Lincoln Reconsidered*, David Donald reaffirms Wilson's view that Lincoln's success derived largely from the fact that he was not weighed down with theories or principles. Lincoln, according to Donald, was characterized by "fundamental opportunism" and "essential ambiguity." Contrary to the "rigid ideologists" who either favored slavery or hated it, Donald argues, Lincoln "joyously played the piano by ear, making up the melody as [he] went." Donald believes this is especially important to remember today, when "frightened if well-intentioned citizens are calling upon historians and teachers to draw up a rigid credo for Americanism and teach 'American values.'" Donald places "American values" in scare quotes because he does not believe there is any such thing and holds that to teach the principles of America as good or true is "to forget Lincoln's nonideological approach." "In our age of anxiety, it is pertinent to remember," Donald instructs his fellow Americans, that Lincoln's "one dogma was an absence of dogma."[16] Donald wrote his book in light of the political question of whether progressives and liberals who championed the New Deal could also champion Lincoln. Donald's answer is clear: there is no conflict between the theoretical principles of progressivism and those of Lincoln because Lincoln had no principles.

Progressives embraced Lincoln for two reasons. First, Lincoln successfully held the Union together during its most difficult trial, and progressives understood that the Union was necessary in order to build a progressive bureaucratic-administrative "state." The progressive political project, in other words, depended upon Lincoln's successfully saving the Union, even though progressives wanted to transform his constitutional union into an evolving, administrative "state."

Second, Lincoln was able to move men and their opinions through his rhetoric; therefore, progressives looked to him as perhaps the best model of what an American progressive "leader" needed to move the people in the direction indicated by the evolutionary forces of history. But the idea of progressive *leadership*, as developed by Woodrow Wilson among others, is strikingly different from the traditional statesmanship of Lincoln. As political scientist Charles Kesler explains, *leadership* is rooted in modern progressive theory and stands at odds against Lincolnian statesmanship:

> Leadership is a term taken from the military side of politics, and all it requires is that you be in the lead, that you be out in front. It arises out of the sense of progressivism that Wilson and others, in the first stage of liberalism, imparted to our politics. If history has a direction, if history is moving towards the ever-more rational, administrative state—the modern state—and building that state is the destiny of the nation, then you need leaders to get out in front to lead you in the direction where you know you are going. The function of leaders is not exactly to pick the direction toward which history itself, or progress itself, is pointing.[17]

Above all, a progressive leader needs *vision* (both "leadership" and "vision," as we use them today, are progressive terms that Woodrow Wilson introduced into the American political vocabulary). A statesman such as Lincoln, by contrast, whose orientation toward political law sprang from the unchanging laws of nature, did not present his arguments in terms of vision. In fact, he never once used the word "vision" to describe his own politics (nor did any of Lincoln's opponents). But the leader's vision, according to Wilson, allows the leader and his people to "see" where history is taking them under the guidance of the leader's leadership. In this way, progressives portrayed the "leader" as a kind of secular prophet whose vision comes not from God but from history, as evolutionary progress reveals its new directions most clearly to the progressive leader who can "see" or "feel" where the historical currents of an evolving social order are moving. To some, Lincoln might have "seemed like an accident," Wilson suggested, "but to history he must seem like a providence."[18]

In an essay titled "Leaders of Men," Wilson argued that progressive leaders are "early vehicles of the Spirit of the Age," the first to detect evolutionary transformations of the human condition and, therefore, not always welcomed by ordinary men and women who do not always welcome change. But a difficult question arises for the progressive leadership theory: how do we who are not visionary leaders, we who are stuck in the present and unable to "see" into the future, distinguish a legitimate leader from a fraud? Wilson offers a perfectly historicist, progressive answer: "Their success is the acknowledgement of their legitimacy."[19] The legitimate leader is the one who is successful, who is able to implement the policies and changes he predicts will happen. The one who cannot carry out his proposals has obviously misread the future; he obviously does not possess a clear "vision" and is therefore not a legitimate *leader*. But is this not another way of saying that legitimacy is conferred on the leader who has the power to implement his will? Is this not simply another way of saying that might makes right?[20]

The Honorable Frank Williams, the current chief justice of the Rhode Island Supreme Court whom Congress recently selected to serve as a member of the Abraham Lincoln Bicentennial Commission, restates the Wilsonian account of leadership in his 2002 *Judging Lincoln*. Throughout his book, Williams praises Lincoln's supposed progressive "vision" over and over. On one page alone of *Judging Lincoln*, Williams praises Lincoln's "rhetorical skill in articulating his national vision," writing that his "moral vision and his willingness to act on it set him apart from the politicians of his age," then (still on the same page) suggesting that Lincoln "used his sophisticated skills to guarantee his progressive vision for the American polity." If we turn the page, we find Williams arguing that the "troops shared Lincoln's vision of a new and better civilization and a more democratic nation" and that Lincoln had become "a prophet and a sculptor of democracy." On the following page, Williams writes that the Thirteenth Amendment was wartime legislation that "related to Lincoln's vision for the nation" and that Lincoln "used the necessary transactional means during wartime especially to achieve his vision of an America" that restored the "values" of the Founders.[21]

It seems Williams is far more comfortable discussing Lincoln's politics in Wilsonian rather than Lincolnian terms. In a chapter questioning whether

Lincoln violated the Constitution when he curbed civil liberties during the Civil War, Williams confidently asserts that Lincoln did not, an opinion not based on any strict interpretation of the Constitution but on the notion that "the verdict of history is that Lincoln's use of power did not constitute abuse."[22] The historical verdict, of course, rests on the fact that Lincoln won the war. Had he lost it, we are left to assume based on Williams' progressive analysis, Lincoln's use of power would have constituted abuse. According to the progressive principles of Williams and Wilson, Lincoln was a legitimate leader because he *won*; his *vision* of America's historical direction was "authentic" because he had the power to get America there.

Herbert Croly, who authored one of the most influential books on progressivism, *The Promise of American Life*, echoed Wilson's celebration of Lincoln's supposed vision, arguing that "Lincoln's vision placed every aspect of the situation in its proper relations."[23] After ascribing the quality of "visionary leadership" to Lincoln, progressives held him up for extolment because they viewed the Union's salvation as history's nod in the direction of the progressive state. As Kesler explains:

> From the progressive point of view, Abraham Lincoln became a kind of Bismarck, the Bismarck of America. His importance was not in reviving natural rights and identifying the moral case against slavery. Those were merely instruments, means in his hands, because they were what he had to work with. From the point of view of Wilson and, to a lesser extent, Teddy Roosevelt, Lincoln had simply been the American Bismarck, the one who imposed national unity upon a fractious, and therefore reactionary, country. Once the nation was in place, you could now have, finally, a nation-state, built along modern lines, along—one might say—Prussian lines. The building of the modern state was the enterprise of Wilson and the other progressives. That is what political liberalism meant: building the modern state, with centralized administrative power and with huge social welfare functions added to it.[24]

Many progressives simply ignored Lincoln's manifest defense of natural rights and insisted that the progressive reform movements of the late nineteenth and early twentieth centuries represented a continuation of the same fight against oppression that Lincoln fought. Vida Dutton Scudder, a founding member of the Society of Christian Socialists, wrote in 1898 about the connection between Lincoln and her own progressive agenda in no uncertain terms:

> The Civil War lies behind us as a great symbol, and its limited and clear-cut struggle may well inspire our generation as we face the more confused

and widespread forces of industrial bondage that hold our laboring classes in a spiritual deprivation as complete in some ways as that of the slaves. Indeed, the same relation binds our present to all the episodes of our great history, even to that most recent episode which lies too close behind us for discussion. Noble and of vast import they have been; yet we begin to question whether they were not all alike the preludes to a vaster conflict for which the forces are slowly gathering: the conflict against industrial slavery, the class-war that threatens the civilized world.[25]

But while early progressives made arguments and prepared the way for an unprecedented expansion of governmental power, it was not until the 1930s, as the Great Depression weighed upon the American people, that progressives (or modern "liberals," as they had begun to call themselves) were presented with an opportunity to put their new theory into practice.

FDR'S NEW DEAL: BUILDING BIG GOVERNMENT

Like earlier progressives, Franklin Delano Roosevelt wanted to prepare American opinion to accept a new, progressive version of the social contract that could form the basis of an unprecedented expansion of the federal government. But Roosevelt differed from his progressive predecessors in his tactics. Whereas earlier progressives openly attacked the political principles of the Founders and Lincoln, Roosevelt opted instead to praise them, presenting his own politics as a continuation of, and addition to, those earlier principles.

Roosevelt's basic message was that earlier principles were useful for earlier times, but new challenges required adding new principles to the old. As he said in a speech in Philadelphia, "This is fitting ground on which to reaffirm the faith of our fathers; to pledge ourselves to restore to the people a wider freedom; to give to 1936 as the founders gave to 1776—an American way of life."[26] In other words, just as the Founders gave Americans in 1776 "wider freedom" and new rights, Roosevelt sought to do the same in 1936.

In his 1932 Commonwealth Address, Roosevelt advanced the progressive theory with great rhetorical skill. According to Roosevelt, "The issue of government has always been whether individual men and women will have to serve some system of government of economics, or whether a system of government and economics exists to serve individual men and women."[27] "The final word," he said, "belongs to no man"; that is, we cannot know for certain whether government serves to protect men and women or whether men and women should serve their government. Yet, "we can still believe in change and in progress." Rejecting the natural rights principles of the Founding, Roosevelt drew from Woodrow Wilson and other earlier progressives, who "saw the situation more clearly."

> Where Jefferson [and the Founders] had feared the encroachment of po-litical power on the lives of individuals, Wilson knew that the new power was financial. He saw, in the highly centralized economic system, the despot of the twentieth century, on whom great masses of individ-uals relied for their safety and their livelihood, and whose irresponsibil-ity and greed, if it were not controlled, would reduce them to starvation and penury.[28]

The task of government, according to Roosevelt, was no longer to protect the equal natural rights of all citizens but to equalize economic power be-tween those with great wealth and those with little. In short, government's new purpose was the redistribution of wealth, taking from the rich and giv-ing to the poor. Building on the scholarship of Merriam and other pro-gressive social scientists who explicitly rejected the idea of a binding social contract between and among free individuals, Roosevelt subtly redefined the old social contract of the Founding:

> The Declaration of Independence discusses the problem of government in terms of a contract. Government is a relation of give and take, a con-tract, perforce, if we would follow the thinking out of which it grew. Un-der such a contract rulers were accorded power, and the people consented to that power on consideration that they be accorded certain rights.

Instead of a contract made among and by the people for their mutual pro-tection, in Roosevelt's account the contract is between the people and gov-ernment, where government is "accorded power," while the people are given "certain rights." Prior to government, in other words, the people had no rights; government determined what rights they would have and, pre-sumably, how they would exercise them. "The task of statesmanship," in Roosevelt's view, "has always been the re-definition of these rights in terms of a changing and growing social order." "Clearly," he said, "all this calls for a re-appraisal of values."

> A mere builder of more industrial plants, a creator of more railroad sys-tems, and organizer of more corporations, is as likely to be a danger as

a help. The day of the great promoter or the financial Titan, to whom we granted anything if only he would build, or develop, is over. Our task now is not discovery or exploitation of natural resources, or necessarily producing more goods. It is the soberer, less dramatic business of administering resources and plants already in hand, of seeking to reestablish foreign markets for our surplus production, of meeting the problem of under consumption, of adjusting production to consumption, of distributing wealth and products more equitably, of adapting existing economic organizations to the service of the people.[29]

Consider who Roosevelt identified in his indictment: builders of industrial plants, creators of railroad systems, organizers of corporations. What kinds of people are these? In a word, they are businessmen. Roosevelt could not have been clearer: in the new progressive, administrative state, the entrepreneurial businessman was "as likely to be a danger as a help." Therefore, the time for protecting equal natural rights or natural liberties had ended, and "the day of enlightened administration [had] come." The day had come when government would administer the affairs of the people.

Roosevelt knew that America was founded in revolution against unchecked and arbitrary governmental power and that Americans might look with suspicion on his New Deal if they maintained the revolutionary spirit of 1776. In his 1936 speech accepting renomination for office, therefore, Roosevelt emphasized that "political tyranny was wiped out in Philadelphia on July 4, 1776."[30] After the Declaration of Independence, political tyranny became impossible, a relic of the past; therefore, Americans of the twentieth century need not be worried about the growing size and scope of Roosevelt's New Deal government.

Besides, Roosevelt would argue elsewhere, a government strictly limited by the Constitution would be unable to provide all the goods progressive government promised to deliver. Central to Roosevelt's redefinition of the social contract was his innovation that the most important rights were what he termed "economic rights," as he called repeatedly for the addition, either formally or informally, of an "economic bill of rights" to the Constitution. As Roosevelt announced in his 1944 message to Congress, the natural rights that the Founders and Lincoln defended have "proved inadequate to assure us equality in the pursuit of happiness."

> We have come to a clear realization of the fact that true individual freedom cannot exist without economic security and independence. . . . In our day these economic truths have become accepted as self-evident. We have accepted, so to speak, a second Bill of Rights under which a new

basis of security and prosperity can be established for all regardless of station, race, or creed.[31]

Among the "economic rights" Roosevelt suggested were the following:

- The right to a useful and remunerative job in the nation's industries, shops, farms, or mines
- The right to earn enough to provide adequate food, clothing, and recreation
- The right of every farmer to raise and sell his products at a return that will give him and his family a decent living
- The right of every businessman, large and small, to trade in an atmosphere of freedom from unfair competition and domination by monopolies at home or abroad
- The right of every family to a decent home
- The right to adequate medical care and the opportunity to achieve and enjoy good health
- The right to adequate protection from the economic fears of old age, sickness, accident, and unemployment
- The right to a good education

According to Roosevelt, "All of these rights spell[ed] security." But Roosevelt's list was not meant to be comprehensive. As he said, "We must be prepared to move forward, in the implementation of these rights, to new goals of human happiness and well-being." As historical progress creates new desires on the part of the people, government must change and grow in order to supply the endless demand for new rights. Roosevelt's lengthy list of economic rights was not meant to be the end; it was only the beginning.

Unlimited government results when people believe that it is the government's purpose to supply everything they might desire, from government-funded jobs to government-funded medical care, government-funded abortions, government-funded farm subsidies, and government-funded after-school programs for children. The only kind of government that can deliver an unlimited number of goods is a government of unlimited power and scope. Further, unlike natural rights, government-created rights need not be equal among citizens. Lincoln could argue that slavery was wrong because all men possess the same natural rights to life, liberty, and property. But progressive or liberal "social justice" authorizes government bureaucrats to determine who gets what kind of rights and how many, dividing Americans into groups based on victimization and needs: racial minorities, women, homosexuals, farmers, union members, the elderly, the poor, and so on.

The liberal view of rights is perhaps best seen in so-called affirmative action policies offering race-based preferences to certain groups while penalizing members of other races. These policies rest on the assumption that the kind and number of rights one has depend on whether one belongs to a victimized group that affirmative action bureaucrats have deemed deserving of special treatment. These policies have the double corrupting effect of misleading Americans into thinking that their rights are gifts from government, while simultaneously justifying massive bureaucracies (most of which are blatantly unconstitutional) that distribute entitlements and preferences to some groups at the expense of others.

The main political obstacle to the New Deal–style big government that FDR wanted to create was a latent belief among Americans that the Constitution should limit the national government. For Roosevelt, the views of liberal New Dealers who wanted big government were not merely different from those of conservatives who favored limited, constitutional government; rather, liberals were right, and conservatives were irredeemably wrong. From Roosevelt's point of view, the New Deal and big government were necessary for, if not synonymous with, the public good; therefore, those who opposed the New Deal and big government were enemies of the public good.

In his 1944 State of the Union Address, Roosevelt stressed that "rightist reaction," that is, conservatism, presented "grave dangers" to the nation, or, more precisely, those who wanted to conserve constitutional government presented a grave danger to the New Deal.

> Indeed, if such [rightist] reaction should develop—if history were to repeat itself and we were to return to the so-called "normalcy" of the 1920s—then it is certain that even though we shall have conquered our enemies on the battlefields abroad, we shall have yielded to the spirit of Fascism here at home.[32]

The "normalcy" of the 1920s that Roosevelt warned against included periods of economic growth and prosperity under Presidents Warren Harding and Calvin Coolidge. Following World War I and the massive costs associated with it, the U.S. economy was suffering at the beginning of the 1920s. This economic downturn prompted President Harding, and later President Coolidge, to cut taxes and government debt and to restore a balanced budget—in general, to restore limited, constitutional government. The American economy responded with a complete reversal, and by 1923 employment levels were so high that there was an employment shortage in many parts of the country.

But for Roosevelt, returning to such a state of affairs would be nothing less than yielding "to the spirit of Fascism here at home." Restoring constitutional government, in other words, would mean that the enemy we beat on European battlefields, Nazi fascism, would triumph here at home.

The New Deal has become sacrosanct in American politics: the crown jewel of the New Deal, Social Security, for example, is arguably more entrenched in our laws and politics today than any of the rights enshrined in the Bill of Rights. Yet, the truth is that New Deal policies likely aggravated, more than they solved, the economic crisis of the Great Depression. The economic crisis persisted throughout the 1930s not because there were too few government programs and regulations but because there were too many. More than a decade of continued confiscation of capital from private ownership and policies hostile to businesses rendered economic recovery increasingly difficult. As economic historian Burton Folsom explains,

> The New Deal was an inevitable economic failure. Roosevelt's formula of substituting government programs for a normal business recovery had no chance of relieving the high unemployment. FDR relied on extracting tax dollars from individuals and corporations to fund government programs, such as the Works Progress Administration (WPA), which hired workers to pick up trash, cut down trees, and build roads, bridges, and schools. The jobs Roosevelt thought he was creating were a mirage. They merely transferred jobs from the productive private sector to the inefficient public one. . . . Unemployment under the New Deal never dropped below 14 percent and averaged over 17 percent.[33]

The economy did not recover until after Roosevelt was gone. The economic costs of Roosevelt's New Deal policies, including widespread bank and business failures, chronic high levels of unemployment, high prices, food shortages, confiscation of private property, and depressed living conditions, are coming under increasing scrutiny, as evidenced by books like Jim Powell's *F.D.R.'s Folly: How Roosevelt and His New Deal Prolonged the Great Depression* and Gary Dean Best's *Pride, Prejudice, and Politics: Roosevelt versus Recovery, 1933–1938*.[34] In his forthcoming *New Deal or Raw Deal? How FDR's Economic Legacy has Damaged America*, Burton Folsom offers perhaps the most comprehensive analysis of the New Deal and its legacy for American economics, politics, and law.[35]

Typically, however, the New Deal is measured not by its poor results but by its good intentions. FDR himself urged as much. In his 1936 acceptance of the renomination for the presidency at the Democratic convention in Philadelphia, Roosevelt said that the new political challenge for Americans was to use the "organized power of government" to put an end to the "despotism" caused by "economic royalists" who profited at the expense of ordinary working Americans. This, in sum, was the goal of New Deal policies. But would those policies produce the desired economic effects? That was not the important question, Roosevelt argued, but rather the question of intentions: "Governments can err, Presidents do make mistakes, but the immortal Dante tells us that divine justice weighs the sins of the cold-blooded and the sins of the warm-hearted in different scales."[36] The New Dealing Democrats were not cold-blooded "economic royalists" interested in making a profit but rather "warm-hearted" friends of working Americans, demonstrated by the fact that they supported a New Deal agenda that purported to help those most in need of help, which is what mattered most in Roosevelt's narrative. Thus, even if New Deal policies were a mistake and caused more economic harm than good—even if "there is considerable evidence that New Deal policies prolonged high unemployment"—even if New Deal policies made it "a crime [for businesses] to increase output or cut prices" at precisely the moment when unemployed Americans would have benefited from lower prices—even if FDR had erred, in other words, Americans should judge New Dealers by their good intentions.[37]

For intelligent liberals, the politics at stake in any assessment of the New Deal are far more important than mere economics. Various New Deal policies might have failed miserably in achieving economic growth and recovery, but those policies enshrined the new liberal view that rights come from government. Intelligent liberals understand how radically this new theory of government departs from the original social contract theory that informed the original Constitution, and they understand that any attack on New Deal policies, in principle, attacks the very ground of modern liberal government. Liberals (I include liberal Republicans no less than liberal Democrats) represent the political class that created, and in large measure continues to control, the new liberal form of government, which is why they must defend it. Defending the New Deal is, for liberals, an act of political self-defense. This is why Senator Obama, for example, encourages Americans to build on "the social contract that F.D.R. first stitched together in the middle of the last century," while ignoring altogether the natural rights social contract that the Founders established and Lincoln defended.[38] It is in his interest and the interest of every progressive liberal that the natural rights ideas of the Founders and Lincoln fade from the American mind.

AMERICAN GOVERNMENT TODAY

The modern administrative-welfare state, which began with the progressives' political philosophy and which New Deal and then Great Society programs later institutionalized, operates largely outside of, and with little regard for, the Constitution. Strictly speaking, the New Deal and the myriad regulatory and administrative agencies it has spawned have no basis in the Constitution. This is not to deny that many people both in and out of government have offered various constitutional apologies for big government, but these usually twist, distort, or ignore the text of the Constitution in ways that turn its meaning on its head.

For decades following the New Deal, for example, Congress and the Supreme Court used the Constitution's Commerce Clause to justify large expansions of federal regulatory power over states and individuals, power that no commonsense reading of the Constitution could ever explain. Article I, Section 8 of the Constitution authorizes Congress "to regulate commerce with foreign nations, and among the several States." Beginning in 1942 with *Wickard v. Filburn*, a case turning on the question of whether Congress possessed constitutional power to regulate the amount of wheat a farmer could grow for his own private consumption, the Supreme Court has argued that Congress can regulate any activity affecting commerce or the economy, however indirect or remote its influence, because it falls within the jurisdiction of "regulat[ing] commerce among the several states."[39] And Congress has been all too willing to oblige. In *Wickard*, the Court argued that while the domestic production and consumption of wheat is neither "commercial" nor "interstate," a farmer who consumes produce grown on his farm is less likely to purchase food at grocery markets, which will have an indirect effect on the economy, which will in turn affect interstate commerce; therefore, Congress may regulate the domestic production and consumption of wheat or other produce under the Commerce Clause in order to achieve desirable prices for the regulated goods in the market. By this reading of the Constitution's Commerce Clause, Congress can regulate any human activity because any human activity can be shown in some way to affect the economy and interstate commerce. Progressive government truly is, in principle, unlimited government.

Lincoln rejected the progressive, evolutionary view of history that progressive liberals used to justify modern big government. Earlier in chapter 4 I quoted Lincoln's 1854 speech in Peoria, demonstrating the immutability of the natural principle of justice and the intrinsic wrongness of slavery: "Repeal the Missouri compromise—repeal all compromises—repeal the declaration of independence—repeal all past history, you still can not repeal human nature."[40] Echoing classical political philosophy, Lincoln maintained that history does not affect human nature, which is the unchanging standard by which we measure and judge historical and political change.[41] For Lincoln, therefore, the only legitimate ends of government are those derived from unchanging human nature: the equal protection of equal, individual natural rights. In defending the idea that all men are created equal in the sense that all men possess equal rights by nature, rights that are antecedent to government, and that the purpose of government is limited to protecting natural rights, Lincoln defended the only firm foundation for limited constitutional government.

Knowing that the American public still largely venerates Lincoln, political liberals since FDR have been almost desperate to reinterpret Lincoln as a supporter of big, liberal government. As journalist Michael Lind observes,

> The progressives—now called liberals—in Franklin Roosevelt's Democratic Party rewrote history. . . . The New Deal liberal sought to enlist Lincoln as a political ancestor. What the New Deal liberal historians and intellectuals did was breathtaking in its audacity. . . . Franklin Roosevelt himself helped orchestrate the campaign to associate his presidency with Lincoln's. In 1940 he hired Sherwood Anderson, author of the popular play *Abe Lincoln in Illinois*, as a White House speech writer. Roosevelt invoked Lincoln to justify recovery programs and his campaign to enlarge the Supreme Court. The struggle for the New Deal[, Roosevelt said], was a "conflict as fundamental as Lincoln's. . . . Lincoln's most famous biographer, Carl Sandburg, an ardent supporter of the New Deal, helped by writing articles with titles like, 'Lincoln-Roosevelt.'" The New Deal intellectuals succeeded in creating a new version of the American past.[42]

New Deal liberals continue in the effort to remake Lincoln in their own image. A recent example is Mario Cuomo's *Why Lincoln Matters: Today More Than Ever*, from which I have already quoted. Cuomo's book illustrates how far prominent liberal politicians will go to exploit Lincoln in order to advance their political agenda.[43]

Cuomo's modus operandi is to invoke an inspirational line from Lincoln, then equate it with a shibboleth of modern liberalism, but only after advising his readers that "conservatives and liberals alike should always resist the impulse to make Lincoln over in their own image." For example, Lincoln explained in his 1861 message to Congress in special session that the Civil War was "essentially a People's contest . . . [presenting] to the whole family of man, the question, whether a constitutional republic, or a democracy—a government of the people, by the same people—can, or cannot, maintain its territorial integrity against its own domestic foes." Cuomo quotes this sentence, then inexplicably draws the conclusion that the administration of George W. Bush wrongly liberated Iraq without permission from the United Nations: "Today, when we need global cooperation the most, our credibility is at a low point because of our perceived arrogance, unilateralism, and bellicosity."[44] Cuomo never pauses to explain the connection between Lincoln's quotation and the present war in Iraq.

The thesis of Cuomo's book hangs on one quotation from Lincoln that he repeats throughout: "The legitimate object of government is to do for the people what needs to be done, but which they can not, by individual effort, do at all, or do so well, for themselves."[45] Cuomo delights in this passage because it lends itself so easily to New Deal–style liberalism. By supporting "internal improvements" such as railroads and canals, writes Cuomo, Lincoln "offered the poor more than freedom and the encouragement of his own good example." From there, Cuomo quickly concludes that Lincoln would have endorsed the kind of liberal policies and redistribution of wealth that Cuomo supports. "Lincoln was too large, complex, and grand to be captured by those shopworn rhetorical labels," meaning we ought not try to label Lincoln as "liberal" or "conservative," yet Cuomo displays a confident certitude throughout his book that Lincoln was a liberal just like Cuomo himself. Senator Obama, also a liberal Democrat, appeals to the very same line from Lincoln as Cuomo in his attempt to place Lincoln on the side of New Deal–style economic regulation.[46]

Cuomo titles one chapter of his book "Today's America: An Unfinished Work," borrowing from Lincoln's dedication to the "unfinished work" advanced by Union soldiers who had given their lives at Gettysburg. But Lincoln is the subject of only two sentences. "Lincoln would have been gratified at how far we have come," Cuomo claims to know, but "disappointed that we have not come far enough." The remainder of the chapter is an advertisement for liberal public policies, stopping along the way to decry President Bush's "tax cuts for the rich" and his supposed unilateralism in international affairs, while serving up plenty of praise for liberal Bill Clinton.[47]

Unlike Lincoln, Cuomo has difficulty embracing the principles of the Declaration of Independence unless he redefines them. According to Cuomo, the Declaration promises "the inalienable right to equality"; the Declaration, of course, does not mention a "right to equality" but rather states that "all men are created equal" because they are "endowed by their Creator with certain unalienable rights," among which are the natural rights to "life, liberty, and the pursuit of happiness." For Cuomo, the problem for America today is that government is not big enough, and not enough private wealth is redistributed. Our top concern should be "that our nation does not become a society of sharply disparate economic classes." In support of his position, Cuomo cites Lincoln's July 4, 1861, message to Congress in special session, in which he argued that the "leading object" of the government is "to lift artificial weights from all shoulders." Of course, Lincoln was referring primarily to the artificial weight imposed by slavery. Lincoln repeatedly affirmed the right of every man to equal opportunity, not an equality of outcome. Indeed, Lincoln thought the freedom America offered was good precisely because the son of a poor man could become rich, while the son of a rich man might become poor. As Lincoln said in an 1859 speech before the Wisconsin State Agricultural Society,

> The prudent, penniless beginner in the world, labors for wages awhile, saves a surplus with which to buy tools or land, for himself; then labors on his own account another while, and at length hires another new beginner to help him. This . . . is free labor—the just and generous, and prosperous system, which opens the way for all, gives hope to all, and energy, and progress, and improvement of condition to all. If any continue through life in the condition of the hired laborer, it is not the fault of the system, but because of either a dependent nature which prefers it, or improvidence, folly, or singular misfortune.[48]

Believing that a man's rights depended in no way on the color of his skin, Lincoln worked tirelessly so that our nation would not become a society of disparate racial classes. When interpreting Lincoln's views on race, Cuomo cites historians who believe that Lincoln favored color-blind law on the one hand and others who condemn Lincoln as an irredeemable racist on the other. Who is correct? Cuomo cannot decide. Regardless, he is sure that Lincoln would favor race-based preferences and affirmative action, bigger welfare programs, government-subsidized housing, and socialized health care.

In the end, it is unclear why Cuomo respects Lincoln, or why he expects us to. But identifying Lincoln with liberal big government programs is not the reserve of Democrats only. Recently, in February 2007, Republican Newt Gingrich cohosted with Cuomo a political forum at New York City's Cooper Union, the spot where Lincoln gave one of his most important speeches in 1860 as he tried to woo support from eastern Republicans. The evening was billed as a "Lincoln-inspired event" intended to "discuss the state of political culture."[49] It is not unusual for Gingrich, who has a long history of public service, to invoke Lincoln; he has on many occasions expressed admiration for the sixteenth president. Interestingly, the Lincoln event with Cuomo was held only a few weeks after Gingrich cowrote an article with fellow Republican Rudy Giuliani, former mayor of New York City, for the *Wall Street Journal* calling for an American-funded New Deal for Iraq: "The [Bush] administration," Gingrich and Giuliani explain, should use funding by Congress to "create an Iraqi Citizen Job Corps, along the lines of FDR's Civilian Conservation Corps during the Great Depression."[50] In a line that could easily be confused with one of FDR's "fireside chats" marketing his New Deal to Americans, Gingrich and Giuliani conclude, "The creation of an Iraqi Citizen Job Corps will help expedite the establishment of a more stable civil society and improve the growing Iraqi economy through the transforming power of an honest day's work."

Whatever might be said of the proposed Iraqi Citizen Job Corps, Gingrich clearly sees little, if any, contradiction in promoting New Deal policies, which rest on principles contrary to Lincoln's views, while conducting forums to remind Americans how to think about politics the way Lincoln did.

Yet, the real Lincoln still matters. For those who believe the principles of the American Founding are *true*, that they do not simply express an eighteenth-century "worldview" or outdated "values" relegated to an irrelevant past, the challenge we face is to recover those true principles. We must revive what Lincoln called our "ancient faith" before we can make real progress in recovering the constitutional government that is rightfully ours. But before we can revive the natural right principles of the Founders and Lincoln, we must take the full measure of modern liberalism, which stands between us and those principles. One of the great failures of statesmanship today, I believe, is an underestimation of how deeply a century of progressivism has already transformed politics (including both political parties), education, and culture in America. Although progressivism has not completely removed the Constitution from American political life, the Constitution is far less relevant to our politics, laws, and government than it used to be. The authority of the Constitution in our politics continues to recede, while government exercises vast power with little or no constitutional authority. Generations have come of age under this new form of big government, producing an American regime and an American people very dissimilar to those of the past. Our progressive politics today owes much to the historicist theories of Hegel, Darwin, Marx, and other modern thinkers. Nothing could be more alien to the natural rights principles of the American Founders. Nothing could be more alien to the politics of Abraham Lincoln.

NOTES

1. Alexander Stephens, "Cornerstone Speech," March 21, 1861, in *Alexander H. Stephens in Public and Private with Letters and Speeches* (Philadelphia: National Publishing, 1866), 721.

2. Herman Belz, *Abraham Lincoln, Constitutionalism, and Equal Rights in the Civil War Era* (New York: Fordham University Press, 1998), 73.

3. Thomas DiLorenzo, *The Real Lincoln: A New Look at Abraham Lincoln, His Agenda, and an Unnecessary War* (Roseville, CA: Prima Publishing, 2002), 273–74.

4. James Madison, "The Virginia Resolution of 1798," The Avalon Project at Yale Law School, www.yale.edu/lawweb/avalon/virres.htm (accessed January 7, 2007).

5. Charles R. Kesler and Clinton Rossiter, eds., *The Federalist Papers* (New York: Signet Classic, 2003), 27.

6. Katherine Hessler, "Early Efforts to Suppress Protest: Unwanted Abolitionist Speech," *Boston University Public Interest Law Journal* 7 (spring 1998): 185–217. See also Michael Kent Curtis, "The Curious History of Attempts to Suppress Antislavery Speech, Press, and Petition in 1835–37," *Northwest Law Review* 89 (1995): 785–849. See also Mark Graber, *Dred Scott and the Problem of Constitutional Evil* (New York: Cambridge University Press, 2006), 231–33.

7. Barack Obama, *The Audacity of Hope: Thoughts on Reclaiming the American Dream* (New York: Crown Publishers, 2006), 152–53.

8. Cf. Thomas G. West and Douglas A. Jeffrey, *The Rise and Fall of Constitutional Government in America* (Claremont, CA: Claremont Institute, 2004), 31–32.

9. John Dewey, "The Future of Liberalism," *Journal of Philosophy* 22, no. 9 (1935): 225–30.

10. Ronald J. Pestritto, ed., *Woodrow Wilson: The Essential Political Writings* (Lanham, MD: Lexington Books, 2005), 175.

11. Woodrow Wilson, *Congressional Government: A Study in American Politics* (New York: Meridian Books, 1956 [1885]), 215.

12. Charles Merriam, *A History of American Political Theories* (New York: MacMillan Co., 1903), 307, 309.

13. Merriam, *A History of American Political Theories,* 312.

14. Merriam, *A History of American Political Theories,* 318.

15. Ronald J. Pestritto, *Woodrow Wilson and the Roots of Modern Liberalism* (Lanham, MD: Rowman & Littlefield, 2005), 57–58.

16. David Donald, *Lincoln Reconsidered: Essays on the Civil War Era* (Westport, CT: Greenwood Press, 1981), 18.

17. Charles Kesler, "Statesmanship for America's Future," June 1, 1998, Claremont.org, www.claremont.org/publications/pubid.497/pub_detail.asp (accessed April 1, 2007).

18. Pestritto, *Woodrow Wilson: The Essential Political Writings,* 89.

19. Pestritto, *Woodrow Wilson: The Essential Political Writings,* 225.

20. Consider the titles that two "leaders" who believed right does make might gave to themselves: Hitler called himself "der Fürher," which means "the Leader," and Mussolini called himself "il Duce," which also means "the Leader."

21. Frank J. Williams, *Judging Lincoln* (Carbondale: Southern Illinois University Press, 2002), 124, 128, 130.

22. Williams, *Judging Lincoln*, 62.

23. Quoted in Eldon Eisenach, ed., *The Social and Political Thought of American Progressivism* (Indianapolis: Hackett Publishing Co., 2006), 6.

24. Kesler, "Statesmanship for America's Future."

25. Eisenach, *The Social and Political Thought of American Progressivism*, 13.

26. Franklin D. Roosevelt, "Acceptance of the Renomination for the Presidency," in *The Public Papers and Addresses of Franklin D. Roosevelt*, ed. Samuel I. Rosenman (New York: Russell & Russell, 1938), 5:231.

27. Roosevelt, *The Public Papers and Addresses of Franklin D. Roosevelt*, 1:743–44.

28. Roosevelt, *The Public Papers and Addresses of Franklin D. Roosevelt*, 1:749.

29. Roosevelt, *The Public Papers and Addresses of Franklin D. Roosevelt*, 1:751.

30. Roosevelt, *The Public Papers and Addresses of Franklin D. Roosevelt*, 2:232.

31. Roosevelt, *The Public Papers and Addresses of Franklin D. Roosevelt*, 13:41.

32. Roosevelt, *The Public Papers and Addresses of Franklin D. Roosevelt*, 13:42.

33. Burton Folsom Jr., "Three Myths of the Great Depression," July 2004, Foundation for Economic Education, www.fee.org/publications/notes/notes/Three Myths.asp (accessed February 22, 2007).

34. Jim Powell, *F.D.R.'s Folly: How Roosevelt and His New Deal Prolonged the Great Depression* (New York: Crown Forum, 2003). Gary Dean Best, *Pride, Prejudice, and Politics: Roosevelt versus Recovery, 1933–1938* (New York: Praeger Publishers, 1990).

35. Burton W. Folsom, Jr., *New Deal or Raw Deal? How FDR's Economic Legacy has Damaged America* (New York: Simon & Schuster, 2008).

36. Roosevelt, *The Public Papers and Addresses of Franklin D. Roosevelt*, 5:235.

37. Powell, *F.D.R.'s Folly*, viii-xvi.

38. Obama, *The Audacity of Hope*, 159.

39. *Wickard v. Filburn*, 317 U.S. 111 (1942).

40. Roy P. Basler, ed., *The Collected Works of Abraham Lincoln* (New Brunswick, NJ: Rutgers University Press, 1953), II:271. Cited hereafter as Lincoln, *Collected Works*.

41. According to Leo Strauss, "Philosophy, in the strict, classical sense of the term, is the quest for the eternal order, or for the eternal cause or causes of all things." Philosophy rests on the premise "that there is an eternal and immutable order within which history takes place, and which remains entirely unaffected by history." See Leo Strauss, *On Tyranny: Revised and Expanded Edition Including the Strauss-Kojeve Correspondence* (New York: The Free Press, 1991 [1963]), 212.

42. Michael Lind, *What Lincoln Believed: The Values and Convictions of America's Greatest President* (New York: Doubleday, 2004), 10–12.

43. Mario M. Cuomo, *Why Lincoln Matters: Today More Than Ever* (New York: Harcourt Press, 2004). My review of Cuomo's book was published in the fall 2004

issue of the *Claremont Review of Books* and is available online at http://claremont
.org/writings/crb/fall2004/krannawitter.html.

44. Cuomo, *Why Lincoln Matters*, 125.

45. Lincoln, *Collected Works*, II:221.

46. Obama, *The Audacity of Hope,* 159.

47. Cuomo, *Why Lincoln Matters*, 32–38.

48. Lincoln, *Collected Works*, III:478–79.

49. Gary Shapiro, "Gingrich, Cuomo to Walk in Lincoln's Footsteps," *New York Sun*, February 26, 2007, http://www.nysun.com/article/49284?page_no=1.

50. Rudy Giuliani and Newt Gingrich, "Getting Iraq to Work," *Wall Street Journal*, January 12, 2007, http://opinionjournal.com/editorial/feature.html?id=110009514.

9

WAS LINCOLN A TYRANT?

Lincoln was an American Pol Pot, except worse. Pol Pot's barbarism was [at least] justified by the Marxian doctrine of class genocide to which he adhered. Lincoln's barbarism was prohibited by the morality of his time and the U.S. Constitution, yet neither deterred him.

—Paul Craig Roberts, Reagan administration official and former *Wall Street Journal* editor, "Lincoln and the War on Terror: A Conservative Reappraisal," March 19, 2002

Let every American, every lover of liberty, every well wisher to his posterity, swear by the blood of the Revolution, never to violate in the least particular, the laws of the country; and never to tolerate their violation by others.

—Abraham Lincoln, speech to the Young Men's Lyceum of Springfield, Illinois, January 27, 1838

In a 1979 essay, Don Fehrenbacher noted that more historians have described Abraham Lincoln as a dictator than any other president.[1] Since then, increasing numbers of scholars and critics have continued to identify Lincoln as a dictator, a tyrant, or both, with heightened invective accompanying the charges. In the first epigraph above, for example, Paul Craig Roberts, who served as Assistant Secretary of the Treasury for economic policy under President Ronald Reagan, compares Lincoln to Pol Pot.[2] Others have compared him to Hitler and Stalin. These critics believe, in the words of Thomas DiLorenzo, that "Lincoln was a glutton for tyranny."[3]

These accusations stem mainly from Lincoln's emergency war measures, which included suspending the writ of habeas corpus, implementing a blockade against Southern ports, and installing military commissions in place of civil courts. These actions constituted nothing less than blatant violations of the Constitution, Lincoln's harshest critics argue. He thereby established the dangerous precedent that a president in particular, and the national government in general, may ignore the Constitution's limitations on governmental power and protections for individual liberty. As Clinton Rossiter writes in *Constitutional Dictatorship*, Lincoln acted with "no precedent and under no restraint," and during most of the Civil War, he "*was* the government of the United States."[4]

Progressive and political liberal scholars, dating back more than a century now, have tended to view Lincoln's actions as a favorable development in American politics, allowing the government to expand and accommodate the growing and changing social problems in America. Although political scientist John Burgess argued at the turn of the last century that Lincoln's actions had transformed the presidency "practically into the position of a military dictator," he concluded nonetheless that Lincoln's was "good political science and good public policy."[5] Lincoln, in this view, offered a "prototype of twentieth-century presidential government, ruling through rhetorical leadership of public opinion rather than an adherence to the text and forms of the Constitution."[6] Although he transgressed the constitutional limitations on presidential power, Lincoln's example is not threatening because, in the words of James G. Randall, "if Lincoln was a dictator, it must be admitted that he was a benevolent dictator."[7] This view of Lincoln as a "benevolent dictator" has gained currency most recently in George Fletcher's *Our Secret Constitution: How Lincoln Redefined American Democracy*.[8]

But some liberals believe Lincoln broke faith with the Constitution and remain unpersuaded that his constitutional infidelity was justified. Mario Cuomo, for example, laments, "I still wish the great Lincoln had stood by the Constitution despite the strong temptation not to." Cuomo goes on to argue that if Lincoln were here advising Americans today in the current War on Terror, he would urge them to ignore his own example of suspending civil liberties in time of war. Cuomo concludes *Why Lincoln Matters* in an odd and rather presumptuous way: he provides the text of a hypothetical speech that might have been given in 2004 before the U.S. Congress, a speech that he, Cuomo, wrote but that he is certain Lincoln would have delivered had it been Lincoln addressing Congress. In this hypothetical speech, Cuomo places the following words into Lincoln's mouth:

Therefore, my disputed actions [suspending civil liberties during the Civil War] in the past are a precedent that may safely be ignored today. Either they will be considered wrong and should be ignored for that reason, or they will be considered right but for reasons that do not pertain in the current emergency [following the terrorist attacks of September 11, 2001].[9]

Lincoln critics writing from a conservative or libertarian perspective consistently deplore Lincoln's example as setting the stage for the largely extraconstitutional growth of American government in the last century and endangering the liberties of American citizens. Willmoore Kendall and George Carey perhaps sounded this theme most clearly in their 1970 *The Basic Symbols of the American Political Tradition*.[10] Many of the Lincoln critics whose arguments I have examined in the preceding chapters repeat this charge of unconstitutional tyranny. In the final analysis, these authors argue, America can never return to a genuinely limited government under the Constitution so long as the American mind holds up Lincoln as the preeminent example of American statesmanship, which is why they labor so tirelessly to discredit him. "As defender of the Union in its most profound crisis," writes Herman Belz, "Lincoln has been regarded as a precursor of the kind of organic nationalism and constitutionalism not bound to the letter of the Constitution nor fettered by states' rights that has characterized American government in the twentieth century."[11]

"The basic question," explains Belz, "in evaluating Lincoln's governance is whether he violated the Constitution in taking emergency actions at the start of the war."[12] First and foremost is the question of secession. If Southern states possessed the legal and constitutional right to secede peacefully, then indeed virtually all of Lincoln's actions in defense of the Union were constitutionally illegitimate. But, as I argue in chapter 5, secession cannot be squared with either the conditions necessary for constitutional government (free elections, majority rule, government by consent, equal protection of equal rights) or the textual provisions of the Constitution. What some Southerners called *secession* was, in light of the Constitution and the social contract principles of the American Founding, *rebellion*.

Once it is agreed that states did not possess a right of secession, the question becomes very different: if the states had waged an armed rebellion against the national government, to what extent, under the Constitution, could the national government use its power to suppress it? In the case of the Civil War, the Southern strategy for victory differed from that of the North. For the South it was mainly a war of attrition. In principle, the

South did not need to win a single battle to secure victory; it needed only for the Union army to tire and go home. For the North, victory, that is, complete suppression of the rebellion, required nothing less than completely vanquishing the hostile Southern forces. How far would the Union go—how far *should* it go—to accomplish this goal? Many Southerners, those who remained, were numb and incoherent by the war's end in April 1865, filled with terror, anxiety, hatred, gloom, and depression. Yet, as commander in chief, Lincoln had a duty to ask hard questions of war strategy.[13] What must the Union army do to win?

Consider also the precedent being set. If a nation of people agrees to settle their political disputes through free elections and ballots, and then some who cannot win that way decide to resort instead to bullets in order to achieve the results they desire, may a president use bullets to vindicate free elections and ballots? If a president does not defend the results of a free election, does that not set the precedent that whatever cannot be attained through free elections may be attained by violence? And if that becomes the accepted standard for settling political disputes, why will anyone place any stock in the importance or value of elections? If violence becomes the standard, is it not wiser to invest in bullets and pay no attention to ballots?

It is a hard truth for many modern critics to accept, but in the face of violent rebellion, violent force on the part of government may be the necessary response. As Lincoln's law partner, William Herndon, asked rhetorically, "Does [Lincoln] suppose he can crush—squelch out this huge rebellion by pop guns filled with rose water?"[14]

LINCOLN CONFRONTS A CRISIS

To remind ourselves of the dangers confronting Lincoln and the U.S. government in 1861, we should recall Lincoln's trip to Washington, D.C., prior to his inauguration and the first days of his presidency. Lincoln departed from his hometown of Springfield, Illinois, on February 11, 1861, traveling by train on a meandering route to Washington, D.C, with multiple stops along the way. At that time, six slave states had already passed ordinances of secession (Texas would soon become the seventh on February 23), and rumors were spreading that Southern sympathizers might attempt to harm Lincoln and prevent his inauguration. When Lincoln's train stopped in Philadelphia, he received credible reports of a plot to assassinate him. This persuaded him to take precautions during the remainder of the trip. Lincoln arrived in Washington, D.C., safely under the cover of night, but his troubles only grew worse.

The day after his inauguration on March 4, he received word from Major Robert Anderson, the commanding officer of the federal garrison at Fort Sumter located in the harbor of Charleston, South Carolina, that the provisions for troops there would last no more than four weeks. The fort was badly in need of resupply. After agonizing about whether to send provisions, and unaware that Secretary of State William Seward had already promised emissaries of the Confederacy, without presidential authorization, that the fort would be abandoned, Lincoln finally decided to send supplies by ship. But before they could reach Sumter, early in the morning of April 12, General P. G. T. Beauregard of the Confederate forces in Charleston opened fire, bombarding the garrison until Anderson surrendered on the morning of April 14.

Lincoln had said in his inaugural address that the government would not assail anyone of the South, stating clearly to the Southerners, "You can have no conflict without being yourselves the aggressors." With the bombardment of Sumter, the South became the aggressor, and Lincoln quickly began to prepare the Union's government to defend itself. Lincoln called for seventy-five thousand volunteer troops (Lincoln's old political nemesis, Stephen Douglas, spoke with him the night before and supported his decision to raise an army, but Douglas thought it wiser to call for two hundred thousand troops). Soon, however, Lincoln learned the extent of Confederate sympathy in places far removed from the Deep South, including Maryland, a slave state that bordered Washington, D.C., to the north.

Maryland was critical for moving troops from Northern states to Washington, D.C., because the rail lines from New York, Philadelphia, and Harrisburg went through Baltimore. When the first numbers of troops arrived in Baltimore on April 18, Southern-sympathizing Marylanders stoned and harassed them. The following day, a full-scale riot broke out in the streets of Baltimore. In his book on Lincoln and civil liberties, the late Chief Justice William Rehnquist describes what happened when the next wave of troops attempted to pass through Baltimore, alarming the administration:

> Four days after Lincoln issued his call for volunteers, a Massachusetts regiment arrived from Philadelphia at Baltimore's President Street Station. . . . The ninth car stopped momentarily, and in a trice all of its windows were broken by rocks and stones. . . . The mob placed rocks and sand on the horse-car tracks, and the soldiers alighted and fell back to the station whence they had come. . . . [In front of them] was a mob of twenty-thousand Confederate sympathizers. The troops decided to fight their way through on foot, and the mob closed in behind as they marched. . . . Soon the crowd loosed a volley of stones at the soldiers, who finally turned and fired their rifles into the crowd. In the final tally, sixteen people were killed, four soldiers and twelve civilians.[15]

Over the next few days, Confederate sympathizers burned railroad bridges leading into Baltimore, effectively cutting off rail transportation into and through the city, and cut telegraph lines between Baltimore and Washington. On April 22, Lincoln responded to a Baltimore committee that had requested he secure peace in Baltimore by stopping all troop movement through the city. Lincoln's frustration is manifest in his language:

> You, gentlemen, come here to me and ask for peace on any terms, and yet have no word of condemnation for those who are making war on us. . . . I must have troops to defend this Capital. Geographically it lies surrounded by the soil of Maryland; and mathematically the necessity exists that they should come over her territory. Our men are not moles, and can't dig under the earth; they are not birds, and can't fly through the air. . . . Go home and tell your people that if they will not attack us, we will not attack them; but if they do attack us, we will return it, and that severely.[16]

Believing that unless the mob violence in Baltimore was immediately contained, it might become impossible to transport troops to Washington, Lincoln finally decided to suspend the writ of habeas corpus, allowing rioters and those attacking troops and preventing their safe transportation through the city to be detained without approval from any court or judge. On April 27, 1861, Lincoln sent the following order to General Winfield Scott, the commanding general of the Army of the United States:

> You are engaged in repressing an insurrection against the laws of the United States. If at any point on or in the vicinity of [any] military line, which is now [or which shall be] used between the City of Philadelphia and the City of Washington, via Perryville, Annapolis City, and Annapolis Junction, you find resistance which renders it necessary to suspend the writ of Habeas Corpus for the public safety, you, personally or through the officer in command at the point where the resistance occurs, are authorized to suspend that writ.[17]

LINCOLN EXPLAINS HIS ACTIONS

Lincoln offered the first full explanation of his emergency wartime measures and addressed publicly the question of whether he had violated the Constitution in his July 4, 1861, message to Congress assembled in special session. The most potent charge against Lincoln held that he had no authority to suspend the writ of habeas corpus and thereby allow the detainment of citizens without benefit of judicial process. This charge stemmed from the assumption that the authority to suspend habeas corpus belonged strictly to Congress because that provision is found in Article I of the Constitution, which creates and enumerates the powers of Congress.

In response, Lincoln noted that "the attention of the country has been called to the proposition that one who is sworn to 'take care that the laws be faithfully executed,' should not himself violate them." Lincoln emphasized that the oath he had taken as president required him to ensure that the laws were executed in *all* states, yet they "were being resisted, and failing of execution, in nearly one-third of the States." He then asked,

> Must they be allowed to finally fail of execution, even had it been perfectly clear, that by the use of the means necessary to their execution, some single law, made in such extreme tenderness of the citizen's liberty, that practically, it relieves more of the guilty, than of the innocent, should, to a very limited extent, be violated? To state the question more directly, are all the laws, *but one*, to go unexecuted, and the government itself go to pieces, lest that one be violated?[18]

Lincoln's question reveals the incredible dilemma of his situation as president. If a president faces the choice of violating one law or allowing all the laws of the Constitution and the constitutional union to go unenforced, what should he do? If he does nothing to resist the rebellion and allows the Union to fall, on the one hand, he fails to execute the laws and violates his oath of office. On the other hand, if he suspends the writ of habeas corpus in order to detain those actively rebelling against the government or those offering assistance to the rebellion, he then will be accused of usurping constitutional powers assigned to Congress, not the president.

Lincoln believed that the Constitution was flexible enough to meet extraordinary threats to its own preservation. In an 1864 letter to Albert Hodges, Lincoln explained,

> By general law, life and limb must be protected; yet often a limb must be amputated to save a life; but a life is never wisely given to save a limb. I felt that measures, otherwise unconstitutional, might become lawful, by becoming indispensable to the preservation of the Constitution, through the preservation of the nation.[19]

In an essay on Lincoln's use of executive power, Benjamin Kleinerman explains, "For Lincoln, the Constitution only countenances actions taken outside its bounds when those actions can be justified by the strictest understanding of necessity, namely the preservation of the document itself."[20]

Therefore, Kleinerman rightly observes, Lincoln's speeches "always paired necessity and constitutionality," teaching the American people why a particularly grave situation that threatens the existence of the Constitution itself might warrant otherwise constitutionally suspicious actions.

John Locke's argument regarding executive prerogative power in his *Second Treatise of Government* informs Kleinerman's observation. Locke defended the principle that the executive branch of government always possesses prerogative power, which he defined as "the power to act according to discretion, for the public good, without the prescription of the law, and sometimes even against it"; "prerogative is nothing but the power of doing public good without a rule."[21] Locke understood fully the danger of prerogative power, by definition illimitable by law, and therefore emphasized that prerogative, rightly understood, does not give an executive the power to do anything he wishes, and it certainly does not entitle him to injure any member of the social compact. Nobody, including the executive, Locke argued, "in the society should ever have a right to do the people harm," and therefore, prerogative power used to "do the people harm" is not a rightful use, but a violation, of prerogative.[22]

Locke's argument for prerogative power springs from the problem of natural right, particularly its infinite malleability or changeability. As Aristotle explained long ago, natural right is everywhere and always changeable. Though no moral relativist, Aristotle understood that what is right depends upon the particulars of a situation; therefore, right changes as situations change.[23] Stated differently, the question of natural right is always the question of the right thing to do, according to nature, here and now. The "here and now" is an important qualification of natural right. Natural right requires judgment, or prudence that considers the particular situation in which a moral determination of what is right is being made. In his folksy way, Lincoln offered a clear example of the changeability of natural right by reference to a problem any frontiersman of his day would have been familiar with:

> [Suppose] on the prairie I find a rattlesnake. I take a stake and kill him. Everybody would applaud the act and say I did right. But suppose the snake was in a bed where children were sleeping. Would I do right to strike him there? I might hurt the children; or I might not kill, but only arouse and exasperate the snake, and he might bite the children. Thus, by meddling with him here, I would do more hurt than good.[24]

What is the right way to deal with the venomous snake? The answer depends on where the snake is. In some situations, it might be right to strike a blow to kill the snake. But in other situations—for instance, as in Lincoln's example, if the snake is discovered in a bed where children are sleeping—it might be wrong to do so. This is not relativism; it is prudence. All natural right is prudential right. Statesmanship comes into sight when prudence is exercised over the weightiest public and political problems.

The problem of natural right and its relation to the rule of law presents human beings with an intractable political difficulty: those who obey the rule of law are bound by it, but those who do not obey the rule of law are not so bound. Lawbreakers, in other words, have an important advantage over those who obey the laws. Is it right for criminals and enemies to have the freedom to employ any power to injure law-abiding citizens while those law-abiding citizens are limited by the law in the power they may employ to protect themselves from enemies and criminals?

Reflecting on this problem, Thomas Jefferson wrote in an 1808 letter to Dr. James Brown: "There are extreme cases where the laws become inadequate even to their own preservation, and where the universal resource is a dictator or martial law."[25] Here, Jefferson was trying to account for the prudential character of natural right and the possible deficiencies of written laws. Laws are general rules for the public good based on certain assumptions. But what happens when a new threat to the public good arises, one that the laws have not addressed? In such a situation, it is the executive's duty, not necessarily according to positive law but under the natural law, to protect the people from the unforeseen threat. As Locke explained:

> For the legislators not being able to foresee and provide by law for all that may be useful to the community, the executor of the laws, having the power in his hands, has by the common law of nature a right to make use of it for the good of the society, in many cases, where the municipal law has given no direction. . . . It is fit that the laws themselves should in some cases give way to the executive power [because] many accidents may happen wherein a strict and rigid observation of the laws may do harm.[26]

Thus, Locke argued, the prerogative power allows the executive the discretion necessary to meet any challenge and promote the common good in the face of any particular situation the laws have not anticipated. From a Lockean perspective, therefore, it might be less important to ask whether Lincoln's actions were legal or constitutional, and more important to ask if they were necessary to protect the public good.

As John Yoo has ably demonstrated, the American constitutional order, as well as the English tradition from which the Americans borrowed in part, has always distinguished the power to declare war from the power to initiate and engage in war, the latter requiring discretion too great to be prescribed by law.[27] In both the American and English political traditions, Yoo argues, the executive branch possesses the right and the power to use military force to protect the common good, while the legislative branch uses its power of the purse, as well as other powers, to check the executive's war-making power when necessary.[28]

The power to declare war, reserved to Congress in Article I, Section 8 of the U.S. Constitution, is the power to make known or announce publicly the existence of a state of war, which has implications for the application of both international and domestic law.[29] But the power to initiate war and engage in acts of military violence is a power reserved to the president, as Article II of the Constitution vests *all* executive power "in a President of the United States" and authorizes him to be "Commander in Chief of the Army and Navy of the United States." The "vestment" clause of the Constitution in particular, argues Yoo, grants the president significant power to use military force whenever and in what manner his discretion determines it necessary for the public good, although Congress and, to a lesser extent, the courts have an important role in checking or countering the executive war power if it is misused.[30] But the process by which the president exercises military power and the Congress checks it is primarily political, not legal, because it is difficult, if not impossible, to anticipate fully all the dynamics of war-making in advance. Much depends on the particulars of any military threat; therefore, it is not only difficult, but potentially dangerous, to legally circumscribe the president's prerogative power because such laws may prevent a president from taking actions necessary to American security.

In his explanation of his actions, Lincoln stated to Congress, "It was not believed that any law was violated." Article I, Section 9 of the Constitution, which lists restrictions on the powers of Congress, declares, "The privilege of the Writ of Habeas Corpus shall not be suspended unless when in Cases of Rebellion or Invasion the Public Safety may require it."

> Now it is insisted that Congress, and not the Executive, is vested with this power. But the Constitution itself, is silent as to which, or who, is to exercise the power; and as the provision was plainly made for a dangerous emergency, it cannot be believed the framers of the instrument intended, that in every case, the danger should run its course, until Congress could be called together; the very assembling of which might be prevented, as was intended in this case, by the rebellion.[31]

To satisfy those who insisted that only Congress possessed the constitutional power to suspend the writ, Lincoln requested that Congress approve retroactively the extraordinary actions he had taken following the bombardment of

Fort Sumter and preceding the special session of Congress. Congress quickly passed an ordinance authorizing all of Lincoln's emergency actions. Or did it? Congress did indeed pass a bill that declared, in part,

> All acts, proclamations and other orders of the President [after March 4, 1861] respecting the army and navy of the United States, and calling out or relating to the militia or volunteers from the states, are hereby approved and in all respects legalized and made valid . . . as if they had been issued and done under the previous express authority and direction of the Congress of the United States.[32]

In *Constitutional Problems under Lincoln*, historian J. G. Randall emphasizes that the bill Congress passed made no explicit mention of the writ of habeas corpus; he concludes that Congress therefore never authorized the suspension of the writ, leaving Lincoln's action constitutionally problematic.[33] But there are at least two reasons to think Randall is wrong. First, some congressmen did not think it was necessary for Congress to authorize Lincoln's suspension of the writ because they agreed with Lincoln that the president possesses the power to suspend the writ in times of emergency when Congress is not in session. That Congress did not explicitly authorize Lincoln's suspension showed, at least in part, an implicit recognition of a rightful exercise of emergency presidential power.[34] Second, the bill Congress passed retroactively authorized all "acts, proclamations and other orders of the President respecting the army and navy." The act by which Lincoln authorized the suspension of the writ was a written order sent to General Winfield Scott and addressed to "The Commanding General of the Army of the United States," authorizing him and his commanding officers to suspend the writ when public safety required it. It is certainly arguable that the bill Congress passed included the suspension because it was in fact an "order of the President respecting the army." Further, it is difficult to argue that Congress did not mention the suspension of habeas corpus because that body did not think it could be done rightfully. Congress certainly had few qualms about suspending the writ, as evidenced by the 1863 act in which it explicitly authorized the president to do so, declaring that "during the present rebellion the President of the United States, whenever, in his judgment, the public safety may require it, is authorized to suspend the privilege of the writ of habeas corpus in any case throughout the United States or any part thereof."[35]

In an 1863 letter to Matthew Birchard, Lincoln responded to Birchard's challenge that he had violated constitutional protections of liberty:

> You ask, in substance, whether I really claim that I may override all the guaranteed rights of individuals, on the plea of conserving the public

safety—when I may choose to say the public safety requires it. This question, divested of the phraseology calculated to represent me as struggling for an arbitrary personal prerogative, is either simply a question *who* shall decide, or an affirmation that *nobody* shall decide, what the public safety does require, in cases of Rebellion or Invasion. The Constitution contemplates the question as likely to occur for decision, but it does not expressly declare who is to decide it. By necessary implication, when Rebellion or Invasion comes, the decision is to be made, from time to time; and I think the man whom, for the time, the people have, under the constitution, made the commander-in-chief, of their Army and Navy, is the man who holds the power, and bears the responsibility of making it. If he uses the power justly, the same people will probably justify him; if he abuses it, he is in their hands, to be dealt with by all the modes they have reserved to themselves in the constitution.[36]

As president, Lincoln would do everything he believed constitutionally permissible to preserve the Constitution's union; if and when the people came to the opinion that he had exceeded or violated his constitutional mandate, they reserved the constitutional power, foremost the power of impeachment, to remove him from office. Perhaps Lincoln displayed his respect for the Constitution nowhere better than in his acknowledgement of the people's constitutional authority over him, as evidenced by his own insistence that the election of 1864, in the midst of the war, take place precisely as required by the Constitution.

THE SUPREME COURT WEIGHS IN

In the 1863 *Prize Cases*, the Supreme Court took up the question of the constitutionality of Lincoln's blockade against Southern ports. The Court began by asking "whether, at the time this blockade was instituted, a state of war existed which would justify a resort to these means of subduing the hostile force." Concluding that indeed a state of war did exist at the time when Lincoln proclaimed the blockade, the Court proceeded to note,

Whether the President, in fulfilling his duties as Commander-in-chief in suppressing an insurrection, has met with such armed hostile resistance and a civil war of such alarming proportions as will compel him to accord to them the character of belligerents is a question to be decided by him, and this Court must be governed by the decisions and acts of the political department of the Government to which this power was entrusted.[37]

One year after Lincoln's death and the conclusion of the Civil War, the Supreme Court addressed the question of whether Lincoln had violated the Constitution with his 1862 order that all persons accused of aiding and comforting the rebels be tried and punished by military commissions rather than civil courts. When a military commission tried and convicted Lambdin Milligan, an outspoken Confederate sympathizer in Indiana, he sued for a writ of habeas corpus, arguing that the military commission had no jurisdiction over him because the civil courts of Indiana had never closed. In *Ex Parte Milligan*, the Supreme Court agreed with Milligan's argument, but only after the war was over and only by using somewhat circular reasoning. As the Court announced,

> No graver question was ever considered by this court, nor one which more nearly concerns the rights of the whole people, for it is the birthright of every American citizen when charged with crime to be tried and punished according to law. The power of punishment is alone through the means which the laws have provided for that purpose, and, if they are ineffectual, there is an immunity from punishment, no matter how great an offender the individual may be or how much his crimes may have shocked the sense of justice of the country or endangered its safety. By the protection of the law, human rights are secured; withdraw that protection and they are at the mercy of wicked rulers or the clamor of an excited people.[38]

Thus, the Court concluded, "if there was law to justify this military trial, it is not our province to interfere; if there was not, it is our duty to declare the nullity of the whole proceedings." Arguing that "the Constitution of the United States is a law for rulers and people, equally in war and in peace," the Court declared that the Constitution "covers with the shield of its protection all classes of men, at all times and under all circumstances." By replacing the jurisdiction of civil courts under the Constitution with military commissions, not only had Lincoln undermined the basic constitutional protections of liberty, but his example represented a serious threat to the very existence of constitutional government: "No doctrine involving more pernicious consequences was ever invented by the wit of man than that any of its provisions can be suspended during any of the great exigencies of government." According to the Court, no emergency can be so great as to require suspension of any constitutional protection. To think otherwise, argued the Court, "leads directly to anarchy or despotism."

But consider the Court's argument. The Court believed "the theory of necessity" with which Lincoln justified the military commissions to be "false" because "the government, within the Constitution, has all the powers granted to it which are necessary to preserve its existence, as has been happily proved by the result of the great effort to throw off its just authority."[39] According to the Court, the government under the Constitution, exercising no more powers than that instrument explicitly grants, possesses all the power necessary to preserve the Constitution against rebellion. How does the Court know this? Because it was "proved by the result of the great effort to throw off its just authority," that is, because the government of the Union was victorious in the Civil War. But the government that won the Civil War was *Lincoln's government*, which *relied on the military commissions* as part of its overall war strategy. Had Lincoln in 1862 acted in accordance with the Court's later opinion, had he not employed military commissions as part of his strategy, the outcome of the war may well have been different. And therefore, the basic premise of the Court's argument fails. This does not deter DiLorenzo, however, in *Lincoln Unmasked*, where he cites *Ex Parte Milligan* authoritatively and argues that Lincoln's Civil War policies were clearly unconstitutional. Interestingly, however, he never mentions the *Prize Cases* in which the Supreme Court upheld the constitutionality of Lincoln's blockade.[40]

THE UNION DESERVED TO BE SAVED

One of the ablest defenses of Lincoln's constitutionalism is Herman Belz's *Abraham Lincoln, Constitutionalism, and Equal Rights in the Civil War Era*, from which I have already quoted. As Belz explains, "Lincoln employed a two-track constitutional justification in explaining the legitimacy of controversial measures adopted under executive authority." The first involved legal arguments based on the text of the Constitution. The second "involved more broadly political arguments concerning the relationship between the Union, the Constitution, and the nature of republican government."[41] It was morally right to preserve the Union, Lincoln believed, because the American union was a morally good one. This was not to say that the Union was, or ever would be, perfect. It will not. But, so long as the Union remains dedicated to the principles of natural justice, the principles of the Declaration of Independence, it is a union capable of redemption.

Perhaps the most eloquent description Lincoln offered of his understanding of the relationship between the principles of the Declaration and the Constitution is found in a fragment of writing dated 1861, which I reproduce here in full:

All this is not the result of accident. It has a philosophical cause. Without the Constitution and the Union, we could not have attained the result; but even these, are not the primary cause of our great prosperity. There is something back of these, entwining itself more closely about the human heart. That something is the principle of "Liberty to all"— the principle that clears the path for all—gives hope to all and, by consequence, enterprise and industry to all.

The assertion of that principle, at that time, was the word, "fitly spoken" which has proved an "apple of gold" to us. The Union, and the Constitution, are the picture of silver, subsequently framed around it. The picture was made, not to conceal or destroy the apple, but to adorn and preserve it. The picture was made for the apple—not the apple for the picture.

So let us act, that neither picture nor apple shall ever be blurred, or bruised, or broken. That we may so act, we must study, and understand the points of danger.[42]

In Lincoln's formulation, the Constitution and the Union are as one; they share the same "philosophical cause." That "philosophical cause," as Lincoln asserted, is the principle of "Liberty to all," foreshadowing his formulation at Gettysburg that America had been "conceived in Liberty, and dedicated to the proposition that all men are created equal." In Lincoln's view, the Constitution and the Union could not be defended without defending the principle of human equality; to forfeit one was to forfeit all. As Belz comments, "Destroy liberty—or allow this sacred principle to be eroded by the spread of slavery—and both the nation and the Constitution would be lost."[43]

Belz calls attention to those parts of Lincoln's 1861 speech to Congress in special session, quoted above, that point toward a philosophical and political argument for preserving the Union, an argument that goes deeper than textual analysis of the Constitution. The Civil War, said Lincoln,

is essentially a People's contest. On the side of the Union, it is a struggle for maintaining in the world, that form, and substance of government, whose leading object is, to elevate the condition of men—to lift artificial weights from all shoulders—to clear the paths of laudable pursuit for all— to afford all, an unfettered start, and a fair chance, in the race of life.[44]

Was it lawful and constitutional for Lincoln to preserve the Union and defend the authority of the Constitution?

Plainly, Lincoln believed it was, and this not mainly in consequence of any construction of positive law or constitutional text, but rather on the self-evident truth that the Constitution justifies extraordinary action to preserve the substance of political liberty that constitutes both its own end and the purpose of the nation.[45]

When the Constitution and the purpose of the American union are understood in light of, and defined by, the principles of the Declaration, Lincoln's actions to preserve the form, functions, and intentions of the Constitution become eminently reasonable. Further, Lincoln's statesmanship is not a prelude to later expansions of governmental power. The powers Lincoln exercised "were crisis powers, not expansions of the commerce and general welfare powers of Congress, or other enumerated powers the delegation of which by the legislature to the executive vastly enlarged the scope of presidential authority in the twentieth century." In short, "Lincoln's actions under the crisis or war powers did not establish precedents for an expanded peacetime role of the presidency in particular or of the federal government in general."[46]

This contradicts the accusations of many libertarian critics who argue that Lincoln, more than anyone, consciously set about dismantling the Constitution in order to expand the power and size of the national government. Consider what happened after Lincoln's presidency. Did his supposed maneuvers for big government stay in place—and expand—or were they quickly removed? The answer is the latter (which is what Lincoln wanted, given his lenient Reconstruction policy). In 1863, America witnessed the suspension of habeas corpus, newspapers were held in check, and an Ohio Congressman was deported to Louisiana. By 1866, all such restrictions on civil liberties were gone. In 1865, Confederate states did not have governments of their choosing, and many former Confederates were disenfranchised. By 1877, federal occupation of Southern states had ended, and except for a handful of former Confederates, all Southern white males were again voting. Without apologizing for the way radical Republicans in Congress handled Reconstruction, but with a full view to the enormous disruption the Civil War caused the Union, one might argue that America returned to constitutional normalcy in a relatively short time.

At any rate, the immediate consequences of the Civil War were not the legacy of a Lincoln who wanted to subvert and overthrow the American constitutional order. Given the magnitude of the rebellion against the Constitution and the authority of the free elections it sanctions, it seems unfair to hold Lincoln accountable for everything that was different *after* the Civil War than it had been *before*. Perhaps, instead, we might ask why so much of the Constitution's authority and its institutions were restored so *quickly* after the terrible civil war America suffered. Why, in the hours of desperation for national survival, did Lincoln go as far as he did to ensure that the Constitution would continue to rule after the war was over, after he would be no more?

Kleinerman offers a broad legal, constitutional, and political overview of Lincoln's presidency. He has distilled three principles to be learned from Lincoln's example of constitutionalism, which I think are worth stating here:

1. Action outside and sometimes against the Constitution is only constitutional when the constitutional union itself is at risk; a concern for the public good is insufficient grounds for the executive to exercise discretionary power.
2. The Constitution should be understood as different during extraordinary times than during ordinary times; thus discretionary action should take place only in extraordinary circumstances and should be understood as extraordinary. Since it is only necessitated by the crisis, the action should have no effect on the existing law. To preserve constitutionalism after the crisis, the actions must not be regularized or institutionalized.
3. A line must separate the executive's personal feeling and his official duty. He should take only those actions that fulfill his official duty, the preservation of the Constitution, even, or especially, if the people want him to go further.[47]

Kleinerman's second point is especially relevant for Americans today as we try to find the right balance between upholding the Constitution on the one hand and protecting ourselves from foreign threats on the other. When a particular threat to American national security requires a military response that might be constitutionally questionable, then "the action should have no effect on the existing law," Kleinerman argues. If the president, for example, determines that certain actions are necessary to prosecute the War on Terror and protect Americans, but those actions perhaps violate the civil rights of American citizens or the standards of international agreements to which America is a party, then those actions should not be "regularized or institutionalized."

In other words, rather than a Patriot Act that institutionalizes prudential war efforts, Kleinerman suggests that it is better for the president to act without law and, in so doing, to explain and defend his actions by speaking openly to the people about the temporary necessities that require such actions. This is preferable, Kleinerman argues, so that when the necessities are gone, there will be no foundation in law for a permanent expansion of governmental power. In the most desperate times, it is not only the laws that matter in judging a president's conduct; it is also his words.

If a president believes it necessary to take questionable actions to protect Americans, they might be constitutionally and morally acceptable if he can explain the unusual threat and why it requires that he take them. Lincoln never for a moment failed to appreciate the importance of communicating to the American people the nature and extent of the threat to the constitutional union, why the Union was essential to their safety and happiness, and why necessity both compelled and justified his actions to save the Union. Lincoln, therefore, was "neither a revolutionary nor a dictator, but a constitutionalist who used the executive power to preserve and extend the liberty of the American Founding."[48]

NOTES

1. Don E. Fehrenbacher, "Lincoln and the Constitution," in *The Public and the Private Lincoln: Contemporary Perspectives*, ed. Cullom Davis (Carbondale: Southern Illinois University Press, 1979).

2. Paul Craig Roberts, "Lincoln and the War on Terror: A Conservative Reappraisal," syndicated column, March 19, 2002, VDARE.com, www.vdare.com/roberts/police_state.htm.

3. Thomas DiLorenzo, *The Real Lincoln: A New Look at Abraham Lincoln, His Agenda, and an Unnecessary War* (Roseville, CA: Prima Publishing, 2002), 162.

4. Clinton Rossiter, *Constitutional Dictatorship: Crisis Government in the Modern Democracies* (Princeton, NJ: Princeton University Press, 1948), 212, 224.

5. John W. Burgess, *The Civil War and the Constitution* (New York: Scribner's, 1901), I:228, 232.

6. Herman Belz, *Abraham Lincoln, Constitutionalism, and Equal Rights in the Civil War Era* (New York: Fordham University Press, 1998), 91.

7. James G. Randall, *Constitutional Problems under Lincoln* (New York: D. Appleton & Co., 1926), 30–47.

8. George P. Fletcher, *Our Secret Constitution: How Lincoln Redefined American Democracy* (New York: Oxford University Press, 2001).

9. Mario M. Cuomo, *Why Lincoln Matters: Today More Than Ever* (New York: Harcourt Press, 2004), 85, 176.

10. Willmoore Kendall and George Carey, *The Basic Symbols of the American Political Tradition* (Baton Rouge: Louisiana State University Press, 1970).

11. Belz, *Abraham Lincoln, Constitutionalism, and Equal Rights in the Civil War Era*, 95.

12. Belz, *Abraham Lincoln, Constitutionalism, and Equal Rights in the Civil War Era*, 91.

13. Jay Winik, *April 1865: The Month That Saved America* (New York: Harper-Collins, 2001), 352–54.

14. Quoted in David Herbert Donald, *Lincoln* (New York: Simon & Schuster, 1995), 317.

15. William Rehnquist, *All the Laws but One: Civil Liberties in Wartime* (New York: Alfred Knopf, 1998), 20–21.

16. Roy P. Basler, ed., *The Collected Works of Abraham Lincoln* (New Brunswick, NJ: Rutgers University Press, 1953), IV:341. Cited hereafter as Lincoln, *Collected Works*.

17. Lincoln, *Collected Works*, IV:347.

18. Lincoln, *Collected Works*, IV:430.

19. Lincoln, *Collected Works*, VII:281.

20. Benjamin Kleinerman, "Lincoln's Example: Executive Power and the Survival of Constitutionalism," *Perspectives on Politics* 3, no. 4 (December 2005): 806.

21. C. B. Macpherson, ed., *John Locke: Second Treatise of Government* (Indianapolis: Hackett Publishing Co., 1980), ch. XIV, 84, 87.

22. Macpherson, *John Locke: Second Treatise of Government*, ch. XIV, 87.

23. Joe Sachs, trans., *Aristotle: Nicomachean Ethics* (Newburyport, MA: Focus Publishing, 2002), 92–93.

24. Lincoln, *Collected Works*, IV:5.

25. Quoted in Leonard W. Levy, *Jefferson and Civil Liberties: The Darker Side* (New York: Quadrangle, 1973 [1963]), 18.

26. Macpherson, *John Locke: Second Treatise of Government*, ch. XIV, 84.

27. John Yoo, *The Powers of War and Peace: The Constitution and Foreign Affairs after 9/11* (Chicago: University of Chicago Press, 2005).

28. Yoo, *The Powers of War and Peace*, 32.

29. Yoo, *The Powers of War and Peace*, 149–51.

30. Yoo, *The Powers of War and Peace*, 144–49.

31. Lincoln, *Collected Works*, IV:430–31.

32. Quoted in Philip Shaw Paludan, *The Presidency of Abraham Lincoln* (Lawrence: University of Kansas Press, 1994), 82.

33. James G. Randall, *Constitutional Problems under Lincoln* (New York: D. Appleton & Co., 1926), 128–29.

34. Paludan, *The Presidency of Abraham Lincoln*, 82–83.

35. Quoted in Randall, *Constitutional Problems under Lincoln*, 130.

36. Lincoln, *Collected Works*, VI:303.

37. *Prize Cases*, 67 U.S. 635.

38. *Ex Parte Milligan*, 71 U.S. 119.

39. *Ex Parte Milligan*, 71 U.S. 121.

40. Thomas DiLorenzo, *Lincoln Unmasked: What You're Not Supposed to Know about Dishonest Abe* (New York: Crown Forum, 2006), 169.

41. Belz, *Abraham Lincoln, Constitutionalism, and Equal Rights in the Civil War Era*, 35.

42. Lincoln, *Collected Works,* IV:168–69.

43. Belz, *Abraham Lincoln, Constitutionalism, and Equal Rights in the Civil War Era*, 38.

44. Lincoln, *Collected Works*, IV:438.

45. Belz, *Abraham Lincoln, Constitutionalism, and Equal Rights in the Civil War Era*, 38.

46. Belz, *Abraham Lincoln, Constitutionalism, and Equal Rights in the Civil War Era*, 42.

47. Kleinerman, "Lincoln's Example: Executive Power and the Survival of Constitutionalism," 808.

48. Belz, *Abraham Lincoln, Constitutionalism, and Equal Rights in the Civil War Era*, 43.

CONCLUSION

"How hard," a young Abraham Lincoln lamented to a friend, "oh how hard it is to die and leave one's Country no better than if one had never lived for it."[1] Little could this precocious young American know how profoundly his life, and death, would affect the destiny of his beloved country.

Among Lincoln's many critics, I have examined historicist historians, libertarians, and modern-day abolitionists. I have considered theoretical assumptions that Lincoln's principles died with Lincoln himself. I have considered those who denounce Lincoln for wrecking the Constitution by doing too much and those who denounce Lincoln as morally irresponsible for not doing enough.

Prudence is the art of the statesman. What a perfect swing is to a baseball player, or perfect harmony is to the musician, wise judgment is to the statesman. Statesmanship requires an understanding of right, as well as of how far it can be advanced in a particular time and place with particular people. With no rule book to consult, statesmen must not attempt too much, yet not do too little. At each step of his political career, Lincoln pushed ahead—to stop slavery from spreading at one time, to maintain the Union at another, and finally to strike a death blow to slavery when he could—judging in each instance how far public opinion and public law would permit him to reach, and he reached for no more. The many criticisms surrounding Lincoln on all sides serve as evidence that his judgment was just about perfect. This seems to have been the opinion of the great antislavery leader Frederick Douglass in his 1876 speech dedicating the Freedmen's Memorial Monument in Washington, D.C.:

> Few great public men have ever been victims of fiercer denunciation than Abraham Lincoln was during his administration. He was often

wounded in the house of his friends. Reproaches came thick and fast upon him from within and from without, and from opposite quarters. He was assailed by abolitionists; he was assailed by slaveholders; he was assailed by men who were for peace at any price; he was assailed by those who were for a more vigorous prosecution of the war; he was assailed for not making the war an abolition war; and he was most bitterly assailed for making the war an abolition war.

"But now behold the change," Douglass argued. "Measuring the tremendous magnitude of the work before him, considering the necessary means to ends, and surveying the end from the beginning, infinite wisdom has seldom sent any man into the world better fitted for his mission than was Abraham Lincoln."[2]

In Lincoln's life, we find a man who rose from poverty and obscurity to the heights of political power and fame. He was able to accomplish this because he understood himself and his place in the world. At six feet, four inches tall, he towered above most men, but he knew that he was small in comparison to that which was truly great, the fixed and eternal principles of right that elevate each individual life and serve as a moral compass for the ship of state. Lincoln also understood that America was unique in the world, built upon and incorporating these natural principles of goodness. This is why Lincoln loved America so dearly, not merely because it was *his* country but because it was a *good* country: "If ever I feel the soul within me elevate and expand to those dimensions not wholly unworthy of its Almighty architect," Lincoln wrote,

> it is when I contemplate the cause of my country, deserted by all the world beside, and I standing up boldly and alone and hurling defiance at her victorious oppressors. Here, without contemplating consequences, before High Heaven, and in the face of the world, I swear eternal fidelity to the just cause, as I deem it, of the land of my life, my liberty and my love.[3]

With the principles of right before him, Lincoln never stopped thinking and working to learn how the right was to be done in America. Elihu Root captures this side of Lincoln perfectly:

> Never concealing or obscuring his ideals, avowing them, declaring them, constant to them, setting them high for guidance as if among the stars, Lincoln kept his feet on the earth, he minded his steps, he studied the country to be traversed, its obstacles, its possible aids to progress. He studied the material with which he had to work—the infinite varieties

of human nature, the good, the bad, and, predominantly, the indifferent; the widely differing material interests of sections and of occupations; the inherited traditions and prejudices, the passions and weaknesses, sympathies and dislikes, the ignorance and misunderstanding, the successive stages of slowly developing opinion, the selfishness and the altruism. He understood that to lead a nation in emergency he had to bring all these forces into such relations to his design and to each other that the resultant of forces would be in the direction of his purpose.[4]

Perhaps the statesman's greatest challenge is connecting the timeless and the timely, knowing how to apply unchanging principles to changing circumstances. In his ability to accomplish this, the statesman is the consummate politician, with a mind and character interested in politics not as a means to political power but as the vehicle through which natural right is transformed into political right. Some might object that such a view of the politician is a view of the low in light of the high, that it portrays the politician as too noble and assumes an idealistic standard of political excellence unattainable by any actual politician. But how else can one judge actual politicians except by counseling the highest goals and noblest purposes of politics? In viewing the low in light of the high, it is true that we risk disappointment when our high expectations are not met. But if we view the high in light of the low, if we assume that all supposedly noble words and deeds are in reality mere dressing for the satisfaction of base appetites, then we risk inescapable cynicism. And is this not characteristic of much of American political life today? Is this not characteristic of the Lincoln critics we have examined? By viewing the high in light of the low, they assume that politicians, Lincoln especially, seek nothing more than power and the satisfaction of selfish desires. They assumed that political rhetoric cannot be edifying, that all speech is mere propaganda.

If we adopt this low point of view, however, our eyes remain closed to the very possibility of statesmanship. We effectively deny the existence of statesmanship before we begin our investigation of it. And thus it turns out to be no point of view at all. It is blindness. We cannot see the goodness of Lincoln because we do not allow ourselves to see the high principles that guided him in the most difficult and trying times.

It will be useful to remember that Abraham Lincoln was a politician. The word is often used as a term of reproach. Such a use indicates the most superficial thinking, or, rather, failure to think. To be a corrupt and self seeking politician ought of course to be a reproach, just as it is a discredit to be a corrupt or unfair businessman. Politics is the practical exercise of the art of self-government, and somebody must attend to it if we are to have self-government; somebody must study it, and learn the art, and exercise patience and sympathy and skill to bring the multitude of opinions and wishes of self-governing people into such order that some prevailing opinion may be expressed and peaceably accepted. Otherwise, confusion will result either in dictatorship or anarchy. The principal ground of reproach against any American citizen should be that he is not a politician. Everyone ought to be, as Lincoln was.[5]

Perhaps Americans can learn no more important lesson today than that we must remind ourselves of the importance of politics, rightly understood, and the principles of right that ought to inform and guide it. While there is much that is low and base in our politics today—there is always much that is low and base in politics—we should remember that politics can be high and noble. Politics, rightly understood, encompasses the knowledge of all the arts and sciences necessary for human happiness. Complete political knowledge includes knowledge of the most beautiful things. Through genuine political education, the kind of education available in the words and deeds of Abraham Lincoln, we can again see with the mind's eye the heights of human potential and human greatness by seeing the idea of statesmanship.

NOTES

1. Quoted in David Herbert Donald, *Lincoln* (New York: Simon & Schuster, 1995), 162.
2. John W. Blassingame and John R. McKivigan, eds., *The Frederick Douglass Papers* (New Haven, CT: Yale University Press, 1991), IV:436, 437.
3. Roy P. Basler, ed., *The Collected Works of Abraham Lincoln* (New Brunswick, NJ: Rutgers University Press, 1953), I:178–79.
4. Elihu Root, "Lincoln as Leader of Men," in *Men and Policies: Addresses by Elihu Root*, ed. Robert Bacon and James Brown Scott (Cambridge, MA: Harvard University Press, 1924), 69.
5. Root, "Lincoln as Leader of Men," 75.

INDEX

abolitionism, 53

abolitionists, 28, 37, 38, 273, 280, 283

abortion: and slavery, 47, 48

Abraham Lincoln Bicentennial Commission, 126, 300

Abraham Lincoln Presidential Library and Museum, 41–42n1

Abraham Lincoln, Constitutionalism, and Equal Rights in the Civil War (Belz), 330

Abraham Lincoln: A Constitutional Biography (Anastaplo), 246

Acton, Lord, 289

Adams, Charles, 14, 146, 147, 175, 176, 189, 192, 193, 198, 207, 209, 214, 254, 263, 266, 280; on secession, 187, 190

Adams, Henry, 196

Adams, John Quincy, 196, 197, 198, 209, 210

Adams, John, 94, 167, 196

Adams, Samuel, 167

affirmative action, 16, 42n10, 306

Alien and Sedition Acts, 182

American Christian theology: German philosophy, influence on, 234

American Founders, 2, 6, 66, 184, 241, 308, 313; America, as idea, 155, 156; blacks, rights of, 78, 85, 89; on freedom, 168; government, views on, 157, 158; and human equality, 93, 125, 126, 155, 156, 186; and human nature, 158, 159, 249; and natural law principles, 6, 297; and reason, 250; revolution, right of, 162, 163; and secession, 145; and slavery, 58, 78, 86, 94, 95, 163; social compact of, 156. *See also* American Founding

American Founding, 111, 127; and human equality, 16; natural rights principles, as philosophy of, 96; natural rights principles, rejection of, 233, 294, 295; principles of, 5; redefining of, 303; religion, influence on, 134; and slavery, 16, 59, 94; social compact theory of, 147; Supreme Court interpretation of, as wrong, 82. *See also* American Founders

American Party. *See* Know Nothing Party

American Protestantism: and social evolution, 234

American Revolution, 198; versus French Revolution, 249, 250

Anastaplo, George, 246, 247, 248, 249, 255

Anderson, Robert, 321
Anderson, Sherwood, 310
Antietam, 58, 281
*The American Political Tradition and the
    Men Who Made It* (Hofstadter), 118,
    275
antislavery movement, 95, 168–69
Apostles of Disunion (Dew), 244
*April 1865: The Month That Saved
    America* (Winik), 20
Aristotle, 121, 132, 133, 223, 225,
    252; on happiness, 217; and natural
    right, 324
Arkansas, 265
Articles of Confederation, 151, 161,
    175, 178, 179, 184, 201n59
Atchison, Dave, 55
Auchampaugh, Philip, 119

Baltimore, 322; riot in, 321
Banneker, Benjamin, 22
Barnum, P. T., 1, 2
*The Basic Symbols of the American
    Political Tradition* (Kendall and
    Carey), 319
Beard, Charles: Civil War,
    interpretation of, 215, 216
Beauregard, P. G. T., 265, 321
Becker, Carl, 118, 138
Belz, Herman, 290, 319, 330, 331
Bennett, Lerone Jr., 13, 34, 35, 36, 37,
    38, 275, 279–80
Benning, Henry, 244
Berwanger, Eugene, 49
Best, Gary Dean, 307
Biden, Joseph, 6, 7
Bill of Rights, 307
Birchard, Matthew, 327
Blackmun, Harry, 80
blacks: and human equality, 125; and
    natural rights, 26, 27; as property,
    89, 107; public opinion toward, 90;
    rights of, 90, 245; slavery, as natural

condition of, 233. *See also* slaves;
    slavery
Bland, Richard, 158
"Bleeding Kansas," 58, 125
Boritt, Gabor, 227
Bork, Robert, 68
Breckinridge, John, 231
Brooks, Preston, 56, 125
Brown, James, 325
Brown, John, 37, 38–39
Buchanan, James, 101, 103, 120, 213
Burgess, John, 318
Burnett, Peter, 105, 106
Burr, Aaron, 180
Bush, George W., 3, 311

Calhoun, John C., 27, 55, 71, 72–73,
    129, 130, 131, 132, 133, 135, 148,
    149, 182, 183, 185, 189, 190, 194,
    198, 207, 216, 220, 229, 237, 296,
    297; American Founding principles,
    rejection of, 164, 165, 166;
    concurrent majority theory of, 165,
    170, 171, 173, 174, 177, 178, 180;
    Constitution, interpretation of, 174,
    175; on disunion, 226; equality,
    critique of, 165, 166, 167, 169,
    170; Thomas Jefferson, denouncing
    of, 168; as nationalist, 224; natural
    rights, denial of, 196; oratory of,
    164; and race, 168; secession,
    defender of, 165, 174, 176, 196;
    secession movement, as father of,
    163; on self-sufficiency, 225; and
    slavery, 165, 176; on slavery, as
    positive good, 169; and states'
    rights, 208; and tariffs, 209, 210,
    224, 258n44
California, 42n10, 104, 105, 106, 230,
    241; as free state, 53, 54, 229; gold
    in, 50, 228, 259n62; slavery, as
    pivotal in, 229
Campbell, John, 82

Carey, George, 319
Caribbean, 34
Catron, John, 82
Central America, 221
Charnwood, Lord, 228
Chase, Salmon, 282
Chesapeake, 197
Chicago, 36
Child, Lydia Maria, 283
Chinn, Julia, 30
Cicero, 132, 133
civil rights era, 15
Civil War, 9, 17, 48, 71, 110, 149,
    265, 274, 301, 310–11; causes of,
    206, 207, 208, 216, 218, 246, 293;
    and Constitution, 109, 177; as
    people's contest, 331; religion, as
    war of, 252; revisionist thesis of,
    119, 120, 121; slavery, as cause of,
    246, 253, 256, 269; and Southern
    honor, 75n7; as unconstitutional,
    146; as unnecessary, 119, 120, 124,
    126
Clay, Henry, 24, 54, 209, 211; and
    American System, 215
Clinton, Bill, 311
Cobb, Howell, 246
colonization, 34, 45n53; defense of,
    35;of slaves, 24
Colorado Territory, 74
common good, 223; and statesmanship,
    10
compact theory, 184
Compromise of 1850: 229; provisions
    of, 54, 55
concurrent majority, 183
Confederacy. *See* Confederate States of
    America (CSA)
Confederate Constitution, 148, 264;
    slavery, protection for, 221, 222,
    291; and tariffs, 220–21, 291
Confederate States of America (CSA),
    148, 155, 198; and inflation, 219;

and limited government, 290, 291;
    and slavery, 191, 291; slaves, arming
    of, 245; and states' rights, 290, 291.
    See also South
Congo, 17
Congress, 309, 327; and Atlantic slave
    trade, 59; war, declaration of, 326
Congressional Government (Wilson), 296
Connerly, Ward, 42n10
Constitution, 9, 95, 127, 151, 156–57,
    184, 272, 286, 333; and Civil War,
    109; Commerce Clause of, 309;
    criticism of, 295, 296; Declaration
    of Independence, relationship
    between, 157, 174, 175;
    diminishing of, 78–79; as living,
    296; and natural law philosophy, 7;
    and natural rights, 72, 193;
    opposition to, 161, 162; as
    perpetual, 150, 268; as racist,
    accusations of, 79; ratification of,
    109, 161; and secession, 154, 180;
    and separation of powers, 160; and
    slavery, 81, 97, 99, 102, 103, 222;
    slavery, compromises over in, 59;
    slavery, and original intent of, 78,
    83, 84, 111; and tariffs, 220, 221;
    Three-Fifths clause in, 59, 96, 97,
    103; and writ of habeas corpus, 326
Constitutional Convention, 59, 175,
    207; and slavery, 94, 96, 97; and
    Three-Fifths Clause, 98
Constitutional Dictatorship (Rossiter),
    318
Constitutional Government (Wilson),
    295–96
Constitutional Problems under Lincoln
    (Randall), 327
Continental Congress, 151
Coolidge, Calvin, 306
Corwin Amendment, 277
cotton: as profitable, 27
Craven, Avery, 119

Croly, Herbert, 294, 301
Cuba, 221, 232
Cuomo, Mario, 14, 47, 48, 49, 71, 72, 74, 84, 310, 312, 318; and Declaration of Independence, 311
Curtis, Benjamin Robbins, 82, 90

Dahomey, 17
Darwin, Charles, 1, 130, 222, 294, 296, 313
Darwinism, 234
Davis, Jefferson, 6, 185–86, 188, 189, 206, 207, 265, 266
The Debates in the Several State Conventions on the Adoption of the Federal Constitution (Elliott), 195
Declaration of Independence, 61, 69, 70, 95, 100, 101, 115, 127, 129, 201n59, 234, 249, 303, 304; American government, as formed by, 158; Constitution, relationship between, 157, 174, 175; equality principle in, 91, 107, 125, 156, 188, 311–12; just versus unjust powers, 189; moral principle of, 4; natural rights principles in, 25, 59, 71, 118, 130, 131, 188, 190, 279; natural rights principles in, as wrong, 295; purpose of, 133; and religion, 134; and secession, 146, 190, 191, 198; and slavery, 58; and states' rights, 190–91; Union, as act of, 151
The Declaration of Independence: A Study in the History of Ideas (Becker), 118
Delano, Columbus, 229
Delaware, 265, 274, 278, 282
Democracy in America (Tocqueville), 10, 31
Democratic Party, 101, 102, 103, 106, 228; split in, 48, 230, 231, 259n62
Democratic Standard (newspaper), 28
democratic tyranny, 3
Dershowitz, Alan, 7

Dew, Charles, 244
Dewey, John, 294, 295
Dickens, Charles, 205, 206, 214
DiLorenzo, Thomas, 49, 107–8, 151, 152, 155, 192, 193, 194, 198, 207, 208, 209, 211, 212, 214, 215, 219, 222, 227, 232, 266, 275, 278, 280, 289, 317, 330; big government, and Confederate states, 291; Civil War, as unnecessary, 119, 124; and Declaration of Independence, 188, 189, 190, 191; on equality, 285; on Abraham Lincoln, as racist, 19, 31; and Jean-Jacques Rousseau, 173; on secession, 146, 187, 190, 196, 197
Disquisition on Government (Calhoun), 170, 173
divine right, 238
Documents Related to New-England Federalism, 1800–1815 (Pickering), 196
Donald, David, 19, 20, 124, 125, 126, 138, 298, 299
Douglas, Stephen, 18, 29, 31, 54, 55, 66–74, 89, 103, 107, 108, 129, 130, 208, 229, 231, 244, 259n67, 321; Declaration of Independence, interpretation of, 71, 72; diversity, defense of, 64, 65, 120; Abraham Lincoln, debates with, 19, 24, 25, 32, 38, 64, 65–74, 115, 116, 121, 125, 126; nonjudgmentalism of, 120; popular sovereignty doctrine of, 38, 48, 56, 62, 68, 69, 70, 73, 230, 259n62; as "pro-choice," 63; racial hierarchy of, 65, 67; South, rejection by, 231–32; tradition, appeals to, 67
Douglass, Frederick, 39, 222, 337, 338
The Dred Scott Case: Its Significance in American Law and Politics (Fehrenbacher), 79
Dred Scott and the Problem of Constitutional Evil (Graber), 80, 99

Dred Scott v. Sandford, 9, 35, 58, 71, 74, 77, 78, 79, 81, 106, 107, 109, 125, 132, 177, 222, 230, 272, 283; personhood, as issue in, 80; and slavery, 104
D'Souza, Dinesh, 17
DuSable, Jean Baptiste Pointe, 36

Earl of Shaftesbury, 43n31
economic determinism, 215, 216, 218
Eisenach, Eldon, 234
Ekelund, Robert, Jr., 216, 217, 218, 219
Electoral College, 96, 160, 177
Elliott, Joseph, 195
Ellis, Joseph, 117, 118, 119, 126, 129, 138
Ellsworth, Oliver, 59
Emancipation Proclamation, 273, 280, 282; consequences of, 283; as controversial, 271; criticism of, 272, 275; issuing of, 281; preliminary version of, 274, 275
Emerson, John, 82
The End of Racism (D'Souza), 17
Engels, Friedrich, 122
England, 27. *See also* Great Britain
equality, 1, 2, 10, 14; mental illness, as suffering from, 28; and statesmanship, 10–11. *See also* human equality
Erler, Edward J., 113n46, 251
The Eve of Conflict: Stephen A. Douglas and the Needless War (Milton), 120
Everett, Edward, 182
Ex Parte Milligan, 329, 330

The Fate of Their Country: Politicians, Slavery Extension, and the Coming of the Civil War (Holt), 124
F.D.R.'s Folly: How Roosevelt and His New Deal Prolonged the Great Depression (Powell), 307

Federalist papers, 3, 41, 96, 97, 99, 136, 137, 156, 157, 159, 160, 163, 175, 178, 180, 182, 292
Federalist Party, 196
Fehrenbacher, Don, 79, 231, 317
Ferguson, Andrew, 41–42n1
Fifteenth Amendment, 113n52
Fifth Amendment, 80, 89, 102
Fillmore, Millard, 53–54
Fisher, George, 278
Fitzhugh, George, 216
Fletcher, George, 318
Florida, 280
Fogel, Robert, 222
Folsom, Burton, 307
Forced into Glory: Abraham Lincoln's White Dream (Bennett), 13, 275
Fort Sumter, 73, 148, 152, 265, 266, 321, 327
Fourteenth Amendment, 44n37, 48, 80, 113n52
France, 17, 197, 275
Franklin, Benjamin, 64, 94
free trade: and freedom, 222
Fremont, John C., 101, 278, 279, 280
French Revolution, 181; versus American Revolution, 249, 250
Fugitive Slave Act, 207
fugitive slave law, 34, 37, 54, 229, 230, 233; support of, 38
Fukuyama, Francis, 218

Gambia, 17
Garrison, William Lloyd, 28, 34, 37, 39, 273
general will, 173; universality of, 172
George III, 95, 190, 191
Georgia, 155, 163, 280
Germany, 270
Gettysburg Address, 4, 6, 134, 175, 246, 248, 255, 331; religious nature of, 247
Gettysburg, 58

Gillespie, Joseph, 74

Gingrich, Newt, 312, 313

Giuliani, Rudy, 313

Golden Rule, 132, 133; and slavery, 2

Gordon, David, 19, 289

government: check on, 160; and
common good, 159; expansion of,
302; and federalism, 160; governed,
consent of, 159, 188; growth of,
293; just versus unjust, 189; as
limited, rejection of, 297; purpose
of, 157; and social compact theory,
159; as threat, 160; wealth,
redistribution of, 303

Graber, Mark, 35, 58, 60, 80, 81, 99,
108, 109, 110, 112n9, 177, 231

Great Britain, 17, 88, 92, 183, 275;
impressment policy of, 197. *See also*
England

Great Depression, 293, 302; and New
Deal, 307

Great Society, 309

Greeley, Horace, 263, 269, 270, 271

Gregoire, Henri, 22–23

Grier, Robert, 82

Gruber, Jacob, 100, 132

Guelzo, Allen C., 271, 272, 278, 283

Gutzman, Kevin, 71, 146, 158,
160–61, 164, 192, 194, 195, 198

Haiti, 45n53

Hamas, 3

Hamilton, Alexander, 3, 64, 94, 178,
179, 180, 185, 208

Hancock, John, 158, 190

happiness, 217

Harding, Warren, 306

Harris, William, 244

Hart, Ephriam, 27

Hartford Convention, 196, 197–98

Hegel, G. W. F., 117, 140–41n1, 173,
222, 238, 294, 313; and Darwinism,
234; and God's will, 238

Heidegger, Martin, 143n44

Herndon, William, 320

Hessler, Katherine, 292

Hill, Anita, 6

historicism, 117, 136, 140, 168, 294;
critique of, 138; as flawed, 137; as
incontrovertible, 118; premise of,
118–19. *See also* multiculturalism

A History of American Political Theories
(Merriam), 296

Hitler, Adolf, 8, 315n20, 317

Hobbes, Thomas, 217

Hodges, Albert, 323

Hofstadter, Richard, 118, 119, 138,
177, 275

Holt, Michael, 124

Hooker, Joseph, 40

Hopkins, John H., 27

Huaqiu, Liu, 115, 136

human equality, 16, 29, 133, 135, 242;
and American Founders, 93, 125,
126, 155, 156, 186; and American
government, 156, 285; human
nature, as rooted in, 155; and
natural rights principle, 74; and
social contract, 26. *See also* equality

human nature, 136, 137, 138; and
common sense, 139; as
evolutionary, 117, 118; government,
need for, 159; and human equality,
155; as unchanging, 117, 118, 122

human reason, 136, 137, 138, 139

human rights, 115

Hunter, David, 280

Hunter, Robert, 246

Illinois black codes, 34; support of, 38

Illinois Whigs, 224

Illinois, 62, 67, 82, 87, 272

incest, 239

Independent Treasury System, 227

Indiana, 87

In Re Archy, 104, 106, 113n46, 241

interracial marriage, 44n37
Iraq, 311, 313
Iraqi Citizen Job Corps, 313
Israel, 3
Italy, 270

Jackson, Andrew, 54, 108, 209, 211
Jaffa, Harry, 127, 128, 129, 130, 132, 135, 285, 286
Japan, 270
Jay, John, 59, 64, 99
Jefferson and Civil Liberties (Levy), 151, 203n118
Jefferson, Thomas, 3, 21, 35, 36–37, 49, 50, 60, 64, 94, 95, 155, 167, 168, 182, 207, 208, 233, 303; on black inequality, 22, 23; Declaration of Independence, purpose of, 133; election of, 267; embargo policies of, 151, 152, 197, 203n118, 225; on majority rule, 184–85, 267; and moral law, 157–58; and natural right, 325; on revolution, 181; slaves, colonization of, 24
Jeffrey, Douglas, 294
Jesus, 121, 132, 133
Johnson, Richard M., 29, 30
Judging Lincoln (Williams), 300

Kansas, 55, 56, 61
Kansas-Nebraska Act, 9, 20, 21, 47–74, 125, 177, 229, 277, 284; consequences of, 58; criticism of, 56; and popular sovereignty, 48, 259n62; and slavery, 56, 104
Kant, Immanuel, 121
Kendall, Willmoore, 319
Kentucky Resolutions, 181
Kentucky, 265, 274, 282
Kesler, Charles, 299
Kirk, Russell, 66–67, 242, 269
Kleinerman, Benjamin, 323, 324, 333, 334

Know Nothing Party, 101, 189
Kossuth, Louis, 187

Laffer curve, 219, 220
Laffer, Arthur, 219, 220
Land of Lincoln (Ferguson), 41–42n1
law: and reason, 137
Laws (Plato), 137
Lecompton, 70, 106, 177
Lee, Robert E., 246
Leopard, 197
Levy, Leonard, 151, 203n118
liberalism, 294, 295, 296, 302, 308, 310, 313. *See also* progressivism
Liberator (newspaper), 28
Liberia, 33
Lincoln (Donald), 124, 125
Lincoln, Abraham, 16, 17, 23, 28, 55, 102, 108, 119, 120, 127, 168, 184, 185, 205, 206, 213, 215, 238, 241, 297, 308, 313, 337, 338, 340; abolitionists, disagreement with, 36, 38; assassination plot against, 320; attacks on, 8, 110, 145, 279, 290; as benevolent dictator, 318; big government, identification with, 310, 311, 312; big government, as originator of, 290; as "Black Republican," 31; colonization, support of, 34, 35, 45n53; and Constitution, 9, 273; Constitution, as perpetual, 150; Constitution, violation of, accusations of, 318, 319, 322, 327, 328, 329, 330; as constitutionalist, 334; Declaration of Independence, interpretation of, 71, 72, 84, 91, 107; Declaration of Independence, and Constitution, on relationship between, 330–31, 332; divine, appeal to, 250, 252, 254; Stephen Douglas, debates with, 19, 24, 25, 32, 38, 64, 65–74, 115, 116, 121, 125, 126; on *Dred Scott* case,

77, 79, 80, 81, 82, 89, 90, 91, 106, 131, 234; election of, 231, 286n2; and Emancipation Proclamation, 271, 272, 274, 275, 281, 282, 283; emotionalism of, 248; on equality, principle of, 93, 125, 312; executive war powers of, 9; first inaugural address of, 128, 251, 255; on freedom, 123, 124; fugitive slave law, support of, 34, 36; and Gettysburg Address, 134, 175, 247, 248, 255; goodness of, 339; and "house divided" speech, 62, 63, 64, 103; and human equality, 2, 4, 69, 73, 132, 189, 242; on human nature, 117; on human nature, as eternal, 121, 310; ideas of, as irrelevant, 126, 135, 137, 140; Illinois black code, support of, 34; inauguration of, 264; and Kansas-Nebraska Act, 58; Kansas-Nebraska Act, opposition to, 48, 49, 60–61, 62, 73; law, preservation of, 36, 37, 38; on liberty, 62; and limited government, 294; and natural rights principles, 5, 6, 25, 66, 74, 81, 92, 111, 324; and New Deal principles, 293; and paper money, 219; on passion versus reason, 136; persistence of, 40; and political economy, 223, 226, 227; political poetry of, divine in, 248, 249; and popular sovereignty, 61; power, limitations of, 277, 280; principles of, 116, 117; and progressives, 298, 299, 300, 301; public opinion, shaping of, 4, 29, 30, 31, 33, 38, 39, 40; as racist, accusations of, 13, 19, 20, 34; and reason, 250, 251; reputation of, as tarnished, 5; on revolution, 186, 187; rhetoric of, 10, 41, 248, 249, 299, 300; and Jean-Jacques Rousseau, 173, 174;

and secession, 177; secession, opposition to, 147, 148, 149, 152–53, 154, 264–65; second inaugural address of, 248, 252, 253, 254; and slavery, 20, 21, 32, 36, 150, 228, 253, 269, 270, 276, 278; slavery, as wrong, 33, 34, 70, 73, 78, 122–23, 243, 244, 264, 271, 305, 309; speeches of, as poetic, 246, 255, 256; statesmanship of, 9, 10, 11, 18, 40, 41, 81, 264, 299; and tariffs, 224, 226, 227; teachings of, as relevant, 5; and Thirteenth Amendment, 284; as tyrant, accusations of, 317, 319; unconstitutionally, acting as, 145, 146; Union, preservation of, 263, 264, 265, 266, 268, 269, 270, 271, 284, 285, 286, 330; wartime measures of, 279, 280, 318, 322, 323, 326, 327, 332; as white supremacist, accusations of, 14

Lincoln at Gettysburg: The Words that Remade America (Wills), 248

Lincoln Day, 5

Lincoln Memorial, 5

Lincoln Reconsidered (Donald), 298

Lincoln scholarship, 289–90; historicist trend in, 139; intellectual framework of, 126

Lincoln the President (Randall), 119

Lincoln Unmasked (DiLorenzo), 49, 108, 124, 151, 215, 219, 330

Lincoln's Emancipation Proclamation: The End of Slavery in America (Guelzo), 271

Lind, Michael, 14, 20, 310

Locke, John, 25, 133, 166, 172; hypocrisy, charges against, 43n31; prerogative power, argument for, 324, 325; and slave trade, 43n31

Lott, Trent, 6

Louisiana Purchase, 50, 55, 207

Louisiana Territory, 82, 88, 89
Louisiana, 274, 282
Lovejoy, Elijah, 39
Loving v. Virginia, 44n37
Lundy, Benjamin, 34

MacIntyre, Alasdair, 7
Madison, James, 25, 41, 61, 64, 87, 94,
    137, 151, 152, 156, 162–63, 175,
    181, 185, 201n59, 222, 258n44,
    291, 292; concurrent majority
    theory, attack on, 180; on
    government, 158–59, 160; on
    justice, 157; and majoritarian
    constitutionalism, 182; on majority
    rule, 182, 183, 184; on slavery, 96,
    97, 98, 99; theory of nullification,
    rejection of, 182
majority rule, 182, 183, 184, 185
Manifest Destiny, 55, 231
Marbury v. Madison, 87
Marshall, Thurgood, 77, 78, 79, 111
Martin, Luther, 59
Marx, Karl, 122, 205, 294, 313; on
    Civil War, 213, 214
Maryland, 192, 195, 196, 265, 274,
    282, 321
Mason, George, 59
Massachusetts Constitution, 165, 166
Massachusetts Federalists, 197
Massachusetts, 59, 90
McLean, John, 82
McClellan, George, 281
McGuire, Robert, 219, 220, 221, 222
McPherson, James, 20, 127
Mencken, H. L., 255
Merriam, Charles, 296, 297, 303
metanarratives, 140; and
    postmodernism, 139
Mexican War, 50, 54, 186
Mexico, 229
Michigan, 42n10, 87
Middle East, 3

Miller, Donald, 214
Milligan, Lambdin, 329
Milton, George Fort, 120
Minnesota, 82, 87
Mississippi, 104; secession of, 6, 245
Missouri Compromise, 21, 50, 55, 61,
    81, 82, 125, 277, 292; repeal of, 56,
    229; as unconstitutional, 81, 86–87,
    88, 89, 102, 107
Missouri, 50, 82, 83, 87, 265, 274,
    278, 279, 280, 282
moral teaching, 121; human nature, as
    unchanging, 122
Morrill tariff, 213
multiculturalism, 15, 68, 137; and
    value judgments, 36. *See also*
    historicism
Mussolini, Benito, 315n20

National Era (newspaper), 56
nationalism, 173
natural law principles, 6, 11; as
    abandoned, 7; rejection of, 28, 130.
    See also natural right principles
natural right principles, 5, 60, 118,
    130, 133, 194, 198, 238, 267, 324,
    325; American Founding, as basis
    of, 96; and blacks, 26, 27; and
    majority rule, 185; rejection of,
    294, 296. *See also* natural law
    principles
Nebraska, 55, 56, 61
Nelson, Samuel, 82
A New Birth of Freedom (Jaffa), 128
New Deal, 293, 304, 308, 309, 310;
    public good, as synonymous with,
    306; as sacrosanct, 307
*New Deal or Raw Deal: How FDR's
    Economic Legacy has Damaged America*
    (Folsom), 307
New England Federalists: and
    secession, 196
New England, 197

New Hampshire, 90
New Jersey Plan, 258n44
New Jersey, 90
New Mexico, 53, 54
New York, 90, 191, 192, 193, 194, 197
Newton, Isaac, 23, 296
Nietzsche, Friedrich, 143n44
Ninth Amendment, 48, 72, 146
Noll, Mark, 235, 252, 255
North Carolina, 90, 265
North, 206, 207, 320. *See also* Union
Northern Democrats: and slavery, 230
Northwest Ordinance, 87
Northwest Territory, 87, 88, 89
Notes on the State of Virginia (Jefferson), 3, 21, 22
Nova Scotia, 197
nullification crisis, 209

Obama, Barack, 14, 293, 308, 311
Ohio, 87
Ottawa (Illinois), 116
Our Secret Constitution: How Lincoln Redefined American Democracy (Fletcher), 318

Paludan, Philip, 30, 126, 127, 128, 129, 130, 131, 132, 134, 138; and ideas, 135; and unfolding meaning, 133
Panama, 45n53
paper money, 218, 219
Patriot Act, 333
Patterson, Orlando, 17
A People's Contest: The Union and Civil War, 1861–1865 (Paludan), 30, 126, 134
Pestritto, Ronald, 298
Pettit, John, 72
philosophy, 315n41
The Philosophy of History (Hegel), 117, 140–41n1, 237

The Philosophy of Right (Hegel), 140–41n1
Pickens, Fort, 266
Pickering, Timothy, 196
Pierce, Franklin, 103
Pierce, Henry, 115
Pillsbury, Parker, 283
Plato, 137
political cynicism, 8
political economy, 223
The Politically Incorrect Guide to American History (Woods), 19, 115, 147, 192
The Politically Incorrect Guide to the Constitution (Gutzman), 71, 146, 158, 164, 192
politics, 8; and self-government, 339–40
polygamy, 239, 240
popular sovereignty, 38, 48, 56, 58, 74, 81, 230, 232; and *Dred Scott* case, 89; as easy way out, 73; liberty, as synonymous with, 62; majority tyranny, as justification for, 61
postmodernism: and metanarratives, 139
Potter, David, 53, 55, 230–31, 266
Powell, Jim, 307
The Presidency of Abraham Lincoln (Paludan), 126, 133
President's Day, 5
Pressly, Thomas, 216
Pride, Prejudice, and Politics: Roosevelt versus Recovery, 1933–1938 (Best), 307
Prize Cases, 328, 330
Progressive Era, 294
progressivism, 295, 302, 310; and leadership theory of, 299, 300; natural rights principles, rejection of, 294. *See also* liberalism
The Promise of American Life (Croly), 301
protectionism, 227, 228

public good, 67–68, 69; and New
Deal, 306

racism, 9, 111, 228; and affirmative
action, 42n10; and white guilt, 15,
16
railroad system, 55, 208
Randall, James G., 119, 124, 318, 327
Reagan, Ronald, 68
The Real Lincoln (DiLorenzo), 49, 107,
146, 187, 214, 275
Rehnquist, William, 321
relativism, 294. *See also* historicism
Republican Party, 6, 101, 102, 103,
107, 125, 228
Revolutionary War, 162
Rhode Island, 191, 192, 193, 194, 195
*The Rise and Fall of the American Whig
Party* (Holt), 124
Roberts, Paul Craig, 317
Roe v. Wade, 48, 80–81
Rogers, Bob, 41–42n1
Roosevelt, Franklin D., 293, 306, 308,
310; and economic rights, 304, 305;
government, purpose of, 303;
progressive theory, advancing of,
302; social contract, redefining of,
303, 304
Roosevelt, Theodore, 294, 301
Root, Elihu, 11, 40, 41, 338
Ross, Fred A., 238, 239, 240, 241, 243
Rossiter, Clinton, 318
Rothbard, Murray, 289
Rousseau, Jean-Jacques, 142n33; and
general will, 172, 174
Royal African Company, 43n31

Sandefur, Timothy, 161
Saulsbury, Willard, 274
Scalia, Antonin: on self-government,
68
Schwartz, Barry, 139; and "fading
hero," 140

Scott, Dred, 82, 83, 86, 87
Scott, Winfield, 332, 327
Scudder, Vida Dutton, 301
secession, 128, 148, 164, 192, 193,
235, 267, 320; anarchy, as essence
of, 149; government, difference
between, 155; in New England,
196, 197, 198; versus rebellion,
319; versus revolution, 186, 187,
188, 198; right of, 145, 146, 147; as
self-destructive, 268; slavery, as
preservation of, 245; and states'
rights, 162, 176, 179
Second Treatise of Government (Locke),
324
self-government, 2, 3, 4–5, 9, 37, 68,
137
September 11 attacks, 3
Seward, William, 321
Shiloh, 58
Silbey, Joel, 207
slavery, 4, 6, 16, 23, 50, 59, 110, 120,
131, 215, 272, 274, 297; and
abortion, 47, 48; and American
Founders, 58, 78, 86, 94, 95, 163; as
beneficial, 241; and Christianity,
235, 236; as Christianizing
institution, 236; and church, 235; in
colonies, 95; and colonization, 34,
35; as commonplace, 17; and
Constitution, 78; Democratic Party
positions on, 81; and *Dred Scott* case,
89, 103, 104, 105; expansion of,
231–32; and Gag Rule, 292; as
God's will, 238, 239, 240, 241; and
Golden Rule, 2, 236; as immoral,
58, 60; justification for, 28, 69, 222;
and limited government, 293;
neutrality toward, 60; and popular
sovereignty, 56, 61; as positive good,
27, 91, 163, 169, 229, 238–39, 243,
273, 276; as profitable, 223;
prohibition of, 284; and property

issue, 97, 98; and public opinion, 276; and Scriptures, 235, 236; and Southern honor, 53; and state law, 272, 276, 277; and tariffs, 211, 212; and Thirteenth Amendment, 284; as wrong, 28. *See also* blacks; slaves
Slavery Ordained of God (Ross), 238
Slavery and Social Death (Patterson), 17
slaves, 272, 273, 275; arming of, 245, 246; confiscation of, 278, 279, 280; humanity of, 98; and person versus property, 97, 98, 102, 103. *See also* blacks; slavery
Sobran, Joe, 146, 198
social compact, 147, 156, 184, 276
social contract: and human equality, 26; redefining of, 303, 304
social justice, 305–6
Social Security, 307
Society of Christian Socialists, 301
South, 108, 319, 320; as aggressor, 321; blockade in, 148; cotton in, 27; economy of, 206; and Emancipation Proclamation, 283; free speech in, 292; and Gag Rule, 292; racism in, 228; and secession, 128, 148, 149, 150, 229, 233, 292; secession, argument for, 153; and slavery, 96, 97, 229, 231, 232, 233, 245, 292; slavery, defense of in, 234; and Southern way of life, 212, 292; and states' rights, 207, 290; and tariffs, 211, 212; and taxation, 207. *See also* Confederate States of America (CSA)
South America, 221, 232
South Carolina, 148, 150, 163, 176, 234, 280, 292; and Ordinance of Nullification, 209; slavery in, 276–77; and Tariff of Abominations, 211
Southern Democrats, 207, 209, 231
Southern Whigs, 207
Spain, 231

Speed, Joshua, 189
Stalin, Joseph, 7, 317
Stampp, Kenneth, 222
statesmanship, 39, 40, 270, 279, 313, 339; and common good, 10; as defined, 263; and equality, 11; as old fashioned, 10; and prudence, 337; rhetoric, art of, 10
states' rights, 9, 179, 180, 181, 190–91, 207, 208; and secession, 198; and sovereignty, 194
state sovereignty, 179
Steele, Shelby, 15, 16
Stephens, Alexander, 28, 155, 191, 205, 206, 232
Stovall, Charles A., 105, 106
Strauss, Leo, 135–36, 138, 252, 315n41
Sumner, Charles, 56, 125
Supreme Court, 309; Abraham Lincoln, constitutional violations, accusations of, 328, 329, 330
Sidney, Algernon, 133, 166

Taney, Roger, 77, 91, 95, 98, 105, 106, 109, 110, 112n9, 129, 130, 131, 133, 135; blacks, as citizens, refusal of, 99; Constitution, interpretation of, 88, 103, 111, 132; Declaration of Independence, interpretation of, 84, 85, 86; defense of, 108; and *Dred Scott*, 79–80, 81, 82, 83, 100, 103, 104, 107; and Missouri Compromise, 89; and Republican threat, 101, 102, 103
The Tariff History of the United States (Taussig), 210
tariffs, 206, 213; and slavery, 211, 212; and Tariff of Abominations, 208, 209, 210, 211, 212, 220
Tariffs, Blockades, and Inflation: The Economics of the Civil War (Thornton and Ekelund), 216
Taussig, F. W., 210, 212
Taylor, John, 207

Taylor, Zachary, 53, 54, 229
Tennessee, 265, 282
Tenth Amendment, 146
Texas, 54, 154, 320
Thirteenth Amendment, 113n52, 284, 300
Thomas, Clarence, 8, 130; natural law principles, defense of, 6
Thoreau, Henry David, 284
Thornton, Mark, 216, 217, 218, 219
Thornwell, James Henley, 234, 235, 236, 237, 238, 243; and God's will, 238; historicism of, 237; and natural rights, 237
Tocqueville, Alexis de, 1, 2, 31
Toombs, Robert, 53
truth, 137, 138, 140–41n1, 143n44; idea of, 1
Turner, Nat, 28
tyranny, 3

Union: and inflation, 219. *See also* North
United States, 14; equality, principle of, 17, 91; moral climate of, decline in, 91; slavery in, 17, 23

Van Cott, T. Norman, 219, 220, 221, 222
Vestiges of the Natural History of Creation (Chamber), 1
Vindicating the Founders (West), 117
Virginia, 191, 192, 195, 265, 274, 282; and Declaration of Rights, 193
Virginia Plan, 258n44
Virginia Resolutions, 181, 182

Wade, Ben, 280
Walker, Leroy Pope, 244
Walker, Robert, 27
War of 1812, 224
War on Terror, 318, 333
Washington, D.C.: slave trade in, abolished, 54

Washington, George, 11, 60, 64, 94, 122, 134, 159, 250, 264
Washington State, 42n10
Wayne, James, 82
Webster, Daniel, 54, 164, 208
"We Cannot Escape History": Lincoln and the Last Best Hope of Earth (McPherson), 127
West, Thomas, 117, 118, 294
West Virginia, 282
When in the Course of Human History: Arguing the Case for Southern Secession (Adams), 146, 187, 214, 254
White Guilt (Steele), 15
Whitney, Eli, 27
Why Lincoln Matters: Today More than Ever (Cuomo), 14, 47, 71, 310, 318
Wickard v. Filburn, 309
Williams, Frank, 300, 301
Williams, Walter, 145, 146, 192, 193, 198, 205, 209, 213, 266, 272, 280, 289
Wills, Garry, 248
Wilmot, David, 50
Wilmot Proviso, 50, 53, 177, 229, 277
Wilson, Clyde, 14, 176, 185, 186, 188, 198
Wilson, Woodrow, 294, 298, 299, 300, 301, 303; Constitution, criticism of, 295
Winik, Jay, 20
Wisconsin, 87
women's suffrage, 272
Woods, Thomas, 19, 115, 137, 138, 147, 192, 194, 196, 198, 209, 266, 270
Works Progress Administration (WPA), 307
World War I, 306
Wyatt-Brown, Bertram, 75n7

Yancey, William, 230
Yates, Robert, 161–62
Yoo, John, 325, 326

ABOUT THE AUTHOR

Thomas L. Krannawitter is an assistant professor of political science and director of the Washington-Hillsdale Internship Program at Hillsdale College (Michigan) and a senior fellow at the Claremont Institute (California). Born and raised in Hays, Kansas, he graduated from Fort Hays State University with degrees in political science and communications. He holds an MA and a PhD in political science from the Claremont Graduate University in Claremont, California. Dr. Krannawitter is coauthor of *A Nation under God? The ACLU and Religion in American Politics* (2005) and a contributing author to *Challenges to the American Founding: Slavery, Historicism, and Progressivism in the 19th Century* (2005). He is also editor for a PBS website on George Washington (www.pbs.org/georgewashington). He has published numerous articles in journals and newspapers and has spoken widely on American politics and history. He lives in Hillsdale, Michigan, with his wife, Lori, and their two children, Claire and Benjamin.